Straight Talk about Your Mental Health

STRAIGHT TALK ABOUT YOUR MENTAL HEALTH

James Morrison, MD

THE GUILFORD PRESS
New York   London

© 2002 The Guilford Press
A Division of Guilford Publications, Inc.
72 Spring Street, New York, NY 10012
www.guilford.com

The information in this volume is not intended as a substitute for
consultation with healthcare professionals. Each individual's health
concerns should be evaluated by a qualified professional.

Printed in the United States of America

This book is printed on acid-free paper.

Last digit is print number: 9   8   7   6   5   4   3   2   1

Library of Congress Cataloging-in-Publication Data

Morrison, James R., 1940–
   Straight talk about your mental health / James Morrison.
        p. cm.
    Includes index.
    ISBN 1-57230-786-2 (hbk. : alk. paper) — ISBN 1-57230-674-2 (pbk. :
alk. paper)
    1. Psychiatry—Popular works. 2. Mental health care—Popular works.
I. Title.
RC460 .M67 2002
616.89—dc21   2002006578

To Geoff, who knows who he is

Contents

PART THREE. Mental Disorders   189

Introduction

During our first visit, Sara seemed distracted. She was a pleasant, middle-aged woman who had never sought care from a psychiatrist. Several months earlier she had begun to feel tired and irritable; she thought she had the flu. When her 25-year-old son called to say that he was getting a divorce, she began to cry. "I worried I had done something to break up his marriage," she told me, dabbing at her eyes. "I felt so guilty." Over the following months she became depressed and so preoccupied that she often forgot to pay bills. She couldn't sleep, cried several times a day, and ultimately broke down, unable even to cook supper for her invalid husband. When I asked why she hadn't come in earlier, when her symptoms first appeared, she replied, "I was afraid I'd find out I was getting Alzheimer's."

In the decades since I first studied psychiatry, many of my 15,000-plus patients have told similar stories about why they put off seeking treatment for mental, emotional, or behavioral problems. Usually their hesitation was rooted in fear about the future.

- **"I thought I might be losing my mind."** Not knowing what symptoms mean prompts many people to keep their feelings to themselves. It is natural to fear what we don't understand, and the powerful emotions of depression, anxiety, or anger can frighten just about anyone into silence. One job of the mental health clinician (and of this book) is to help you understand that, just as the fears we imagine in the dark yield to the light of day, fear of the unknown fades in the light of facts. Fortunately, we have learned enough about mental illness that we can predict, with considerable accuracy, what will happen in the course of a particular patient's illness. One purpose of Part III of this book is to provide the information you need to feel reassured that we know a lot about—and can do a lot for—the mental disorder that concerns you.
- **"Only crazy people see psychiatrists."** Assuming that "crazy" means psychotic (out of touch with reality), under 5% of those who consult mental health pro-

1

fessionals are so seriously affected. Influenced by films like *One Flew Over the Cuckoo's Nest,* many people worry that "mental illness" means schizophrenia. On the contrary, most people who consult clinicians have problems with depression, anxiety, or the misuse of substances.

• **"I was afraid I'd never get well." "I thought I'd have to be hospitalized." "They'll have me committed."** When something goes wrong with body or brain, we tend to imagine the worst. The dire predictions I've just quoted reflect two common myths: (1) all mental illness is basically the same, and (2) once you become mentally ill, you're sick for life. The truth is quite different. Over the past 150 years, clinicians have come to recognize dozens of ways in which people can have mental or emotional problems. In the course of this book we will visit the more serious of these problem areas and explore the many roads to recovery. Most people diagnosed with a psychiatric disorder recover or stabilize to the point where they are comfortable, happy, and productive. Most patients never stop working; of those who do, most start again once they have recovered. Few mental patients ever need hospitalization; most who do need it enter voluntarily—and leave greatly improved.

• **"What will my family think? What will my boss do?"** In my professional lifetime the stigma of mental disease has declined, but some people still fear having it known that they have sought care. I've even known psychiatrists and psychologists who felt this way upon falling ill!

• **"No one will ever want to marry me."** This reflects the fear that mental illness leaves you permanently scarred. However, you can't distinguish most mental patients from everyone else; properly treated, mental disorders need not preclude happy and productive lives.

• **"I hate to be weak."** Many people believe that if only you resist mental symptoms strongly enough, you will stay healthy. Some, including even a tiny handful of psychiatrists, believe that mental illness isn't a disease but a myth—that psychosis, depression, and anxiety are expressions of cultural influence, personal autonomy, or loose morals. In reality, mental disorders are similar to other medical conditions: they run in families and are often inherited; they run a well-defined course; they respond predictably to treatment; and some are associated with abnormalities in body chemistry, physiology, or anatomy.

• **"My first wife was in treatment for 15 years, and it never helped her a bit." "My uncle takes drugs for his emotions, and he's a zombie."** Every medical specialty has its share of bad outcomes. Fortunately, as treatments have improved and practitioners have become better trained, positive outcomes have increased considerably. Now we know that, if your uncle is a zombie, he should be on a different medicine, and if your wife hasn't been helped, she should consider changing doctors.

The list of reasons to delay seeking treatment is endless.

• **"It seemed so trivial at first, I thought it would go away."** Wishful thinking and unfamiliarity with the usual course of mental disorders can encourage delay.

- **"It's God's will."** Thousands of ministers and other clergy who provide counseling services would disagree.
- **"I'm in therapy already with my minister."** Although pastoral counseling can be an excellent choice for some situations, sometimes the help of other health care professionals may be necessary. To make sure they address all needs, many pastoral counselors work closely with psychologists and psychiatrists.
- **"I tried it once before, but my psychiatrist was sicker than I was."** Sure, some doctors have emotional problems, and psychiatrists are no exception. In Chapter 3 I discuss choosing an appropriate mental health care provider.
- **"I can't afford treatment."** Most states and communities offer diagnostic and treatment services that are either free or affordable through a sliding-scale fee.

The bottom line is that mental illnesses are eminently treatable—though, like cooking a meal for company, therapy nearly always succeeds better if you get an early start. If you delay, what might otherwise be managed with a few outpatient visits could get complicated and require prolonged treatment.

No book can substitute for competent professional help, but when well informed, patients, their friends, and their relatives are better equipped to join their doctors in their efforts to help them overcome mental illness. To help you become informed, I have spent countless hours researching the latest journal articles, databases, and online resources. I have measured all of what has been written against my own clinical experience of over 30 years to give you my best recommendations about finding a doctor, what to watch for in the diagnostic process, which treatments are most likely to work for your disorder—in short, the inside information that will light your way to mental health.

USING THIS BOOK

How you use this book will, of course, depend on your own needs. I write to you, the reader, as though you are the patient. If you are a relative, spouse, or close friend, you should find the information equally useful in understanding and helping the person you care about. My main focus is mental health treatment, the subject of Part II and the core of this book. People who are considering seeking professional help usually have dozens of questions about medication, psychotherapy, herbal remedies, and other forms of treatment they have heard about. How can they know what's best for them? How will different treatments affect the rest of their lives? In Part II I offer current information on how treatments work and which problems they address, along with straight facts that will clear up persistent myths and, I hope, assuage fears.

If you are new to the field of mental health, you should probably begin with Part I. There I explain where to go for help, how clinicians determine what is wrong, and your role in your own treatment. Consult Part III to learn about the symptoms and course of the various mental health diagnoses and about the treatments that are most likely to work. Understanding what your diagnosis means and what options are available to improve your mental health is critical to getting the best professional help available. Realizing that no book, however complete, can possibly tell you all you need and want to know, I've also provided an appendix that lists resources for obtaining further information and guidance about mental disorder and its treatments.

To provide information that is clear and easy to use, I've condensed certain facts into tables that allow quick reference and easy comparison. For example, a number of the chapters in Part II end with tables showing which disorders can be treated best with treatments discussed in that chapter. Information about side effects, drug interactions, tablet size, and price are also presented in the tables. How to use these tables is explained in Chapter 5.

Generally I've used brand names for medications throughout the book, because they are somewhat simpler than generic names and are almost always more familiar to consumers. The tables at the end of each medication chapter in Part II tell you when there is a generic drug that is just as effective.

I use the terms "mental health professional" and "clinician" to refer to psychiatrists, psychologists, social workers, and other professionals who help those with mental and emotional problems. In recent years, the mental health field has sometimes been called "behavioral health," reflecting a broad sphere of activity that includes treatment of substance use as well as traditional mental disorders. It all means basically the same thing, so I stick with the more familiar terminology.

The people I describe are based on real people, though to protect their privacy, I have always changed identifying details and often created composites from several of the patients I have treated. I believe you'll find your own experiences and concerns reflected in some of these illustrations, which are intended to give you a closer look at what might be ahead.

I truly hope you will find help and comfort in my approach to mental and emotional problems. As to Sara, whom I introduced on page 1, what became of her? Once she got up the courage to seek consultation, she started treatment for depression. You can read about her response to treatment in Chapter 15.

ACKNOWLEDGMENTS

Of the many people who helped in the creation of this book, I especially want to thank my editors at The Guilford Press, Kitty Moore and Chris Benton, who helped develop and refine the concept of this book, then worked with me throughout the writing. For their patience and support, I am deeply indebted. I also want to acknowledge the fine work of Margaret Ryan and Anna Nelson.

I also thank my wife, Mary, for her unstinting encouragement and incisive reading, especially of the early drafts. I gratefully acknowledge others who have provided assistance at various stages of this work, including Andrew Henry, Al Lewy, MD, Joanne Renz, RN, Kelsea Thayne, LSW, George Ainslie, MD, and Stephen Cavicchia, PsyD.

Finally, I wish I could express my appreciation individually to the thousands of patients whose lives have crossed mine over the years, leaving each of us, I believe, the richer.

PART ONE

SEEKING HELP

Some time ago I ran into Leslie, a friend I'd known for years. We began talking about the time we had met. "It really concerned me, meeting a psychiatrist," Leslie said. "I was sure that you'd know all about me just from our conversation." Although we both laughed, it made me feel slightly uncomfortable. I've heard this expressed dozens of times, as have most professionals in the mental health field. For some reason, people have the mistaken belief that we can magically "psychoanalyze" our families, friends, and casual acquaintances, almost as though we could read minds. Of course, we evaluate the people who come to us for help, and in doing so we use our powers of observation. But we don't have any extraordinary abilities, and, as you will see, most of what we learn about you comes from what you tell us.

In the Introduction I mentioned the fears that keep people who need help from seeking it. Another big deterrent is a lack of understanding about what the mental health profession can do for those who need help. In the chapters of Part I, I discuss how mental health problems are diagnosed, what help you can expect, where you can get it, and what your role is. First, though, let me clear up some common misconceptions about what you will get if you seek help from a mental health professional.

- **"If you see a psychiatrist [or psychologist or social worker], you'll be labeled mentally ill whether or not something is wrong with you."** When diagnosing a mental disturbance, clinicians must be especially careful that it can be sustained by well-proven criteria. The science-based criteria of the fourth edition of the *Diagnostic and Statistical Manual of Mental Disorders* (DSM-IV, page 13) have given us a handle on this problem, but we haven't yet grasped it firmly enough. Clinicians who promote the idea of "subclinical" illnesses may, for example, diagnose someone who has very few depressive symptoms as having a "minor depressive disorder." Followed to its extreme, this line of thinking risks making the unusual the norm and bringing us perilously close to diagnosing mental illness in half the population! I believe that you don't have to have a mental disorder to be unhappy, and that much of what some choose to call subclinical illness may be simply problems of living. These, too, often require help—as was the case for Sidney.

When he was 21, Sidney left home for the first time to begin graduate school. Feeling lonely, he proposed marriage to a girl he had met only a few weeks earlier. When she agreed and made plans for Sidney to meet her parents, he began to feel intensely anxious. His heart pounded and he was so short of breath he could barely concentrate in class. After a week of increasing symptoms, he made an appointment at student health. He poured out his story to a clinician, who listened attentively for half an hour, almost without interruption. "And that's about it," Sidney finished up. "What do you think is the cause?" The doctor replied, "Now, start over and tell it all again." When he was about halfway through his second recitation, Sidney stopped and said, "You think it's my engagement, don't you?" With this insight, Sidney's symptoms subsided, and he pondered how he really felt about being engaged. Some clinicians might have given Sidney a diagnosis of anxiety disorder; I think he had an acute problem of living and needed just a minor intervention to spotlight the connection to his symptoms. Most of this book, however, focuses on well-researched disorders that nearly everyone would agree are problems that need treatment.

- **"A shrink is just a paid friend."** Of course we like to be paid, and we try to be friendly—only we call it "rapport," the good feeling that exists when people like and respect one another. However, friends are often too close to be objective, and most don't have the training needed to be helpful in alleviating the problem itself—though their supportiveness is appreciated. Clinicians have spent years studying mental disorder, so they can offer you not just friendship but relief from your symptoms.

- **"All you doctors do is prescribe Prozac or Valium." "Treatment is just endless psychotherapy."** These contradictory statements contain a germ of truth—two germs, actually. Medication is the preferred approach for many mental disorders; it is certainly the approach HMOs and other third-party payers prefer, because it is relatively cheap. Although psychotherapy can sometimes seem interminable, the shorter forms that I discuss in Chapter 13 can bring improvement within a few sessions, and the whole process might last only a matter of months. Clinicians recognize that medication and psychotherapy are both important in effective and lasting mental health care.

- **"Psychiatrists and psychologists are into control and domination."** Actually, we work very hard to help patients retain or regain self-control. You'll find examples throughout this book.

- **"I'll have to talk about stuff I don't want to."** Partly correct. You may well have thoughts, experiences, or memories that you feel uncomfortable exploring. As you get into therapy, however, you will probably come to see that you need to discuss them and will feel better once they are out in the open. But no one, not even a therapist, can make you say anything you wish to keep secret.

- **"Treatment costs too much."** At last! A statement that nearly everyone can agree with. It is no secret that medical costs are high; psychiatric hospitalization is in the stratosphere. There are some solutions, however, which I discuss in Chapter 3.

YOUR RIGHTS, OUR RESPONSIBILITIES

The preceding list is just a glimpse into the myths about mental health professionals that I continue to debunk in the following chapters. Even more important are the positives—what you should expect from us. This is how I view the responsibilities of any mental health clinician. The flip side, of course, is that they are also your rights as a patient:

- We must be able to recognize the symptoms of mental disorder. Symptoms are not always out in the open, where anyone can see them, so we must also know how to dig for hidden symptoms.
- We must understand what is wrong and make a clear diagnosis that will point the way to its resolution. If the diagnosis is not immediately apparent, we must know how to clarify it.
- We must know which approach is best to take. For most problems, there are several possible solutions, and those we recommend must be based on studies that demonstrate what works the best and the most quickly.
- In case the first attempts at treatment don't pan out, we must present you with an organized plan that estimates the time needed for improvement and lists alternatives.
- We must inform you clearly and completely about the risks of treatment (and of withholding treatment).
- We must inform you of any possible conflict of interest we may have, such as a financial investment in particular treatment facilities or experimental drugs.
- With your permission, we will work with your relatives and friends to help them understand your condition and overcome its consequences for you and all your family.
- We will, in effect, regard you as a full partner in making informed decisions about your care.

CHAPTER 1

Taking Charge of Your Care
What Mental Health Clinicians Do

In this chapter I outline how clinicians go about the business of taking care of their patients—how we gather information and how we use it to make a diagnosis and recommend treatment. Any mental health professional is likely to approach your problem using an approach similar to this one.

GATHERING INFORMATION

Like others who do detective work, clinicians don't intuit our findings, we deduce them from information obtained from many sources. The first step is simply to ask what is troubling you. This usually occurs during an interview that lasts an hour or more, during which you'll reveal the clues that will identify the nature of your illness. Such clues are called symptoms,* which can include a huge variety of behaviors, emotions, ideas, and thoughts—just about anything that is unusual or abnormal for a particular person or in a given culture.

Some of the areas covered in the interview may surprise you, because they don't seem immediately pertinent to your problem. Suppose you're being evaluated for anxiety symptoms. You'll probably be asked about your sex life, drinking habits, and how you get on with your relatives—information that may seem off the point but that can have a bearing on nearly any mental disorder. To develop the fullest picture possible of you as a person, you'll be asked about many areas of your life. Even the

---

*Technically, a *symptom* is something you complain about (such as anxiety attacks or depression), whereas a *sign* is anything that I notice about you (a furrowed brow or weeping). For simplicity, I use the same word for both meanings.

most sincere patient in the world will have certain blind spots, such as areas of character development or past experience that appear quite different when viewed by others. That's why 21st-century clinicians also recognize the importance of obtaining any records of previous evaluations, hospitalizations, treatments—any possible clue to the cause and appropriate treatment of what is troubling you. Another potential source of information is your physical exam. Mental or emotional symptoms can be caused by endocrine disorders, head trauma, tumors, and other medical conditions. That is why you may be referred to an internist or family doctor for a complete medical workup.

Sometimes your doctor may want to consult with your relatives, friends, or other physicians and medical caregivers—anyone who can help complete the picture of you as a person. Although clinicians know that it is sometimes in a patient's best interest to share information with family and others, as well as to seek information about you from them, we are honor-bound to maintain confidentiality. Only with your express permission can we talk about your symptoms, treatment, or prognosis, even with your spouse or trusted friend. (If a patient is not competent to give such permission, we would have to obtain the consent of the person legally designated to act as guardian or conservator.) Only if a life is seriously, immediately threatened can we breach the duty of complete confidentiality. The bottom line is this: Barring exceptional circumstances, the only people who will learn about your mental health consultations are those you yourself tell.

MAKING A DIAGNOSIS

Once we have obtained all the relevant information, we look for familiar patterns of symptoms—in short, a diagnosis. The value of identifying a specific diagnosis has been questioned in the past: why not just treat the obvious complaint? If I had done that with Dorothy, a young homemaker I saw several years ago who complained of anxiety, I might have prescribed Valium. On further inquiry, I learned that she was also depressed. Should I have offered her Prozac instead? Perhaps, when I found out that she had been drinking, I should have prescribed Antabuse and recommended Alcoholics Anonymous. Finally, though, I discovered that throughout her adult life she had experienced many physical and mental symptoms. I diagnosed her as having somatization disorder, which doesn't respond to medication, but does—as did Dorothy—respond to regular office visits for psychotherapy.

From Dorothy's example, you can see how strongly context determines the meaning of symptoms. Coughs can be caused by a cold or by cancer; auditory hallucinations can be caused by dementia, substance abuse, schizophrenia, or a mood disorder. Words express thoughts only when put into a sentence; symptoms require the context of diagnosis (the sentence) to tell the full story of your mental or emotional problem. This is why it is important for your clinician to learn all about you before prescribing a specific treatment.

Some clinicians worry that diagnosis somehow harms patients by "pigeonholing" them in a category with a meaningless label that diminishes their value as individual human beings. Suppose you had a sudden pain in your abdomen and, in great agony, you went to your doctor. Would you want your doctor to say, "Gee, I wouldn't devalue your humanity by trying to classify you. Your pain is unique to you; it could be anything. We'll just have to wait and see"? Perhaps you'd prefer to hear, "Based on your symptoms, age, and physical exam, it's probably appendicitis. We'll do some tests to make sure, and we may need to operate." There's no contest. Of course you can have a diagnosis and retain your individuality; all you stand to lose is your appendix. The same reasoning is just as valid applied to your depression, hallucinations, or insomnia.

However, I would criticize the tendency of some to confuse people with their diagnoses. When we call someone "an alcoholic," we imply that alcoholism defines the person. If we say "Oh, you can't take Murray too seriously—he's manic–depressive," we imply that Murray's (episodic) disorder drives all of his actions, thoughts, and feelings, all of the time. We don't do this with medical illnesses, such as diabetes or heart disease, and it's not right to do it with mental illness. Careful clinicians try to avoid this sort of harmful labeling by using phrases such as "a patient with schizophrenia" instead of "schizophrenic."

Properly used, diagnosis helps us decide which treatment program is likely to help. We know what would be likely to happen if a doctor prescribed only aspirin to someone whose chronic headaches were caused by high blood pressure or a brain tumor. Now imagine the effect if your anxiety or depression was physically caused, but an antidepressant was the full extent of your treatment. We need the whole story, in context, to determine how best to proceed. Diagnosis also relieves individual patients of the need to be pioneers—today's patients can benefit from all that we have discovered about symptom patterns and effective treatments.

Diagnosis enables us to communicate about disease and extend the benefits of scientific advances to people around the world. Today, two diagnostic manuals are used worldwide to help clinicians identify and talk about disorders. In North America the DSM-IV (*Diagnostic and Statistical Manual of Mental Disorders,* fourth edition, of the American Psychiatric Association) is the standard. Throughout most of the rest of the world the ICD-10 (*International Classification of Diseases,* 10th edition) is used. For most disorders, these manuals substantially agree as to the types and diagnostic features of mental illness. Making a specific diagnosis is not a matter of arbitrarily attaching a label to a person; it should mean determining, through a careful evaluation, that a person meets the well-defined, science-based criteria for that disorder in DSM-IV or ICD-10.

RECOMMENDING TREATMENT

Even today, treatment frightens many people, whose impressions of it seem based on reruns of early Hollywood versions of mental health care. Take, for example, the

1950 movie *Harvey*, in which a psychiatrist plans to use "Formula 977" to make a grumpy misanthrope of happy, lovable Jimmy Stewart, who has a harmless friendship with an invisible 6-foot-tall white rabbit. In the 1964 *Shock Treatment*, Lauren Bacall plays an evil psychiatrist who experiments on healthy people by administering electroshock. In reality, patients today have a broad range of treatment options (described in full in Part II). When you're considering seeking professional help, it's useful to think of these options in terms of three broad categories: psychological, biological, and social. Together, they make up a three-legged approach to treatment that all mental health professionals are familiar with.

Psychological

For more than a century, psychotherapy has been the mainstay of mental health treatment. Perhaps you are like many people who think that psychotherapy means psychoanalysis, in which the patient spends years talking to a doctor who takes notes and doesn't say much. This is one style of psychotherapy, but we now have available many newer, more quickly effective psychological treatments. Probably the most popular of these is cognitive-behavioral therapy; it certainly has the most research demonstrating its effectiveness in a variety of disorders behind it. I discuss effective forms of brief psychotherapy in Chapters 13 and 14.

Biological

Today, effective medications are the mainstay of treatment for many mental disorders. That wasn't the case when *Harvey* was filmed. In fact, most of the drugs we use today were introduced only within the past two decades. With medication we can now treat such major problems as depression, mania, psychosis, and anxiety, as well as disorders of appetite and sleep. We'll talk about all of these medications in upcoming chapters. Other biological therapies I discuss include bright light therapy, useful for some mood and sleep disorders, and electroconvulsive therapy (though not as used by "Dr. Bacall"!)

Social

A variety of social problems can result from mental or emotional discomfort; sometimes they even cause it. Your clinician may suggest measures to deal with them. For example, consider Arnold, an 85-year-old depressed widower who lives alone. He may benefit from homemaker services, Meals on Wheels, and transportation to a senior day-care center. Mary, arrested for stealing food from a bakery, is a homeless patient with schizophrenia who needs shelter and legal services. She may do best under case management, in which a field worker would visit regularly to make sure she is taking her medicine, keeping her medical appointments, and getting adequate nutrition. Other interventions that address social aspects of problems include vocational counseling and job retraining, social skills training, providing for child care, help obtaining disability payments, and counseling for domestic violence, neglect, or abuse. Although these approaches don't reduce symptoms directly, they can enhance a patient's ability to use other treatment options.

With so many possible treatments and so many issues to consider for each individual patient, how do we know which treatment will be appropriate for you? Modern-day clinicians use the results of studies that compare outcomes in groups of patients carefully selected on the basis of scientific criteria (see sidebar). Even though choosing the best treatment for each individual is still partly an art, several principles generally apply:

- If a given treatment helped during a previous episode of your disorder, it probably will again.
- A treatment that has helped a close blood relative is likely to help you, too.
- Of course, both you and your clinician will prefer treatments that are safe and have few unwanted effects.
- You should begin to see improvement shortly after beginning treatment. With medications, that can be as short a time as 2–3 weeks, and sometimes within the first couple of days. All physical treatments, such as drugs, bright light, or electroconvulsive therapy, are likely to work faster than most forms of psychotherapy.
- Patients with personality traits such as suspiciousness, isolation, or dependency will respond more slowly.

In Part III of this book you'll read how clinicians use these principles to recommend the best treatment for a wide variety of mental disorders.

Regardless of the treatment employed, one of the most important considerations is your safety—and that of those around you. Suicide is a risk that every clinician must consider for every patient, every visit. In the general population, the chance of suicide is about 1 in 100; many mental disorders carry a much greater risk. A clinician would be especially wary if you were depressed, psychotic, or using alcohol, conditions that entail the greatest risk of suicide, or if you had made previous attempts. I would especially worry about an elderly man who is also medically ill, unemployed, owns a gun, and lives alone—each of these characteristics increases the risk of suicide.

I would move very quickly to protect such a person. Most of the time, patients agree that hospitalization is an appropriate step, and remain hospitalized voluntarily until sufficiently improved to return home. However, the occasional patient may have to be detained involuntarily. Although the laws vary slightly depending on the jurisdiction, involuntarily hospitalized patients have the right to argue before a judge (with the help of an attorney) why the commitment should be terminated. Then the judge must decide whether to order a release. If release is refused, the commitment will usually be extended briefly (perhaps 2 weeks) before another judicial review.

Although most psychiatric disorders respond readily to treatment, your road to health could still involve some wrong turns. In some of the following circumstances, your clinician might ask a consultant to help map other avenues to explore:

1. **When your response to treatment is less than expected.** An outcome that differs from predictions doesn't mean that either you or the clinician has failed. It does suggest that another pair of eyes and added brainpower may help devise an approach that works better.
2. **If your doctor proposes new or controversial treatments.** Research drugs or medications that haven't been approved for your condition are two examples.
3. **Whenever electroconvulsive therapy seems warranted.** Many states require consultation in such a case.
4. **When you need reassurance.** If you have serious reservations about diagnosis or treatment, some clinicians will suggest a second opinion. If your clinician doesn't suggest this step, you may have to act as your own advocate and ask.

HOW WE DETERMINE WHICH TREATMENTS WORK

Treatment is only therapy if it works—that is, it either hastens your recovery or increases the degree to which you improve. Although it is relatively simple to tell when someone has improved, it isn't so easy to know why. Until we know why, we don't know which treatments are effective and which are not. Let's say you have a cold that you "treat" by drinking orange juice. In a few days, your cold is gone. Does that mean that the OJ worked? Or has the course of time taken care of your cold? To judge the effectiveness of an intervention (even orange juice) requires knowing about two things: the natural history of the disease and the results of what are called "double-blind studies."

To establish a baseline from which to assess the effects of treatment, mental health practitioners rely on knowledge of the natural history of disease. This is the course a given illness is likely to take if left untreated (the natural history of your cold is one of improvement after 3 days). Over the years, clinicians have conducted many studies to determine what happens to patients who have, say, schizophrenia, Alzheimer's dementia, or mania. Most of these studies date from before the development of the first effective treatments—before 1940, for many disorders. For example, researchers could see that most people with carefully diagnosed bipolar mood disorder recovered, though many had subsequent episodes of either depression or mania.

Our other invaluable tool is the double-blind study. Scientists have used this device since the 1930s to guarantee that outcome studies are not biased by expectations. For example, about 30% of depressed patients who take only a placebo (sugar or some other substance that has no medical effect) feel better; some even have to discontinue the "medication" because they seem to have side effects. Here's how the double-blind study works to eliminate any unconscious bias on the part of patient or clinician. The treating physician gives a bottle of capsules to the patient. Although the patients all know they are taking part in a study, neither patients nor physician knows who is getting capsules that contain the drug being studied and who is getting a placebo or a drug already proven effective for the particular disorder. Which patients get which drug is known only by a third person, who does not reveal the key except in an emergency. Once the last pill has been taken and its effects have been studied, the code is broken and results from all patients are gathered to determine how well the new drug has worked.

A treatment is considered "possibly therapeutic" when patients taking it seem to improve faster than the natural course of the disorder would predict. It only advances to "therapeutic" on the basis of double-blind studies. Although you are safest trying a treatment that has been proven effective scientifically, your response could differ from the majority of study participants. You could also respond well to a treatment that hasn't yet been supported by double-blind studies. Evaluating your own progress, or having someone close to you monitor your progress, is an important way to determine the therapeutic benefit of any treatment you try; see the list of questions under "Is My Treatment Working?" on pages 41–42 in Chapter 4.

A QUICK GUIDE TO THE CLINICAL INTERVIEW

If your history is relatively straightforward, such as a recent onset of depression with no prior psychiatric treatment, your initial mental health interview will probably take an hour or less. A more complicated history could require several hours to produce enough information for accurate diagnosis. However long it takes, your clinician can then propose a treatment plan. In Chapter 4 I explain how you can prepare for this visit to speed the flow of information to your clinician. Here's what to expect from the initial diagnostic process.

Chief Complaint

At your first meeting, you'll be asked why you came for a consultation. You should state your main reason(s) for concern, referred to as the "chief complaint." Over the next few minutes, most clinicians will want you just to talk about your problem, starting from the time it began and running right up to the present. There will probably be a number of threads to your story—one that concerns your symptoms (depression? anxiety?), another about the difficulties you've had at work or school, still others about the effects your problems have had on your family, or your family on your problems. During these first few minutes of the interview, your mental health clinician will listen carefully to learn what sorts of symptoms you have (discussed in greater detail in Chapter 2).

History of the Present Illness

Once you have described the issues that motivated you to seek treatment, your clinician will begin to explore them more thoroughly. Expect a large number of specific questions that will help you and your clinician pinpoint the nature of your problem. For example, did you experience any serious stresses that might have triggered this episode? Have you had prior episodes? What sort of treatment did you receive then? If you have previously taken medications, which ones seemed to help most? You will also be asked what consequences your problem has had for your marriage, sex life, friendships, finances, work, or school. Have you had legal problems? Changes in your usual interests? All of this information will help your clinician better understand the breadth of your problems.

Medical History

Medical disorders are important for several reasons.

1. Physical handicaps, childhood illnesses, even allergies can influence how people see themselves; or the medical disorders may suggest a history of dependence on medical care systems.
2. Drugs you take for medical disorders may alter the effectiveness of any new medicines you might be prescribed.
3. Many medications, including herbal remedies, can also produce mental symptoms.
4. As we noted earlier, just about any mental symptom can be caused by medical illnesses. For example, Horace had faithfully attended Alcoholics Anonymous for 25 years, so his therapist was surprised to observe, during several midmorning sessions, that he had begun to slur his words. When asked, Horace revealed that he was worried about his diabetes. An adjustment to his in-

sulin dose and harder work on his diet resulted in better control and no more slurred speech.

Personal History

Health care professionals don't treat illnesses; we treat people. This means learning all about the context in which your problems occur—your personal, social, and family background, beginning with childhood family relationships, right up to your current living situation—including information about your education and work, any military experience or legal problems, your religion and sexual and marital history. Such extensive material may take more than one session to gather, but the result will be a better understanding of your treatment needs.

For several years, Henry had had increasingly severe anxiety attacks and difficulty relating to other people. However, during his initial interview he showed no emotional response until he was asked about his years in the army, and then he began to cry. He related a number of episodes as a Ranger in Vietnam, during which close friends had been killed by mortar attacks and booby traps. On one particularly horrible Friday afternoon, a sniper had pinned down Henry's squad in an open field and methodically picked them off, one by one. The clinician diagnosed posttraumatic stress disorder.

Family History

Many mental problems run in families. Some are inherited, others seem to pass from one generation to another by learning or imitation. Therefore, your clinician will want to know whether any relatives, especially parents, children, or brothers and sisters, have had mental or emotional problems.

Mental Status Examination

Much of the assessment of your current mental condition, which we call the mental status examination (MSE), takes place quietly during the course of normal conversation. Your clinician will make general observations (your apparent age, hygiene, nutritional state, condition of clothing), and note your activity level (high, medium, low), any peculiar behaviors, mood, and flow of speech (do words and sentences convey meaning?)

However, other parts of the MSE require certain questions. For example, you may be asked whether you hear or see things not apparent to others (hallucinations), have false ideas (delusions, such as receiving transmissions from outer space through your microwave oven), and other troubling experiences (fears, anxiety attacks, obsessive thoughts, compulsive behavior, ideas about violence or suicide). It is also routine to judge cognitive status (memory and ability to think) by asking you to perform small tasks: give the correct date, month, and year; recall three items after the passage of a few minutes, such as a name, a color, and a street address; subtract 7's repeatedly from 100 (93—86—79—and so forth); name five presidents in order, beginning with the most recent; name ways in which an apple and an orange are similar.

Other Information

What you have just read is the barest outline of a mental health evaluation. Much more may be needed, such as old records, especially when there has been a history of prolonged previous treatment, perhaps with several clinicians. You may be given specialized psychological tests to quantify the degree of your depression, anxiety, or dozens of other emotional or mental characteristics. Once again, I'll mention the physical examination, which can help find medical causes for symptoms or assess the degree to which a mental illness might have impaired your general health.

Character structure is difficult to describe briefly, let alone assess, but your clinician will try to judge your important strengths and personal resources and how well you have coped with life's hardships. To determine what sort of person you are, or were, before your illness began ("premorbid personality") may require additional information; interviews with relatives and friends are often vital, even for intelligent adult patients who can relate a history that is coherent, concise, and nearly complete.

CHAPTER 2

Will Treatment Help Me?

The short answer is *yes*. Nearly every mental health problem imaginable can be helped. Unfortunately, many people view their problems as personal inadequacies and therefore believe no one and nothing can help them. Take Wayne, for example, who had been a taxi dispatcher for several years. Recently he began to doubt that he was up to his job. "When 5 P.M. rolls around and traffic picks up, I'm losing it," Wayne complained. "I can't stand the tension anymore—I'm just not a big enough person. I even broke down and cried when I talked to my boss last week. I've become a high-maintenance employee. How can you help someone who is basically a failure?"

You're not alone if you blame your emotional problems on failure to meet the demands of a job, finances, or interpersonal conflict. In reality, mental illnesses are caused not by personal failure or moral decline but by heredity, physical disease or injury, or stresses inflicted by changes in the environment. In this chapter you'll see that we have effective treatments for an enormous range of mental, emotional, and behavioral problems, most likely including yours. Part III provides details on individual disorders, but right now you want to know if your symptoms can be helped. The types and severity of symptoms that call for attention are listed briefly in the following pages.

CONDITIONS WE CAN TREAT EFFECTIVELY

Mental, emotional, and behavioral problems can make people feel isolated, as if no one else has suffered the same combination of circumstances and problems. In this isolation, it is hard to appreciate that even complex mental illnesses can be categorized and understood and therefore treated. The following groupings show how clinicians think about mental disorders in a way that points to effective treatment. You will see that many others have experienced problems similar to yours, and effective treatments *have* been developed.

Major Mental Illnesses

These include such well-recognized disorders as depression and mania, alcoholism and drug dependence, panic disorder and specific phobias, even psychoses, of which schizophrenia is the best known. Such illnesses are major in that the symptoms are obvious and their consequences can be dire. These disorders affect so many people that nearly everyone has relatives or friends who have suffered from one or more of them. Any of them can create personal and social problems like Wayne's. Because these disorders impair lives so severely when left untreated, much research has been devoted to them, and each now has treatment that studies have proven effective.

Mental Disorders Caused by Medical Problems

Although many people don't realize it, physical disease can also cause mental and emotional symptoms. For example, strokes can produce depression, epilepsy can lead to psychosis. I've seen anxiety symptoms caused by thyroid disease, and nearly every clinician has encountered patients whose depressions lifted once their blood pressure medicine was adjusted. Of course, brain disease, such as tumors and infection, can produce problems with thinking that we call cognitive disorder, but it can also be responsible for anxiety symptoms, depression, and psychosis. In all such cases, the obvious treatment is to cure or arrest the underlying medical disease process. Analogous arguments can be made for depressions, anxiety states, and psychoses caused by the use of alcohol and street drugs.

Personality Disorders

Even thoroughly ingrained patterns of dealing with other people, though they often cause serious consequences for both individuals and those who associate with them, can yield to vigorous treatment with psychotherapy.

Interpersonal Issues and Problems of Living

Finally, we come to the sort of problem Wayne thought he had. Problems of living include trouble getting along with spouse, siblings, parents, or friends—areas that can affect anyone, with or without a diagnosable mental disorder. Using medications or other physical means as interventions is rare; even the need for intensive psychotherapy would be unusual, though couple therapy would be a possibility.

WHAT SYMPTOMS MIGHT INDICATE THE NEED FOR TREATMENT?

Some of the symptoms that suggest the need for a mental health evaluation are listed below. Before you read through it, however, please note these very important warnings:

1. A couple of symptoms don't make you abnormal; nearly everyone has symptoms sometimes.
2. Even the most severely ill patient will have only some of these symptoms; no one has them all.
3. The list is hardly complete; there are far more possible symptoms than I could squeeze onto a page.
4. Some symptoms, such as palpitations and shortness of breath, can also indicate a physical illness; your clinician will need to evaluate you for both possibilities.
5. Some symptoms are common to several mental disorders.
6. Most patients have symptoms that fit more than one group. In Part III you'll see how symptoms fit together to make a diagnosis.

Mood Disturbance

A problem with mood is a common reason for a mental health evaluation. Whereas many patients are well aware of their feelings (people have told me, "I feel depressed" as they walked into my office for the first time), others don't recognize that their mood is abnormal.

Anxiety/panic
Depression
Guilt
Hostility/anger
Mania
Unnatural happiness (mania)

Difficulty Thinking

Although we usually associate trouble thinking with brain disease such as dementia, cognitive (thinking) symptoms also occur in other mental disorders.

Confusion
Distractibility
Faulty judgment

Faulty memory
Incoherent speech
Loss of consciousness
Poor concentration

Social and Personality Problems

Certain quirks of character—loosely defined as the way people interact with one another—make social problems more likely to develop. Problems in this area can also
be found in every psychiatric disorder I can name.

Distrustful or suspicious
Few friends
Frequent change of jobs
Marital conflict
Physical fighting
Repeated legal difficulties
Social withdrawal

Unusual Behavior

In assessing for mental disturbance, clinicians don't just look for the unusual, but for
any changes from a person's normal behavior. Such shifts may involve:

Bizarre (not understandable) behavior
Compulsive behavior
Excessive drama
Excessive fidgeting
Frequent crying
Heavy drinking
Hyperactivity
Impulsiveness
Loss of interest in usual activities
Muteness
Rapid or loud speech
Reduced activity level

Thought Content

What a person thinks about (and talks about) provides important clues to mental illness.

Death wishes, suicidal ideas
Delusions
Excessive worrying
Fear of dying or becoming insane
Fear of objects or situations
Feeling worthless
Hallucinations
Obsessions

Physical and Physiological Symptoms

These symptoms can indicate medical (physical) disease, and they need to be investigated as such, but they are also often found in many mental conditions.

Appetite loss or gain
Chest pain
Decreased interest in sex
Dizziness
Excessive sleepiness
Fatigue
Insomnia
Irregular or rapid heartbeat (palpitations)
Nausea, vomiting
Shortness of breath
Sweating
Trembling
Weight loss or gain

HOW CAN I TELL IF MY SYMPTOMS ARE SERIOUS?

If most people have symptoms at one time or another, how can you tell when a problem is serious? Sometimes the need for treatment seems obvious, as with suicidal depression, phobias that keep a person housebound, or delusions of persecution by aliens. But what about the occasional anxiety attack or a depression so mild that you continue to function at home and on the job? An almost endless variety of human behavior is normal in the sense of not requiring treatment. Sadness, anxiety, anger, envy—all of these emotions are a part of the human condition. It is when they are carried to extremes that they may require the services of a mental health clinician. Untreated, a mild depression can become incapacitating as symptoms accumulate or worsen. Is it better, then, to seek treatment at once, or should you wait to see whether the symptoms abate? Though there is no single, correct answer to such a question, let me point out some warning signs that would warrant an early evaluation:

- **Severe symptoms.** These are the problems that demand an immediate, careful evaluation by a qualified professional. The really serious symptoms are usually pretty obvious—suicidal or homicidal ideas, delusions, or hallucinations. However, symptoms that one person might find merely uncomfortable could incapacitate another. For example, heavy drinking or drug use may be quite serious in someone who has never done so before.

- **Many symptoms.** Symptoms that individually don't seem so serious may, by sheer number, become alarming. Consider Pam, a school teacher I saw years ago, not long after the fall semester had begun. During student orientation week she noticed that her appetite had fallen off and she couldn't focus on her new students. By the second week of school, she was awakening earlier than normal, had lost weight, and felt that she was failing as a teacher. The fact that she was experiencing more and more symptoms was what finally persuaded her to seek help.

- **Lasting symptoms.** If you've felt upset for a short time, you might not pay it too much attention—as long as the feeling goes away within a few days. It is the persistence of symptoms that seems to grind you down, eventually affecting your work, leisure time, and personal relationships. As symptoms endure for weeks or months, they become more worrisome and suggest the need for consultation.

- **Alarming consequences.** Sometimes it's the fallout from symptoms that waves the red flag. Consider Bob, whose six-pack-a-day drinking seemed about normal for his family. His brothers, who enjoyed "knocking back" a few themselves, finally took notice of Bob's drinking when he was fired for chronic absenteeism from work and his wife took the kids and left.

Of course, warning signs are helpful only if they are heeded. Some people don't realize when they are becoming mentally ill. In such an instance, it is more important than ever for others to contribute their viewpoints. If you are worried about the health of someone you care about, you may need to use a list of the symptoms you have noticed as the basis for a frank talk. If you are the person with the symptoms and those who know you well have begun to voice concern, perhaps you are too close to the problem to be able to judge your own behavior accurately. Then you should make the list and request the frank discussion.

CHAPTER 3

Where Can I Go for Help?

Once you've decided to seek evaluation or treatment, either for yourself or for a friend or close relative, where do you go for help? You can consult practitioners from a sometimes confusing array of professional disciplines, each of which has its positives and negatives. Of course, your selection will be guided, in large part, by your type of problem and how far you have come in identifying it. Following is a list of the professional disciplines, in approximate decreasing order of expense.

• **Psychiatrist.** A psychiatrist is a physician (doctor of medicine or osteopathy) who has spent four years in medical school followed by another four in specialty training. Like all other physicians, psychiatrists must be licensed by the state in which they practice. They are trained in doing initial evaluations and can provide psychotherapy as well as medication, though not all psychiatrists have equal facility with both. Of all the professions mentioned here, psychiatrists can provide the widest scope of service, usually at the greatest expense, though insurance will often defray part of the fee.

• **Psychologist.** Clinical psychologists have studied human behavior and the science and art of psychotherapy; they cannot prescribe medication or other forms of somatic treatment. Many psychologists have doctorate degrees, either PhD (doctor of philosophy) or PsyD (doctor of psychology). The latter degree is granted by institutions where training emphasizes evaluating and treating patients. Although PhD programs also provide clinical training, some of these graduates are more interested in doing research. After college, doctoral-level psychologists spend 4 years in training and a year of postgraduate experience, then must pass a state licensing examination. Clinical psychologists may specialize in psychological testing, such as administering and interpreting intelligence tests, personality inventories, and evaluations for cognitive disorders such as dementia. Others may spend all or most of

27

their time providing initial evaluations and doing behavioral therapy or psychotherapy. Fees are close to those of a psychiatrist and may be covered by insurance.

• **Family doctor.** Family doctors receive training in psychiatric drugs and other treatments, but their level of interest in mental health problems varies widely. Most will feel comfortable in prescribing medication for anxiety and depression; some have a wider interest in diagnosis and psychotherapy.

• **Social worker.** Originally, these professionals addressed patients' social needs such as assuring adequate housing, child care, and recreational and sanitary facilities. Today, many psychiatric social workers specialize in individual and group counseling, similar to that provided by psychiatrists and psychologists. Training for social workers varies enormously, ranging from as little as a bachelor's degree for a social work associate to a doctorate. Most who specialize in treating mental patients have had training at the master's-degree level. Hundreds of hours of supervised casework with patients are required for social workers at all levels. Depending on their degree of training, locality, and whether they are certified as qualified, diplomats, licensed, clinical, independent, or associate, social workers may have any of the following degree/licensing designations: LCSW, LSW, ISW, SWA, LICSW, LSWA, QCSW, and DCSW.

• **Advanced practice nurse and physician's assistant.** A registered nurse with master's-level education and training, plus many hours of supervised practice (an advanced practice nurse, or, for short, AP nurse), can become expert in diagnosis and treatment of certain disorders. In the field of mental health, such a person could be licensed as a clinical nurse specialist or psychiatric nurse practitioner, depending on the state granting the license. Physician's assistants (PAs) are neither nurses nor doctors, but have had intensive medical training and, under the supervision of a physician, do much the same sort of work as an AP nurse. Both PAs and AP nurses can prescribe certain medicines.

• **Marriage and family therapist.** These professionals (MFTs, for short) are trained to provide marital and individual therapy to adults, adolescents, and children. Their therapy seeks to improve relationships within the family, and often the approach involves more than one family member. Three years or more of classroom and casework are needed to complete this course of study. A licensure exam includes both written and oral sections. Although their professional titles are usually given as MFT, in some states they are known as marriage, family and child counselors (MFCCs).

• **Drug and alcohol addiction counselor.** These professionals assess drug and alcohol disorders, manage treatment plans, and provide individual, family, and group counseling. States credential them at various levels, depending on education, supervision, and work experience.

• **Pastoral counselor.** These clergy (ministers, priests, rabbis) provide counseling to individuals, couples, and families. Some have had master's-level training offered by divinity schools and may hold a MDiv degree, which designates the mastery of counseling techniques applied in the context of the religious experience.

Who you contact also depends on the services you need, which you may not know until after your initial appointment. However, here are some guidelines.

- **Recent onset of symptoms, no previous diagnosis.** You need someone skilled in interviewing and diagnosis. A psychiatrist or psychologist is probably your best bet. If it turns out that you don't have a major mental problem, such as a depression, anxiety disorder, or substance use problem, but rather a problem of living, the diagnosing clinician may even refer you to a different therapist.
- **Likely to require medication.** Patients with depression, anxiety, or psychosis often need medication. Most psychiatrists will prescribe medication, though a few practice only psychotherapy. Family physicians also prescribe medication and can be a perfectly sound choice for uncomplicated depression or anxiety.
- **Likely to need psychotherapy.** The "talking cure" is likely to be the treatment of choice for a variety of disorders, including problems of living, somatization disorder, eating disorders, some anxiety disorders, many substance use problems, and personality problems (indicated by a lifelong history of trouble getting along with most people). If you know that your diagnosis is one of these, any of the professionals listed above can work with you in a large variety of psychotherapy models, though most will prefer their favorite techniques. For specialized psychoanalytic psychotherapy, you'd need either a psychiatrist or a psychologist with analytical training.
- **Likely to need family or couple therapy.** If the problem has been diagnosed as one of family relations, and not an illness in an individual family member, a family therapist (MFT or MFCC) will often be appropriate. So will many social workers who practice family and couple therapy.
- **Adolescents or children.** Many mental health professionals treat both adults and children, but child disorders, which are beyond the scope of this book, require a professional who has special training and experience with this age group. Any of the professionals mentioned above may have received such subspecialty training.

Depending on your circumstances, any of these professionals could provide the right combination of service and cost. Absent the need for medication, the personality, experience, and dedication of the therapist matters more than the initials that follow the name. The finest psychotherapist I have ever known is a social worker by training who practices in a university town and helps train psychiatric residents. Also consider that you can probably tolerate almost anyone long enough to get a diagnosis, but ongoing therapy requires a person you like and trust; lacking this, no degree of learning or fame matters very much. Finding that person is a little like eating out: the new restaurant in the mall may sound terrific in a printed review, but it takes a meal or two to know whether you'd care to return on a regular basis.

FINDING A CLINICIAN

Once you've decided which type of professional you need to see, how can you locate the right one? There are significant problems with some of the more traditional methods of choosing a clinician, such as asking a friend or consulting the Yellow Pages. Asking a friend is likely to yield a sample of one, whereas the Yellow Pages, like any type of advertising, provides little basis for an informed decision. Local medical, psychiatric, or psychological societies will give you names of practitioners but, like the phone book, without evaluations. Magazines and newspapers sometimes try to boost circulation by publishing lists of the "best doctors" in a given community, but these lists often boil down to who is the best connected or best known. I wouldn't pay them much mind.

I'd also be wary of Internet search engines, which will return the names of health care providers in your area. However, these results attest principally to the enterprising nature of these individuals, which is not the same as the quality of their care. Although you may learn something about the type of therapy offered, you should further check the credentials and other characteristics of these potential caregivers. Don't be put off if your browser turns up a Scientology page that vilifies psychiatry and mental health treatment, in general; these opinions are a matter of belief, not science.

You can compile a short list of names to check out with your family doctor (who, we will assume, does not treat mental illness personally). Ministers, rabbis, and priests can also be good resources, because they often ask how well treatment is going with therapists they have recommended to their congregation. Of course, if you are already in individual treatment and you also need some other type of therapy (couple or drug treatment, for example), your current clinician may have a good recommendation for you.

One of my favorite techniques is to ask a nurse. Nurses, especially those who work on a psychiatric ward (or in a general hospital that admits psychiatric patients), get to see a large number of health care givers in action, and if you can find one who is willing to discuss the question with you, you'll get a ground view of the local mental health care scene. A potentially informative question, which I also ask physicians and other psychiatrists, is this: "Where would you go if you had [name your problem]?" Regardless of your final choice, check with your referring source to learn: "Why do you think this person is right for me?" The best answer is: "I've seen excellent results in others who have your kind of problem."

You may not have the luxury of choice if you receive care through a college or university student health service, a community mental health center, or a health maintenance organization (HMO). Although any of these organizations may have limited options, you should still do your best to evaluate the characteristics of your clinician and to reevaluate the care you receive periodically.

You may have two clinicians, one to prescribe medication and one to provide the psychotherapy. Such an arrangement occasionally tempts a patient to engage in what we call "splitting"—that is, to pit the two clinicians against one another, perhaps by idealizing one while denigrating the other. This circumstance works to everyone's disadvantage, but mostly to the patient's. Sharing patients can work well if both clinicians are well trained, have worked together for a long time, respect one another's judgment, and consult each other frequently. You should always be seen at least once by the physician for an evaluation, and preferably at intervals thereafter.

Especially in the larger metropolitan areas, you'll encounter newspaper or television ads recruiting research subjects with particular emotional symptoms, such as depression, anxiety, or psychotic thinking. These researchers are looking for people to take drugs that have not yet been approved by the Food and Drug Administration (FDA). Sometimes, this is a terrific idea—after all, every new drug, like every new therapist, has to start somewhere. For no money you might receive high-quality ethical treatment. However, some of these programs are far more concerned with the researchers' needs than the patients', even to the extent of falsifying test scores and laboratory data to squeeze more subjects into an extremely profitable operation. There is no convenient way to tell which is which, though your chances may be better in a program administered through a university or medical school department of psychiatry. Important questions to ask at the outset include:

"Will I continue to receive care once the study is finished?"
"If the medication is successful, can I continue to receive it once the study has run its course?"
"What are the chances I'll get a placebo, and if I do, would I later get an active medication?"

CHECKING QUALIFICATIONS

Once you have developed a list of potential clinicians, check these important details before you make your selection:

• **Schooling.** In general, the more complicated your problem, the more training your therapist should have. Diagnosis "from scratch" will usually require the evaluation of a psychiatrist or a doctoral-level psychologist, though you may be referred to someone with less training for the actual delivery of psychotherapy. Although many little known or foreign schools can provide fine educations, you may feel more secure if your therapist attended a school with a familiar name. Resources for checking out the qualities of professional schools include the *U.S. News & World Report* annual college issue, and the Internet. Search for a professional school by name.

- **Certification.** If a psychiatrist, is your doctor certified by the American Board of Psychiatry and Neurology? This certification requires passing rigorous written and oral examinations that cover all phases of diagnosis and treatment. Up to 1994, this board issued credentials that were good for the lifetime of the physician, so you might ask how your clinician keeps current. Reading journals? Attending meetings? Teaching at a medical school? Continuing medical education is now required by most states for license renewal.

- **Fellowship.** Becoming a fellow in a professional organization sounds impressive, but it is typically an honor bestowed for service to the profession rather than for demonstrated level of expertise. It's a nice extra, but don't put much store by either its presence or its absence.

- **Experience.** Ask how much experience this clinician has had with your particular disorder or problem. A reassuring answer would be, "This sort of problem has constituted about 10% of my practice for the past 15 years." An OK answer would be, "There is someone good I usually refer this sort of problem to, if that turns out to be the case." More troubling: "I don't usually see this sort of problem, but I'm willing to try" or "I've done a lot of reading."

- **Network.** Can this clinician consult other professionals for advice, or is this therapist a solo practitioner? There is nothing inherently wrong with the latter, but the ability to ask directions when in unfamiliar territory is a real plus in any caregiver.

- **Range of therapies.** Some therapists are guided more by a theoretical orientation than by the problem. If you see such a clinician, you risk procrustean tailoring of your problem to a one-size-fits-all treatment philosophy. (This narrowness can also characterize clinicians who specialize in prescribing medications.) Obviously, your treatment should be based on what works best for your problem. A phone call to the therapist (or secretary) will reveal what types of therapy this person uses— medication, individual psychotherapy, family counseling, marriage therapy, and so on. If you see a nonphysician counselor, ask how medication would be provided, if you should need it. Some nonphysician counselors are experienced and well informed about when drugs should be used and which ones work well; others are not.

Beyond credentials, what does it take to succeed with your therapist? The better your working relationship with your therapist, the more likely a good outcome will be. This can be just as true for treatment with medication as with psychotherapy. To stand a good chance of benefiting from the treatment, you must like your therapist and feel that you are understood. Whether you are referred or select someone from a list, you may want to interview more than one potential therapist. For couple or family therapy, be sure that both spouses are involved in the selection process. Otherwise you risk adding the therapist to the list of potential battlegrounds for parties who are sometimes at war with one another.

It is usually better to choose a therapist who isn't involved in the care of your relatives. Try as they might, it would be hard for most clinicians to keep straight what they have heard from whom, and who is privy to what secrets. Exceptions to this recommendation might be clinicians who mainly provide medications, other physical treatments, or behavior modification therapy.

Some people look for a therapist of their own age, sex, ethnicity, or religious preference. All the evidence I've seen suggests that these personal factors don't much affect the outcome of treatment. It is far more important for your therapist to get the diagnosis right and have the necessary treatment skills; mental health treatment is an equal opportunity healer. If your therapist has not personally had experiences or life conditions (divorce, being gay, particular religious beliefs) that are germane to your problem, you can provide that education. A good clinician will learn and adapt to your new information.

COST OF TREATMENT

The total cost of therapy depends most on the complexity of your problem, though hourly rates do vary with the type of practitioner you select. An initial evaluation from a psychiatrist or psychologist will probably run $200 or more; subsequent appointments can range from $50 to $150. Other caregivers may charge less. (Unlike lawyers, clinicians expect to be paid from the first session.) All fees may be partly offset by contributions from your health insurance plan. Most clinicians will expect you to pay for uncanceled appointments, which *won't* be covered by insurance.

Unhappily, many Americans are not covered by mental health insurance, are retired, or are otherwise unable to afford much for mental health care. Though options may be somewhat limited, some treatment facilities accept low-fee patients. If you live near a medical school or other training facility, check to see whether a department of psychiatry or psychology offers sliding-scale fees. If they do, you will probably be assigned to a resident, perhaps even a medical student, who will provide treatment under the close supervision of a faculty clinician. The trainee gets experience and you receive inexpensive care. Aside from the inexperience of your clinician, a major drawback is the fact that every few months trainees move on to other services; if continuity of care is an absolute must, this plan is clearly not for you. You might also consider a community mental health clinic that operates under similar payment conditions. If you are a veteran who was discharged honorably from the military, you will probably qualify for mental health care from a VA outpatient clinic, where your visits may be partly or entirely underwritten by the government.

That still leaves the cost of medication, should one be prescribed. VA clinics and

TABLE 3.1. Selected Pharmaceutical Manufacturers That Supply Free Drugs for Needy Patients

Company	Telephone number	Drug name(s)
Abbott	800-441-4987	Depakote
Boehringer Ingelheim	800-556-8317	Serentil
Bristol-Myers Squibb	800-332-2056	BuSpar, Desyrel, Prolixin, Serzone
Ciba	800-257-3273	Ludiomil
Eli Lilly	800-545-6962	Prozac, Zyprexa
Forest	800-851-0758	Celexa
Glaxo SmithKline	800-546-0420	Paxil, Wellbutrin
Hoechst Marion Roussel	800-221-4025	Norpramin
Janssen	800-652-6227	Risperdal
Novartis	800-257-3273	Clozaril, Tegretol
Organon	800-241-8812	Remeron
Ortho-McNeil	800-797-7737	Haldol
Pfizer	800-646-4455	Navane, Neurontin, Sinequan, Zoloft
Roche	800-285-4484	Klonopin, Valium
Schering/Key	800-656-9485	Trilafon
Solvay	800-256-8918	Lithobid, Luvox
Wyeth-Ayerst	800-568-9938	Effexor, Surmontil
Zeneca	800-424-3727	Seroquel

community mental health clinics often provide medicine very inexpensively. Of course, generic medications (those that have been on the market long enough that they are out of patent and are now provided by multiple manufacturers) usually cost far less than brand-name drugs, but many of our most effective and safest drugs are not yet produced as generics. Some companies have special programs through which they will provide brand-name drugs free for patients who cannot otherwise afford them. By calling 202-835-3450, your doctor can request a directory published by the Pharmaceutical Research and Manufacturers Association. Table 3.1 lists telephone numbers for some companies that will require supporting documentation from your physician.

HOW IS MY CLINICIAN DOING?

Above all else, your doctor or other mental health provider should be a professional who, during the time you sit together, has only your well-being at stake. Such a person manifests an attitude of caring that reflects a genuine concern for your happiness and well-being. In addition to the list of responsibilities I've given in the introduction to Part I, a good clinician:

- Listens well, to give your problems a complete evaluation.
- Takes a complete history.
- Considers a variety of diagnoses and reevaluates your diagnosis if new data come to light.
- Lists the benefits and risks of treatment options and is aware of new treatment methods.
- Frequently reevaluates your progress and suggests changes if improvement lags.
- Can handle after-hours and weekend emergencies, either personally or through an on-call associate.
- Listens to any complaints you may have and works to resolve them appropriately.
- Sticks with you, regardless of your rate of progress or whether your insurance runs out.

CHAPTER 4

What Is My Role
in Treatment?

Earlier generations of patients were regarded as passive vessels into which clinicians poured treatment; doctors prescribed, patients complied. For at least the past couple of decades, this one-way street has been under heavy reconstruction. Clinicians now recognize that they can provide far better care when patients (and families) actively participate in the entire treatment process. With this in mind, in this chapter I outline some ways in which you can become a better partner with your clinician.

PREPARING FOR THE EVALUATION

There are a number of ways to prepare for your first meeting with your new clinician. If you were referred to this clinician, ask the person who referred you (family doctor, for example) to send the clinician a summary of the findings that prompted the referral. Whether referred or self-directed, for this first meeting, bring all relevant information, such as old treatment records, and a complete chronology of your illness. Compile a list of previous treatments—what worked well, what didn't? Your new clinician will also want to know about family history; you can save some valuable initial interview time if you bring in a typed list of relatives who have had any form of mental disorder (see details in Chapter 1). Even if this is your first experience in the mental health field, you can speed things along by bringing a summary of your physical health, including past illnesses, allergies to medications, hospitalizations, operations, and a list of all medicines you currently take, with dosages.

REVIEWING THE EVALUATION

The first interview should produce enough information to suggest a diagnosis and a plan of action. Be sure that you clearly understand everything your clinician says. As hard as we try to use plain language, all of us occasionally slip into mental health jargon. If you hear words or concepts that are unfamiliar to you, don't be embarrassed to ask for clarification.

Every treatment plan should include alternatives, which you should take pains to understand. If none is presented, ask, even if it is only for the option *not* to begin treatment at this time. You may have to ask specifically about treatments (or diagnoses) that have not already been discussed. Of all the treatment choices you discuss, usually one will stand out. Before starting this treatment, be sure that you also understand its drawbacks—there will always be some—and reevaluate: based on what you've read previously and heard in the interview, does it match your own goals for treatment?

Suppose, however, that the choices seem so muddled that you can't make up your mind. Unless there is some sort of dire emergency (such as serious thoughts of harming yourself) that cannot wait, take a little time to think over the alternatives. Discussing the options with a spouse, relative, or trusted friend may help. If you do wait to decide, keep in mind a couple of warnings.

1. Don't delay too long—action delayed could be improvement denied. Sometimes it feels safer having choices than it does taking action.
2. Advice of friends and family could be clouded by lack of information or fear of the unknown.

Your therapist has the most relevant information and the most experience with problems like yours, but even so, you may want to check out the advice you get. You can read about your diagnosis in Part III of this book; also check the treatment recommendations in Part II to see whether they support the advice you received. If you still feel uncomfortable, a frank discussion with the therapist about your concerns may clear the air. You could also request a second opinion (page 42).

If you have secret fears about the nature of your problem ("Could my problem be due to AIDS?" "Could I pass it on to my children?"), this is a terrific time to bring them up. What you hear will probably reassure you, but if you don't ask, you may always wonder.

YOUR RESPONSIBILITIES DURING TREATMENT

Once the diagnosis is made, learn all you can about the scientific underpinnings of your illness and its treatment. The more you know, the better you can participate in making decisions that affect your health. If you encounter something you don't understand—perhaps your therapist uses the word *cognitive* or mentions the diagnosis of "bipolar disorder"—even if the issue itself is not critical to your care, request an explanation. At a minimum, you'll be helping the therapist understand how best to communicate with you in the future. Many resources can help you learn; you are reading one of them, and Appendix A mentions others. Appendix A will also get you started with some basic Internet resources devoted to disorders, treatments, and general mental health issues. Your browser will lead you to many more.

As the relationship with your therapist progresses, you will find many opportunities to facilitate your own improvement. In most cases, one or two visits won't fix your problem, so you'll need follow-up appointments. Be sure to keep them. If all goes well from the first, you may not need many, but treatment is often a matter of trial and refinement as patient and clinician come to understand the problems they face together.

A major responsibility is sticking to your treatment plan. This may involve more than just taking medicines on time. You may be asked to keep a treatment log, for example, or to follow through with recommended tests, exercises, or family discussions. Taking medicine as directed is an important task, one too often honored in the breach. It has been repeatedly documented that about half the time patients don't follow their medication schedules. Sometimes it's no big deal, especially if it is only a matter of taking evening pills at 9 P.M. instead of at 6, but there can be more at stake, depending on the medication.

At every visit with a patient, even if it is the 50th visit, I ask, "Just what medicine are you taking and how are you taking it?" The answer often differs from the program I thought I had prescribed. That doesn't mean that what my patient has done is wrong—the change may have been due to side effects or to a simple misunderstanding. In any event, it must be discussed and recorded: no physician can provide competent care without knowing your exact drug schedule.

On page 56 I list causes of medication noncompliance; similar reasons may apply to other problems people have following a clinician's suggestions. Repeatedly missing appointments, for example, may relate to a fear of what might be learned; neglecting to discuss symptoms with relatives may fulfill an unconscious wish that the whole illness problem would just go away. Whatever the reason, any problem following treatment recommendations should be the subject of future discussions with your clinician.

However, don't wait to be asked about medications or any other changes in your life. Of course you'd mention something as obvious as symptoms that crop up (or disappear), but also bring up other possible stressors, such as new relationships, a change in diet or exercise habits, or problems in your family. Write these down as they occur so you'll be sure to remember them all during your appointment.

Most of the questions that you'll want to discuss can wait until your next appointment. You can even tolerate an urgent problem if you know that you have an appointment in a day or two, but you might have trouble coping if relief is a week away. If that is the case, you should call. Here are a few rules of thumb as to what constitutes a problem that needs immediate attention:

- Alarming symptoms, such as increasing depression, suicidal ideas, worsening hallucinations, episodes of falling, or dizziness
- New side effects of medicines
- Any issue about which your doctor has asked you to call right away
- A personal crisis—marital separation, death in the family, being laid off work

If you can't decide whether your issue is urgent, *call*. I have been worried far more often by overly considerate patients who didn't call soon enough than by the tiny handful who call too often.

Finally, resist the temptation to make your therapist a personal friend. That can be hard. After all, this *is* a friendly person who is intelligent, sympathetic, who likes and helps you, with whom you have shared feelings and thoughts, as you would with a close friend. But one reason therapists are effective sources of help is that they don't have a personal relationship with you to conflict with the job of helping you feel better. When a therapist and patient do become friendly, even intimate, personal motives intrude upon what should be an objective view of your problems by someone who is supposed to have only your interest at heart. The result is often a terrible muddle in which the problem that initiated treatment is drowned in a sea of changing relationships and conflicted emotions.

THE IMPORTANCE OF ADVOCACY

A variety of state and federal agencies oversee health care in the United States. The FDA regulates the manufacture and use of drugs and devices. Each state has a variety of quality assurance boards (they go by various formal names) that oversee the work of clinicians. If you have a problem with billing, professional ethics, or medical practice regarding a physician, psychologist, or social worker, you can write, call, or e-mail the appropriate board for assistance. Many clinicians belong to their respective professional societies, such as the American Psychiatric Association, American Psychological Association, and National Association of Social Workers. These associations and societies, which have branches in each state as well as in many larger counties, can also help resolve problems with health care providers.

However, these agencies and associations mostly offer repair services after an accident, whereas what you would really like is accident prevention. For that, you must rely on your own resources. I'd encourage you to have a confidante. This may be a friend or relative who has been in treatment and knows the ropes. Of course, you probably won't share everything, but if any aspect of your treatment troubles you, bounce it off your confidante. Even without hearing all the intimate details, this person can probably reassure you—or validate your concerns.

For example, as treatment progresses, you could encounter disquieting behaviors in your therapist. Does your clinician sometimes seem not to pay attention to you? I've even known a few who fall asleep, especially during sessions right after lunch. What about flexibility? A good clinician will have an open mind. Not long ago I encountered a young man who had a psychotherapist in mind and wanted a psychiatrist who would just prescribe medication; the doctor had refused, and the patient had gone elsewhere. In addition, a good clinician will *not*:

- Take personal phone calls during your time together, except in a rare emergency
- Burden you with personal problems
- Outside of office hours, encourage or allow contact with you, whether personal, social, sexual, or financial
- Take you off a treatment that is working well to try an experimental treatment, especially when there is a risk that you could get a placebo

WHEN IS A PROFESSIONAL BEHAVING PROFESSIONALLY?

Professionalism is accomplishment married to attitude; it includes the following characteristics of service:

- Professionals have attained special education and training designed to address complex problems or issues.
- As they accumulate experience in this field, they develop a sense of how to approach a given situation. At the same time, professionals know their limitations and sense when they themselves need advice.
- They maintain high ethical standards and take pride in doing the best job possible without regard for personal gain.
- They adhere to core humanistic values of compassion, honesty, respect, and trustworthiness.
- They recognize their own errors and learn from them.
- They hold themselves accountable for their own and their colleagues' actions.
- Professionals place the needs of their patients/clients/customers above all else.

Obviously, this definition of a professional applies to fields of endeavor far beyond the realm of medicine. I know furniture restorers who fit the above criteria, and, unhappily, I've known doctors and lawyers who could never qualify. It's your right to expect this level of professionalism from any mental health care provider you consult. You may not be in a position to judge your caregiver on every item, but if you see evidence of serious shortcomings, go find someone with higher standards.

It is vital that treatment be customized to fit your needs. For example, an antidepressant medicine that is appropriate for many patients may be wrong for you, but only because you have medical problems that the side effects of this medication may worsen. Beware the cookie-cutter approach of some clinicians who prescribe the same treatment (drugs or otherwise) for most patients or who overdiagnose a particular illness, such as borderline personality disorder and depression. You might learn of this tendency by comparing notes with friends or speaking with other patients in the waiting room.

IS MY TREATMENT WORKING?

Rarely does a medical specialist prescribe treatment and then never see the patient again. Mental health treatment is no different in this regard. In fact, we are probably somewhat more assiduous than most about insisting on follow-up appointments to evaluate the reduction of symptoms, the emergence of side effects, and impact of treatment on your interpersonal relationships and ability to work. For some problems, such as a relatively mild depression or anxiety disorder, this may mean no more than a few visits. If you require prophylaxis (such as for bipolar disease) or extensive treatment (such as for schizophrenia), you could be at the start of a lifelong relationship.

However long your treatment lasts, periodically ask yourself, "How am I doing now compared with before I started therapy?" In particular, do you:

- Notice reduction in your target symptoms?
- Feel that you understand yourself and your relationships better, that you communicate more easily with friends and relatives?
- Participate in your usual activities and hobbies?
- Hear from friends, relatives, or coworkers, "Gee, you seem like your old self," or "You've got your smile back," or "It's just like old times"?
- Sleep and eat normally once again?
- Focus on issues and problems other than yourself?
- Start thinking, "Why am I taking this medicine—I feel so good?" (*Warning*: the appropriate response is *not* to stop, but talk to your doctor about how you feel.)

Even if your progress is not 100%, you should see something in the way of improvement within a few weeks—sooner, if your main treatment is drugs. If you don't seem to be following this pattern, you could need additional interventions. It is far better to deal with your concerns at once; waiting to see "if it will all work out" invites frustration and worse. What are your options?

Your best approach would be to speak frankly with your doctor about your concerns. For example, suppose that, contrary to your expectations, you are prescribed a course of treatment within the first half-hour of meeting your new doctor—before you've even discussed the area that concerns you deeply. You respond, "I'm worried that we seem to be going too fast. What should we do?" Of course, there may be an excellent explanation—perhaps the doctor has learned a lot about you from the family physician who referred you, or a relative might have called. More likely, however, your comment will prompt a thorough discussion of your history. You could end up with the same treatment recommendation, but because of your action, your comfort with your clinician's overall understanding will improve. Other expressions of concern could result in a change of medication or a new psychotherapeutic approach. The vital bottom line: you have been heard and feel a part of the therapeutic team.

If you find it hard to talk in a way that suggests criticism, ease into the topic with "I feel uncomfortable about something that's really hard for me to talk about." Of course, your therapist will ask you to go on, which will be easier once you've been invited. If you cannot bear the thought of a personal confrontation, you might try to explain your feelings in a letter or e-mail. And if even letter writing seems too daunting, ask a relative or friend to intercede on your behalf. As hard as this process may seem, it is far better to discuss your reservations than to bury them.

Sometimes (it happens eventually to every clinician) doctor and patient hit a discordant note that is nobody's fault—or perhaps everybody's. Then you need a second opinion from another clinician. Your own doctor may suggest someone who can carefully reappraise your situation from the ground up. Failing that, you can try some of the same resources I suggested in Chapter 3. The second opinion may only reassure you that your current treatment course is the best available. However, you could be handed a list of suggestions for alternative approaches—possibly a different medication or a change in dose. If an entirely different type of treatment is suggested, you should take the opportunity to discuss with the consultant the scientific rationale for what could be a radical change in course. With perhaps some urging on your part, the two clinicians might confer and agree on a plan of action that combines the best of both points of view. Ultimately, you may have to decide which course (and, by inference, which health care professional) is the more credible.

THE FUTURE OF MENTAL HEALTH CARE

What can we expect in the next 50 years by way of developments in the mental health field? While I'm looking around for my crystal ball, let's briefly recap how the mental health field has progressed during the last half century.

- As recently as the 1950s, your mental health diagnosis would almost certainly have been based on a hunch—formal criteria were almost unheard of prior to the early 1970s. Today, diagnoses are based on scientific criteria derived from thousands of careful studies of tens of thousands of patients.

- In the 1950s, mental hospitals bulged with over half a million chronic patients whose only prospect was lifelong institutionalization. Now, with nearly twice as many Americans, fewer than 100,000 remain chronically hospitalized.

- Unless you received electroconvulsive therapy (ECT), your physical treatment would have been ineffective for your condition. We didn't even completely understand how many mental patients recover spontaneously, regardless of treatment. Today there are over 30 medications with efficacy proven by scientific studies. Nearly every mental health diagnosis in the DSM can be favorably affected by drugs or other physical treatments.

- Depth (analytic) psychotherapy was the principal psychological treatment offered. Today, hundreds of scientific studies are proving the value of brief therapies for many illnesses.

- Mental health professionals waged war on two fronts: Psychoanalysts and nonanalysts battled for mainstream acceptance, while psychologists and psychiatrists duked it out for patients. Today, the professions coexist in an atmosphere of increasing mutual respect, affording patients the benefits that each has to offer.

- No one understood that patients had any rights at all. Now, patient rights are explicitly acknowledged, including the right to confidentiality, informed consent for treatment, and even mental health coverage that is often equivalent to other medical insurance.

In short, mental health treatment was far more art than science, and at that, the art was fairly abstract. Clinicians are alive today who have practiced throughout much of this era, which witnessed several scientific revolutions in therapy. Based on the past half century, here's what I believe the next 5–10 years holds:

- General physicians (and the general public) will learn even more about mental disorders, leading to earlier, more effective treatment.
- Psychotherapy and drugs will become less competitive and more coordinated as complementary treatment modalities.
- The FDA will continue to approve currently available medications for new indications.
- New medications will be developed that are more specific, act faster, and have fewer side effects.
- Behavioral programs, similar to those that have been successful with anorexia nervosa, will be aimed at other behavioral problems.
- Improved education will afford patients and their families even more protection and leverage in the medical marketplace.

And here's what we may expect beyond the next decade:

- We will greatly improve our ability to predict the onset of serious disorders such as Alzheimer's dementia, schizophrenia, and bipolar mood disorder.
- Of all the mental disorders discussed in this book, Alzheimer's dementia seems the closest to a definitive treatment.
- The application of molecular techniques to identification of the genetic underpinnings of many mental disorders could result in another therapeutic revolution many years into our new century.
- Some scientists predict that it may become ultimately possible to design medications for a given disorder that fit exactly into an individual patient's molecular structure, completely relieving symptoms while causing no side effects at all.

PART TWO

TREATMENT OPTIONS

In the past several decades, the science of treatment has galloped forward, with far-reaching results:

- More disorders than ever before have at least one specific, effective treatment. (We also recognize many more disorders, but that's another story.)
- Many of these disorders have several treatments—not just multiple drugs, but different modalities of therapy.
- Current treatments are more effective than those we relied on decades ago. Partly this increased efficiency is because clinicians have better defined the mental disorders they treat, and can therefore target the disorders more effectively. Newer medications often work better and with fewer side effects, and effective alternatives to drug therapy have also been introduced.
- The effectiveness of new forms of psychotherapy for many disorders has been demonstrated beyond doubt.
- We have finally learned that the effects of psychotherapy and drug therapy can be additive.

If one thing has stayed about the same, it is this: I still hear the same complaints about mental health treatment that were current decades ago, when I was a resident. Some writers (in books, articles, and now on websites) continue to make the same extravagant claims—that electroconvulsive therapy (ECT) damages the brain and that medications "flood the brain with neurotransmitters." The beauty of the scientific method is that it uses evidence generated from controlled investigations to judge the truth of any testable assertion. For example, sophisticated radiographic studies have shown that ECT doesn't produce anatomical changes in the brain.

Other scientific studies show that, rather than creating a flood, psychiatric medications tend to normalize the streams of chemicals in the brain that have slowed to a trickle, in some cases, or swollen to torrent proportions in other cases.

These critics advocate substituting "human caring" and protective environments as the solution to mental illness. Now, I care as much about human caring as the next person, but we should worry about any solution to mental illness that blows off all the scientific studies of the past 60 years in favor of institutionalization. The truth is that all of the treatment methods I'll talk about in this section—medications, electroconvulsive therapy, bright light, new forms of psychotherapy such as cognitive-behavioral therapy—have come into extensive use because more studies each year prove that they work.

Our critics also state that we use medications because we have been "bought by the drug industry," that we are "pill pushers" who would tranquilize everyone into compliant zombies. I won't pretend that all clinicians use treatments wisely and well. In truth, I have known psychiatrists who *are* pill pushers who basically owe their souls to the drug companies. But these are only a tiny fraction of all the mental health professionals, the vast majority of whom work hard every day to provide the best care available, and who constantly read and attend courses to keep up to date on the newest research. We are truly fortunate that we are so accustomed to good doctoring that it only makes news when it is conspicuously absent.

Conspicuously present in this book is one goal—to help you recognize and understand a reasonable approach to a given mental condition. I hope this information will help you sort out the claims you will read, to decide which have the ring of scientific truth and which are unsubstantiated nonsense.

CHAPTER 5

Introduction to Psychiatric Drugs

People have used drugs as long as they've had access to alcohol, tobacco, and the myriad roots, herbs, and potions we now call "natural medicine." But the first *manufactured* medication effective in treating mental disorders was dextro-amphetamine, which in 1937 was found to improve attention span and reduce excessive activity in hyperactive children. Another 15 years elapsed before the next effective psychiatric medication arrived (Thorazine, in 1952). After that, medications emerged rapidly—the first antidepressants in 1957, the first antianxiety agent in 1960. Nowadays, psychiatric patients in the United States can turn to over 90 drugs, and many more are currently in development; some of these new drugs are already available in other countries. Magazine ads for medications have become so commonplace that patients come in not only self-diagnosed but ready to self-treat.

WHY SHOULD I TAKE PSYCHIATRIC MEDICATION?

Many people still don't like to take medications. The very word *drug* can seem threatening, partly because we so often use it to mean a substance of abuse and we fear being addicted or "hooked." However, physicians use *drug* to mean a medication that can heal or relieve symptoms. It is mainly that sense in which I use the word in this book.

Another comment I've often heard is this: "I don't want to depend on drugs, I want to lick this thing myself." I respect this desire, but I also respect the power psychiatric illness can have over people, and I know how dramatically the right drug can improve the life of someone caught in the coils of a mental disorder. In the 21st century, medications should be considered for most mental illnesses, but that doesn't mean they should always be used.

HOW DO PSYCHIATRIC MEDICATIONS WORK?

A common misperception is that psychiatric medications mask symptoms without attacking their cause. Sometimes that's true, in the same way that aspirin or insulin doesn't address the cause of headaches or diabetes. Most psychiatric drugs actually do relieve symptoms; some can even prevent symptoms from developing. Lithium and the other mood stabilizers are good examples of this sort of brain "preventive maintenance."

All brain activity is conducted by electrical impulses passing along nerves. However, unlike the wiring in your house, nerves don't actually touch one another—they are separated by tiny gaps called "synapses." For an impulse to travel from one nerve to another, it must first jump across the synapse. The jump occurs when a chemical, called a "neurotransmitter," physically moves across the gap between neurons. At the far side, it fits into a receptor site of the receiving nerve, creating an electrical excitation there. Eventually, another synapse is reached, and the whole process begins again. The impulse travels through the brain, with many more impulses following the same path, resulting in, perhaps, a stable mood, a steady hand and placid brow, or an ear unassailed by the voices of monsters.

Scientists currently believe that many mental disorders occur because a neurotransmitter fails to carry impulses across synapses, or the reverse, that excessive neurotransmitter activity results in too much traffic at that particular intersection. The cause could be anything that affects the manufacture, release, or subsequent metabolism of a neurotransmitter, or something that affects its reception at the far side of the synapse. I said "scientists currently *believe*" because no one has proven the existence of a connection between neurotransmitters and disease. We believe there is a causal relationship, but many details—and the proof—are still lacking. We do know that a number of different neurotransmitting chemicals help regulate brain activity. These include norepinephrine (similar to adrenaline), serotonin, dopamine, and gamma-aminobutyric acid (GABA). For example, an increase in the activity level of dopamine may be partly at the root of schizophrenia and other psychoses. Serotonin and norepinephrine have both been implicated in depression (not enough of these two and you feel despondent, have trouble sleeping, perhaps even feel suicidal). Anxiety symptoms may spring from a variety of sources, including noradrenaline, serotonin, and GABA.

Psychiatric medications work in several ways to normalize the balance of these neurotransmitters. Some block the reuptake of a neurotransmitter into the nerve ending, leaving more neurotransmitter in the synapse to transport impulses. Others prevent enzymes from destroying neurotransmitters. Still others imitate the way the neurotransmitter works; in effect, they trick the receiving cell into thinking it has been stimulated by a nerve impulse. Whatever the actual mechanism, the result is that brain neurons fire often enough to keep you from feeling depressed, panicky, or otherwise unwell.

CHOOSING A DRUG

Several features of the "ideal drug" will help you and your doctor decide which one to try.

1. An ideal drug must do a good job of reducing or eliminating symptoms.
2. It must be safe. Of course, it shouldn't produce physically dangerous side effects such as abnormal heartbeats, shallow breathing, or seizures. However, safety in the mental health field has the additional meaning that, accidentally or purposely taken in an excessive dose, the drug won't cause death or devastating illness.
3. It shouldn't interact with another medication to produce side effects or alter the effectiveness of either drug.
4. It should be convenient to use—for example, a tablet that is easy to swallow and can be taken just once a day.
5. It should be inexpensive.

Although today's drugs are better than those of a generation ago, none meets all the standards I've just mentioned. In addition to these drug characteristics, your doctor will consider the following factors about you when deciding what to prescribe:

- **What are your target symptoms?** Target symptoms (the problems you are trying to change) are different for each disorder and often vary for each individual patient. One common cluster of target symptoms would include low mood, poor appetite, and trouble getting to sleep.
- **Do you have more than one diagnosis?** Unfortunately, many people with more than one mental problem are treated with multiple medications, one for each diagnosis, when one drug might be able to do all of the jobs with safety and economy. For example, if you had both depression and panic attacks, an antidepressant such as Zoloft or Nardil might relieve both problems. With drugs, less is often more.
- **Do you currently take medications for a medical illness?** If so, you may need to avoid certain psychiatric drugs that can change how your body me-

tabolizes other drugs. At the very least, you may have to start the new medication at a low level and cautiously increase the dose.

- **What has been your prior drug response history?** Clinicians like to quote an old saying, "Past behavior is the best predictor of future behavior." If, during a previous episode of depression, you responded well to Effexor, you probably will do so again.
- **Has a close relative responded well to a particular drug?** Just like mental disorders, drug response can be inherited. If Paxil helped a close relative (parent, child, brother, or sister), perhaps you should try it first.
- **Does anything hinder your ability to take medicine?** A patient who is especially forgetful, perhaps due to a cognitive impairment, might not remember to take medicine; a psychotic patient might refuse; someone with physical disability might have trouble swallowing. Each of these problems can be solved by methods crafted to fit individual needs.
- **Could your age or medical health hinder the work of a particular drug?** Most drugs are metabolized in the liver, eliminated by the kidneys, or both. Severe disease of either organ could greatly influence the choice of psychiatric drug. Advancing age can also reduce the efficiency of your liver and kidneys. If you are 60 or over, many drugs should be started at low doses and increased cautiously.

For many medications, you will have to decide whether to use a generic version. The term is used to mean a particular medication without specifying a brand name. For example, the generic drug aspirin has a number of brand, or trade, names, including *Bayer* and *McKesson*. Once a new drug has been patented and FDA-approved, the company that developed it has exclusive rights to make and market it. Although the nominal duration of patents is 17 years, much of that time is spent evaluating safety and effectiveness. When the period of exclusive rights expires, the drug is said to be "out of patent" and other manufacturers can produce it. Although a generic tablet will look different, it is formulated to work just the same as the trade-named drug; the significant difference is the price, which usually plummets due to competition. If you are taking an expensive brand-name drug, ask your doctor or pharmacist whether it is available generically; it could save half or more of the total cost. Tables in Chapters 6–11 state whether a generic is available.

SIDE EFFECTS

A side effect is any consequence of treatment other than what is intended; almost always, side effects are unwanted. Chapters 6–11 contain tables that lists the main side effects for all drugs discussed in this chapter. Throughout the text, I have mentioned especially dangerous side effects in special sections, to be sure that you notice them. Your doctor and your pharmacist will point out major side effects when you start taking a drug. You can look up minor or less common side effects in resources such as the *Physicians' Desk Reference* (PDR). Package inserts and newsletters printed by drug companies and some HMOs also provide side-effect information.

As you consult these resources, keep two issues in mind:

1. Some of them, especially the PDR, list many side effects, some so rare that they have been reported in only one or two patients out of the millions who may have taken the drug.
2. As you learn about an illness, you may begin to imagine that you have some of its typical symptoms. This happens so often among physicians in training that it is called "medical student disease." As you read about side effects, you may also temporarily experience symptoms that are "not really there."

What is a serious side effect? Obviously, all life-threatening consequences of treatment are serious; they include interference with the functioning of heart or lungs, marked changes in blood pressure, and convulsions. Although drowsiness by itself might not seem so serious, it could prove lethal to a long-distance trucker. For many patients, seriousness hinges on a drug's tendency to create discomfort (such as itching, headaches, dry mouth), inconvenience (such as increased need to urinate), or fear (skipped heartbeats can be quite scary). However, most side effects, though inconvenient, won't require you to stop taking the drug.

Freda began taking Prozac for a depression that, though relatively mild, had persisted for several months. By the third day, she complained of feeling jittery and nauseated, to the point that she began carrying a motion sickness bag when she went out. Within 2 weeks she reported that the nausea had diminished and she was feeling less "wired." By the end of a month her depression had remitted completely, and she had "forgotten about ever having those side effects."

Also started on Prozac, Monica began feeling less depressed within the first week and had neither nausea nor nervousness. But after her husband returned from an extended business trip to Hong Kong, she found that she could no longer experience climax with sexual intercourse. Reducing the dose helped a little, but then her depression worsened. Reluctantly, she agreed she should change antidepressants.

FIRST AID FOR SIDE EFFECTS

Because your medication will almost certainly produce some adverse effects, it is useful to know how to deal with them. As the vignettes of Freda and Monica illustrate, some will diminish with time, and some will require you to reduce the dosage or perhaps stop the medication altogether. Still others may yield to a little "first aid." Although each of the following suggestions is logical and nearly risk-free, always discuss the symptom and your proposed solution with your doctor.

- **Constipation.** Keep on a regular schedule, drink plenty of fluids, eat adequate amounts of fiber-containing vegetables, fruits, and cereals. You might also try stool softeners (such as Senekot) and bulk expanders (such as Metamucil or Colace).
- **Faintness.** Some medicines cause dizziness or even fainting when you sit up or stand up, a condition called postural hypotension (positional low blood pressure). One remedy is support stockings; another is to avoid hot tubs and long, hot showers—and move more slowly than usual when you change positions.
- **Increased appetite.** This can be quite distressing if it leads to weight gain. With your doctor's blessing, reduce the calories in your diet (such as by eating less fat) and increase the amount that you exercise.
- **Nausea.** Take drugs with meals to get them through your stomach before they create discomfort. Nausea and upset stomach often remit with time.
- **Dry mouth.** Especially likely with the older antidepressants dry mouth can be alleviated by sucking on hard candy—sugar-free, if you value your teeth.
- **Sedation.** For drugs that stay in your body a long time, your doctor may suggest taking all or most of the day's dose at bedtime. While you're working on this problem, be extra careful not to drive or operate machinery. Drowsiness often remits with time.
- **Flushing or sunburn.** Some drugs increase skin sensitivity to sunlight. Wear protective clothing and hats, use a sunscreen with a high SPF rating, and strictly limit your sun exposure to a few minutes a day (you'll be doing your skin a favor, in any case).
- **Difficulty urinating.** Although it can bother men or women, older men with enlarged prostates may suffer especially. Running water from a tap or holding your hands in warm water can sometimes help get the urinary stream started, but this problem may require the prescription drug Urecholine (bethanechol).
- **Blurred vision.** If this problem doesn't right itself within a few weeks, you may need a different eyeglass prescription while you are taking the drug. Reading through a pinhole can help in a pinch.
- **Excessive sweating.** Reduce your overall activity, ensure adequate ventilation when in the sun, and increase fluid intake.
- **Tremor.** Some drugs (such as lithium) can cause a fine trembling that usually affects the hands and isn't very severe. If it is bothersome and you can't reduce the dose, Inderal (propranolol) can sometimes reduce the tremor.

STARTING A MEDICATION

There is an art as well as a science to drug use. Although your history and symptoms will give a fairly clear idea about which drug to choose, your physician may speak of its use as a "therapeutic trial." In this mini-experiment, you are the only subject and you agree to try a drug to see whether it improves your target symptoms without causing serious side effects.

It's important to begin any medication trial with realistic expectations. Perhaps it is because we seem to accomplish everything so quickly—fast food, flowers by wire, movies downloaded by satellite, aspirin and other remedies relieve our headaches and arthritis in less than an hour—that we expect instant relief from our psychiatric drugs. Some, such as the antianxiety drugs, do take effect rapidly, but most of the medications you will read about in this book need days or weeks to work their magic. Many drugs require you to start with a small dose and increase gradually ("start low, go slow" has been the clinician's watchword for generations). Drugs work by altering brain chemistry at a cellular level, and this takes time. Try to rush the process and you increase the danger that side effects will elbow their way in before your target symptoms can step aside. This can mean unnecessarily rejecting drug after drug, subjecting yourself to trial after therapeutic trial. Try to be patient if your doctor wants you to boost your dosage just a little at a time to learn how little it will require for improvement.

One problem with therapeutic trials is the placebo effect. This means that your hopes for improvement raise your expectations so that you think you feel better at first, but it doesn't last. This doesn't mean that your original symptoms are "all in your head"—placebo effects are so common that nearly everyone experiences them at one time or another. It just gives you one more reason to be patient through a full trial to see how much your drug will really help.

If you have pneumonia and take penicillin, the infection goes away and you are done with it. With many mental disorders, it isn't realistic to expect this sort of "cure," even with the best possible medication. As you probably realize by now, how long you take a drug depends heavily upon your diagnosis, its severity, the natural course of your particular illness, and how completely you respond to a given treatment. For an acute episode of major depression, you might need an antidepressant for 6–9 months, but if you also need medicine to prevent the recurrence of mania or depression, you could decide to take it for a very long time—perhaps years. When patients worry that mental illness means a lifetime of medication, I point out that "forever" is a word, not a sentence. Down the road, there is always the option of stopping medication to see how they do. You and your doctor will have to sort out your particular situation, but remember that no one can read the future, and most people can eventually reduce or discontinue medication.

Every person's goal should be to achieve the highest level of function and comfort with the least possible intervention. It is especially important to use hypnotics (sleeping pills) and antianxiety drugs as briefly as possible, because they can be abused. Happily, in managing many mental disorders, those drugs are often required for only a few days—perhaps just until other, more specific medications or psychotherapy start working. In any event, worries about becoming addicted to your medication are needless. I tell my patients that they will eventually be able to stop their medicines without much difficulty, but that until their mental disorder has been fully corrected, they'll feel better with the drug.

MONITORING YOUR DRUG TRIAL

Your doctor's alertness and your own powers of observation are key to the success of the trial. It is important to record and report all of your observations about unwanted effects as well as improvement in your symptoms, whether they be depression, panic attacks, or auditory hallucinations. It will help you and your doctor communicate about any such changes if you use a simple numerical scale, such as 1 (minimal or no anxiety), 3 (moderate anxiety), 5 (marked anxiety), to evaluate your symptoms and side effects. Your doctor will also want to know when any adverse effects occur, how severe they are, and what you do to make them better. For a drug that is causing insomnia, you might use a similar scale to report how well you sleep. You should also inform your doctor if you change your diet or if you start or stop other medications.

You'll make better sense of all this if you keep a daily diary to record symptoms and side effects, as well as other important observations, such as what you eat, how much you sleep, and any unusual stressors you may be experiencing. On page 55 I've included a sample page that you can duplicate to use in reporting your experiences with treatment.

WHY THERAPEUTIC TRIALS FAIL

Used appropriately, psychiatric medicines work well more than half the time; often, when one medicine doesn't work, another one will. For that reason, I'd like you to read the word *fail* very loosely. For most disorders, you are likely to respond so favorably to medication that you will want to continue. If not, or if side effects are too bothersome, you and your doctor will need to determine why the first trial failed so that you can pick another medication that might serve you better. Here are the main reasons that drugs seem to fail:

- **Wrong diagnosis.** It seems obvious that anyone treated for the wrong diagnosis could have a disappointing drug response. Suppose you have a depression that causes you to feel panicky. If you start with an antianxiety agent like Valium, the panic will probably subside, but your low mood, insomnia, and poor appetite—and the panic—may return. An incomplete diagnosis has caused you and your doctor to focus on the wrong target symptom.
- **Inadequate treatment.** Too often, patients take too little medicine for too short a time before deciding that it isn't working.
- **Side effects and drug interactions.** Up to 10% of patients have to discontinue psychiatric medications due to side effects such as severe sedation, protracted nausea, dizziness, or impotence. More alarming problems, such as seizures or blood disorders, are far less common.

Therapeutic Diary

Week beginning:	Drug	Drug	Drug	Observations	Stressors
Monday					
morning					
noon					
evening					
night					
Tuesday					
morning					
noon					
evening					
night					
Wednesday					
morning					
noon					
evening					
night					
Thursday					
morning					
noon					
evening					
night					
Friday					
morning					
noon					
evening					
night					
Saturday					
morning					
noon					
evening					
night					
Sunday					
morning					
noon					
evening					
night					

Duplicate and use as a reminder to take your medication (or other treatments) and as a record of appetite, sleep, stressors, and side effects of therapy.

- **Tolerance.** In its specialized medical context, *tolerance* means that the cells of your body have become so accustomed to the effects of a medicine that it no longer seems to work. This sort of problem develops over time (days to weeks) and is especially likely with antianxiety medications.
- **Noncompliance.** It's pretty obvious that if you don't take the medication, it won't work, but even doctors sometimes forget that under half of patients take their medications exactly as directed. Lack of compliance is therefore a common reason for failure. The emergence of side effects is one reason for poor compliance, but forgetfulness, complicated instructions, and rejection of the whole idea of being ill also play roles.

A number of other factors may affect your willingness to take medication as directed. If you have a good education, a treatment program that is easy to follow, a trusting relationship with your physician, and good support from your family, you start out on the plus side of the compliance ledger. It isn't too hard to figure out the factors that contribute to noncompliance: a low level of trust, poor family support, and a complicated treatment regimen that is expensive or fraught with side effects. Any one of three diagnoses could also suggest trouble: psychosis, a cognitive disorder such as dementia, or any form of substance abuse. If any of these diagnoses applies to you or your relative, your physician will probably take extra pains to construct a treatment plan that will be easy to follow.

IF AT FIRST YOU DON'T SUCCEED . . .

If you and your doctor decide to try another drug, you'll want to keep the following caveats in mind:

1. If you are taking two or more psychiatric drugs, change only one at a time. Even clinicians who are expert in drug treatment can become confused by the often intersecting effects of drugs that fight depression, anxiety, and psychosis. Adjust one drug and you know what is responsible for a change in symptoms or side effects; adjust two, and you may have to flip a coin.
2. Because it is often important not to leave yourself "uncovered" with medication when making a change, you may have to taper off one drug while starting another. In such a case, it is important to make sure that the two drugs don't gang up to produce additional unwanted side effects. Table 2 at the end of each chapter (6–11) will help you identify possible drug interactions.
3. If you need to add one drug to another for their combined effect, it is more important than ever to keep careful records of your observations.

CONTINUING TREATMENT TO MAINTAIN YOUR GAINS

Let's say your medication trial has been such a rousing success that you and your doctor decide you should keep taking the drug to stay well. Keep the following practical matters in mind:

- **Maintenance monitoring.** Even though the trial is over and you have stabilized on your present dose, you'll still have to pay attention to changes in side effects and, for that matter, to the possibility that target symptoms could return later on. Faithfully report any of these changes to your doctor, if necessary by telephone or during an extra appointment.
- **Blood levels.** For some drugs, blood levels can be obtained. Physicians use drug blood levels in two ways.

  1. Some drugs, especially mood stabilizers such as lithium and Depakote, must be present in just the right concentration to do their work—below that level they are ineffective, and above it they become toxic. The ideal part of the range is sometimes called a "therapeutic window," which can best be determined by measuring the blood level.
  2. If a medicine seems ineffective, a blood level is sometimes used to determine whether it is being absorbed into the body once swallowed, or whether it is being swallowed at all—noncompliance is probably the most important cause of medication failure.

- **Drinking on drugs.** Technically, a small amount of alcohol won't conflict with most medicines. Two notable exceptions are red wine in combination with MAOIs (monoamine oxidase inhibitor antidepressants), a potentially dangerous combination, and any form of alcohol with Antabuse, which will always produce severe symptoms. However, many medications can increase alcohol's tendency to impair attention, coordination, and judgment. My advice is to limit alcohol to no more than one drink (12 oz. beer, 6 oz. wine, 1 shot hard liquor) per day.
- **Storing medication.** To delay their deterioration, most medicines should be stored at room temperature, out of the sun, in a tightly closed container. Of course, if small children ever enter your home, always use the childproof container lids provided by your pharmacy and keep drugs in a place inaccessible to inquisitive fingers.

STOPPING MEDICATION

It takes time for the body to become used to any medication, so it stands to reason that the same would hold if you reversed the process—your cells could react with displeasure if you suddenly withdrew something they have come to depend on. The answer is to reduce drugs gradually. If you take more than one psychiatric medicine, your doctor will probably advise you to reduce them one at a time. Should you need surgery, be sure to tell the surgeon and anesthesiologist about your medications, so they can adjust their techniques accordingly. If you have had trouble in the past with mood changes around the time of your menstrual periods, try to reduce or eliminate medications at the time your period begins. That way, you'll have 3 weeks to evaluate the medicine change before your hormones are likely to cause confusion.

SPECIAL PATIENT GROUPS

Children and Adolescents

Young people who need psychiatric medicines pose additional treatment problems— they are not simply miniature adults, and their body and brain chemistries impose special limitations on drug use. Although some drugs can be taken in adult doses, others are dangerous and should not be used by children at all. Still others may require doses that are, pound for pound, higher or lower than an adult would receive. Although this book focuses on adult diagnosis and treatment, Appendix A lists resources relevant to child diagnosis and treatment.

Geriatric Patients

Older people metabolize some drugs slowly, and they are especially vulnerable to certain side effects—dizziness, for example, which can lead to falls and fractured hips. Physical illness may require them to take medications that can interfere with the metabolism of psychiatric drugs. If you are over 60, your doctor may start your drug at a dose lower than recommended for younger adults.

Medically Ill Patients

Some illnesses, especially liver and kidney disorders, reduce the rate at which drugs are metabolized or excreted. The bottom line is, if you have a serious medical illness, you may need to start psychiatric drugs in lower doses and increase them more gradually than would be the case for other adults of your age.

Pregnant Women and Nursing Mothers

In the PDR you'll see warnings like this: " . . . should be used during pregnancy only if the potential benefits outweigh the potential risks." Although most medications haven't been proven harmful to developing babies, they haven't been proven safe, either. Pregnant women should use psychiatric drugs only if a physician emphasizes their importance. Because lithium and anticonvulsants can definitely produce fetal malformations, they must be used with special care. Many drugs are secreted in the milk, so you should also avoid breast-feeding when taking psychiatric drugs.

HOW DO NEW DRUGS GET APPROVED?

As a rule, the United States approves drugs for general use somewhat more slowly than do other countries. This is because our Food and Drug Administration (FDA) takes great care in evaluating each new drug. We can feel profoundly grateful for this comprehensive deliberation. Without it, we undoubtedly would have far more in the way of tragic medication side effects than we do now. Remember thalidomide, which caused limb deformities in thousands of European babies whose mothers took it to combat insomnia and morning sickness? Because the drug had not been approved for use here, it affected only a tiny handful of American babies.

Of course, such infinite care has a downside. We sometimes get to use new drugs years later than do citizens of other countries, and the laborious process is almost unbelievably expensive, helping to create some of the highest drug prices in the world.

Drugs are often approved for only one or two indications, even though they are probably effective for other purposes. Good examples are the antidepressants, many of which work well for anxiety disorders, though most have not been officially approved for these indications. Once approved, physicians can prescribe a drug for any indication if, in their judgment, it will help the patient. Sometimes a drug will receive additional approvals after it has been used for years. For example, in 1991 Zoloft was approved for major depression; in 1997 it was approved for panic disorder and obsessive–compulsive disorder (OCD), and in 1999 for posttraumatic stress disorder (PTSD).

On the other hand, not all drugs should be used for their approved indications. Years ago the FDA approved barbiturates for treating anxiety and insomnia. Now there are far safer, more effective treatments for these indications, but in the *Physicians' Desk Reference*, you'll still find Nembutal and Mebaral listed for these conditions.

TABLES

Use the tables that end each chapter in Part II as a handy reference when you are about to start a new drug, or whenever you have questions about one of your medications. For example, you might want to make sure your starting dose is reasonable, or learn whether you can save money with a generic. You can also learn what other drugs could conflict with your medication and what serious side effects you should report right away, without waiting for your next appointment. Starting any new medication can result in information overload, so here's a resource to which you can turn for a quick refresher course. Most of the information in these tables is self-explanatory; here's a quick kick-starter, using Elavil as the new medication.

Table 6.1

Recent FDA approval means a longer wait until a generic equivalent becomes available. The date also tells us how many years clinicians have had to accumulate data concerning interactions with other drugs. "Starting treatment" gives the dose most people start with and how often they are to take it. In the case of Elavil, you would start with 25 milligrams (mg), which you might take just once a day if you are older, three times a day if you are younger and in good physical health. When you increase the dose, it would be by either 25 or 50 mg (at the discretion of your doctor), but only after 7 days have passed since you started the medicine.

The next two columns should be read as a unit. "Adult dose range" states the range needed for therapeutic effect—for Elavil, that's from 50 to 300 mg/day—and the number after the slash is the amount that most people need (150 mg for Elavil). The "Divided into" column tells you the number of times per day you'll take this amount of medicine, once you've arrived at the dose that is right for you. Because Elavil often causes drowsiness, it will probably be taken just at bedtime, but with many other drugs, the dose will be split into smaller amounts taken two, three, or even four times during the day.

"Dosage size" gives the milligram strength of tablets or capsules you can buy. Some drugs are also available as suppositories, for intravenous injection (IV), or as an oral liquid, which can be given in juice for people who have trouble swallowing tablets and capsules. "$/day" states a ballpark figure for a day's effective dose. The PDR Red Book (my resource for wholesale drug prices) says that 150 mg of Elavil, in three 50-mg tablets, would be available most economically at a thrifty 21¢ per day. I say *ballpark* because many factors can influence the cost of medicine. The price I state is (usually) for 100-tablet lots; if you buy fewer, they'll usually cost more per dose. It may also matter whether you buy from a local pharmacy, a drug store chain, or a mail-order plan. Drug companies carefully track sales and their competition, resulting in prices that rise and fall, depending on what the market (that's you) will bear. Of course, the price you pay will be some percentage above wholesale.

For many drugs, we know a range of numbers that constitutes the ideal blood level. This range is stated in terms of nanograms (ng), or one billionth of a gram, per milliliter (ml), which is equivalent to detecting half an aspirin tablet dissolved in a backyard swimming pool. These figures can be helpful if, for example, you haven't improved when taking what should be an adequate dose (see page 57 for discussion).

The half-life of a drug reflects the time it stays in the body; specifically, it is the time your body needs to eliminate half the remaining amount. For example, suppose you are taking Elavil and your blood level is 200 ng/ml. About 36 hours from the time you stop taking the drug, your level will have fallen to 100; another day and a half and it will be just 50. By the time you've been off the drug for a week, your blood level will be down around 6. This rather esoteric figure tells you:

1. How long it will take for a daily dose to yield a steady amount of the drug in your system (longer half-life means a longer time to steady-state). Also, the shorter the half-life, the more times each day you will need to take the drug to keep a constant supply of it in your system.
2. Longer half-life also means lower risk of withdrawal symptoms when you stop taking the drug (you have more time to get used to decreasing amounts).
3. If your first drug trial doesn't do the job, one with a shorter half-life will require a shorter washout period before you start taking a different medication.

"Time to work" is a best guess about the number of weeks it may take for a good response to a given drug. This time range varies considerably depending on your metabolism and how rapidly you have increased the dose. You could feel somewhat better right away, for example, if you have been having trouble sleeping and your new medication has the side effect of drowsiness. However, full effectiveness will usually require a time that falls somewhere within the limits indicated. Time to full trial is that period you'd need to take a full dose before you and your doctor could be sure it wasn't going to work.

Table 6.2

Most of the material in this table is straightforward, but the side-effects columns require a little discussion. Of course, what you should report to your physician at once versus what is benign and can wait until your next appointment is a matter of judgment and will depend on the individual patient and physician. For example, I included "positional low blood pressure" in the report column, even though I've also suggested some "first aid" for it on page 52. Because it can lead to falls and fractured hips, I like to have the opportunity to assess each patient's situation for myself. However, not every physician will feel the same, and many instances of positional low blood pressure will be so mild or fleeting that they can probably safely wait until the next office appointment. The same reasoning applies to some of the other symptoms listed in the "report right away" column.

"Important cautions" will be of interest if you have special conditions such as older age (usually, above 60, though it can vary quite a lot) or liver or kidney problems. By the way, this statement is generally interpreted to mean *serious* liver or kidney problems—you can lose a lot of function and still have enough left to be chemi-cally normal. I've listed drug interactions that you are likely to encounter as an outpatient. They are not the only ones possible—there is a lot more to be discovered. Don't become a case in a medical journal: *Tell your doctor if you are taking other medi-cations.*

Table 6.3

The *a* in the Elavil column indicates that it has been approved by the FDA for the treatment of major depression. The *b*'s mean that it is also commonly used for bulimia and panic disorder. Double plus marks indicate that it is highly dangerous in overdose; a single plus mark refers to its sedative qualities.

CHAPTER 6

Antidepressants

When antidepressant drugs were first introduced, the name made sense. Now, the name seems almost unfortunate because these medications can treat many other conditions—anxiety disorders (panic, posttraumatic stress, social phobia), pain (chronic pain syndrome, migraine), attention-deficit/hyperactivity disorder, autism, bulimia, enuresis, irritable bowel syndrome, insomnia, and premenstrual syndrome. Today's antidepressants are about equally effective in relieving symptoms in clinical depression. All have side effects, some far more serious than others; for that reason alone, none of them has all the qualities of an ideal drug (see page 49). They aren't super drugs, either—they won't raise your spirits if you are not clinically depressed. They won't take away the natural feeling of unhappiness anyone would experience with commonplace ordeals such as failing an examination, being rejected by a lover, or experiencing the death of a close friend. If you took an antidepressant in such a situation, you'd get only side effects to add to your misery.

But if you have a mental disorder, how would you and your doctor decide which antidepressant to try first? Of all the issues you have to consider, among the most important is your safety. Compared to the older drugs, the SSRIs and all other antidepressants introduced from the late 1980s onward are less likely to produce side effects and far less likely to cause death if taken in overdose, either accidentally or on purpose. For that reason alone, I recommend starting with one of them. This doesn't mean that the older drugs are obsolete. Sometimes I might advise using an antidepressant that has been around even longer than I've been a psychiatrist. Though they have some significant drawbacks, they are often cheaper and may be uniquely effective if you have an extremely severe depression or one that has not responded to first-line antidepressants. I make diagnosis-specific recommendations in Part III.

SELECTIVE SEROTONIN REUPTAKE INHIBITORS (SSRIs)

When Prozac was introduced in 1988, it attained instant success. It has since been joined by similar drugs, some of which may be even better first choices. Today, the SSRIs account for over half of all prescriptions written for antidepressants. These drugs take their group name from their main action. They prevent the neurotransmitter serotonin from being taken back up into the neurons that release it; the effect is greater availability of serotonin in the synapse for message transmission.

SSRIs are often effective against depression at their starting doses. This means they don't require a gradual increase to get the desired effect, so they are easier and quicker to use. Their side effects are usually mild, and they are safe, even if taken in overdose. Cheap, however, they are not.

Uses

Part of their popularity results from the fact that SSRIs can effectively treat so many different emotional and mental conditions (see Table 6.3). Currently, four of the five are FDA-approved for use in depression. The fifth, Luvox, is approved only for the treatment of obsessive–compulsive disorder (OCD), but some doctors may also use it for depression. SSRIs have also been used to treat bulimia, dysthymia (a relatively mild, long-lasting form of depression), social phobia, premature ejaculation, pain syndromes resulting from migraine or diabetes, alcohol dependence, and posttraumatic stress disorder (PTSD). Those with borderline personality disorder sometimes take an SSRI to reduce impulsiveness. Some patients with schizophrenia may experience improved mood and reduced aggression. A frequent side effect, delayed ejaculation, has been turned to good account as a remedy for premature ejaculation.

Drawbacks

The more common side effects (see Table 6.2) are likely to decrease as you get used to your SSRI. The less common ones will probably persist, but you may be able to manage them by reducing the dose. Even if this is not possible, with time you may come to accept them as a cost of feeling better. One especially irksome side effect is sexual dysfunction, which in both men and women can mean reduced interest in sex and trouble achieving orgasm. This effect may continue as long as you take the medication. However, if you are taking one of the shorter-acting SSRIs, such as Paxil, you might be able to take a brief "drug holiday" that sometimes allows the temporary return of normal sexual functioning.

Nearly all antidepressants can trigger an episode of mania in bipolar patients (see Chapter 16). Drug-induced mania occurs in people with bipolar depression perhaps 3% of the time. Although it tends to be less severe than a naturally occurring mania, you and your relatives should watch out for an abnormal rise in mood, increased activity level, and talkativeness.

Prozac, Luvox, and Paxil are most likely to interact with other drugs, so keep your doctor informed about any other medications you take, including over-the-counter drugs and herbals such as St. John's wort. No one knows for sure whether SSRIs can harm a fetus in the womb, but a general rule applies: if you are pregnant, take any drug only if it seems absolutely essential and only after your doctor has carefully explained any possibility for harm. In 2001 a study found that the tiny amount of Zoloft secreted into breast milk was probably safe for infants. Although the same probably holds for all SSRIs, I still recommend that you plan not to nurse your baby if antidepressant drug treatment is essential.

Finally, I'll mention the discontinuation syndrome, which probably occurs more often than drug companies would like you to believe. If you discontinue your medication you may experience an uncomfortable feeling, rather like the flu, with a whole lot of possible symptoms—dizziness, fatigue, headache, muscle aches and pains, numbness or tingling of your hands or feet, weakness, vivid dreams, tremors, and nausea. You could also experience anxiety, irritability, and crying spells, so that you might even think your depression was coming back. Symptoms begin a few days after stopping the SSRI and usually last for a week or more. It is much more likely if you stop taking your medication suddenly, and it occurs more often with drugs that are rapidly metabolized. (It's nearly unheard of with Prozac, which has a long half-life and so is nearly impossible to discontinue abruptly). Though unpleasant, the discontinuation syndrome doesn't usually cause serious problems; your doctor will probably just have you restart the drug and gradually reduce the dose. (However, a class action lawsuit has been instituted by patients who claim that they cannot discontinue Paxil.)

Special Precaution

A rare but life-threatening condition is the serotonin syndrome, caused by using two or more different types of drug that increase serotonin levels; the combination of an SSRI with a monoamine oxidase inhibitor (MAOI) is especially dangerous. This syndrome is unrelated to dose and could start any time, from minutes to weeks after you begin taking the second drug. Symptoms include abdominal pain, diarrhea, fever, sweating, rapid heartbeat, high blood pressure, delirium, muscle twitching, agitation, and mood changes (irritability or hostility). This condition is no joke—when really severe, it can kill. Prevention is key: if you need to start a new antidepressant, your doctor will ask you to wait 2 weeks or longer for the old drug to wash out of your system. However, don't be alarmed; it is only when certain drugs are combined that there is any danger. Antidepressants are safe if you take them as directed.

Using SSRIs

Most of these drugs can be taken just once a day, with or without food. For treating depression, the SSRI range of effective dose is relatively narrow (see Table 6.1). This means that the dose you start with may work just fine—for depression. However, OCD, panic disorder, and bulimia often require much higher doses. If you have panic disorder, you'll be more likely to have side effects, so you will have to start low (for example, 10 mg of Prozac) and gradually increase the dose, watching for the emergence of anxiety or insomnia.

Specific SSRIs

Celexa (citalopram)

The newest of the SSRIs, Celexa has been FDA-approved only for treating depression, though it is often used effectively for anxiety disorders. Some patients develop drowsiness, nausea, or dry mouth, but side effects and interactions with other drugs are somewhat less likely than with other SSRIs. The dose must be titrated upward somewhat more often than with other SSRIs; this could increase the time it takes you to feel better.

Luvox (fluvoxamine)

Although many countries have approved Luvox for treating depression, the United States has approved it only for OCD. Among SSRIs, it is the grand champion of side effects, in both seriousness and number, so your doctor will probably ask you to start it at less than the recommended effective dose and increase it gradually. As with some other antidepressants, smokers may more quickly metabolize this drug and therefore need a higher total daily dose.

Paxil (paroxetine)

Paxil is FDA-approved for a variety of disorders, including major depression, OCD, panic disorder, PTSD, and social anxiety disorder. However, it carries greater risk of weight gain and constipation than other SSRIs, and at higher doses it is likely to interfere with sleep. As with any antidepressant, dosing begins low in panic disorder, to avoid a sudden worsening of agitation. However, the target dose for panic is 40 mg/day, approached gradually with increases of only 10 mg/day each week.

Prozac (fluoxetine)

Partly because it is officially approved for so many disorders, partly because of name recognition, many clinicians choose Prozac first for patients who have depression complicated by a variety of other problems. These include atypical depression, obsessions, panic attacks, excessive drowsiness, premenstrual dysphoric disorder (which is an especially severe form of premenstrual syndrome, or PMS), and bulimia. Prozac is the only SSRI available as a liquid, which means that people who have trouble swallowing tablets can take it in juice. A weekly 90 mg timed-release capsule offers greater dosing convenience, though with more diarrhea and slightly increased risk of relapse. (And how often do you have an opportunity to swallow capsules that cost nearly $20 each?) In 2001, regular Prozac went generic and the price plummeted.

With its long half-life, improvement may take longer, and it takes longer to eliminate completely, once you stop taking it. Typically it is effective at its starting dose of 20 mg/day, but if for some reason (perhaps a medical illness, or if you are elderly) you need to titrate it upward, Prozac can take much longer than most of the other antidepressants to reach a steady state in your body. Of the SSRIs, it has the greatest number of documented drug interactions, but that could just reflect the fact that it has been around the longest; with time, other SSRIs may yet catch up.

Zoloft (sertraline)

Less activating than most other SSRIs, Zoloft may still cause nausea, diarrhea, insomnia, and in higher doses, sedation. Like Celexa, it is less likely to interfere with other drugs you may be taking. Besides depression, Zoloft is approved for OCD, PTSD, and panic disorder. For panic disorder, you'd start at 25 mg/day.

OTHER NEWER ANTIDEPRESSANTS

Like the SSRIs, the next four antidepressants are of relatively recent vintage, though their mechanisms of action are somewhat different. I have grouped them here because they are good alternatives to the SSRIs, safer than the other antidepressants listed farther along in this chapter.

Effexor (venlafaxine)

At low doses (75 mg/day), Effexor inhibits serotonin; at high doses (close to 375 mg/day) it also inhibits norepinephrine. Both neurotransmitters have been implicated in causing depression. It is an effective antidepressant at low doses; a 2001 summary of several controlled studies found Effexor somewhat more effective than SSRIs. The timed-release version (Effexor XR, for extended release) can be taken once a day. Though it has more gastrointestinal side effects (especially nausea) than SSRIs, it may work faster, and its relative lack of drug–drug interactions can be an advantage for those who must take other medications. Effexor is likely to cause a discontinuation syndrome unless it is carefully tapered.

Special Precaution

At higher dose levels, elevated blood pressure can develop. Though it may diminish with time, you should have your blood pressure checked before starting Effexor and periodically thereafter, especially at doses of 300 mg/day or greater.

Remeron (mirtazapine)

Though used for years in other countries, Remeron is a relative newcomer for Americans. It is effective in depressed patients, including those who also have anxiety, and at least one study has found that it may be more effective than SSRIs in severe depression. It doesn't cause diarrhea or sexual dysfunction, and it may even help reduce SSRI-induced nausea. However, it is so sedating that some patients cannot take it at all. Increased appetite and weight can be useful in depressed cancer patients but distressing to many others. It is safe in overdose and relatively free of interactions with other drugs. Remeron SolTab dissolves on the tongue in half a minute, without water.

Special Precaution

In early trials, 3 of 3,000 patients developed agranulocytosis—low white blood cell count that can impair the body's ability to fight off infection. However, later experience has not been especially alarming in this regard, and the manufacturer now advises that you should have a white blood cell count only if you develop fever or infection.

Serzone (nefazodone)

Less sedating than Remeron, Serzone improves sleep and decreases anxiety. Although it has generally fewer side effects than some other antidepressants, those that occur are often dose-related. Therefore, you should start at low doses and increase gradually (not a good choice for severe depression that must be addressed rapidly). Its brief half-life means twice-a-day dosing, a disadvantage for most of us.

Wellbutrin, Zyban (bupropion)

Less likely than most other antidepressants to cause a switch to mania, Wellbutrin may be especially useful if you have a history (or family history) of bipolar disease. Marketed as Zyban, it is also approved for use in patients attempting to quit smoking. It isn't sedating (some patients even complain of insomnia or agitation), and it doesn't hamper sexual functioning.

Special Precaution

Wellbutrin's release to the market was delayed because it caused seizures, especially in patients with bulimia. If you have either bulimia or anorexia, you should not take it. For everyone else, at doses greater than 450 mg/day it is more likely than other antidepressants to produce seizures. To minimize the amount in your bloodstream, take it in two or more doses per day, with no two doses closer than 4 hours apart.

TRICYCLIC ANTIDEPRESSANTS (TCAs)

If you'd had depression 35 years ago, your doctor would probably have prescribed a TCA. These drugs, named for their three-ring chemical structure, have fallen out of favor for the initial treatment of depression, but they still account for about 20% of all antidepressant prescriptions—much of this for chronic pain and treatment of migraine. For acute depression, they are at least as effective as any other drug; for severe depression with melancholia (see Chapter 15), they may be better. They are probably not as effective in depressions accompanied by psychosis. TCAs are also effective against dysthymia—imipramine and desipramine have been best studied, though any of them should work. Although never specifically approved for indications other than depression, the TCAs are also reportedly effective in OCD, panic disorder, PTSD, and chronic fatigue syndrome.

Drawbacks

As shown in Table 6.2, the second group of TCAs is somewhat less likely to produce side effects. The side effects that are especially likely include dizziness, constipation, dry mouth (often producing a characteristic "sticky speech"), tremors, sweating, and fatigue, though these may diminish with time. Positional hypotension (lowered blood pressure when you sit up or stand up) is a big problem, causing perhaps 10% of those who try one of these drugs to stop taking it. Rapid heartbeat is especially common in younger patients, and rashes can occur in patients of all ages. All are somewhat more likely than the SSRIs to precipitate a mania. Some of them also produce drowsiness, which can be seen as either an advantage or a disadvantage, depending on whether you want to sleep or operate heavy machinery. Although TCAs have not been clearly implicated in fetal malformation, if you are pregnant (or nursing), you should take this (or any) medication only after thorough discussion with your physician. In high dose, tremor and anxiety are possible, and some patients may experience moderately increased blood pressure.

Special Precautions

All TCAs affect electrical conduction in the heart. This isn't ordinarily a problem, but if you already have heart disease, you could suffer irregular or slowed heartbeat. Occasionally, this effect has proven fatal. Even healthy older patients should have an electrocardiogram prior to starting a TCA. Anyone who might take an overdose, through mistake or intent, should be strictly limited to a one-week supply or less. Rarely (perhaps only in 1 out of 1,000 patients) a TCA will induce hepatitis, which can also prove lethal.

Using TCAs

The effective dose range is much greater for TCAs than for most other antidepressants, and side effects can begin at low doses. I've known patients who didn't respond on amitriptyline until they reached 350 mg a day, others who slept all day on 25 mg. This means that your doctor will probably want you to start low and increase cautiously until you reach the right level (mood improves or you notice marked dry mouth). For panic disorder, you'll start at even lower doses than those listed in Table 6.1.

If you are taking a usual therapeutic dose without getting any benefit, a drug blood level (also in Table 6.1) could help determine whether you are getting enough of the medication. For most TCAs, more than 300 ng/ml risks severe side effects (delirium, seizures, stupor, problems with electrical conduction in the heart). If you got that far, still without adequate relief from your depression, you and your doctor would need to consider other treatment options.

As with the SSRIs, abrupt discontinuation can result in poor appetite, nausea, vomiting, diarrhea, headache, muscle aches and pains, weakness and generally feeling blah. Taper gradually over a period of several weeks.

Specific TCAs

Anafranil (clomipramine)

This is the only TCA approved for OCD; others probably work less well. It isn't used much for depression in this country due to its side effects: nearly everyone who takes it has dry mouth, and half get headaches. Constipation, insomnia, and sexual dysfunctioning, especially impotence and the inability to ejaculate, are worse than for other TCAs. To combat the upset stomach, start with multiple doses; later you can try it as a single bedtime dose.

Elavil, Endep (amitriptyline)

An old standby, amitriptyline is an effective antidepressant that is markedly sedative and quite likely to give you the other typical TCA side effects, especially at higher doses. The drowsiness can be an advantage if your symptoms include insomnia or anxiety. Elavil is commonly used in low doses (up to about 75 mg/day) for chronic pain and migraine.

Sinequan, Adapin (doxepin)

Like Elavil, Sinequan produces considerable drowsiness. It is a comparatively weak antidepressant, so you could need a somewhat higher dose than with other antidepressants. There are better choices.

Surmontil (trimipramine)

In the heyday of the TCAs, every drug company scrambled to produce its own version. Each of these "me-too" drugs differed slightly in chemical structure, with few substantive features to distinguish them from the pack—hence, Surmontil, a good (if expensive) drug that is barely remembered anymore.

Tofranil (imipramine)

Another well-tested standby, Tofranil also has been approved for the treatment of bed-wetting ("enuresis"). It bears the full range of TCA side effects.

Norpramin (desipramine)

Because the usual TCA side effects (dry mouth, constipation, trouble urinating, blurred vision) are not so intense as in some TCAs, Norpramin is considered a drug of choice in this class. However, it may be less effective for severe depression, and it has been reported to be the most lethal in overdose. In younger patients, it may increase blood pressure.

Pamelor (nortriptyline)

This is another TCA of choice, partly because positional low blood pressure is less likely. The usual effective dose is somewhat low and the effective range is narrow, so many clinicians will want to monitor it with periodic blood levels.

Vivactil (protriptyline)

As its name suggests, this drug is alerting, so take it in the morning and don't use it at all if severe insomnia is one of your target symptoms. A person who is depressed and lethargic might find it especially useful.

BEWARE COMBINATION TABLETS

Many years ago, when antidepressants and antipsychotic drugs were first developed, two brands, Etrafon and Triavil, were created by combining an antidepressant (Elavil) with an antipsychotic agent (Trilafon). These combination drugs are still in use, marketed as treatment for patients with both depression and anxiety. In my opinion, you should avoid them for two reasons:
(1) They contain too little antidepressant to do most people much good.
(2) With rare exceptions, people who aren't psychotic shouldn't take antipsychotic medications. Another combination, Elavil with Librium, is marketed as Limbitrol for depression with anxiety and bears similar criticisms.

MONOAMINE OXIDASE INHIBITORS (MAOIs)

Originally created to combat tuberculosis, the first of these drugs was made from V-2 rocket fuel left over from World War II. Because of its toxicity, it was soon discontinued. However, it was noted that TB patients who took later MAOIs (free of rocket fuel!) seemed less depressed. Quickly it became apparent that these drugs also improved mood in physically healthy but depressed patients. Though they have lost popularity in the face of drugs with fewer side effects and no dietary restrictions, for some patients they seem to work when nothing else does.

The MAOIs work by inhibiting monoamine oxidase, the enzyme that destroys neurotransmitters; this "enemy of my enemy is my friend" strategy increases the amount of neurotransmitter available for carrying messages across nerve synapses. MAOIs work well for severe major depression, atypical depression, and depression mixed with anxiety, panic, or phobia. Nardil and Parnate may help some people with borderline personality disorder. I haven't listed half-lives for the MAOIs because, though they are very brief, it can take 2 weeks for the body to make new enzymes (Manerix is the exception; as a reversible MAOI, its effects last only a couple of days).

Common side effects of the three MAOIs available in the United States include insomnia, weight gain, and positional low blood pressure. Swelling of the extremities also occurs in some patients. Similar to the SSRIs, both men and women may report loss of ability to climax with intercourse.

Special Precautions

As mentioned, the serotonin syndrome (page 65) is a potentially deadly reaction that can occur when different classes of antidepressants are used together, most notably an MAOI with an SSRI. As with so much else in life, prevention is the better part of treatment. Wait 2 weeks when switching from one drug to another if they are listed in Table 6.2 as potentially causing serotonin syndrome when used in combination (5 weeks if switching from fluoxetine, because of its long half-life).

If you take an MAOI, you must follow a special diet that avoids tyramine, an amino acid breakdown product that can cause extreme high blood pressure (splitting headache, stiff neck, nausea). The syndrome is a true medical emergency, hence the name of this episode—hypertensive *crisis*. Most people don't have this reaction, but those who do are at great risk for stroke and even death. Pay careful attention to the foods and drugs you must avoid while taking an MAOI. The prescription drug Procardia (nifedipine), dissolved under the tongue, is a rapidly effective antidote to hypertensive crisis. Discuss with your doctor whether you should keep some on hand.

Some lists of dietary restrictions exclude everything from chocolate to banana skins (yes, *skins!*). A sensible list includes only those foods that are high in tyramine. The main food that could cause you difficulty is **aged cheese**—hence the name "the cheese reaction" that is sometimes given to hypertensive crisis. Avoid all cheeses except cottage, cream, ricotta, and mozzarella. Also stay away from other foods formed by fermentation, including **aged meats and fish** (pastrami, salami, sausage, pickled herring). Liver, liverwurst, and pâté, especially any that has sat around for a while, can contain dangerous amounts of tyramine, so don't eat them. Also avoid the **pods of broad beans** (Chinese pea pods, fava beans), **red wine**, and **tap beer** (other alcoholic beverages are okay, except that when you take any psychiatric medication, you should carefully limit your drinking—no more than one shot or beer or 6-oz. glass of wine per day. Also avoid **soy sauce** and **yeast extract**, though baked products made with yeast, such as bread, are perfectly safe.

You must also scrupulously avoid certain drugs, including some over-the-counter items: **cold remedies**, **sinus medicines**, and **allergy** and **hay fever** preparations; **diet pills** and **amphetamines**; pain relievers such as **cocaine** and **Demerol**, and injectable anesthetics that contain **epinephrine**. It is fine to take aspirin, Tylenol, and ibuprofen. In my experience, once patients see how much their MAOI helps them, they become highly motivated to be careful with drugs and diets.

Suddenly stopping an MAOI can create a discontinuation syndrome that includes feeling "wired"; the solution is to taper gradually.

Specific MAOIs

Marplan (isocarboxazid)

This drug was so little used that for eight years it was withdrawn from the market, then reintroduced in 1998. An acceptable antidepressant, Marplan has never really caught on in the United States.

Nardil (phenelzine)

I've always liked Nardil best because it is highly effective with relatively few side effects.

Parnate (tranylcypromine)

In very high doses (100 mg/day or even higher), Parnate has been reported especially useful in treating depressions that haven't responded to other medications. It is more likely than Nardil to disturb sleep.

Manerix (moclobemide)

This is a reversible MAOI, which means that there is less likelihood of food and drug interactions, and that it takes much less time (within 48 hours) for the effects to wear off and another drug started, if that is needed. Manerix users are less often troubled by side effects, including tyramine reaction. You should still avoid eating great quantities of the foods mentioned above. Manerix is currently available in Canada and the United Kingdom but not in the United States.

ANTIDEPRESSANTS WITH SPECIAL PROBLEMS

After the first rush of development, drug companies tried to find newer treatments that would have a competitive edge. Three have serious side effects that require careful consideration before you use them. (Still others have been withdrawn due to even more serious side effects.) In my opinion, they are definitely "last choice" drugs that might be used in depressions that have not responded to other treatments.

Asendin (amoxapine)

The advantage of this drug is that, like Norpramin and Ludiomil, its side effects are generally less troublesome than those of the TCAs. It may start working a little faster than other antidepressants. However . . .

Special Precaution

Because it is closely related to the older antipsychotic medications, there is a chance that anyone who takes it could develop a movement disorder, tardive dyskinesia (see page 118). There is no need to risk such a serious outcome in the quest for an antidepressant, so Asendin goes on my "Not Recommended" list.

Desyrel (trazodone)

Originally developed as an antidepressant, trazodone causes enough drowsiness that a bedtime dose is now often used as a non-habit-forming sleeping medication. This same tendency to produce drowsiness makes it especially helpful to those whose depression is accompanied by anxiety, insomnia, or agitation, and in those who have insomnia induced by another antidepressant (especially the SSRIs). However, if a feature of your depression is lethargy and lack of pep, Desyrel probably won't suit you. Because of its dual effects on sleep and depression, some patients with posttraumatic stress disorder find it quite useful. Because it doesn't worsen psychosis, it can even be used in depressed patients with schizophrenia.

Special Precaution

Although side effects are mild overall and it is relatively benign in overdose, around one in 10,000 men develops priapism (it can also affect women). This is a persistent, painful erection that, if not relieved, can lead to serious disability. It usually occurs in the first month of treatment and is more likely at higher doses. Priapism is no joke; it is a true medical emergency that must be dealt with at once.

Ludiomil (maprotiline)

The side effects of this drug are similar to those of Norpramin.

Special Precaution

All of the older antidepressants carry at least some risk of seizures. Below 225 mg/day, Ludiomil is no worse than the rest, but at higher doses, the risk escalates. However, it may be useful for some people who don't respond to a variety of other antidepressant medications—which is what keeps it *off* the "Not Recommended" list.

St. John's Wort (hypericum)

This herbal remedy has become quite popular in the past several years. Some studies claim that it works about as well as mainstream antidepressants, but at least two facts make me feel less than sanguine about it. First, a 2001 study found it useless against moderately severe depression. The discrepancy with other studies was laid to the methodological flaws of the earlier studies (too few patients to draw firm conclusions, inadequate diagnostic criteria, and inadequate controls). The second fact that worries me is the herb's ability to affect blood levels of many drugs, including prescription antidepressant drugs and other medical preparations. If you need *real* help for even a mild depression, choose a *real* antidepressant with proven benefits.

SAM-e

An antioxidant food supplement, *S*-adenosylmethionine (called SAM-e for short) has been touted lately as another "natural" treatment for depression. The final data have yet to be reported, but there are indications that this substance could be of some benefit in depression. Right now, there simply aren't enough data to support a recommendation.

ANTIDEPRESSANTS FOR OLDER PEOPLE

Older patients should start many antidepressants at half the usual dose.

ANTIDEPRESSANTS FOR THE MEDICALLY ILL

If you have liver or kidney impairment, you must use any drug cautiously, due to the reduced rate at which these organs metabolize and eliminate drugs. As listed in Table 6.1, I recommend starting many antidepressants at half the usual dose. A number of medical conditions—heart disease, positional low blood pressure, ventricular arrhythmia, and Parkinson's disease—would make an SSRI the drug of choice. Wellbutrin may also be safer for patients with active heart disease. If you have a seizure disorder, avoid Anafranil and Wellbutrin in favor of Norpramin, SSRIs, MAOIs, Remeron, or Desyrel. Cancer patients might want to exploit the appetite-stimulating effects of some of the TCAs.

TABLE 6.1. Antidepressants Currently Prescribed in the United States

Brand name	Generic name, year of FDA approval	Generic?	Starting treatment	Adult dose range/usual dose effective for moderate depression (mg/day)	Divided into # doses/day	Dosage size (mg)	$/day, average daily dose	Ideal blood level (ng/ml)	Half-life (hr)	Time to work (wk)/full trial (wk)
Selective serotonin reuptake inhibitors (SSRIs)										
Celexa	citalopram, 1998	N	Start 20 mg 1x/day; ↑ by 20 mg each 7 days	20–60/40	1	20, 40, IV	$2.19		L	2–4/4
Luvox	fluvoxamine 1996	N	Start 50 mg 1x/day; ↑ by 50 mg each 4–7 days	50–300/100	1 (2 if over 100 mg/day)	25, 50, 100	$2.62		M	2–4/4
Paxil	paroxetine, 1993	N	Start 20 mg 1x/day; ↑ by 10 mg each 7 days	10–60/30	1	10, 20, 30, 40	$2.60		M	2–4/4
Prozac, Sarafem	fluoxetine, 1988	Y	Start 20 mg 1x/day; ↑ by 20 mg each 28 days	10–80/20	1	10, 20, 40, 90; oral liquid	$0.85	200–700	L	2–4/5–6
Zoloft	sertraline, 1992	N	Start 50 mg 1x/day; ↑ by 50 mg each 7 days	50–200/100	1	25, 50, 100; oral liquid	$2.25	30–190	L	2–4/4
Tricyclic antidepressants (TCAs)										
Anafranil	clomipramine, 1991	N	Start 25 mg 1x/day; ↑ by 25 mg each 5 days	50–250/150	3 (with meals)	25, 50, 75	$2.66	200–300	L	2–4/4
Elavil, Endep	amitriptyline, 1961	Y	Start 25–75 mg/day (take in 1–3 doses); ↑ by 25–50 mg each 7 days	50–300/150	1	10, 25, 50, 75, 100, 150; oral liquid	$0.21	100–250	L	2–4/4
Norpramin	desipramine, 1964	Y	Start 50–75 mg/day (take in 1–4 doses); ↑ by 25–50 mg each 7 days	50–300/175	1–3	10, 25, 50, 75, 100, 150; oral liquid	$1.09	125–300	M	2–4/4
Pamelor, Aventyl	nortriptyline, 1964	Y	Start 25–50 mg/day (take in 1–2 doses); ↑ by 25 mg each 7 days	50–200/75	1	10, 25, 50, 75; oral liquid	$0.42	50–100	M–L	2–4/4
Sinequan, Adapin	doxepin, 1969	Y	Start 25–75 mg/day (take in 1–3 doses); ↑ by 25–50 mg/d each 7 days	75–300/200	1	10, 25, 50, 75, 100, 150; oral liquid	$0.54	125–250	M	2–4/4
Surmontil	trimipramine, 1979	N	Start 25 mg 3x/day; ↑ gradually to 150 mg/day	50–300/150	1–3	25, 50, 100	$3.40	250–300	M–L	2–4/4
Tofranil	imipramine, 1959	Y	Start 50–100 mg/day (take in 1–4 doses); ↑ by 25–50 mg each 7 days	50–300/150	1	10, 25, 50, 75, 100, 125, 150; IM	$0.18	150–250	M	2–4/4
Vivactil	protriptyline, 1967	Y	Start 15–30 mg/day (take in 3 doses); ↑ by 10 mg each 7 days	15–60 /30	3 (with meals)	5, 10	$1.92	100–200	L	2–4/4

(continued)

TABLE 6.1. (*continued*)

Brand name	Generic name, year of FDA approval	Generic?	Starting treatment	Adult dose range/usual dose effective for moderate depression . . . (mg/day)	Divided into # doses/day	Dosage size (mg)	$/day average daily	Ideal blood level (ng/ml)	Half-life (hr)	Time to work (wk)/full trial (wk)
				Monoamine oxidase inhibitors (MAOIs)						
Manerix	moclobemide (Canada & UK)	N	Start 100 mg 3x/day; ↑ gradually by 100 mg/day	300–600/450	3 (after meals)	100, 150	$1.00		—	2-4/4
Marplan	isocarboxazid, 1959	N	Start 10 mg 2x/day; ↑ by 10 mg each 2–4 days	20–60/40	2–4	10	$2.96		—	2-6/6
Nardil	phenelzine, 1959	N	Start 15 mg 3x/day; ↑ quickly to 60 mg/day	15–90/60	1	15	$2.08		—	2-6/6
Parnate	tranylcypromine, 1961	N	Start 10 mg 3x/day; ↑ by 10 mg each 2–3 wks	10–60/40	1	10	$2.40		—	1-6/6
				Other antidepressants						
Asendin	amoxapine, 1980	Y	Start 50 mg 2–3x/day; ↑ to 100 mg after 7 days	100–400/300	1–2	25, 50, 75, 100, 150	$4.60	200–500	M–L	1-4/4
Desyrel	trazodone, 1981	Y	Start 50 mg 3x/day; ↑ by 50 mg each 3–4 days; take with food	150–600/300	2–4	50, 100, 150, 300	$1.23	800–1600	M	2-4/4
Effexor	venlafaxine, 1993	N	Start 75 mg/day (take in 2–3 doses); ↑ by 75 mg each 4 days	75–375/150	2–3	25, 37.5, 50, 75, 100	$1.75		M	1-2/4
Ludiomil	maprotiline, 1980	Y	Start 25 mg 3x/day; ↑ by 25–50 mg each 7 days	50–225/150	3 (or bedtime)	25, 50, 75	$1.86	150–250	L	1-4/4
Remeron	mirtazapine, 1996	N	Start 15 mg/day at bed; ↑ by 15 mg each 1–2 wks	15–45/30	1 (bedtime)	15, 30, 45	$2.73		L	1-4/4
Serzone	nefazodone, 1994	N	Start 100 mg 2x/day; ↑ by 100–200 each 7 days	400–600/400	2	50, 100, 150, 200, 250	$2.66		S	2-4/4
Wellbutrin, Zyban	bupropion, 1989	Y	Start 100 mg 2x/day early in day; ↑ to 100 mg 3x/day after 3 days	200–450/300	3 (6 hrs apart)	75, 100, 150, 200	$2.88	25–100	M	2-4/4

S = short (< 6 hr); M = medium (6–24 hr); L = long (> 24 hr); Y = yes; N = no; IM = Intramuscular; IV = intravenous

78

TABLE 6.2. Side Effects and Precautions for Antidepressants

Brand name	Report right away	Discuss at next visit	Important cautions, tests	Symptoms of toxicity	Interactions with other drugs
			Selective serotonin reuptake inhibitors (SSRIs)		
Celexa, Luvox, Paxil, Prozac, Zoloft	*Dizziness*	*Diarrhea, decreased appetite, drowsiness, dry mouth, headache,* reduced libido, trouble with orgasm, impotence, *insomnia, nausea, nervousness* (less of a problem for Celexa, Paxil, Zoloft), sweating, *tremor,* weakness/fatigue	• Serotonin syndrome: do not use with other SSRIs, St. John's wort, MAOIs, tryptophan • Can precipitate mania • For elderly: start at about half adult dose, increase slowly (especially true for Paxil, Prozac). Celexa: start 10–20 mg/day; ↑ to 20 mg after 7 days (40 mg maximum) • Liver or kidney impairment: may need to start at half dose, increase slowly	Nausea, vomiting, drowsiness, dilated pupils, rapid heartbeat, restlessness, confusion, dizziness, sweating, tremor	• Avoid: Mellaril, MAOIs, tryptophan, Propulsid • May ↑ impairment in thinking and motor skills caused by alcohol, other CNS depressants • SSRIs may ↑ the effects of: TCAs (for example, Tofranil), beta blockers (for example, Inderal), antipsychotics (for example, Haldol, Clozaril), anticonvulsants (for example, Tegretol, Dilantin), benzodiazepines (for example, Xanax, Halcion), methadone, Cognex, theophylline, Coumadin, anti-arrhythmics (for example, Rythmol, Cardizem, Propulsid) • SSRIs may ↑ or ↓ effects of lithium • The following may ↑ effects of SSRIs: Tagamet, grapefruit juice • The following may ↓ effects of SSRIs: Dilantin, barbiturates, cigarette smoking • Antimigraine "triptans" (for example, Imitrex) may cause weakness, incoordination
			Novel antidepressants		
Effexor	*Dizziness,* increased blood pressure (at higher doses), vomiting	*Constipation, decreased appetite, drowsiness, dry mouth, headache, insomnia, nausea, nervousness, sexual dysfunction (males: delayed orgasm, impotence), sweating, weakness, weight loss*	• High blood pressure: check blood pressure often • If moderate liver impairment, start 50% less • Kidney impairment: start 25–50% less • Watch for serotonin syndrome	Drowsiness, altered heartbeat rates, low blood pressure, dizziness, seizures, coma	• Avoid: MAOIs, Propulsid • May ↑ impairment in thinking and motor skills caused by alcohol, other CNS depressants • May ↑ effects of: TCAs, antipsychotic drugs (for example, Stelazine), dextromethorphan • May ↓ effects of Crixivan • The following may ↑ effects of Effexor: Norvir, Tagamet • Could cause serotonin syndrome: Ultram, pentazocine

(continued)

79

TABLE 6.2. (*continued*)

Brand name	Report right away	Discuss at next visit	Important cautions, tests	Symptoms of toxicity	Interactions with other drugs
			Novel antidepressants		
Remeron	Drowsiness, disorientation, forgetfulness, rapid heartbeat	*Constipation*, fatigue, *drowsiness, dry mouth, increased appetite, weight gain*	• Low white blood cell count (rare) • Can increase cholesterol level • If infection, obtain white blood cell count • Watch for serotonin syndrome • Elderly: start at 7.5 mg; increase every 1–2 weeks • Liver, kidney impairment: start low, ↑ slowly	Drowsiness, disorientation, forgetfulness, rapid heartbeat	• Avoid MAOIs • May ↑ impairment in thinking and motor skills caused by alcohol, other CNS depressants • Remeron may ↓ effects of Catapres
Serzone	Dizziness, confusion, postural low blood pressure	Blurred vision, nausea, dry mouth, constipation, weakness, drowsiness, abnormal dreams, headache, increased appetite	• Watch for serotonin syndrome • Seizures • Elderly: start 50 mg 2x/day; ↑ as for adult • Liver impairment: start low, ↑ slowly	Nausea, vomiting, drowsiness	• May ↑ impairment in thinking and motor skills caused by alcohol, other CNS depressants • Avoid: Seldane, Propulsid, Orap, MAOIs, Tagamet, Tegretol • May ↑ effects of benzodiazepines (especially Xanax, Halcion), Prograf, Pletal, antiviral drugs (for example, Crixivan, Viramune, Norvir). BuSpar, cyclosporine, digoxin, ergotamine, Evoxac, Haldol, Lipitor, methadone, Mevacor, Pletal, Provigil, Targretin, Tikosyn, Zocor • The following may ↑ effects of Serzone: Norvir, Rescriptor • The following may ↓ effects of Serzone: Nevirapine, Sustiva • The following may encourage serotonin syndrome: St John's wort, SSRIs, dextromethorphan, Meridia, Ultram, Desyrel, amphetamines
Wellbutrin, Zyban	Confusion, *dizziness*, seizures (especially likely with anorexia or bulimia), *vomiting*	*Agitation, blurred vision, constipation, dry mouth, headache, insomnia, nausea*, rash, *sweating, weight loss*	• Risk of seizures ↑ above 450 mg/day • Obtain EKG, liver function (blood) tests, complete blood count • For elderly or liver or kidney impairment: may need to reduce initial dose	Fever, muscle rigidity, low blood pressure, rapid heartbeat, hallucinations, seizures, coma	• Avoid MAOIs • The following may ↑ Wellbutrin effects: Norvir, Dilantin, Tagamet, barbiturates, levodopa • The following may ↓ Wellbutrin effects: Tegretol, barbiturates, Dilantin • The following may ↑ risk of seizures: alcohol, amphetamine, antipsychotics, benzodiazepines, cocaine, TCAs, theophylline, Ultram, weight loss medications • Wellbutrin may ↑ effects of: levodopa • Wellbutrin may ↓ effects of: codeine • Use of nicotine patch may ↑ blood pressure in some patients

Tricyclic antidepressants (TCAs)

Anafranil, Elavil (Endep), Sinequan (Adepin), Surmontil, Tofranil	Confusion, *dizziness, positional low blood pressure, rapid or irregular heartbeat, urinary hesitancy or retention* Anafranil: seizures	Agitation, *blurred vision, constipation, drowsiness, dry mouth,* insomnia, nausea, *sweating, weight gain* Anafranil: *Headache, muscle spasms, trouble with orgasm*	• Don't use if recent heart attack, certain abnormal heart rhythms • Use cautiously in glaucoma, markedly enlarged prostate, seizure disorder (Anafranil) • Extremely dangerous in overdose • Obtain EKG (especially if over age 50) • Elderly: start at ½ – ⅔ usual adult dose; ↑ slowly • Liver impairment (Anafranil, Sinequan): start low, ↑ slowly	Agitation, confusion, poor concentration, dilated pupils, drowsiness, muscle rigidity, irregular or rapid heartbeat, decreased blood pressure, sweating, visual hallucinations, vomiting	• May ↑ impairment in thinking and motor skills caused by alcohol, other CNS depressants • Avoid: MAOIs TCAs may ↑ effects of: SSRIs, beta blockers (for example, Inderal), Ismelin or Catapres, antipsychotics (for example, Haldol, Clozaril), Rythmol • The following may ↑ TCA effects: antipsychotics (for example, Thorazine), codeine, lithium, oral contraceptives, quinidine, Tagamet, thyroid replacement drugs • Smoking may reduce effectiveness of TCAs • Use of TCAs with antipsychotics and drugs used to treat side effects of antipsychotics (for example, Artane, Cogentin) may interfere with the body's heat regulation; especially in hot weather, heat exhaustion may result
Norpramin (Pamelor), Aventyl, Vivactil	Confusion, *dizziness, positional low blood pressure (less with Pamelor),* rapid or irregular heartbeat, *urinary hesitancy or retention*	*Blurred vision, constipation,* drowsiness, *dry mouth,* nausea, *sweating, weight gain (less likely with Vivactil),* sexual dysfunctioning Vivactil: *Agitation, insomnia*	• Don't use if recent heart attack, certain abnormal heart rhythms • Use cautiously in glaucoma, markedly enlarged prostate (Pamelor, Aventyl) • Extremely dangerous in overdose • Obtain EKG (especially if over age 50) • **For elderly:** Norpramin: start at 25 mg/day, ↑ by 25 mg each 7 days to 150 mg; Pamelor: start at 10–25 mg/day, ↑ by 25 mg each 3 days to 150; Vivactil: start at 15 mg/day, ↑ by 10 mg each 7 days to 30 mg max and watch for heart arrhythmias • Liver impairment (Vivactil): start low, ↑ slowly		

(continued)

TABLE 6.2. (continued)

Brand name	Report right away	Discuss at next visit	Important cautions, tests	Symptoms of toxicity	Interactions with other drugs
			Monoamine oxidase inhibitors (MAOI)		
Nardil, Marplan, Parnate	Difficulty urinating, dizziness, *postural low blood pressure*, severe headache with palpitations and (especially) neck stiffness	*Ankle swelling, headache, insomnia, muscle twitching, sexual difficulties (especially trouble having orgasm), tremor, weight gain,* drowsiness	• Defer elective surgery while on drug • Avoid if pheochromocytoma, a rare, adrenaline-producing tumor • Use cautiously in hyperthyroidism, high blood pressure, heart disease • Serotonin syndrome • Carefully maintain diet low in tyramine • Check blood pressure each visit • Elderly: start with one dose/day; ↑ slowly; avoid Parnate if over 60 • Liver or kidney impairment: use with caution; avoid if severe	Anxiety, blood pressure changes, confusion, dizziness, drowsiness, faintness, headache, heart palpitations, sweating, weakness. **More severe:** agitation, hallucinations, muscle rigidity, convulsions, coma	• May ↑ impairment in thinking and motor skills caused by alcohol, other CNS depressants • Due to risk of severe hypertension (see warning page 73), avoid: amphetamines, BuSpar, cocaine, cold and allergy remedies, Demerol, dextromethorphan, epinephrine, excessive caffeine, guanadrel, guanethidine, L-dopa, L-tryptophan, L-tyrosine, meperidine, pentazocine, phenylalanine, reserpine, Ritalin, SSRIs, St. John's wort, TCAs, Wellbutrin, or Zyban • Follow dietary precautions to avoid high protein foods that have undergone breakdown by aging • MAOIs may ↑ effects of: doxapram • Avoid Comtan, Tasmar, Ultram, valerian
Manerix (Canada and UK)	Postural low blood pressure, rapid or irregular heartbeat	*Blurred vision,* constipation, *dry mouth, headache, insomnia, nausea,* drowsiness, sweating, tremor	• Risk of hypertensive crisis is far less than for other MAOIs • Stop drug 2 days before elective surgery • Elderly or liver impairment: start at half the usual dose	Agitation, drowsiness, slurred speech, confusion, low blood pressure, hallucinations, sweating	• Most of the same drug interactions as listed for the other MAOIs apply • Diet is less important, but avoid large quantities of tyramine-rich food

82

Older antidepressants

Asendin	Abnormal mouth movements, urinary hesitancy, *positional low blood pressure, irregular heartbeat*, seizures	Blurred vision, *constipation, drowsiness, dry mouth, insomnia, weight gain*	• Risk of neuroleptic malignant syndrome, tardive dyskinesia (see page 118) • Avoid if recent heart attack Elderly: start 25 mg; ↑ to 50 mg in 7 days; 300 mg max (100–150 is usual effective dose) • Liver impairment: start low, ↑ slowly	Drowsiness, delirium, lethargy, seizures, rapid heartbeat	See tricyclic antidepressants
Desyrel	Confusion, *dizziness*, persistent erection, postural low blood pressure	*Blurred vision*, constipation, drowsiness, *dry mouth, headache*, fatigue, *nausea*, sweating, weight gain	• Persistent erection (priapism) can be dangerous; a medical emergency • Elderly or liver impairment: start low, ↑ slowly • Watch for serotonin syndrome	Weakness, low blood pressure, seizures, worsening of any side effect	• May ↑ impairment in thinking and motor skills caused by alcohol, other CNS depressants • Avoid: buspirone, SSRIs, St. John's wort, TCAs, MAOIs • Desyrel may ↓ effects of Coumadin, anticonvulsants (for example, barbiturates, Dilantin) • Desyrel may ↑ effects of hypertension drugs • The following may ↓ effects of Desyrel: barbiturates, Tegretol
Ludiomil	Confusion, heartbeat irregularities, positional low blood pressure, seizures, urinary hesitancy	Agitation, *blurred vision, constipation, drowsiness, dry mouth, tremor, weight gain*	• Avoid if: glaucoma, markedly enlarged prostate, certain abnormal heart rhythms, history of seizures • Elderly: start 25 mg at bed; ↑ 25 mg each 7 days to 225 max • Liver impairment: start low, ↑ slowly	Breathing slowed, confusion, dilated pupils, dizziness, fever, heartbeat rapid or irregular, low blood pressure, muscle spasms and rigidity, restlessness, seizures, staggering, tremor, vomiting, coma	• Avoid: MAOIs • May ↑ impairment in thinking and motor skills caused by alcohol, other CNS depressants • Ludiomil may ↓ effects of hypertension drugs (Catapres, Ismelin, methyldopa, reserpine) • Ludiomil may ↑ effects of: adrenalin, Dilantin, Ritalin • The following may ↑ effects of Ludiomil: antipsychotics (for example, Thorazine), beta blockers (for example, Inderal) • The following may ↓ effects of Ludiomil: barbiturates, contraceptives, Dilantin, Tegretol

Boldface italic = more common (10% or more of patients); ↑ = increase; ↓ = decrease

TABLE 6.3. Indications, Advantages, and Risks of Antidepressants

Legend:
a FDA approved
b non-FDA approved
c Canada only
++ strongly yes
+ yes

	Anafranil	Asendin	Celexa	Desyrel	Effexor	Elavil	Ludiomil	Luvox	Manerix	Marplan	Nardil	Norpramin	Pamelor	Parnate	Paxil	Prozac	Remeron	Serzone	Sinequan	Surmontil	Tofranil	Vivactil	Wellbutrin	Zoloft
Used for:																								
Major depression	b	a	a	a	a	a	a	a	b	c	a	a	a	a	a	a	a	a	a	a	a	a	a	a
Atypical depression									b	b	b			b		b								
Dysthymia										b				b										b
Mixed anxiety/depression																		a		a				
Premenstrual dysphoric disorder			b					b					b		b	a								b
Panic disorder		b	b		b			b			b	b	b		a	b			b		b			a
Generalized anxiety disorder			b		a										b									
Obsessive–compulsive disorder	a		b					a			b				a	a								a
Agoraphobia			b											b										
Social anxiety disorder								b	b						a	b								b
Posttraumatic stress disorder								b							a	b								a
Anorexia nervosa																b								
Bulimia nervosa				b				b				b	b			a					b			
Insomnia				b																				
Smoking cessation																							a	
Cocaine withdrawal				b																				
Premature ejaculation	b														b	b								b
Enuresis (bed-wetting)																					a			
Advantages:																								
Effective at usual starting dose			+		+			+							+	+								+
Few drug interactions					+				+	+	+		+	++										
Side effects unlikely to cause dropout					+																		+	
Older patients may tolerate well				+	+				+	+	+													
Sedating	+					+											++	+	+	+				
Low risk of switch to mania																							+	
Low risk of weight gain																							+	
Low risk of sexual dysfunction																	+	+					+	
Risks and drawbacks:																								
Activating			+					+				+			+	+						++	+	+
Agranulocytosis (low white blood cell count)																	+							
Central serotonin syndrome			+					+		+	+			+	+	+								+
High blood pressure					+					+	+			+										
Positional low blood pressure											+	+	+	+						+	+			
Lethal in overdose	++	++				++				++	++	++	++	++					++	++	++	++		
Tardive dyskinesia (movement disorder) possible		+																						
Seizures	+	+																					++	
Sexual dysfunctioning			+		+			+		+	+			+	+	+								+
Special diet required									+	++	++			++										

84

CHAPTER 7

Mood Stabilizers

Two decades ago, we would have discussed just one drug in this chapter: lithium. Now there are others that stabilize the highs and lows of mood in bipolar disorder, notably Depakote and Tegretol, first used to prevent epileptic seizures. Although we aren't yet sure how they control mood, they probably increase the effectiveness of GABA (gamma-aminobutyric acid), yet another in our lengthening list of neurotransmitters. To one degree or other, all of the mood stabilizers:

- **Moderate the symptoms of acute mania.** Although they may need short-term help in the form of an antipsychotic or Ativan (a benzodiazepine), within a few weeks these drugs control the hyperactivity, euphoric mood, excessive speech, and decreased need for sleep that characterize the manic phase of bipolar disorder.
- **Modify the course of bipolar disease.** Although they don't provide a cure, when used long term they can reduce the number and severity of manic and depressive episodes.
- **Augment the effects of antidepressants.** If your depression doesn't respond well to an antidepressant alone, you may do better if you add a mood stabilizer. This holds true for both bipolar and unipolar depressions (see Chapters 15 and 16 for an explanation of the distinctions between these types of depression).
- **Treat schizoaffective disorder.** Mood stabilizers are especially likely to help when mood symptoms are more pronounced than psychotic symptoms.
- **Reduce aggression.** Mentally retarded people who cannot otherwise control outbursts of aggression may obtain relief from one of these drugs.

With any of these drugs, you could notice improvement in acute mania within a few days, although it can take several weeks to reach full effect. However, people are often more interested in how long they should continue to take this sort of drug. My answer is often, "To prevent relapse, just keep taking it." On the other hand, about 10% of patients have only one episode, so if this is your first, after a year or two of complete stability, you and your doctor might discuss the risks and benefits of coming off the medicine completely. If you do, taper very gradually, to avoid any possible rebound side effects, and watch carefully for the first sign of recurring manic or depressive symptoms. Those who have multiple episodes may experience 5 years or more between first and second episodes. Subsequently, the interval between episodes shortens.

Although mood stabilizers are among the most useful medications available to mental health patients, each has its downside. There are numerous side effects, some of which can be extremely serious. They interact with many other drugs, increasing or decreasing the amount of them your body needs. And several must be regulated with blood level measurements. The time of day at which you have your blood drawn matters a lot. A few hours after you take any medicine, your blood level increases rapidly, then declines more slowly and eventually levels out. All of this usually takes about 12 hours, so you should get your test done just about 12 hours after your last dose. If you miss it by an hour in either direction, it won't make that much difference—your doctor will be able to make sense out of the results.

Perhaps most alarming is the potential impact of the mood stabilizers on a growing fetus. I've known women who have conceived and delivered normal children when taking lithium, but they took a fearful risk. Mood stabilizers can produce malformations such as heart and spinal column defects. Expectant parents and women who might become pregnant must discuss the risks and benefits with their doctors. The decision to carry a child to term while the mother is taking a mood stabilizer should be made only when both spouses are aware of the risks and emotionally stable enough to make a sound decision. Because these drugs are secreted into breast milk, they should not be used by nursing mothers.

Table 7.1 gives the facts and figures of the various mood stabilizers, and Table 7.2 lists their side effects.

SPECIFIC MOOD STABILIZERS

Depakote (valproic acid)

Although there are several forms of this medicine, in your stomach all forms turn to valproic acid. For several reasons, Depakote is the mood stabilizer usually tried first. It is the quickest to work—often within just a few days. Unlike lithium, Depakote can help patients whose moods swing up and down frequently (four or more times a year). It also has the fewest side effects. It has been a godsend for the 20% or so of patients who can't or won't take lithium, or who aren't helped by it.

Your doctor may prescribe Depakote by itself, with an antidepressant, or with another mood stabilizer. Added to lithium or Tegretol, Depakote may stabilize a bipolar patient who hasn't responded well to just one of these drugs. The serum level needs to be greater than 50 micrograms (µg)/ml; much above 100 µg, however, side effects mount but the effectiveness doesn't. For those who have trouble swallowing capsules and tablets, Depakote can be sprinkled on food such as applesauce.

Drawbacks

For the most part, Depakote's side effects (Table 7.2) are mild and tend to diminish spontaneously. It can sometimes impair mental alertness, so be careful when driving a car or engaging in other activities that require good motor coordination. The most feared side effect is also one of the rarest: potentially fatal liver toxicity (tiredness, facial swelling, loss of appetite, and vomiting are early symptoms). Although liver toxicity occurs almost exclusively in children, even for adults the drug manufacturer recommends weekly liver tests during the first few months, and once every 6 months or so thereafter. Depakote has also produced pancreatitis, albeit rarely, with symptoms of severe abdominal pain, nausea, and vomiting. Although Depakote often causes mild forms of these symptoms without serious import, be safe: telephone your physician if they develop.

Lithium

Lithium is the only psychiatric drug that is an element—a building block of the universe, like carbon or hydrogen. It is neither grown nor chemically synthesized; rather, it is dug out of rocks (*lithos* is Greek for *stone*). It is also one of the few drugs that is far more commonly known by its generic name than by any of its trade names. One of the oldest psychiatric drugs still in use, lithium chloride used to be promoted as a salt substitute, until indiscriminate use led to deaths from toxicity. Then in 1949 its role in treating mania was accidentally discovered. Although the response rate (about 80%) is generally excellent, it goes to work so slowly that it is often combined with an antipsychotic or a benzodiazepine to accelerate the improvement.

You will probably start on lithium carbonate at 900 mg/day. Although the long half-life means that you could take all the medicine just once a day, you may need to divide the dose and take it with food to decrease nausea, diarrhea, or other side effects that many people experience. After a week you'll get a lithium blood level; depending on the result, you may need to increase your dose by 300 mg. If you can't swallow tablets or capsules, there is an oral solution available, lithium citrate, a teaspoon of which contains the same amount of active drug as a 300-mg lithium tablet.

A good maintenance level is usually between 0.4 and 1.0 mEq/l (which stands for milliequivalents per liter).* However, there is a great deal of individual variation;

---

*An equivalent is a fancy way of measuring chemicals that takes into account their electronic charge.

some people relapse at the 0.4 level; others may notice intolerable side effects at 1.0. For some, the effective blood level will be as high as 1.4. You and your doctor will have to experiment to learn what works best for you.

Drawbacks

A major problem with lithium therapy is treading the line between too much and just right. Clinicians sometimes call this margin the "therapeutic ratio"—for lithium, it is razor-thin. You could go wrong in a number of ways, among them:

- **Taking too much.** Just a couple of tablets a day extra could push you into mild lithium toxicity. Keep carefully to your schedule; if you forget a dose, don't try to make it up.
- **Dehydration.** You'll need to drink plenty of liquid (the equivalent of at least 3 quarts of water a day) and report immediately to your doctor if you suffer vomiting, diarrhea, fever, or increased urination.
- **Low salt intake.** Should you reduce the amount of table salt in your diet, your kidneys will respond by retaining more lithium; if you increase salt intake, your lithium level could decline enough to become ineffective. Of course, we all vary our salt intake somewhat from day to day, which shouldn't be a problem. Just don't make a major change in your diet without the approval of your doctor.
- **Kidney disease.** Lithium isn't metabolized at all (you can't change an element except by radioactive bombardment). Nearly all of it is excreted in urine, and anything that alters kidney functioning can affect your lithium level.
- **Advancing age.** As people get older, they need less lithium to produce the same effects. If you are over 60, your doctor may increase the frequency of your lithium levels to track changes in your requirements.
- **Certain drugs.** Special precautions may be needed if you take any of the drugs listed in Table 7.2.

Early symptoms of toxicity include trouble speaking clearly, staggering or stumbling when you try to walk, and trembling that is coarser than the fine hand tremor so many people experience with lithium. Any of these symptoms should prompt an immediate call to your doctor. If toxicity worsened, impaired consciousness, coma, and even death could ensue. All of this is preventable, which is why you will need to take a blood test every week or so at first. Once stabilized, you'll need to get blood levels perhaps twice a year.

You may notice an increase in urine volume. This is usually temporary and doesn't cause much inconvenience, but lithium makes some people urinate far more than normal (well over the 3 quarts/day). The loss of body fluid produces tremendous thirst, so they drink much more liquid than normal. This condition is called "nephrogenic diabetes insipidus" (NDI). It has nothing to do with the disease we usually just call "diabetes"; it is only a descriptive name that means that the kidney produces excessive but diluted urine. If you notice that you are drinking far more liquid than usual, or if you get up many times during the night to urinate, notify your doctor at once. You will probably have to reduce the lithium dose or add one of several special medications to counteract the problem.

Perhaps 4% of people (mostly women) who take lithium develop hypothyroidism, or low thyroid functioning. They notice that their skin becomes rough and coarse, that they perspire less, or that they feel colder than usual. They may feel slowed down, even depressed; some develop an enlargement in the neck called a goiter. Hypothyroidism is easily treatable, but first it must be detected. That is why you will need a thyroid test when you first start lithium, and yearly repeats.

Tegretol (carbamazepine)

Tegretol works about as well as lithium for acute mania, though it is probably less effective against bipolar depression. It prevents recurrences of both mania and depression, and it can stabilize rapid cycling, similar to Depakote. Tegretol is usually effective at blood levels of 8–12 micrograms/ml; the manufacturer recommends weekly monitoring of blood levels until they are stable, then monthly for 6 months, one to two times a year thereafter. Although you would have to take the regular tablets several times a day, there is an extended release form that allows once-a-day dosing. If you need to discontinue Tegretol, taper slowly to prevent any possibility of seizures.

Drawbacks

A serious but fortunately rare side effect is agranulocytosis, a condition in which the bone marrow produces too few of the white blood cells you need to fight off infection. If you should develop fever, sore throat, mouth ulcers, or easy bruising while taking Tegretol, telephone your doctor at once. Most other side effects are relatively mild and decrease after a few days. It is sedating, so you will want to take most of your dose at bedtime. Nausea and the sensation of slowed thinking are especially a problem if you take this medicine just once a day or if you increase it rapidly. And Tegretol has an extensive list of potential side effects. (None of them should be cause for avoiding Tegretol; just watch carefully for problems.) On the positive side, Tegretol is unlikely to cause you to gain weight the way both lithium and Depakote do.

Tegretol absorbs moisture readily, which causes it to lose potency. Keep the lid on tightly and store it someplace dry at room temperature.

OTHER MOOD STABILIZERS

The chances are excellent that Depakote, lithium, or Tegretol will work for you. If not, your doctor may suggest two or three of them in combination. (As you will note from Table 7.2, simultaneous use can cause drug interactions; usually, these can be managed by careful testing and gradually adjusting the dose.) Still, a tiny fraction of people will need to reach out further for the mood stabilizer that is right for them. Several other drugs have been used, alone or with more conventional mood stabilizers, to treat bipolar disorder. Mostly, you should consider these drugs only if the better-studied medications discussed so far don't work well or if side effects make it impossible for you to use them.

Lamictal (lamotrigine)

Double-blind studies have shown Lamictal to be effective in treating both mania and bipolar depression. It may be less likely than the other mood stabilizers to promote a switch to mania, and less likely than the antidepressants to increase the frequency of mania–depression cycles. About 10% of patients who take Lamictal with other drugs develop a rash. In most cases it is benign, but very rarely such a skin rash can become life-threatening. Therefore, if you take this drug, you must *immediately* report any of these symptoms to your physician:

- Skin rash, itching
- Fever
- Painful sores in your mouth, eyes, or nose
- Swelling of your face, lips, or tongue
- Swollen lymph glands

Neurontin and Topamax

Two other new drugs have shown promise in stabilizing mood disorders, but they haven't had enough scientific scrutiny to merit a recommendation. Still, if for some reason you can't use the mood stabilizers I've already discussed, you and your doctor might want to consider Neurontin or Topamax.

Neurontin (gabapentin) has been used to treat amyotrophic lateral sclerosis (ALS, or Lou Gerhig's disease) and the aggression that occurs with dementia. At least one study suggests that it is useful for bipolar patients who are resistant to lithium. Side effects are usually insignificant, but users need to take multiple doses throughout the day; relatively large doses are only partly absorbed.

In some open (that is, *not* double-blind, placebo-controlled) studies, Topamax (topiramate) has stabilized patients with acute mania or rapid cycling who have not responded well to more conventional treatment. It has two other attractions: blood levels are not needed, and it sometimes actually promotes weight loss.

MOOD STABILIZERS FOR OLDER PEOPLE

Because of reduced kidney and liver function, older patients may need less lithium; they certainly need frequent monitoring. (For example, a tall, extremely manic 94-year-old man I knew required only 600 mg of lithium for stabilization.) Also, the medicines older people are likely to be taking for other illnesses and conditions may conflict with mood stabilizers. This fact creates a certain prejudice against using lithium for older people (my 94-year-old patient notwithstanding). Lithium works, but Depakote is less likely to create problems with diet, other illnesses, loss of kidney filtering capacity, and sensitivity to side effects.

MOOD STABILIZERS FOR THE MEDICALLY ILL

None of these drugs is without risks if you have impaired liver or kidneys. Except in the most extreme cases, however, this doesn't mean that you cannot take a mood stabilizer, only that you must take it with care. If you must use a mood stabilizer, you should take every precaution against becoming pregnant.

TABLE 7.1. Mood Stabilizing Medications Currently Prescribed in the United States

Brand name	Generic name, year of FDA approval	Generic?	Starting treatment	Adult dose range/ usual effective for maintenance (mg/ day)	Divided into # doses/day	Dose strength (mg) (tablet or capsule)	$/day, average daily dose	Ideal blood level	Half-life includes metabolites	Time to work (wk)/Full trial (wk)
Depakote, Depekene	divalproex, valproic acid, valproate, 1995	Y	Start 250 mg 3x/day; ↑ by 250 mg each 2–3 days	750–2000/ 1500	3 with food	125, 250, 500	$5.15	50–125 µg/ml	M	1–2/3
Eskalith, Lithobid, Lithane, Lithonate	lithium, 1970	Y	Start 300 mg 3x/day; ↑ by 300 mg each 5 days	600–2400/ 1200	1–2 with food	150, 300, 450; oral liquid	$0.70	0.8–1.0 mEq/l	L	1–2/3
Lamictal	lamotrigine, 1994	N	Start 50 mg/day for 2 wks; then 50 mg 2x/day for 2 wks; then ↑ by 100 mg/day to total of 300–500/day	50–250/200	2	25, 100, 150, 200	$4.58	—	L	1–2/3
Tegretol, Atrelol, Epitol	carbamazepine, 1968	Y	Start 200 mg 2–3 x/day; ↑ by 200 mg each 4 days	200–1600/ 1000	3–4 with food	100, 200, 300, 400; oral liquid	$1.05	8–12 µg/ ml	M	1–2/3

M = medium (6–24 hr); L = long (> 24 hr); ↑ = increase; µg/ml = micrograms/milliliter; mEq/l = milliequivalents/liter

TABLE 7.2. Side Effects and Precautions for Mood Stabilizing Medications

Brand name	Report right away	Discuss at next visit	Important cautions, tests	Symptoms of toxicity	Interactions with other drugs
Depakote	Abdominal pain (with loss of appetite, nausea, vomiting, a symptom of rare pancreatitis); jaundice, weakness, nausea, loss of appetite (rare liver toxicity in children)	*Drowsiness, nausea, upset stomach, vomiting* often ↓ with time; easy bruising	• Liver toxicity (lethal, rare) in young children • May impair mental alertness, coordination • Don't stop abruptly • Obtain liver and thyroid function tests, complete blood count; repeat monthly for 6 months, then every 6–12 months. • EKG if over 45 • Known to cause fetal malformations • If elderly or liver impairment: start low, ↑ slowly • Avoid if severe liver disease	Drowsiness, irregular heartbeat	• Avoid Klonopin • May ↑ impairment in thinking and motor skills caused by alcohol, other CNS depressants • Depakote may ↑ the effects of: barbiturates, Dilantin, Lamictal, Mysoline, phenobarbital, Tegretol, TCAs (for example, Elavil, Pamolar), Valium, Zarontin • The following may ↑ Depakote effects: Felbatol, isoniazid • The following may ↓ Depakote effects: cholestyramine, Dilantin, Lamictal, Lariam, Merrem, phenobarbital, Rifadin, Tegretol
Lamictal	*Dizziness, rash*, sores, bruising, ↑ bleeding tendency, sore throat, yellowing of skin	*Headache, drowsiness, blurred vision*, nausea, vomiting, *weakness*	• Toxic rash is rare—1 in 1,000; seen especially in young patients who start with high dose and ↑ rapidly • For elderly and those with kidney or liver disease: start low, ↑ slowly	Trouble walking, nausea, vomiting, nystagmus, unconsciousness	• Use care when operating machinery • Lamictal may ↑ the effects of: Tegretol • The following may ↑ Lamictal effects: Depakote • The following may ↓ Lamictal effects: Celontin, Dilantin, Mysoline, Norvir, phenobarbital, Rifadin, Tegretol, Zarontin

(continued)

TABLE 7.2. (*continued*)

Brand name	Report right away	Discuss at next visit	Important cautions, tests	Symptoms of toxicity	Interactions with other drugs
Lithium	Severe thirst, markedly ↑ urination, symptoms of hypothyroidism (feeling cold, tired; dry skin), vomiting	*Mild to moderate ↑ thirst/urination, tremor, ↑ appetite, weight gain, acne, slowed thinking,* reduced creativity, headache, dry mouth; *stomach upset, nausea, and diarrhea* often decrease with time	• Maintain fluid intake (↑ if fever) • Obtain thyroid and kidney function tests at baseline and yearly); EKG if over 40 • For elderly, those with kidney disease, or if on diuretics: start at half dose and ↑ very gradually • Known to cause fetal malformations • Use carefully if history of heart or kidney disease (lithium can worsen irregular heartbeat)	Blurred vision, confusion, diarrhea, dizziness, drowsiness, muscle twitching, nausea, tremor, vomiting	• Take special care if using diuretics, which can increase lithium to toxic levels • The following may ↑ effects of lithium: Indocin and Feldene, Flagyl, ACE inhibitors (for example, lisinopril, enalapril, and Capoten), calcium channel blockers (such as Cardizem and verapamil), antidepressants (TCAs and SSRIs), Aldomet, Tegretol • The following may ↓ effects of lithium: Diamox, urea, theophylline, sodium bicarbonate • Used together, lithium and antipsychotic drugs have produced delirium, confusion, seizures
Tegretol	*Dizziness,* fever, sore throat; any infection, mouth ulcers, easy bruising (all symptoms of rare agranulcytosis): stop medication at once and call doctor	*Drowsiness, nausea, vomiting, unsteady walking* (often ↓ with time)	• Avoid if history of bundle branch block, agranulocytosis • Before starting, obtain CBC, liver and kidney tests, EKG; repeat each 2 weeks for 2 months, then every 3–6 months • Obtain periodic slit lamp eye exam • Known to cause fetal malformations • Use extra care if history of liver damage	Dizziness, drowsiness, nausea, restlessness, trouble walking, tremor, flushing, vomiting	• Avoid MAOIs, Darvon • The following may ↑ effects of Tegretol: antibiotics (erythromycin, Tao, Biaxin), Cardizem, Claritin, Danocrine, Darvon, Depakote, grapefruit juice, isoniazid, lithium, niacinamide, nicotinamide, Nizoral, Prozac, Serzone, Sporanox, Suprax, Tagamet, verapamil • The following may ↓ effects of Tegretol: Adriamycin, Dilantin, Felbatol, Mysoline, phenobarbital, Rifadin, St. John's wort, theophylline • Tegretol may ↓ the effects of: anticoagulants (for example, Coumadin), antipsychotics (for example, Clozaril, Haldol, Risperdal, Zyprexa), Celontin, contraceptives, Depakote, Dilantin, Gabitril, Klonopin, Lamictal, narcotics (for example, methadone), Serzone, theophylline, Topamax, Tylenol, Viagra, Vibramycin, Xanax, Zarontin • Anti-HIV drugs may have complicated interactions with Tegretol

Boldface italic = more common (10% or more of patients); ↑ = increase; ↓ = decrease

94

TABLE 7.3. Indications, Advantages, and Risks of Mood Stabilizers

a FDA approved b non-FDA approved ++ strongly yes + yes	Depakote	Lamictal	Lithium	Tegretol
Used for:				
Depression			b	b
Acute mania	a	b	a	b
Bipolar prophylaxis	a	b	a	b
Agitation in dementia	b			
Migraine prophylaxis	a			
Schizoaffective disorder	b		b	
Agitation in dementia	b			b
PTSD		b		
Advantages:				
Useful in rapid cycling				+
Few drug interactions		+		
Available as oral liquid			+	+
Low cost			+	
Risks and drawbacks:				
Potentially lethal in overdose			++	

CHAPTER 8

Drugs to Treat Anxiety and Insomnia

Anxiety is central to many mental disorders and accompanies many others. Just a few decades ago, if you needed a drug for either anxiety or sleep, what you got was likely to harm you in the long run. That was before the first of the modern antianxiety drugs was approved for use in the United States. Now, with over 20 drugs to choose from, your odds of receiving genuine help are greatly improved. Although *anxiety* and *insomnia* cover a lot of ground, the medications used to treat them are strikingly similar. In reading this chapter, remember that other classes of drugs, especially the antidepressants, may be better for the treatment of anxiety or insomnia in depression, social phobia, obsessive–compulsive disorder, even panic disorder and generalized anxiety disorder. See Chapters 6 and 17–20 for details.

BENZODIAZEPINES AND THEIR CLOSE RELATIVES

Most of the drugs discussed in this chapter belong to a class called "benzodiazepines," named for the chemical structure they have in common. With over 30 of them on the world market, they have become the medications of choice for insomnia and anxiety. Benzodiazepines also have suffered more than their share of controversy and bad press. Whole books—and now websites, too—are devoted to disparaging these medications. However, if you use them with some thought and care, they are remarkably safe and effective.

The benzodiazepines increase the effects of a neurotransmitter called gamma-aminobutyric acid, or GABA, which can reduce anxiety, promote sleep, relax muscles, and reduce the likelihood of epileptic seizures. Some of these medications have been approved for use in specific disorders, but often this reflects the marketing strategies of individual drug companies. They are all effective in a variety of disorders, including obsessive–compulsive disorder, posttraumatic stress disorder, generalized anxiety disorder, and just plain anxiety. In high doses, some are used to combat the effects of alcohol or drug withdrawal, such as occur in delirium tremens (the "DTs"). Which drug you take will be determined largely by side effects, interactions with other drugs you're taking, your physician's preference, cost, and advertising. Unless otherwise stated, the doses and other information given in the tables at the end of this chapter apply to the treatment of moderate anxiety or insomnia, regardless of your underlying diagnosis.

Drawbacks

The main side effect of benzodiazepines is sedation. You may feel drowsy or slowed down, even falling asleep during the day, but you will probably adapt quickly. Until you do, you could encounter problems performing certain tasks: be especially careful when driving a car or operating power tools. A benzodiazepine taken with alcohol or certain other drugs (such as antihistamines) will make you drowsier than would either substance alone. Although depression doesn't occur often with the benzodiazepines, if you start to feel sad or gloomy, contact your doctor immediately. Occasionally, someone experiences a loss of voluntary control, called *disinhibition*, which can lead to reckless behavior such as erratic driving, unprovoked arguing, or impulsive stealing. There is no way to predict this unusual side effect, but anyone who has had such an experience should avoid benzodiazepines thereafter.

Benzodiazepines are neither truly addicting nor, contrary to some of our worst fears, often abused. However, stopping them suddenly can cause withdrawal symptoms, which may tempt you to restart the medication. The original symptoms of insomnia or anxiety may return, perhaps more intensely. You could also experience irritability, fatigue, nausea, depression, and increased sensitivity of smell, taste, and touch. Withdrawal symptoms are more likely with drugs that have short half-lives, which is especially the case with Xanax. These symptoms generally disappear after a week or two, but it is better to avoid them by tapering slowly. Though there is no evidence that these drugs pose a risk to a fetus, they do cross the placental barrier, so you would need a mighty good reason to use them if you are pregnant. They are also secreted into breast milk; though we know little about their effect on a newborn or young infant, take the prudent course and don't nurse if you must take medicine for anxiety or sleep.

Using Benzodiazepines

You would usually start at a standard dose, then monitor your symptoms carefully for improvement, increasing the dose every few days until you find relief. The longer-acting ones can be taken just once a day (almost always in the evening), but some people prefer the feeling of control they get from taking medication only when symptoms appear. This is a defendable strategy, but I believe that it is generally better to prevent than to treat. Control the symptoms, then learn other (perhaps behavioral) ways to deal with the blips of anxiety that affect us all through the course of a day. As with most medications, remember that *less is more*, and take them for the shortest time possible. Every few weeks your doctor will probably suggest that you try to reduce the dose.

SPECIFIC ANTIANXIETY AGENTS

Librium (chlordiazepoxide); Tranxene (clorazepate); Valium (diazepam)

I've listed these three drugs as a group because, as far as your anxiety is concerned, they are just one drug, differing very little in action or side effects. Your body breaks each one down to the same active chemical—something called desmethyldiazepam, which takes a long time for the body to eliminate. Even so, the drugs are absorbed rapidly after swallowing and start working within an hour. Although the popularity of these three drugs has been eclipsed by the benzodiazepines that are eliminated more quickly, such as Xanax and Ativan, these three are safe and effective. Your doctor might recommend one from this group because they act quickly or because of price: generic Valium is both inexpensive and effective. Librium was the first commercial benzodiazepine, and it retains much of its popularity today.

Ativan (lorazepam)

Ativan is quite short-acting—something that is useful if you need relief quickly but briefly, as when you face a time-limited situation sure to cause significant anxiety. Ativan will be out of your system and gone without leaving metabolites behind to make you drowsy later. An intramuscular form is sometimes used to calm people who are acutely psychotic due to mania or schizophrenia.

Klonopin (clonazepam)

For years Klonopin was officially approved only for treating seizure disorders, but in recent years it has been approved for panic disorder as well. However, Klonopin also effectively treats other anxiety disorders, such as social phobia. Sometimes it is used to prevent recurrence of mania in patients who don't respond well to some of the more commonly used mood stabilizing drugs (see Chapter 7).

Serax (oxazepam)

Because Serax is so short-acting, you would have to take it several times a day to ensure evenness of action and prevent anxiety symptoms from breaking through. Its brief duration of action also carries the danger that you could develop tolerance to its effects after several weeks and become anxious or wakeful at night.

Xanax (alprazolam)

Effective in panic disorder and social phobia, Xanax may also have some antidepressant effect, but it is not useful as a solo treatment in severe depression. Withdrawal symptoms can make it harder than other benzodiazepines for some patients to discontinue its usage. In fact, because some people have such extreme difficulty stopping it, I usually recommend that patients stay away from Xanax.

BuSpar (buspirone)

The only drug in this section that is not a benzodiazepine, BuSpar has no anticonvulsant, muscle relaxant, or sedative qualities, though it may have some antidepressant function. It has few interactions with other drugs (however, *avoid* it if you also take a monoamine oxidase inhibitor) and no withdrawal symptoms. As best we can tell, it doesn't create dependence. With these recommendations, why shouldn't everyone use it? For one thing, despite its short half-life in the body, it takes several weeks to start working. Furthermore, if you have been taking a benzodiazepine, you may not respond to BuSpar; at minimum, you would have to taper off the benzodiazepine, then wait a month before you start the BuSpar. Because it takes so long to work, the rate at which you adjust the dose will be a lot slower than with the other antianxiety agents.

BETA BLOCKERS

The beta blockers are a different class of drugs from the benzodiazepines. They get their name from the way they act, which is to block the activation of certain nerves that are stimulated by noradrenaline and other neurotransmitters acting at their beta (second) site. These drugs are also used to treat high blood pressure and irregular heartbeat, and to prevent migraine. In the mental health field, beta blockers effectively treat the tremor caused by lithium, the motor restlessness ("akathisia") caused by antipsychotic drugs, and violent or aggressive behavior. In one type of social phobia called performance anxiety, they can reduce the shaking, sweating, heart palpitations, and flushing that typically occur when you take a test or perform in public. You'll probably still feel somewhat nervous, but you don't have to worry that other people will notice, and your level of anxiety won't incapacitate you.

Drawbacks

The beta blockers are safe for most people to take, though they can reduce heart rate and blood pressure. *You shouldn't take them at all* if you have diabetes, asthma, or other respiratory illnesses. Used occasionally, as for performance anxiety, they should produce essentially no side effects. Taken chronically, as you might for akathisia or migraine, they produce mild side effects, which people tend to get used to after a time. The beta blockers are secreted into breast milk, so avoid them if nursing. If you use them only occasionally to reduce performance anxiety, there is very little to worry about in the way of drug interactions or other medical problems.

Using Beta Blockers

Don't wait until you must perform to use a beta blocker for the first time—always try the drug out at some time when the chips *aren't* down and you can afford to experience side effects. The amount you need may be quite different from the next person; start with the lowest dose and increase only if necessary. If you have taken one of them for a time, don't stop suddenly. When quitting, taper to avoid blood pressure rebound.

There are quite a few beta blockers available; here I've mentioned the two used most for anxiety. The doses mentioned in Table 8.1 are only for performance anxiety; your doctor will advise you about the amount to take for other purposes.

Inderal (propranolol)

In performance anxiety, 10–40 mg half an hour or so before taking a test can help focus concentration and even raise test scores. Because Inderal has such a short half-life, you'd have to repeat the dose several times a day for it to continue to work. High doses (half a gram per day or even more) have been used to reduce violent behavior. However, people who are sensitive to its tendency to lower blood pressure feel weak and dizzy, even with small doses.

Corgard (nadolol)

Corgard has a long half-life, which might get you through an entire day's performance. It would also be more convenient for someone who finds beta blockers useful for ongoing generalized anxiety, migraine prevention, or reduction of akathisia.

DRUGS USED MAINLY TO INDUCE SLEEP

Problems with sleep are so common that hardly an adult hasn't experienced a sleepless night at some time. Even people who don't usually have insomnia occasionally spend a longer time than usual getting to sleep, or awaken during the night or before it is time to arise. For millions, the solution is to take a sleeping pill, perhaps one of the prescription drugs I discuss in this chapter. It could also be something you've purchased without a prescription, which I mention a little later on—and even less favorably than the prescription kind. I say that because there are many approaches to insomnia that are safer and ultimately more satisfying to patients than pills. Before using sleeping pills, I strongly urge you to read about "sleep hygiene" and other approaches in Chapter 24. Sleeping pills (some are benzodiazepines, some not) do have their place, however—four places, to be exact:

- In the case of severe depression or other mental or emotional disorder, the short-term use of sleeping pills, while waiting for definitive treatment (such as antidepressants) to kick in, can be helpful.
- The brief management of jet lag. Not all clinicians agree that this is a valid use for sleeping pills, but I can hardly avoid recommending that which I have found useful myself. Short-term (2–5 days) use of Ambien or Sonata can ease the burden of intercontinental travel.
- Brief use to help combat the difficulty sleeping that can accompany any acute stress, such as death of a loved one.
- Until recently, physicians advised using benzodiazepines only short-term (2–4 weeks). Now we are more willing to consider longer-term use of drugs when insomnia hasn't responded to other measures.

Regardless of the reason, your goal in taking a sleeping pill should not be the rapid loss of consciousness but normal sleep.

If you need to take a sleeping pill, you want it to work quickly and be out of your system by morning. Rapid absorption means that you can take it only after you have tried, without success, to fall asleep naturally. A very short half-life (the time necessary to eliminate half the dose from the body) means that you won't feel drowsy or inattentive the next day. Some of the drugs included here act so fast that you should be ready for bed when you take them. Some take so much longer to begin working that you may even want to take them an hour before bedtime. Whichever your doctor recommends, it may take a couple of evenings before you arrive at the right dose and the right time to take the drug.

Drawbacks

Most of these drugs can have any of the side effects common to benzodiazepines. You risk rebound insomnia, defined as insomnia that is worse than what you had before you took drugs, with the shorter half-life drugs. Regardless of half-life, remember that the more you take, the more likely you are to encounter side effects the next day. Take the pill on an empty stomach; food, especially if high in fat content, will delay the onset of action. Of course, the usual cautions about pregnancy and breast-feeding also apply.

If you use a benzodiazepine sleeping aid for several weeks, you could very well have two sorts of problem. First, most sleeping aids seem to lose their effectiveness after as little as 2 weeks of continuous use. Second, you could experience a withdrawal syndrome—rebound insomnia, restlessness, and anxiety. People who have had problems with addiction to other substances may be especially prone to this difficulty. All of these symptoms would eventually go away—but who needs them? Much better to use the drug so sparingly that you don't risk these complications.

People whose responsibilities require them to be instantly alert should avoid sleeping pills on nights when they are on duty. Examples include those who provide care for sick relatives or a new baby, or professionals on-call such as firefighters and doctors. I recall one family physician whom, years ago, we interns learned never to call at night: if we could understand him at all, his instructions were often totally unreliable. A year later I admitted him to our psychiatric ward—severely addicted to sleeping pills.

Ambien (zolpidem)

Ambien and Sonata are the two best sleeping aids currently marketed in the United States. Ambien is not a benzodiazepine and doesn't have muscle relaxant properties. At least one study found that it continued to be effective even after 6 months of use (which I *don't* recommend), whereas older drugs, such as Halcion, begin to lose effectiveness after a couple of weeks. Remarkably free of side effects, Ambien's major drawback (expense) should be improved when it becomes available generically.

Sonata (zaleplon)

An extremely short onset of drowsiness (within 30 minutes) and a duration of action that is only about 4 hours make Sonata a nearly ideal sleeping pill. (A high-fat meal will lengthen these times somewhat.) There is minimal chance that it will cause dependence or a withdrawal reaction, though you could experience some rebound insomnia after stopping it suddenly. Although drug build-up after taking it for many nights is unlikely, I would still urge you not to depend on it, or any other sleeping pill, for longer than a few nights at a time. Older patients should handle it about as well as younger patients.

Halcion (triazolam)

With a short duration of action, you won't be hung over the day after taking Halcion. There have been reports that at higher doses it causes amnesia, a problem that can theoretically affect patients taking any of the benzodiazepines. If it happens to you, of course you should avoid taking this class of drug.

Dalmane (flurazepam)

Dalmane is a benzodiazepine with an active half-life of 4 days. That means it can leave you feeling drowsy the next day, and there is a risk of building up concentrations of the drug in your blood if you take it for several days in a row. Once considered the leading medication for insomnia, today there are better choices. You still might consider it if your problem is mainly staying asleep, not getting to sleep.

Doral (quazepam); ProSom (estazolam); Restoril (temazepam)

Although these drugs aren't as long-acting as Dalmane, daytime drowsiness may still occur. They may also help keep you asleep at night, if waking up is your problem. They have all the other potential drawbacks of the benzodiazepines. Although their onset isn't as rapid as with the newest drugs, otherwise they work just fine. Overall, they don't offer anything really special other than, perhaps, price.

OTHER DRUGS SOMETIMES USED FOR SLEEP

I've already mentioned that I feel it is better to use a prescription sleeping preparation than something you can buy over the counter (OTC). Several important factors justify the extra expense of going to a doctor and paying for the prescription drug.

1. Your self-made diagnosis could be correct, but your "just sleeping" problem could really be a symptom of something else. Physicians look for just this sort of issue—physical or mental disorders that affect your sleep—when they evaluate a patient for insomnia.
2. Your doctor might advise you about lifestyle changes (diet, exercise, work habits) that would improve your general health and your sleep, without the need for chemicals. See the sidebar on pages 296–297 for some suggestions.
3. The OTC tablet you select could produce side effects that add to your discomfort.
4. You might end up taking a medication that stays in your body so long that you feel groggy the next day.
5. Your brain could become so used to medication that you can't sleep without it.

For me, the bottom line is this: if an OTC sleeping medicine works well for you and you use it sparingly, go ahead and take it. But I believe that you'll be happier in the long run with a more holistic approach to your sleeping problem.

Antihistamines

When this group of drugs was introduced over half a century ago to combat allergy symptoms, patients and clinicians quickly learned that drowsiness was a prominent side effect. Ever since, they have been prescribed as Atarax, Vistaril, Benadryl, and others to treat insomnia, and more recently they've appeared in countless OTC preparations such as Sominex, Nytol, and Excedrin PM. The trouble is, these drugs have many other effects on the body, some of which (dry mouth and nose, restless legs) may *worsen* your insomnia. They can also cause difficulty thinking and problems coordinating motor movements. The last straw: users rapidly accommodate to the sedative effect, meaning that after a few days none of these drugs is likely to work very well. I don't know of any expert today who thinks they are as good as the prescription drugs specifically meant to induce sleep.

Valerian

A "natural" product (valerian is a plant, a relative of the heliotrope), there is little evidence that it has more than a mild effect on sleep. Furthermore, it has never been carefully studied for safety and effectiveness. There are few if any side effects, but long-term use has been reported to produce headache, restlessness, sleeplessness, and disorders of cardiac function. As with many herbal remedies, you can never be sure just how much active substance you are getting in a tablet. There is also the possibility of an additive effect with other drugs. Though some people swear by it, I cannot recommend valerian for sleep.

Melatonin

The report on another "natural" substance is more positive, though the explanation requires a nodding acquaintance with some physiology. Made in the pineal gland of the brain, melatonin is a hormone that controls our circadian rhythms: when daylight fades, melatonin production increases and it permeates our bodies, making us sleepy. Light falling on the retinas of our eyes reduces the amount of melatonin we produce. That's why we tend to feel alert on sunny days. It also accounts for the confusion we feel when jet travel forces our internal clocks to cycle rapidly through periods of dark and light—our melatonin encounters serious production snafus.

In the late 1990s, 3–5 mg of melatonin became very popular for insomnia and nervousness. Some studies suggest that its effect on sleep is pretty minimal, but other experts feel that it is valuable, especially in treating jet lag. A recent in-depth review strongly supported its use. Melatonin appears to have no side effects, so if you've tried it and it helps, go for it. If you are traveling west to east, you could try melatonin a half-hour before bedtime for 4 days after you arrive. East to west travel isn't generally as much problem (people adapt to it more readily), but a similar strategy may help, anyway. The 2-mg slow-release form is less effective than the standard (and cheaper) formulation. Melatonin can be artificially synthesized or extracted from the brains of slaughtered animals. It is hard enough to know the quality and purity of any unregulated drug, but artificial synthesis seems safer to me.

Two groups of people should probably not use melatonin: those who have a seizure disorder, and those who take an anticoagulant such as Coumadin. Combining melatonin with a standard sleeping drug may produce a lot of additional side effects, and I would definitely recommend against taking it on a chronic basis.

Desyrel (trazodone)

Clinicians have increasingly prescribed some of the older antidepressants, such as Desyrel, Elavil, and Sinequan, to promote sleep, especially for patients who are depressed. None of these drugs has been adequately studied as a sleeping agent, but they are probably effective, even when used long term. Significant drawbacks are their many side effects and the fact that they can be lethal in overdose. Depending on the presence of other diagnoses (most notably, depression), doses range upward from 50 mg at bedtime.

STILL APPROVED, BUT NOT RECOMMENDED

Drug approval is a bit like obtaining a college degree—once you've earned it, it's yours for life. As a consequence, many once-popular drugs are still "indicated" for anxiety or insomnia that, for a variety of reasons, go on my "Not Recommended" list. Most deficient are those that carry a serious risk of addiction or death by overdose, sometimes in amounts available within a single prescription bottle. This group includes barbiturates such as Nembutal and Seconal, chloral hydrate (Noctec), Placidyl, and meprobamate (Miltown, Equanil). Please, *scrupulously avoid these drugs.*

Other drugs that aren't nearly so risky in terms of safety have simply outstayed their welcome. For example, the generic drug hydroxyzine (Atarax, Vistaril) was approved by the FDA in 1957, but recent information suggests that for it to have much antianxiety effect, it must be prescribed in excess of the 400 mg/day suggested as the top adult dose. It was developed in the era before rigorous testing for efficacy was required, and it has just hung around ever since. Whether for anxiety or sleep, there are better choices.

ANTIANXIETY/SLEEPING MEDICATIONS FOR OLDER PEOPLE

As we age, benzodiazepines—especially the shorter-acting drugs such as Halcion—increasingly affect our concentration and ability to learn new material. Furthermore, older people metabolize benzodiazepines more slowly, so they need smaller doses. Therefore, if you are 60 or older, your doctor will probably ask you to start with a dose that is half (or even less, depending on your age and other health issues) of the usual adult dose and to increase very slowly until you get the desired effect. Sonata could prove a significant exception to this general rule.

ANTIANXIETY/SLEEPING MEDICATIONS FOR THE MEDICALLY ILL

Although we know that liver or kidney disease can reduce the rate at which the body eliminates many drugs, in many cases we simply don't have enough experience to predict exactly how (or whether) to modify the dose and frequency. Therefore, in Table 8.2 I have sometimes indicated to start low and increase slowly, which means that your doctor will probably ask you to start with the smallest dose possible and increase very gradually, watching carefully to see the effect of each change of dose on symptoms and side effects. Benzodiazepines can also interfere with how deeply you breathe, so if you have chronic lung disease or sleep apnea, your doctor will advise you on the degree to which you can safely take anxiety or sleeping medications.

TABLE 8.1. Antianxiety and Sleeping Medications Currently Prescribed in the United States

Brand name	Generic name, year of FDA approval	Generic?	Starting treatment for mild to moderate symptoms	Adult dose range/usual dose effective for moderate symptoms	Divided into # doses/day (mg/day)	Dose size (mg)	$/day average daily dose	Half-life with metabolites	Time to work (min)/full trial (days)/full dose (days) at full dose
Antianxiety drugs									
Ativan	lorazepam, 1977	Y	0.5 mg 2–3x/day; ↑ carefully if needed	1–10/4	2–3	0.5, 1, 2; I	$1.01	M	15–30/2
BuSpar	buspirone, 1986	Y	5 mg 3x/day; may ↑ by 5 mg/day each 2–3 days	15–60/30	2–3	5, 10, 15	$3.06	S	2–4wks/4wks
Corgard	nadolol, 1989	Y	20–40 mg taken once	20–40/20	1	20, 40, 80, 120, 160	$0.73	M	60/7
Inderal	propranolol, 1967	Y	20–40 mg taken once	10–80/40	1	10, 20, 40, 60, 80; I	$0.03	S	60/7
Klonopin	clonazepam, 1975	Y	0.25–0.5 mg 2–3x/day; ↑ carefully if needed	0.5–4/2	2–3	0.5, 1, 2	$0.45	L	20–60/2
Librium	chlordiazepoxide, 1960	Y	5–10 mg day; ↑ carefully if needed	15–100/30	3–4	5, 10, 25; I	$0.08	L	30–45/2
Serax	oxazepam, 1965	Y	10–20 mg 3–4x/day; ↑ carefully if needed	30–120/60	3–4	10, 15, 30	$1.20	M	60–120/2
Tranxene	clorazepate, 1972	Y	7.5 mg 1–2x/day; ↑ carefully if needed	15–60/30	2–4	3.75, 7.5, 11.25, 15, 22.5	$0.82	L	30–60/2
Valium	diazepam, 1963	Y	2–5 mg 1–2x day; ↑ carefully if needed	4–40/10	1–4	2, 5, 10, 15; O, I, R	$0.25	L	30–60/2
Xanax	alprazolam, 1981	Y	0.25–0.5 mg 2–3x/day; ↑ carefully if needed	1–4/2	3–4	0.25, 0.5, 1, 2	$2.40	S	15–30/2
Sleeping pills									
Ambien	zolpidem, 1993	N	10 mg	5–10/10	1 bed	5, 10	$2.63	S	15–30/1–2 nights
Dalmane	flurazepam, 1970	Y	15 mg	15–30/30	1 bed	15, 30	$0.21	L	15–30/1–2 nights
Doral	quazepam, 1985	N	15 mg	7.5–15/15	1 bed	7.5, 15	$2.90	L	30–60/1–2 nights
Halcion	triazolam, 1982	Y	0.25 mg	0.125–0.5/0.25	1 bed	0.125, 0.25	$0.60	S	15–30/1–2 nights
ProSom	estazolam, 1990	Y	1 mg	0.5–2/1	1 bed	1	$0.89	M	30–60/1–2 nights
Restoril	temazepam, 1981	Y	15 mg	7.5–30/30	1 bed	7.5, 15, 30	$0.13	M	45–60/1–2 nights
Sonata	zaleplon, 1999	N	10 mg	5–20/10	1 bed	5, 10	$2.23	S	15–30/1–2 nights

R = rectal suppository; O = oral solution; I = injectable; half-life: S = short (< 6 hr); M = medium (6–24 hr); L = long (> 24 hr)

TABLE 8.2. Side Effects and Precautions for Antianxiety Medications

Brand name	Report right away	Discuss at next visit	Important cautions, tests	Symptoms of toxicity	Interactions with other drugs
Librium, Tranxene, Valium	Confusion, dizziness, trouble walking	Blurred vision, *drowsiness*, fatigue, nausea	• Beware driving, operating machinery • Avoid use with: sleep apnea, respiratory disease • Discontinue gradually • For elderly: start at half the usual adult dose and ↑ slowly • If liver impairment: use cautiously; consider using Ativan instead	Confusion, drowsiness, coma	• Avoid: valerian, smoking • May ↑ impairment in thinking and motor skills caused by alcohol, other CNS depressants • Benzodiazepines may ↑ the effects of: digitalis • Benzodiazepines may ↓ the effects of: Aralen • The following may ↑ benzodiazepine effects: Antabuse, Benemid, contraceptives, Depakote, erythromycin, isoniazid, Luvox, melatonin, Prilosec, Sporanox, Synercid, Tagamet • The following may ↓ benzodiazepine effects: Rifadin • Klonopin can either ↑ or ↓ Dilantin effects; monitor carefully
Ativan	Confusion, dizziness, *memory loss*, weakness	*Drowsiness*	• Beware driving, operating machinery • Dependence, withdrawal symptoms are risks • Avoid use with glaucoma • For elderly: start at half adult dose	Blood pressure loss, confusion, drowsiness, lethargy, trouble walking	
Klonopin	Depression, poor coordination, trouble walking	*Drowsiness*, tiredness	• Beware driving, operating machinery • Dependence, withdrawal symptoms are risks • Avoid use with: sleep apnea, respiratory disease, glaucoma • If kidney impairment: start low, ↑ slowly	Confusion, drowsiness, coma	
Serax		*Drowsiness*	• Beware driving, operating machinery • Dependence, withdrawal symptoms are risks • Avoid use with: sleep apnea, respiratory disease, glaucoma • Elderly usually tolerate adult dose, but start at 10 mg	Confusion, drowsiness, coma	• Avoid: valerian • May ↑ impairment in thinking and motor skills caused by alcohol, other CNS depressants • Serax may ↓ the effects of contraceptives • The following may ↑ Serax effects: Benemid, melatonin

Xanax	Confusion, *dizziness*	*Drowsiness*	• Dependence, withdrawal symptoms are risks • Discontinue gradually • For elderly: start at half adult dose • If liver or kidney impairment: start low, ↑ slowly	Drowsiness	• Avoid: valerian, Tagamet, Luvox, Posicor, Serzone • May ↑ impairment in thinking and motor skills caused by alcohol, other CNS depressants • Xanax may ↑ effects of: digitalis, Norpramin, Tofranil • The following may ↓ Xanax effects: Actos, barbiturates, Dilantin, Mycobutin, Rifadin, Tegretol, Trileptal, Viramune • The following may ↑ Xanax effects: Accolate, amiodarone, Antabuse, Biaxin, Cardene, Cardizem, contraceptives, cyclosporine, Danocrine, Darvon, ergotamine, erythromycin, grapefruit juice, isoniazid, Luvox, melatonin, mifepristone (RU-486), Nizoral, Prilosec, Procardia, Prozac, quinidine, quinine, Rescriptor, Serzone, Sporanox, Sustiva, Synercid, Tagamet, Tao, verapamil, Zoloft
BuSpar	Agitation, *dizziness*, restlessness	*Drowsiness*, headache, nausea	• For elderly: start 5 mg 2x/day; ↑ by 5 mg every 2–3 days to 15–30 mg/day • For severe liver or kidney impairment: start low, ↑ slowly	Ataxia, dizziness, drowsiness, nausea, vomiting	• Avoid: MAOIs (including Zyvox) • May ↑ impairment in thinking and motor skills caused by alcohol, other CNS depressants • BuSpar may ↑ the effects of: Haldol • The following may ↑ BuSpar effects: verapamil, Cardizem, grapefruit juice • Use cautiously with: SSRIs, Effexor (due to serotonin syndrome) • BuSpar may not be effective if benzodiazepines used in past month
Corgard, Inderal	Dizziness, positional low blood pressure	Fatigue, heart rate slowed	• Avoid use with: serious heart arrhythmia, congestive heart failure, chronic lung disease • Use with caution with: diabetes, hyperthyroidism, myasthenia gravis, psoriasis • Corgard: for elderly or kidney impairment, start low, ↑ slowly • Inderal: for elderly or liver impairment, start low, ↑ slowly	Fainting, heartbeat slowed	• Avoid: Lariam, theophylline • Beta blockers may ↑ the effects of: Cardizem, Coumadin, ergotamine, older antipsychotics (for example, Thorazine), verapamil • The following may ↑ beta blocker effects: Cardizem, MAOIs, older antipsychotics (for example, Thorazine), Tagamet, antihypertensive drugs (for example, Catapres, Ismelin, Procardia, reserpine), verapamil • The following may ↓ beta blocker effects: barbiturates, Cytomel, Feldene, Indocin, levodopa, naproxen, Rifadin, vitamin C
Ambien	Amnesia, dizziness	Daytime drowsiness	• Take right at bedtime • Do not operate machinery • Use with caution if lung disease • For elderly or liver impairment: start at 5 mg	Drowsiness, trouble breathing	• Avoid: melatonin, valerian • May ↑ impairment in thinking and motor skills caused by alcohol, other CNS depressants • The following may ↑ Ambien effects: BuSpar, Nizoral, Norvir, SSRIs • The following may ↓ Ambien effects: Rifadin, Viramune

(continued)

TABLE 8.2. (*continued*)

Brand name	Report right away	Discuss at next visit	Important cautions, tests	Symptoms of toxicity	Interactions with other drugs
Sonata		**Headache**, trouble with memory	• Take right at bedtime • Avoid use with: severe liver impairment	Blood pressure low, breathing shallow, drowsiness, lethargy, trouble walking, coma	• Avoid: valerian • Tagamet may ↑ Sonata effects • The following may ↓ Sonata effects: Dilantin, phenobarbital, Rifadin, Tegretol
Halcion	Dizziness, trouble with coordination or walking	Daytime drowsiness	• Risk of dependence • Use cautiously if: lung disease, myasthenia gravis, porphyria • For elderly or liver impairment: start at 0.125 mg	Confusion, drowsiness, poor coordination, slurred speech, coma	*See Xanax entry*
Dalmane, Doral, ProSom, Restoril	Confusion, dizziness, incoordination, trouble walking	***Daytime drowsiness***, depression, dry mouth, fatigue, headache, tremor	• Risk of dependence, withdrawal • Use cautiously with: lung disease, sleep apnea, myasthenia gravis, porphyria • For elderly or liver or kidney impairment: start at lowest dose and watch carefully	Breathing shallow, confusion, drowsiness, poor coordination, slurred speech, coma	• May ↑ impairment in thinking and motor skills caused by alcohol, other CNS depressants, including melatonin, valerian. • The following may ↑ effects of sleeping medications: Antabuse, Benemid, Biaxin, contracptives, Diflucan, erythromycin, isoniazid, Luvox, Nizoral, Norvir, quinine, Rescriptor, Serzone, Sporanox, Sustiva, Tagamet • The following may ↓ effects of sleeping medications: barbiturates, Dilantin, Rifadin, Tegretol, theophylline, Viramune

Boldface italic = more common (10% or more of patients); ↑ = increase; ↓ = decrease

TABLE 8.3. Indications, Advantages, and Risks of Antianxiety Medications

a FDA approved b non-FDA approved ++ strongly yes + yes	Ambien	Ativan	BuSpar	Corgard	Dalmane	Doral	Halcion	Inderal	Klonopin	Librium	ProSom	Restoril	Serax	Sonata	Tranxene	Valium	Xanax
Used for:																	
Anxiety, cause unstated		a	b						b	a			a		a	a	a
Panic disorder			a						a								a
Generalized anxiety disorder																	a
Alcohol withdrawal		b								a			a		a	b	
Premenstrual syndrome																	b
Muscle spasm																a	
Calming psychosis		b															
Insomnia	a	a			a	a	a				a	a		a			
Performance anxiety				b				b									
Lithium-induced tremor				b				b									
Mania prophylaxis									b								
Relieve akathisia (restlessness due to antipsychotics)				b				b									
Advantages:																	
Low cost								+		+							
Risks and drawbacks:																	
Low pulse, blood pressure								++									
Respiratory arrest in lung disease, sleep apnea		+			+	+					+	+					
Withdrawal symptoms, addiction		+			+	+			+	+	+	+	+		+	+	++
Very long time to take effect			++														

111

CHAPTER 9

Antipsychotic Medications

The first modern medicine for psychosis became generally available in 1954. Discovered by scientists looking for a better anesthetic, Thorazine was quickly found to dramatically decrease, and even eliminate, the hallucinations and delusions that plague victims of schizophrenia. It also had a remarkable calming action, reducing hyperactivity, agitation, and violence. In effect, it fought the tendency toward asocial behavior and helped patients integrate better into their families. And when taken as maintenance over long periods of time, it often prevented recurrence of symptoms. Under its influence, thousands of patients were able to leave the mental hospitals they might otherwise have called home forever.

Thorazine and the dozen or so similar drugs that came along within a few years also quelled the delusions and hallucinations caused by other psychotic illnesses. These include mania, psychotic depression, delusional disorder, Alzheimer's dementia, and schizoaffective disorder (in which patients have symptoms of both schizophrenia and mood disorder at the same time). In addition, Thorazine was found to effectively suppress the agitation and impulsiveness that can occur in severe neurological conditions such as Huntington's disease and Tourette's disorder, and in autism and other developmental disorders of childhood. It also helped suppress the delusions and hallucinations that arise in psychosis induced by alcohol or other drugs. Some clinicians even found low doses of antipsychotic drugs useful for nonpsychotic conditions, such as borderline personality disorder.

For all their virtues, antipsychotic drugs also have their drawbacks. They frequently cause serious neurological side effects, and they do not relieve some symptoms of psychosis. When a new type of antipsychotic drug was introduced in the United States in 1990—one which was not only broadly effective against the symptoms of psychosis but also caused far fewer side effects—it sparked a revolution in the care of psychotic patients.

THE NEWER ANTIPSYCHOTIC DRUGS

By the close of the 20th century, it had become obvious to practitioners that most patients who require an antipsychotic agent should first try one of these newer drugs. These drugs subdue hallucinations and delusions about as well as the older antipsychotic agents but also work much better for the "negative" symptoms, such as the lack of will to get things done and the absence of emotional responsivity (which appears as little or no facial expression, no matter what happens). There is also good evidence that these drugs reduce the agitation and psychosis in acute mania, and when combined with antidepressants, help treat previously resistant cases of obsessive–compulsive disorder.

Another important difference is that the newer drugs are far less likely than their predecessors to cause harmful neurological side effects. I describe these problems in detail in a few pages, but for now let's just say that the older drugs are quite likely to produce movements of arms, legs, and other body parts that can be extremely distressing to patients and those around them. With the elimination of these side effects, patients feel more comfortable and consequently take their medication more reliably, improving still further the overall outcome. Of course, the newer drugs do have unwanted side effects, which are detailed below and in Table 9.2a. Although terrifically expensive, they can reduce the likelihood of hospitalization and improve attendance at work, thereby lessening their overall cost.

A final difference, though not necessarily an advantage, is that the new antipsychotics have chemical structures that are quite distinct from the older drugs—a difference that might be obvious only to a chemist. For this reason, your doctor might refer to the newer drugs as novel or atypical drugs and to the older drugs, as traditional or typical.

Using the Newer Antipsychotics

As with all antipsychotics, how these drugs are used will be governed by the person's symptoms. For acute agitation, treatment will probably begin with an intramuscular injection of Risperdal or Geodon, followed by oral medication. If speed isn't essential, one of these medications will probably be started at a low dose and increased over 3 or 4 days, until the recommended dose is reached. All of these drugs have an almost immediate calming effect, though it will take them a week or more to diminish hallucinations or delusions. So far, none of the newer drugs is available as a long-acting injectable.

Once the drug has begun to work, it is extremely important to take it regularly. Many patients hate to admit that they are ill and will stop their medication once they start to feel better. Then the symptoms are almost certain to start all over again, especially in the case of schizophrenia and when there have been previous episodes of psychosis. In a first episode, some clinicians will agree that medicine can be discontinued after a year. Though a defendable strategy, it nonetheless runs the risk of setting the stage for a recurrence, sometimes even after many months off medication.

A major reason to use a newer antipsychotic is the low risk of neurological side effects, especially the movement disorder called "tardive dyskinesia" (see sidebar on page 117). However, this is not to say that there is no risk, and with tardive dyskinesia, any risk at all is too great to ignore. Therefore, as with the older antipsychotics, patient and doctor must stay alert for the appearance of a movement disorder. Every 6 months an AIMS (Abnormal Involuntary Movement Scales) test should be taken. This test takes just a few minutes and involves simple tasks such as observing the patient's open mouth, outstretched hands, walking, and thumb-tapping with each finger in succession. Recently it has become clear that these drugs are associated with the onset of diabetes; therefore, the physician will want to monitor glucose levels, especially for patients who are overweight.

If the medication doesn't seem to be working after several weeks on a full dose or greater, either a different newer drug or one of the older antipsychotics should be tried. The last choice would be to try Clozaril; although it is probably the most effective of all the antipsychotics, side effects make it the riskiest.

Specific Newer Antipsychotic Agents

Zyprexa (olanzapine)

Three features of Zyprexa give it practical advantages: a long half-life (about 30 hours) means that it can be taken just once a day; a low risk of positional low blood pressure means that it can be started at a dose that is often fully therapeutic; and its metabolism is little affected by other drugs. Seizures are unlikely, though weight gain may be greater and affect more patients than with the other new antipsychotics. Some of the typical neurological side effects have been reported (restlessness, acute muscle spasms), but their incidence is low. Because Zyprexa is such a new drug, we still don't know how it compares with other new drugs, though a 2001 comparison with Risperdal came out slightly in favor of Zyprexa overall.

Seroquel (quetiapine)

As of this writing, Seroquel is the antipsychotic drug that seems least likely to cause neurological side effects, including tardive dyskinesia. However, longer experience could write a different story. It has the usual problems with positional low blood pressure and dizziness, and at higher doses it can make people drowsy. Because animal studies have found cataract development with this drug, and some people have developed lens changes, eye exams with a device called a slit lamp should be performed at least twice a year.

Geodon (ziprasidone)

The newest drug on this list, Geodon (called Zeldox abroad) may be better tolerated than some of its predecessors, though how well it will perform compared to similar drugs remains to be seen. Weight increase is less, and because it can cause nausea, it should be taken with food. It is on schedule for approval in intramuscular form in the United States.

Risperdal (risperidone)

Risperdal is the least sedating of the newer drugs; in fact, because it can cause wakefulness, it should be taken in the morning and late afternoon, not at bedtime. Some clinicians feel that Risperdal performs best with a dose closer to 4–5 mg/day, though many people will need more. It can be given by injection. In doses above 6 mg/day, it can cause neurological side effects of restlessness and muscle cramping (page 117). Even a few cases of tardive dyskinesia have been reported, though the risk is much lower than with the older drugs.

Clozaril (clozapine)

The oldest of the new antipsychotic drugs, Clozaril probably performs the best overall, indeed, some patients who have not been helped by any other antipsychotic respond to it. Abnormal excitement usually decreases within 5 days of beginning treatment. Delusions and hallucinations disappear next, whereas negative symptoms may still be improving 6 weeks later. In fact, it can take months of treatment to see all the benefits of Clozaril. A blood level of about 350 ng/ml is thought to produce an optimal response.

Special Precautions. Clozaril doesn't appear to produce neurological side effects, probably not even tardive dyskinesia, though we still don't know for sure. However, it does carry a significant risk of one side effect so serious that it delayed FDA approval for 30 years. About 2% of users experience a reduction in white blood cells (WBCs) that, if not recognized, can lead to a potentially fatal loss of the ability to fight off infection. The risk may be even greater if the drug is taken with Tegretol. Identified and treated in time, nearly everyone survives, but even the possibility requires special precautions. Watch carefully for fever or infection (such as sore throat), especially during the first 4 months of treatment. To continue receiving the medicine, each week the patient will have to visit the doctor and take a WBC count. A count of less than 2,000 requires immediate discontinuation of Clozaril. The blood tests contribute to Clozaril's cost, which is somewhere over $5,000/year, making it the most expensive psychiatric drug currently on the market. Fortunately, none of the other new antipsychotics has this complication.

As with the other newer antipsychotic drugs, Clozaril can cause weight gain. Because some patients may develop a rapid heartbeat or positional low blood pressure (which can lead to collapse of the cardiovascular system), anyone with a history of cardiac problems must be monitored carefully. Clozaril also has a peculiar side effect that no one has yet satisfactorily explained: although some patients report dry mouth, about a third find that they salivate excessively. Some can combat the drooling by taking other drugs, such as Catapres, Elavil, or Cogentin, but others find it so distressing that they quit taking Clozaril.

THE OLDER ANTIPSYCHOTIC DRUGS

For nearly half a century, Thorazine and other drugs with similar chemical structures and identical treatment effects were the mainstay for the treatment of schizophrenia. Although no longer the first choice for most patients, they are still an important option for psychosis; they may even be prescribed first for people who have previously done well with them. Nearly a dozen are available in the United States, and even more are sold in other countries.

According to dose, they are usually divided into three groups that can help predict the likelihood of side effects. High-dose (low-potency) drugs such as Thorazine are somewhat less likely to produce the neurological effects of acute dystonia, akathisia, and parkinsonism (see page 117), but they are more likely to cause drowsiness and positional low blood pressure. Low-dose (highly potent) drugs such as Haldol and Prolixin more often cause neurological side effects but less often play havoc with blood pressure. The side effects of middle-dose drugs fall somewhere between these two extremes.

The older antipsychotics are thought to exert their effect by decreasing the activity of the neurotransmitter called "dopamine." They are especially effective at reducing the positive symptoms of schizophrenia (delusions, hallucinations), but they are not nearly as effective as the newer drugs for negative symptoms such as blunted affect, emotional distancing, decreased social interaction, and disorganized thinking. They also calm the agitation, excitement, and even violence that sometimes accompany schizophrenia and mania. For that reason, they have been called "major tranquilizers" and used for anxiety or nervousness not related to psychosis. However, they should not be prescribed for people who are "only" depressed or anxious. They are too potent and their side effects potentially far too grim to use them for anything other than psychosis or, sometimes, the agitation of dementia.

Drawbacks

Because all of the older drugs have similar effects on psychosis, their most important differences reside in their side effects. The high-dose drugs (such as Thorazine and

Mellaril) are especially likely to affect heartbeat or cause faintness (due to low blood pressure) upon sitting up. They can also cause constipation, drowsiness, dry mouth, and difficulty urinating. Patients who take Thorazine may notice that they become much more sensitive to sunburn. All of the older antipsychotics increase the risk of seizures, especially in those who already suffer from epilepsy. And all are quite likely to interfere with sexual functioning—men have trouble attaining and maintaining erections, women may not experience orgasm or may lose interest in sex altogether. On the positive side, these drugs do not appear to be especially risky to a developing fetus.

The most important, and in many ways the most serious, side effects of the older antipsychotics are several varieties of movement disorder. For descriptions, along with one other side effect that should be considered a medical emergency, see the sidebar below.

CAUTION: THE SERIOUS SIDE EFFECTS OF OLDER ANTIPSYCHOTICS

Acute dystonia can occur within a few hours of taking the first dose, and it almost always occurs within the first 3 or 4 days. Dystonia means an abnormality of muscle tension, and acute dystonia is a sudden onset of spasms of the head and neck, often causing a person's eyes to roll upward and head to twist painfully to the side. No one who has once experienced this frightening side effect will ever forget the experience. It occurs in perhaps 5% of patients who take older antipsychotic drugs, especially in young males.

Another side effect that patients tend to remember is **akathisia**, a distressing inability to sit still. Usually beginning 2–5 days after starting the medication, the patient experiences a need to keep moving or walking, even if it is only stepping in place. Over half of those who take the older antipsychotic drugs experience some degree of akathisia.

The **drug-induced parkinsonism** that affects around 20% of patients strongly resembles the naturally occurring disease. Beginning gradually after a week or two on medication, a rigid facial expression that seems never to vary, rapid back-and-forth tremor of hands, and shuffling gait develop. Parkinsonism is especially likely in those who are elderly or have pre-existing neurological illness. When severe, symptoms can result in disability. Another feature of parkinsonism is **akinesia** (literally, "without movement"). Akinesia can sometimes involve a freezing of motion, though more often people experience it as slowing down, like trying to run in a swimming pool. Akinesia affects perhaps a third of patients and usually begins within the first 3 weeks of treatment. Each of the above disorders can be treated rapidly with an injection or tablet of Benadryl or Cogentin (see sidebar on page 121).

The last neurological side effect is by far the most notorious. Because it can take several months or longer to develop, it is called **tardive** (late) **dyskinesia** (difficult or abnormal movement). Although not uncomfortable— in fact, patients often don't even seem to notice that they are affected— tardive dyskinesia (TD) consists of abnormal movements such as facial grimaces, lip smacking, or rapid protrusions of the tongue. It may affect up to 20% of those who take the older antipsychotic drugs on a long-term basis. Women and the elderly are especially vulnerable, and it is more likely to occur in people who have other neurological side effects, diabetes, or a mood disorder. The really serious problem with TD is that some degree of the movement disorder can persist, perhaps forever, though recent reports suggest that the newer antipsychotic agents (e.g., Zyprexa) may greatly diminish the symptoms.

Because it is so serious, it is best to identify tardive dyskinesia (TD) early, when symptoms are minor and perhaps still reversible. You can actually screen for early symptoms yourself, before they become obvious. Ask to look inside the person's mouth (the tongue should be at rest, not protruded). Do you see any tiny tongue movements? Observe the person at rest, with hands dangling between the legs or over the knees. Are there any small movements of the hands or fingers? If so, a physician should make a formal evaluation. If TD is confirmed, changing medications should be seriously considered.

Another serious side effect is the **neuroleptic malignant syndrome** (NMS). This condition causes marked muscle rigidity, fever, and sometimes sweating, confusion, and high blood pressure. It occurs infrequently, though more often in patients who have been given large doses of a high-potency medication or who also take lithium or antidepressants. It is especially likely to happen within a couple of weeks of first starting a drug or increasing its dose, particularly if the dose is high or given by injection.

NMS is a true medical emergency: untreated, it can prove fatal. The drug must be stopped immediately and careful medical management begun. This sounds easy, but it happens so infrequently (perhaps 1 in 100 patients) that even clinicians sometimes forget to consider NMS when a psychotic patient develops typical symptoms. Being always alert to the possibility will facilitate the diagnosis and perhaps save a life.

Using the Older Antipsychotics

Once you get above a certain critical threshold, low doses of the older antipsychotics work just as well as high doses, and you reduce the risk of side effects. For someone who is psychotic but calm, a modest initial dose with increases every few days usually works just fine. For someone who is acutely agitated, perhaps even violent, starting with a larger dose (perhaps by injection) may be essential to provide rapid relief. Once calmed down, the same drug can then be taken orally. Eventually, over a period of weeks or even months, the dose can be decreased to the lowest level that will keep symptoms in check. Women respond to the older antipsychotics better and at lower doses than do men, whereas smokers of either sex may need more. Because the half-life for most of the older antipsychotics is about a day, once-a-day dosing should eventually be possible.

Although hallucinations and delusions may begin to fade within a week or two, it usually takes 6–8 weeks to feel the full effect of these medications. It is vitally important for the patient to keep taking the medicine as long as it is prescribed. For schizophrenia, this could mean months or even years to prevent recurrence of symptoms. It is equally important for patients with mania or psychotic depression to stop taking an older antipsychotic as soon as the symptoms have been stabilized. To do otherwise risks tardive dyskinesia.

Two drugs, Prolixin and Haldol, are available in long-acting forms that can be injected once or twice a month. This is a godsend for someone who doesn't like to take medicine by mouth or refuses to take it at all—it is far easier to get someone to a doctor once or twice a month for an injection than to try to persuade the same person to swallow medicine every day!

Specific Older Antipsychotic Agents

Thorazine (chlorpromazine)

After nearly half a century, Thorazine is still an excellent choice for patients who are both psychotic and agitated. However, the drugged, drowsy feeling and the "Thorazine shuffle" make it less attractive for long-term treatment. Once the acutely excited phase of the illness comes under control, a different antipsychotic drug may be preferable. Because it can lower blood pressure, Thorazine would be a poor first choice for elderly patients and for those with heart or blood pressure problems.

Mellaril (thioridazine); Serentil (mesoridazine)

Although the potential for pathology in the retina of the eye has long restricted prescribing Mellaril at a top dose of 800 mg/day, it has been a clinical mainstay for decades. Recently it has been found sometimes to produce a potentially fatal condition known as ventricular tachycardia (severe rapid heartbeat). As a result, it is now recommended only for those who cannot take or do not respond to any other drug—in essence, nobody. Serentil, the breakdown product of Mellaril, has been tarred with the same brush: its manufacturer has also labeled it a drug of last resort. These two drugs could disappear within the next few years.

Loxitane (loxapine); Moban (molindone); Trilafon (perphenazine)

Each of these three steers a middle course between the high-dose and low-dose drugs. This is not to say that they have no side effects; in fact, they do have side effects typical of both the high-dose and low-dose groups. But on balance, side-effect intensity may be such that a patient can tolerate a drug in this group better than one from either of the extremes. Moban may be less likely than most older antipsychotics to cause seizures in a person who already has that tendency. It is also much less likely to produce weight gain.

Stelazine (trifluoperazine)

One of the earliest low-dose drugs, Stelazine won't produce drowsiness but may cause most of the other side effects mentioned above for the older antipsychotics.

Navane (thiothixene)

Another low-dose antipsychotic drug that is effective and yet causes the usual side effects.

Haldol (haloperidol)

One of the old standbys, Haldol is still used for a variety of conditions, including severe tics in Tourette's disorder—one of the tiny handful of nonpsychotic indications for any antipsychotic drug. It is one of only two drugs available in the United States that can be given by long-acting injection (Haldol Decanoate). Because it has a half-life of 21 days, this form can be taken as infrequently as every 4 weeks.

Prolixin (fluphenazine)

Similar to Haldol, Prolixin is a low-dose drug that can be given in tablet form or by long-acting injection (Prolixin Decanoate). Its half-life is 14 days, so it would have to be taken a bit more often than Haldol Decanoate.

Orap (pimozide)

Orap is marketed only to combat the motor and vocal tics of Tourette's disorder, and it has a greater potential for causing fatal heart arrhythmias, especially in interaction with other drugs. Therefore, it should not be used routinely to treat schizophrenia and other psychoses. However, mainly on the basis of a lot of anecdotal information, some clinicians believe that Orap is especially effective in treating delusional disorder.

TREATING NEUROLOGICAL SIDE EFFECTS OF ANTIPSYCHOTICS

If a neurological side effect described on pages 117–118 should develop, one of the drugs listed below could come to the rescue. The first four, which belong to a class called "anticholinergics," have been used for 40 years or more to treat the symptoms of naturally occurring Parkinson's disease (tremor, rigidity, and loss of mobility) as well as acute dystonia and other movement disorders caused by antipsychotic medication. Although drugs like Artane and Cogentin are used for akathisia, benzodiazepines such as Ativan sometimes provide greater relief.

Sometimes doctors routinely prescribe an anticholinergic drug to prevent the onset of movement disorders, but because such drugs can have side effects of their own, other clinicians start one only if neurological symptoms actually develop. I favor the second view. These drugs can worsen the symptoms of glaucoma, peptic ulcers, enlarged prostate, and myasthenia gravis, and they can affect how the body regulates temperature, increasing the risk of heat prostration during hot weather.

The doses listed below are for acute dystonia; symptoms of parkinsonism may require higher doses. Prices are for an average daily dose.

- **Artane (trihexyphenidyl).** 2 mg three times/day costs 54¢. Some people seem to like the effects of Artane a little too much and want to increase the dose. I'd stick to one of the other drugs.
- **Cogentin (benztropine).** 2 mg twice/day costs 21¢. Cogentin can also be given by injection for acute dystonia.
- **Akineton (biperiden).** 2 mg three times/day costs $1.11.
- **Kemadrin (procyclidine).** 2.5 mg three times/day costs 98¢.
- Another old stand-by is **Benadryl (diphenhydramine)**, an antihistamine that can relieve acute dystonia either by injection or by mouth—50 mg three times/day costs about 10¢.
- **Symmetrel (amantadine)** was created to fight viruses; it was later found to be effective against parkinsonism and other neurological effects of antipsychotics—100 mg twice/day costs 60¢.

None of these antidotes has much effect on tardive dyskinesia, which sometimes improves when a patient switches to one of the newer antipsychotics. However, the safest approach is to prevent TD by starting out with one of the newer antipsychotic drugs.

ANTIPSYCHOTIC AGENTS FOR OLDER PEOPLE

Older people should avoid the high-dose older drugs, which often cause postural low blood pressure. Geriatric dosage for each of the older antipsychotics is generally lower than for younger adults, due to lower metabolism and slower elimination from the blood by kidneys. This is especially the case in the very old (over 80 years), who also have greater sensitivity to parkinsonism symptoms. For the newer antipsychotics, patients older than 60 should generally decrease the initial dose by half.

ANTIPSYCHOTIC AGENTS FOR THE MEDICALLY ILL

Because all of the antipsychotics are metabolized in the liver and excreted through the kidneys, anyone with a medical illness involving those organs should start at about half the usual adult dose.

TABLE 9.1. Antipsychotic Medications Currently Prescribed in the United States

Brand name	Generic name, year of FDA approval	Generic?	Starting treatment	Adult dose range/ usual dose effective for psychosis (mg/day)	Divided into # doses/day	Dosage size (mg)	$/day, average daily dose	Half-life (hr)	Time to work (hr)/full trial (wk)
Newer antipsychotics									
Clozaril	clozapine, 1990	N	Start 12.5–25 mg day 1; ↑ by 25–50 mg every 2 days	250–600/400	2	25, 100	$13.31	M	1-3/8
Geodon	ziprasidone, 2001	N	Start 20 mg 2x/day; ↑ every 2 days to 80 mg 2x/day	40–160/120	2 with food	20, 40, 60, 80	$8.12	M	1-3/4
Risperdal	risperidone, 1993	N	In 1 or 2 doses: start 2mg day 1; 4 mg day 2; 6 mg day 3	4–8/5	1	1, 2, 3, 4; I	$9.64	L	1-3/4
Seroquel	quetiapine, 1997	N	Start 25 mg 2x/day; ↑ to 300–400mg/day by day 4	150–600/400	2–3	25, 100, 200, 300	$9.74	S	1-3/4
Zyprexa	olanzapine, 1996	N	Start 5 or 10 mg 1x/day; ↑ to 10 mg in 3–4 days	10–20/12	1	2.5, 5, 7.5, 10	$12.09	L	1-3/4
High-dose, low-potency older antipsychotics									
Mellaril	thioridazine, 1959	Y	Start 10–50 mg 3x/day; add 10–50 mg/day each 4–7 days	50–800/300	2–4	10, 15, 25, 50, 100, 150, 200; O	$0.59	M	1-2/4
Serentil	mesoridazine, 1970	N	Start 50 mg 3x/day; add 50 mg each 4–7 days	100–400/150	1	10, 25, 50, 100; O, I	$2.52	L	1-2/4
Thorazine	chlorpromazine, 1954	Y	Start 25–50 mg 3–4x/day; add 25–50 mg each 3–4 days	300–2000/400	1–3	10, 25, 30, 50, 75, 100, 150, 200, 300; O, R, I	$1.30	L	1-2/4

(continued)

123

TABLE 9.1. (*continued*)

Brand name	Generic name, year of FDA approval	Generic?	Starting treatment	Adult dose range/usual dose effective for psychosis (mg/day)	Divided into # doses/day	Dosage size (mg)	$/day, average daily dose	Half-life (hr)	Time to work (hr)/full trial (wk)
Moderate-dose, medium-potency older antipsychotics									
Loxitane	loxapine, 1975	Y	Start 10 mg 2x/day; add as needed over 7–10 days	20–250/60–100	2–4	5, 10, 25, 50; O, I	$4.89	S	1–2/4
Moban	molindone, 1974	N	Start 50–75 mg/day; add 25–50 mg each 3–4 days	15–225/100	1–2	5, 10, 25, 50, 100; O	$6.54	M	1–2/4
Trilafon	perphenazine, 1957	Y	Start 4–8 mg 3 x/day; add 8 mg each 7 days	9–64/24	1–2	2, 4, 8, 16; O, I	$1.05	L	1–2/4
Low-dose, high-potency older antipsychotics									
Haldol	haloperidol, 1958	Y	Start 1–2 mg 2–3x/day; ↑ gradually as needed	2–60/15	1–2	0.5, 1, 2, 5, 10, 20; O, I	$0.21	L	1–2/4
Navane	thiothixene, 1967	Y	Start 2–5 mg 2–4x/day; ↑ gradually as needed	6–60/20–30	1–3	1, 2, 5, 10, 20	$1.80	L	1–2/4
Orap	pimozide, 1984	N	Start 1–2 mg/day; ↑ 1–2 mg every other day as needed	2–10/6	1–2	1, 2	$2.61	L	1–2/4
Prolixin	fluphenazine, 1959	Y	Start 1–10 mg/day in 2–3 doses; ↑ 5 mg each 7 days	1–40/15	1–2	1, 2.5, 5, 10; O, I	$1.14	L	1–2/4
Stelazine	trifluoperazine, 1958	Y	Start 2–5 mg 2x/day; ↑ gradually as needed	5–60/15–20	1–2	1, 2, 5, 10; O, I	$1.10	L	1–2/4

R = rectal suppository; O = oral solution; I = injectable; half-life: S = short (< 6 hr); M = medium (6–24 hr); L = long (> 24 hr); ↑ = increase

124

TABLE 9.2a. Side Effects and Precautions for the Newer Antipsychotics

Brand name	Report right away	Discuss at next visit	Important cautions, tests	Symptoms of toxicity	Interactions with other drugs
Clozaril	Fever, sore throat, symptoms of infection, *dizziness*, seizures, urinary retention, bed-wetting; muscle rigidity, fever (symptoms of NMS); watch for TD	Blurred vision, *constipation*, *drowsiness*, dry mouth, excessive salivation, headache, nausea, *rapid heartbeat, weight gain*	• Low white blood cell count in 1–2%; can be lethal. Obtain counts weekly for 6 months, then semiweekly • Seizures above 600 mg/day • For elderly, kidney disease: start low, ↑ slowly; lower total doses likely • Liver disease: start low, ↑ by no more than 25mg 1–2x/week	Drowsiness, delirium, rapid heartbeat, low blood pressure, trouble breathing, drooling, coma	• Avoid Propulsid • May ↑ impairment in thinking and motor skills caused by alcohol, other CNS depressants • Use cautiously with lithium, which may lead to seizures, confusion, neuroleptic malignant syndrome • May ↑ the effects of: Coumadin, digoxin, hypertension drugs • The following may ↓ Clozaril effects: barbiturates, caffeine, cigarettes, Dilantin, Mycobutin, Rifadin, Tegretol • The following may ↑ Clozaril effects: erythromycin, grapefruit juice, heart drugs (for example, Cordarone, Rythmol, and quinidine), Norvir, SSRIs (for example, Luvox, Paxil, Zoloft), Tagamet
Geodon	Dizziness; watch for TD	Drowsiness, nausea	• If heart disease: avoid • For elderly: no dosage adjustment • If liver impairment: start at lower dose and ↑ slowly	Drowsiness, slurred speech	• Due to possible fatal heart arrythmias, avoid: Adriamycin, Anzemet, arsenic trioxide, Asendin, Avelox, Betapace, Biaxin, Cardizem, certain antibiotics (Tequin, Raxar, Levaquin), Cerubidine, Cordarone, erythromycin, local anesthetics, Lorelco, Lozol, Ludiomil, Mellaril, Norpace, Orap, pentamidine, Pronestyl, Propulsid, quinidine, Rythmol, Sandostatin, Tambocor, Tao, terfenadine, Tikosyn, Tonocard, tricyclic antidepressants, Vascon, verapamil, Zagam • May ↑ impairment in thinking and motor skills caused by alcohol, other CNS depressants • May ↑ the effects of hypertension drugs • The following may ↓ Geodon effects: Tegretol • The following may ↑ Geodon effects: AIDS drugs, Nizoral, Diflucan, Luvox, Prozac, quinine, Serzone, Sporanox, Tagamet

(continued)

TABLE 9.2a. *(continued)*

Brand name	Report right away	Discuss at next visit	Important cautions, tests	Symptoms of toxicity	Interactions with other drugs
Risperdal	Dizziness, seizures; watch for TD (rare under 6 mg); muscle rigidity, fever (symptoms of NMS)	**Agitation, anxiety,** constipation, **headache, insomnia,** nausea, **runny nose, sexual dysfunction,** sunburn, **weight gain** At high doses: lactation, absent menses	• EKG if previous heart trouble • Monitor blood pressure • For elderly: start at .5 mg 2x/day, ↑ slowly to 5 mg/day • Liver or kidney impairment: start at half dose, ↑ slowly	Drowsiness, rapid heartbeat, low blood pressure, seizures	• Avoid Propulsid • May ↑ impairment in thinking and motor skills caused by alcohol, other CNS depressants • May ↑ the effects of: Clozaril, hypertension drugs • May ↓ the effects of: dopamine, levodopa • The following may ↓ Risperdal effects: Tegretol
Seroquel	**Dizziness,** seizures; muscle rigidity, fever (symptoms of NMS); watch for TD	Constipation, **drowsiness,** dry mouth, **headaches,** rapid heartbeat, upset stomach, weakness, **weight gain**	• Obtain slit-lamp survey for cataracts and repeat each 6 months • For elderly: start same but may need slow ↑ • If impaired liver: start same, but may need slower ↑, lower endpoint	Drowsiness, rapid heartbeat, low blood pressure	• Use Propulsid cautiously • May ↑ impairment in thinking and motor skills caused by alcohol, other CNS depressants • Seroquel may ↑ the effects of: hypertension drugs • Seroquel may ↓ the effects of: dopamine, levodopa • The following may ↓ Seroquel effects: barbiturates, Dilantin, Rifadin, Mellaril, Tegretol • The following may ↑ Seroquel effects: antifungal drugs (for example, Nizoral, Sporanox, Diflucan), erythromycin, Tagamet
Zyprexa	**Dizziness,** seizures; muscle rigidity, fever (symptoms of NMS); watch for TD	**Agitation,** constipation, **drowsiness,** dry mouth, upset stomach, tremor, **weight gain**	• If history of liver disease: obtain blood tests • For elderly: start 5 mg/day, ↑ by 5 mg/wk if needed	Drowsiness, slurred speech	• Use Propulsid cautiously • May ↑ impairment in thinking and motor skills caused by alcohol, other CNS depressants • May ↑ the effects of: hypertension drugs • May ↓ the effects of: dementia drugs (cholinesterase inhibitors), dopamine, levodopa • The following may ↓ Zyprexa effects: Prilosec, Rifadin, Tegretol • The following may ↑ Zyprexa effects: cigarettes

Boldface italic = more common (10% or more of patients); ↑ = increase; ↓ = decrease

TABLE 9.2b. Side Effects and Precautions for the Older Antipsychotics

Brand name	Report right away	Discuss at next visit	Important cautions, tests	Symptoms of toxicity	Interactions with other drugs
High-dose: Thorazine, Mellaril, Serentil; *Medium-dose:* Loxitane, Moban., Trilafon; *Low-dose:* Stelazine, Navane, Haldol, Prolixin, Orap	• Irregular heartbeat, dizziness, **urine retention, acute muscle spasms, severe restlessness, parkinsonian tremor** (greatest risk in low-dose drugs; intermediate risk in middle-dose drugs; lowest risk in low-dose drugs) • Tardive dyskinesia (abnormal motions of mouth or tongue) • Seizures: greatest risk in low-dose drugs; intermediate risk in middle-dose drugs; lowest risk in low-dose drugs • Neuroleptic malignant syndrome: fever; muscle rigidity; rapid heartbeat, low blood pressure, sweating	• May improve with time: **Blurred vision, constipation, drowsiness, dry mouth** (least risk with low-dose drugs; greatest with high-dose drugs) • Abnormal coloring of skin, weight gain • Breast enlargement, milk production (women and men) • Sunburn and ↑ ultraviolet sensitivity (especially on Thorazine)	• Tardive dyskinesia (abnormal facial movements that may become permanent) are a serious risk for patients who take any of these drugs • Neuroleptic malignant syndrome • Use care driving, operating machinery • Use cautiously if: enlarged prostate, glaucoma, paralytic ileus, urinary retention, heart disease • Avoid in the case of breast cancer • Because of heart toxicity, Mellaril and Serentil are now recommended only for those who don't respond to anything else • Orap is especially likely to cause irregular heartbeat, which can be fatal; obtain EKG before starting • For elderly: start at about half adult dose and ↑ gradually; consider low-dose antipsychotics (reduced risk of low blood pressure) • Liver or kidney impairment: start low, ↑ slowly	Agitation, blurred vision, confusion, dilated pupils, drowsiness, dry mouth, fever, heartbeat irregularities, muscle rigidity, nasal congestion, vomiting, coma	• May ↑ impairment in thinking and motor skills caused by alcohol, other CNS depressants • May ↑ seizures in those who take anticonvulsants, Wellbutrin, Ultram • Lithium may ↑ risk of seizures, delirium (may be especially a problem with Haldol, though not proven and probably infrequent) • Risk of heat intolerance ↑ when used with TCAs, drugs for neurological side effects (for example, Artane, Cogentin), other anticholinergic drugs • Older antipsychotics may ↑ the effects of: hypertension drugs (for example, Catapres, Ismelin, Aldomet), Inderal • Older antipsychotics may ↓ the effects of: lithium, parkinsonism drugs (for example, Levodopa, Permax, Mirapex, Requip) • The following may ↑ effects of older antipsychotic drugs: antifungals (for example, Nizoral, Sporanox) Effexor, erythromycin, grapefruit juice, Inderal, malaria drugs (for example, Aralen), SSRIs (for example, Prozac, Paxil, Zoloft) • The following may ↓ effects of older antipsychotic drugs: amphetamines, antacids containing aluminum or magnesium, barbiturates, cigarettes, Dilantin, lithium, Mycobutin, Rifadin, Tagamet, Tegretol *Additional interactions for Mellaril and Serentil:* • The following may cause fatal heart complications: anti-arrhythmia drugs (Vascon, Propulsid, Norpace), antibiotics (Tequin, Raxar, Zagam), Betapace, Corvert, Effexor, Geodon, Lorelco, Orap, Pronestyl, quinidine, some SSRIs (Prozac, Luvox, Paxil, Zoloft), Tikosyn,Tambocor, Tonocard Additional interactions for Orap: • The following may also cause fatal heart disease: AIDS drugs, anti-arrhythmic agents (Vascon, Propulsid, Norpace, Tikosyn, Tambocor, Corvert) antibiotics (Biaxin, dirithromycin, erythromycin, Raxar, Tao, Tequin, Zagam), antifungals (Nizoral, Diflucan, Sporanox), Betapace, Cardizem, Cipro, Cognex, Geodon, Lorelco, Noroxin, Orap, Pronestyl, quinidine, SSRIs (Cilexa, Luvox, Paxil, Zoloft), Tagamet, Tonocard, Zyflow

Boldface italic = more common (10% or more of patients); ↑ = increase; ↓ = decrease

127

TABLE 9.3. Indications, Advantages, and Risks of Antipsychotics

a FDA approved b non-FDA approved ++ strongly yes + yes	Atypical "newer" drug					High dose			Moderate dose			Low dose				
	Clozaril	Geodon	Risperdal	Seroquel	Zyprexa	Mellaril	Serentil	Thorazine	Loxitane	Moban	Trilafon	Haldol	Navane	Orap	Prolixin	Stelazine
Used for:																
Psychotic depression			a			a		a	a		a		b		a	
Mania	b				a		b					b				
Schizophrenia, acute psychosis	a	a	a	a	a	a	a	a	a	a	a	a	a	b	a	a
Delusional disorder														b		
Dementia	b		b	b	b	b	b	b	b		b		b		b	
Tourette's disorder		b	b									a		a		
Agitation	b		b	b	b	a	b	b	b		b	b	b		b	
Advantages:																
Reduces negative symptoms	+	+	+	+	+											
Safer for older patients	+	+	+	+	+							+	+	+	+	+
Available as oral liquid						+	+	+	+	+	+	+			+	+
Weight gain less likely			+													
Few drug interactions			+													
Low risk of tardive dyskinesia	++	++	+	++	++											
Risks and drawbacks:																
Seizures	++															
Agranulocytosis	++															
Sedating						+	+	+								
Activating			+													
Positional low blood pressure						++	++	++								
Marked risk of movement disorders						++	++	++	++	++	++	++	++	++	++	++
Drooling	++															
Risk of diabetes	+	+	?	+	+											

128

CHAPTER 10

Drugs for Dementia

If you have a parent, spouse, or other relative with Alzheimer's dementia, you probably already know that several drugs for the treatment of this disorder have been available since 1993. Though they are no miracle, one of them could, at least for a time, modestly improve the ability of an Alzheimer's patient to think and to pursue activities of daily living. As you would hope, these drugs can also ease the burden on spouses and others who provide home care. With one of these drugs, for example, your relative might become less apathetic, more aware of time and date, better able to bathe and dress, work independently at hobbies, even handle money. Patients with dementia due to other causes, such as strokes or Parkinson's disease, may also benefit from these drugs, though these uses haven't been well studied yet.

Although intended for people who are mildly to moderately demented, these drugs may also help people who are more severely impaired. Case reports and the experience of some clinicians suggest that agitation, delusions, and hallucinations may decline to the point that antipsychotic medication can be reduced or eliminated. However, the scientific studies needed to prove benefits for severely demented patients have not yet been reported.

How do the antidementia drugs work? A neurotransmitter called "acetylcholine" is an important link in the process that allows us to think and to control our behavior. The brains of Alzheimer's patients gradually lose the ability to make this chemical. Antidementia drugs improve the efficiency with which the brain uses what acetylcholine is available. (The way they accomplish this is by inhibiting a brain enzyme called *cholinesterase*, which is why these drugs are called "anticholinesterase inhibitors.") The average improvement is modest, and some people aren't helped at all. But when the drugs do work, they can improve enjoyment of family life and prolong the time before nursing home care becomes necessary. They may help for only a few months, or sometimes much longer, depending on how fast the dementia progresses. Once the disease advances to the point that the brain makes hardly any acetylcholine, the drugs stop working and the patient deteriorates rapidly.

DRAWBACKS

Perhaps the greatest drawback overall is the fact that side effects prevent many patients from taking antidementia drugs at their fullest doses, where they are probably most effective. To help limit side effects, the doctor may advise gradually increasing the dose to as high as the patient can tolerate. Any of the four antidementia drugs will probably work about as well as the next. Which one your relative uses will depend mostly on side effects and convenience. They all can cause some degree of diarrhea, nausea, vomiting, and insomnia, which may abate with time. Sometimes these drugs can worsen problems with breathing, so people with a history of asthma or obstructive lung disease will need extra watching by their physicians. Peptic ulcer disease or heart disease will also prompt special attention to the monitoring process. If your relative needs an operation, special care must be taken—the antidementia drugs can increase the effects of medications used in either local or general anesthesia.

Under what circumstances should the decision be made to take the patient off the antidementia drug? The doctor will probably advise this step (1) if your relative doesn't tolerate the drug well or complies poorly with taking it; (2) if, despite 3–6 months of treatment, the mental condition continues to deteriorate at about the same rate; and (3) certainly if the rate of deterioration increases. The drugs should be tapered, if possible, to lessen the chance of abrupt deterioration of behavior or cognitive function.

INDIVIDUAL ANTIDEMENTIA DRUGS

Aricept (donepezil)

Aricept has two advantages: it can be taken just once a day, and there is but a single step from initial to maximum dose (5–10 mg). It produces no increase in liver enzyme activity, so it doesn't require the repeated blood studies needed for Cognex. The side effects, though typical of the drugs in this class, usually aren't very bothersome.

Exelon (rivastigmine)

Although similar to Aricept, Exelon requires twice-a-day dosing, and it takes more steps to get to the maximum effective dose. Starting with 1.5 mg twice a day with meals, the dose should be increased by an additional 1.5 mg every 2 weeks, as long as well tolerated, up to 6 mg twice a day. If the patient cannot tolerate the most recent increase because of abdominal pain, loss of appetite, vomiting, or weight loss, the drug should be stopped for several doses, then restarted at the same dose level or one level lower.

Exelon is also offered as an oral liquid, an advantage because so many demented people have trouble swallowing capsules. The side effects are about the same as for the other drugs, and no change in dose is necessary for someone who has liver or kidney disease. Very few interactions with other drugs have been proven, nor are they likely to be: Exelon is metabolized by different liver systems than are responsible for handling so many other drugs.

Reminyl (galantamine)

Originally found in the bulbs of daffodils, Reminyl is the newest of the four approved antidementia drugs, with the same pluses and minuses. By the time you read this book, it should also be available as an oral liquid.

Cognex (tacrine)

The first of the antidementia drugs to be approved, Cognex remains by far the most difficult to use. It is so rapidly metabolized that it must be taken 4 times a day. Food markedly decreases its absorption, so it should be taken on an empty stomach if at all possible. However, the side effects (poor appetite, nausea, vomiting, diarrhea) sometimes demand that it be taken with food! As a result, many people simply cannot take enough Cognex to do them much good. As with Exelon, very gradual increases (over several months) may help reduce side effects. Cigarette smoking lowers blood levels.

Cognex will affect the liver in nearly half those who take it; usually this means a rise in liver enzymes but no symptoms. Although actual liver toxicity is rare, it is extremely dangerous, sometimes fatal, so the doctor must be sure that blood enzyme levels (especially ALT, or alanine aminotransferase) are not too high before each increase. This determination requires a blood test every other week for the first 4 months, and if ALT is stable, every 3 months afterward. If liver enzymes increase by two to three times normal values, very careful monitoring will be needed; if by four times, the dose will have to be reduced; if by five times or more, the medication must be discontinued until levels recede.

STILL APPROVED, BUT NOT RECOMMENDED

Over the years, the FDA has approved some treatments for dementia that are almost surely worthless. Examples include urecholine, nicotine, Hydergine, and Gerimal. If your relative is already taking one of these drugs and seems to be benefiting from it, it will probably do no harm to continue. In my opinion, however, though still promoted and prescribed, they are a waste of money and time.

DRUGS THAT SLOW THE ALZHEIMER'S DISEASE PROCESS

The four anticholinesterase inhibitors merely improve symptoms of dementia while the disease process continues on its destructive path. Wouldn't it be better to prevent whatever is causing the problem in the first place? For that, we'd have to know what causes Alzheimer's, and we don't. One theory is that, with aging, our metabolism promotes increased formation of "free radicals," molecules that contain unpaired electrons (most stable molecules have electrons that are paired). These free radicals are thought to play a role in the destruction of neurons—hence Alzheimer's, and a number of other diseases. Some clinicians believe we can protect neurons either by taking antioxidant drugs that reduce the production of free radicals, or by taking "radical scavengers"—drugs that inactivate free radicals before they can cause damage. Although the evidence is still not clear, there is reason to consider using some of the following antioxidants:

- **Selegiline**, which goes by several trade names (including Eldepryl, Atapryl, and Carbex), may delay by several months the time until a mildly to moderately demented person can no longer be cared for at home. Limited data suggest it may even improve some patients' ability to think. The dose identified as helpful was 5 mg twice a day. Most common side effects include nausea, dizziness, and abdominal pain. Although selegiline is also a monoamine oxidase inhibitor (MAOI), similar to Nardil, there are no explicit dietary restrictions.
- In the one controlled study that has been completed, **vitamin E** had about the same benefits for Alzheimer's patients as selegiline. The dose usually cited is 2,000 IU (international units) a day, roughly 20 times the amount contained in a multiple vitamin tablet. Side effects, usually mild, include diarrhea, nausea, tiredness, and weakness. You can buy vitamin E without a prescription, but of course you should discuss it with the doctor before giving it to your relative.
- You don't need a prescription to buy **ginkgo biloba**, either. EGb 761, an extract of the leaves of this exotic tree, may act as an antioxidant and is sold under various trade names. The studies have not been conclusive. Some find only a tiny effect, others that it works about as well as Aricept. Except in patients who must take medicine to thin their blood (anticoagulants like coumadin), it probably won't do any harm, though it has been known to cause mild intestinal upset, rash, and headache. The usual dose is 120 mg divided into two or three doses a day.
- Controlled trials of **estrogen hormone replacement therapy** for women with dementia have yielded conflicting results. At least one has suggested that it may help; others have not. The jury is still out, but my hopes are not high for a favorable verdict—as treatment. Although a 2002 report has raised doubts about their effectiveness, several studies have shown that estrogens reduce the risk of developing Alzheimer's and, when it does develop, it may begin at a later age than in women who don't take estrogens. If you have had a hysterectomy or are otherwise

postmenopausal, you are probably already on hormone replacement therapy, which could yet decrease your chances of developing Alzheimer's. Ask your doctor!

Finally, there is the question of prevention. The final data are not yet in, but early results of several studies suggest that anti-inflammatory drugs such as Naprosyn or Advil (usually for arthritis) greatly reduce the risk of Alzheimer's. Of course, these drugs have risks of their own, and no one is prescribing them for dementia prevention—yet.

DEMENTIA DRUGS FOR OLDER PEOPLE

Of course, nearly everyone who becomes demented is older. But what about patients who are 85 or over, the so-called "very old"? Such people are often not only old but frail and more likely than ever to need additional medications. Tolerance for side effects such as nausea will be less than ever, and even greater watchfulness than usual will be necessary.

DEMENTIA DRUGS FOR THE MEDICALLY ILL

Any of the four anticholinesterase inhibitors could be contraindicated by serious liver or kidney disease. Under those circumstances, one of the alternative medications mentioned above might be tolerated better.

TABLE 10.1. Medications for Dementia Currently Prescribed in the United States

Brand name	Generic name, year of FDA approval	Generic?	Starting treatment	Adult dose range/ usual dose effective for maintenance (mg/day)	Divided into # doses/day	Dosage size (mg)	$/day, average daily dose	Half-life includes metabolites
Aricept	donepezil, 1996	N	Start with 5 mg, ↑ to 10 mg after 6 weeks, if needed	5–10/10	1 (bed)	5, 10	$4.48	L
Cognex	tacrine, 1993	N	Start with 10 mg 4x/day; ↑ dose by 40 mg/day at 4-week intervals, as tolerated	120–160/160	4 (between meals, if possible)	10, 20, 30, 40	$5.09	S
Exelon	rivastigmine, 2000	N	See text	6–12/12	2 (with meals)	1.5, 3, 4.5, 6; O	$4.34	M
Reminyl	galantamine, 2001	N	Start 4 mg 2x/day with meals; after 4 weeks, ↑ to 8 mg 2x/day; ↑ to 12 mg 2x/day after 4 more weeks, as tolerated	16–24/24	2 (with meals)	4, 8, 12	$4.32	M

O = oral solution; half-life: S = short (6 hr or less); M = medium (6–24 hr); L = long (> 24 hr)

TABLE 10.2. Side Effects and Precautions for Antidementia Medications

Brand name	Report right away	Discuss at next visit	Important cautions, tests	Symptoms of toxicity	Interactions with other drugs
Aricept	Dizziness, vomiting	*Nausea*, insomnia, *diarrhea*, *headache*, muscle aches, loss of appetite, weight loss	• Avoid with: active intestinal bleeding, severe liver disease, jaundice • Use cautiously with: asthma, enlarged prostate, impaired kidney functioning, irregular heartbeat, obstructive lung disease, seizures	Severe nausea, vomiting, salivation, sweating, slow heartbeat, low blood pressure, breathing	• Motrin and other NSAIDs may cause stomach bleeding • The following may ↑ the effects of Aricept: AIDS drugs, Cardizem, Cordarone, erythromycin, Nizoral, quinidine, Rescriptor, Rythmol, Serzone, Sporanox, SSRIs (for example, Prozac), Synercid, verapamil • The following may ↓ the effects of Aricept: antihistamines (for example, Benadryl, chlorpheniramine), Asendin, atropine, barbiturates, Clozaril, dexamethasone, Dilantin, Flexeril, Ludiomil, Mycobutin, Norflex, Norpace, older antipsychotics (for example, Thorazine), Provigil, Rifadin, St. John's wort, Sustiva (may induce or inhibit), Symmetrel, TCAs, Tegretol, Viramune, Zyprexa
Cognex	*Dizziness*, vomiting	*Diarrhea, nausea, headache*, muscle aches, appetite loss, upset stomach, weight loss	• Avoid with: active intestinal bleeding, severe liver disease, or jaundice • Measure liver enzymes 2x/month • Use cautiously with: asthma, obstructive lung disease, impaired kidney functioning, irregular heartbeat, enlarged prostate, seizures • Take on empty stomach (1 hour before or 2 hours after eating)	slow and shallow, muscle weakness, seizures	• Motrin and other NSAIDs may cause stomach bleeding • Cognex may ↑ the effects of: Haldol, theophylline • Cognex may ↓ the effects of: Librium, Rilutel, Valium, Zyflo • The following may ↑ the effects of Cognex: estrogens, Luvox, Tagamet • The following may ↓ the effects of Aricept: antihistamines (for example, Benadryl, chlorpheniramine), Asendin, atropine, cigarettes, Clozaril, Flexeril, Ludiomil, Norflex, Norpace, older antipsychotics (for example, Thorazine), St. John's wort, Symmetrel, TCAs, Zyprexa
Exelon	Dizziness, *vomiting*	Abdominal pain, appetite loss, headache, insomnia, nausea, weight loss	• Avoid with: active intestinal bleeding, severe liver disease, or jaundice • Use cautiously with: asthma, enlarged prostate, impaired kidney functioning, irregular heartbeat, obstructive lung disease, seizures		• Motrin and other NSAIDs may cause stomach bleeding • The following may ↓ the effects of Aricept: antihistamines (for example, Benadryl, chlorpheniramine), Asendin, atropine, Clozaril, Flexeril, Ludiomil, Norflex, Norpace, older antipsychotics (for example, Thorazine), smoking, Symmetrel, TCAs, Zyprexa
Reminyl	Dizziness, *vomiting*	Abdominal pain, *diarrhea*, upset stomach, *nausea*, loss of appetite, weight loss, headache	• Avoid with: active intestinal bleeding, severe liver disease, jaundice • Use cautiously with: asthma, obstructive lung disease, impaired kidney functioning, irregular heartbeat, urinary obstruction (such as large prostate), seizures • With moderate liver or kidney impairment: top dose of 16 mg/day		• Motrin and other NSAIDs may cause stomach bleeding • The following may ↑ the effects of Reminyl: Accolate, alcohol, AIDS drugs, antibiotics (for example, Biaxin erythromycin), Cardizem, Cordarone, Lamisil, Luvox, Nizoral, Norvir, Paxil, Prozac, quinidine, quinine, Serzone, Tagamet, verapamil • The following may ↓ the effects of Aricept: Actos, antihistamines (for example, Benadryl, chlorpheniramine), Asendin, atropine, barbiturates, Clozaril, Dilantin, Flexeril, Ludiomil, Mycobutin, Norflex, Norpace, older antipsychotics (for example, Thorazine), Rifadin, St. John's wort, Symmetrel, TCAs, Tegretol, Zyprexa

Boldface italic = more common (10% or more of patients); NSAIDS, nonsteroidal anti-inflammatory drugs; ↑ = increase; ↓ = decrease

TABLE 10.3. Indications, Advantages, and Risks of Antidementia Drugs

a FDA approved b non-FDA approved ++ strongly yes + yes	Aricept	Cognex	Exelon	Reminyl
Used for:				
Alzheimer's dementia	a	a	a	a
Dementia	b	b	b	
Advantages:				
Once a day dosing	+			
Few drug interactions			+	
Available as oral liquid			+	
Drawbacks:				
Liver disease		++		
Weight loss	+	+	+	
Frequent blood tests required		+		
Frequent dosing required		++		

CHAPTER 11

Medications to Treat Substance Abuse

Medications that treat substance abuse either reduce the attractions of the habit or "punish" the user. (A quick analogy: to reduce bank robberies, you could keep less cash in the vault or legislate longer prison sentences.) The medications available to treat nicotine and opioid addiction all reduce the attractions; alcohol abusers have available medications in both categories. Whichever treatment seems right for you, don't rely on medication alone: all antidrug drugs work best when they are part of a complete program that includes social support groups such as AA and Smokenders, and psychological approaches such as cognitive-behavioral therapy (Chapters 13 and 25).

MEDICATIONS FOR SMOKING CESSATION

Nicotine Replacement Therapy

Nicotine is one of the most powerfully addicting drugs ever discovered, so kicking the tobacco habit could be one of the hardest jobs you've ever faced. Withdrawal symptoms commonly include anxiety, depression, trouble concentrating, irritability, restlessness, and insomnia. At least temporarily, your weight will probably increase by around 10 pounds. And you may find yourself fighting the temptation to smoke long past the time you are under active treatment—off and on for years the craving can crop up, prompted by sights and situations you've long associated with lighting up.

Nicotine replacement therapy (NRT) reduces withdrawal symptoms by substituting for the addictive drug in cigarette smoke but without the harmful tars and other components that cause cancer. NRT is especially useful for someone who must quit immediately, perhaps necessitated by an upcoming hospitalization or an employer who doesn't permit smoking, and it often works better for moderate to heavy smokers. If you are serious about quitting, you should probably try some form of NRT—studies have repeatedly shown that it can double your chances of success. If you don't succeed the first time, try again as soon as you can. There is little that will benefit your health more than giving up tobacco.

Nicotine replacement is available as a gum, a nasal spray, an oral inhaler, and a patch. These delivery methods are about equally effective, but because none of them provides the nearly instantaneous, habit-forming nicotine rush of inhaled smoke, they may not work at all. Getting free of nicotine addiction takes time, often longer than the maximum 6 months recommended by the manufacturers, regardless of the method. Whatever form of NRT you prefer, start attending a support group such as Smokenders or smoking cessation classes run by a local health agency. Group support and shared misery (and success) will help see you over the hurdles.

Usage and Drawbacks

The gum and patch are safe enough that you can buy them without a doctor's prescription. However, you should consult your doctor before self-medicating, especially if you have had heart disease, irregular heartbeat, diabetes, high blood pressure, ulcer, or thyroid disease. Don't use NRT unless you actually reduce your tobacco use—you don't want your medicine to increase the strength of your habit or increase your risk of hypertension and heart disease. Although there is inadequate evidence as to NRT's long-term safety, many patients (and physicians) believe that it is less harmful than smoking. Use during pregnancy hasn't been studied adequately, but a developing fetus probably gets less nicotine from NRT than from a smoking mother, certainly less of tobacco smoke's myriad other deadly constituents. A safety review in 2001 advised that, because little nicotine is secreted into breast milk, NRT could be used during breast-feeding.

Patch

The idea behind the patch is to provide a constant supply of nicotine, so you won't crave tobacco. All brands come in different strengths; beginning with a high dose, you wean yourself from nicotine. If you smoke 10 or more cigarettes a day, start with the highest-dose patch for about 6 weeks, then move to the next-highest dose for 2–4 weeks, then to the lowest for another 2–4 weeks. Lighter smokers (under 10 cigarettes/day) would start at the middle dose. Apply the patch to clean, dry, hairless skin of your arm or body at about the same time each day. (You can clip body hair, if necessary, but don't shave—irritation or cuts can affect absorption of nicotine.) Patches can cause rash and itching, so once you've used an area of skin, give it a rest by selecting different areas for the next several days. If you have insomnia or vivid dreams—the most frequent side effects of the patch—remove it at bedtime. The Nicotrol patch is meant to be worn just 16 hours a day, but the 24-hour patches may forestall your morning craving. Keep unused patches tightly sealed to prevent evaporation. Dispose of used patches carefully: they retain enough nicotine to poison a small child.

Gum

Set a quit date, then substitute chewing for smoking. The manufacturer suggests using a piece every hour or 2 for the first 6 weeks, every 2–4 hours for the next 3 weeks, and every 4–8 hours for the last 3 weeks. Most people need about 15 sticks per day, and you shouldn't use over 24. To avoid side effects, chew slowly—perhaps 5 chews, followed by a rest with the gum parked in your cheek. Wait a minute or so until the tingling in your mouth goes away, then begin chewing again. Don't use the gum while drinking or eating; acid substances in your mouth can interfere with absorption of nicotine. Although the gum comes in 2-mg and 4-mg strengths, only the higher dose seems to work very well. If you are still smoking after 4 weeks, stop using the gum and try another approach. After you've been off cigarettes for several months, gradually discontinue using it. If you find yourself unable to discontinue the gum, talk to your doctor.

This gum takes so much strength to chew it can cause jaw pain and even loosen fillings. Belching is quite common, but slow chewing should reduce it. Nicotine is absorbed through the lining of the mouth; any that you swallow will be destroyed and won't do you any good (or harm, either, if you swallow the whole wad by mistake). If you do develop irregular heartbeat or other symptoms of nicotine toxicity, stop chewing and call your doctor.

Nasal Spray

Next to smoking, nasal spray is the fastest way to deliver nicotine to your system. It is also rather inconvenient, and it routinely produces coughing and local irritation. However, some studies find that it is the most helpful method for heavy smokers. The usual dose is one squirt into each nostril when you feel the desire to smoke, with a maximum of five doses (10 squirts) every hour and 40 doses a day. You'll need to use it at least eight times a day to get any benefit from it. The bottle contains a lot of nicotine, so keep it safe from children.

Inhaler

This device is seriously misnamed. You don't inhale the nicotine at all; nearly all is absorbed through the lining of your mouth after you suck it out of a cigarette-like tube. That's the stated advantage of the inhaler—it provides some of the familiar "feel" of moving a cigarette to your lips. But it can be a nuisance to use, and you have to puff hard to get the nicotine. And, it delivers less nicotine when it is cold (less than 50° F). Each tube contains 4 mg of nicotine, which requires about 20 minutes to extract (you don't have to use all that is in a tube at one time). Still, those who use it seem to like it. You'll probably use 6–16 tubes a day.

Zyban (bupropion)

The same chemical as the antidepressant Wellbutrin (pages 68–69), Zyban reduces the desire to smoke. It probably works because it eases the irritability, poor concentration, restlessness, and depressed mood that typically occur during withdrawal. Your doctor might recommend Zyban if NRT, with or without psychotherapy, hasn't helped or if you have also had depression. You would probably start at 150 mg/day for three days and increase to 150 mg twice a day for 7–12 weeks, though if you had depression, you might need to continue much longer. Due to the risk of seizures, your doctor will advise you not to use more than 300 mg/day and to take your doses at least 8, preferably 12 hours apart. You should plan to stop smoking in about the second week. Your doctor might well recommend Zyban with a nicotine patch—the success rates are a little higher than for either product used alone.

MEDICATIONS FOR TREATING ALCOHOL ABUSE

Antabuse (disulfiram)

Used for half a century to prevent alcohol abuse relapse, Antabuse relies on what most medications seek to avoid: toxicity. If you drank even a small amount of alcohol (a tablespoon of vodka can do it) while taking Antabuse, you would feel extremely ill within just a few minutes. The symptoms—nausea, vomiting, throbbing headache, sweating, dizziness, weakness, anxiety, and rapid heartbeat and breathing—would persist for an hour or so, until all the alcohol was out of your bloodstream; afterward, you would probably sleep. The fear of becoming sick should keep you from drinking, but once you stopped taking Antabuse, you could resume drinking within a few days.

Some people feel tempted to drink while on Antabuse, just to see if it really works, but you shouldn't risk the complications of liver damage or circulatory collapse that have occurred, though rarely. You should carry a card or wear a bracelet identifying yourself as an Antabuse user. Although you should not take this medication if you have heart disease, it really isn't as scary to use as it sounds. The risks from taking Antabuse are probably far less than the risks from continued heavy drinking. Antabuse works like a conscience with consequences, reminding you not to drink; if you think that you might ignore this advice, don't use Antabuse. You can see why Antabuse is most useful for someone who is highly motivated to quit drinking but needs assistance getting past the temptation alcoholics feel every day to "have just one." Some people comply better when they take Antabuse under the supervision of a relative or pharmacist.

Drawbacks

As long as you don't use alcohol, you won't ordinarily notice any side effects of Antabuse. When taking Antabuse, you need to remain under your physician's watchful eye: even the small amounts of alcohol contained in foods, candy, and medicines—cough syrups are a notorious example—can produce symptoms. Although extreme Antabuse reactions are unusual, episodes of unconsciousness and even death have occurred. If you ever experienced a reaction with alcohol, you'd need immediate medical attention to ensure that your vital functions remained intact until the reaction stopped.

ReVia (naltrexone)

A medication developed to combat narcotics abuse, ReVia also blunts the craving for alcohol and the pleasurable "buzz" alcohol produces. Alcohol abusers may drink less when taking 50 mg of ReVia a day. It is not the approach most clinicians would choose, though it may be useful if physical or emotional pain puts you at risk for relapse. However, a 2001 study of heavy alcohol abusers did not confirm the value of ReVia. See page 143 for details of its use.

MEDICATIONS TO FIGHT NARCOTIC ADDICTION

Methadone; ORLAAM (levomethadyl acetate)

When a person repeatedly succumbs to using illegal drugs, the only solution may be another drug that will silence the siren call of addiction. Methadone and ORLAAM are called *opioid agonists* because they act like heroin and other narcotics to produce drowsiness and euphoria and reduce perception of pain. However, methadone and ORLAAM are not attractive for recreational use because they provide little "rush" and they block heroin's euphoric high. They suppress the addict's craving for narcotics, thereby reducing the drive that leads to crime and dirty needles. By gradually reducing the dose to zero, methadone is sometimes used to wean patients from other narcotics. During detoxification, the user will probably experience mild flu-like symptoms such as nausea and muscle pain. The withdrawal process takes several weeks—longer than withdrawal from shorter-acting narcotics.

The U.S. government so carefully controls the distribution of methadone and ORLAAM that most physicians cannot even prescribe either; the drugs are available only at federally approved clinics. To be eligible, patients must have been opioid-dependent for at least a year. Once admitted to a maintenance program, they take liquid methadone once a day, closely supervised to make sure none of the drug is sold on the street. Weekend take-home doses are offered only to those patients with time-tested reliability. Beginning dose is usually 25 mg/day, with weekly 5-mg increases, until illicit drug use stops. Some studies indicate that the best results require at least 80 mg/day.

ORLAAM, which stands for "oral solution of levo-alpha-acetylmethadol," a synonym for levomethadyl acetate, is effective when taken just three times a week, so no weekend dosing is needed. In fact, federal regulations don't permit take-home doses. Its usual starting dose is 20–40 mg, depending on the severity of the habit, and each dose is increased by 5–10 mg weekly. The average patient needs about 90 mg, three times a week.

An important problem with both drugs is inadequate dosage. Although experts recommend gradual increases until heroin use stops, physicians sometimes prescribe doses lower than addicts need. A second problem is stopping treatment too soon, which often guarantees relapse to heroin use; such patients should probably continue methadone or ORLAAM for years. If you use either drug, the decision to stop is one that you and your doctor should discuss carefully and agree on.

Using methadone during pregnancy is actually encouraged—just about the only time you'll read such a thing in this book. Factoring in malnutrition, hepatitis, HIV, and other sexually transmitted diseases, the risks to a developing baby from methadone are far less than from continuing heroin use. However, even some weeks after birth, a baby whose mother is taking methadone can have withdrawal symptoms.

You may encounter some clinicians who feel that using methadone or ORLAAM only masks the addiction and does not give the individual the chance to deal with its underlying causes. It is also pointed out that methadone is used by some heroin users to "top off" while they continue with their primary addiction, and that methadone diverted from clinics and hospitals has itself caused the death of some users. In my view, however, used with group and other psychotherapies, methadone represents a final chance at salvation for those who cannot control their craving in any other way.

WHAT'S IN A NAME?

Ever wonder why medicines have several names? It comes from the competing interests of a word simple enough for the consumer to remember (and evocative of the medication's function) yet complicated enough to distinguish it from other similar medications. ReVia, the brand name for naltrexone, suggests renewed life for substance abusers. Mortals can neither pronounce nor remember the chemical name, which would allow a chemist to reconstruct the drug from scratch: 17-(cyclopropylmethy)-4,5a-epoxy-3,14-dihydroxymorphinan-6-one hydrochloride.

ReVia (naltrexone)

As an opioid antagonist, ReVia blocks the high that addicts feel when they inject heroin. It doesn't relieve pain or produce a high itself, so it has no value on the illegal market. You don't have to be in a special program to receive ReVia—any physician can prescribe it. It also reduces the craving for drugs and has no withdrawal symptoms. So, why not prescribe ReVia for every opioid user? The answer is that most opioid abusers don't comply with the 7–10-day detoxification period necessary before ReVia can be started. And of those who actually start ReVia, most simply stop taking it; within about 3 days the effects of ReVia are gone, and the patient can resume the use of heroin. However, ReVia is an excellent alternative to methadone and ORLAAM for truly motivated patients, such as health care professionals and imprisoned addicts trying to win release. Your chances of complying will improve with an established routine for taking ReVia, such as arranging for a nurse or pharmacist to watch you swallow each dose.

If you were dependent on opioids and took ReVia without going through the detoxification period, you would develop the typical symptoms of opioid withdrawal (see Table 25.1). If you were heavily dependent, your breathing or heart could stop. That is why your doctor might worry that you have used opioids recently and ask you to take a ReVia challenge test: Following a small injected dose, you would be observed carefully to be sure that no symptoms of withdrawal occur. Then, you could start regular 50 mg/day dosing. Because of a very long duration of action, many people find they can take 100 mg on Mondays and Wednesdays and 150 mg on Fridays for the weekend. This flexibility of dosing may help you remain on the medication. A few patients find they need a higher dose of the medication each day to be effective. You should carry a card warning that you are taking ReVia. Once you discontinue it, you could find that you are then more sensitive to the effects of opioids.

TABLE 11.1. Drugs Used to Treat Substance Abuse in the United States

Brand name	Generic name, year of FDA approval	Starting treatment	Generic?	Adult dose range/ usual dose effective for maintenance	Dosage size (mg)	$/day, average daily dose	Half-life (hr)	Time to work
Dolophine, Methadose	methadone, 1947	Start 15–20 mg/day; ↑ as needed	Y	20–120/80 mg/day	5, 10, 40; O, I	$0.68	M–L	1 hr
ORLAAM	levomethadyl acetate, 1993	Start at 20–40 mg every other day; ↑ as needed by 5–10 mg per dose every wk or 2	N	60–140/90 mg 3x/wk	O	$4.32	L	3–5 days
Antabuse	disulfiram, 1951	500 mg/day for 1–2 wk; then 250 mg/day	Y	125–500/250 mg/day	250, 500	$0.07	L	12 hr
ReVia	naltrexone, 1984/1995	Alcoholism: 50 mg/day; opioid addiction (see text)	Y	50–100/50 mg daily or every other day (see text)	50 mg	$4.28	M	1 hr
Nicorette	nicotine gum, 1984	Chew 1 when urge to smoke arises	Y	8–24/15 pieces/day (see text)	2, 4	$6.52	S	3 months
Nicoderm	nicotine patch, 1991	For 10+ cigs/day: highest dose 4–12 wk; next highest 2–4 wk; lowest 2–4 wk	Y	Wear patch 24 hrs/day	21, 14, 7	$3.00–$4.50	L	3+ months
Habitrol					21, 14, 7			
Prostep		Under 10: start with second highest dose			22, 11		M	
Nicotrol				Wear Nicotrol patch 16 hrs; discard at bedtime	15, 10, 5			
Nicotrol NS	nicotine nasal spray, 1996	1 spray each nostril when urge to smoke arises	N	8–40/15 doses/day	.5 mg/spray (100-mg/ bottle)	$6.00	S	3 months
Nicotrol inhaler	nicotine oral inhaler, 1997	Puff 20 minutes, 6–16 cartridges/day x 12 wk; then gradual reduction	N	6–16/6 cartridges/day	4 mg/cartridge	$5.70	S	3+ months
Zyban	bupropion, 1999	150 mg 2x/day	Y	150–300/300 mg/day	75, 100, 150	$3.05	M	2 wk

O = oral solution; S = short (< 6 hr); M = medium (6–24 hr); L = long (> 24 hr); ↑ = increase

TABLE 11.2. Side Effects and Precautions for Drugs Used to Treat Substance Abuse

Brand name	Report right away	Discuss at next visit	Important cautions, tests	Symptoms of toxicity	Interactions with other drugs
ReVia	*Dizziness, jaundice,* vomiting	*Abdominal pain, anxiety, headache, insomnia, muscle or joint pain, nausea, nervousness, tiredness*	• At high doses, can cause liver toxicity • Avoid if: hepatitis or acute liver failure • Obtain baseline liver function tests, then monthly for 3 months, then each 3–6 months • Can cause withdrawal symptoms if you are dependent on opioids; may thwart benefits of opioid medicines • If impaired liver or kidney, may need to reduce dose	—	• Should probably avoid Antabuse (each can be toxic to the liver) • May cause excessive drowsiness with antipsychotic drugs
Methadone	Trouble breathing, heart palpitations, dizziness, fainting, seizures, clammy skin	Often decrease with time: abdominal cramping, *appetite loss, constipation, low sex interest,* drowsiness, *dry mouth,* headache, insomnia, itching, muscle or joint aching, nausea, sweating, *trouble urinating,* vomiting	• Once begun, withdrawal symptoms can make it hard to stop • Taper to minimize withdrawal symptoms • Elderly or impaired liver or kidney: may need reduced dose	Slow, shallow breathing, dizziness, drowsiness, nausea and vomiting, pinpoint pupils, low blood pressure	• Avoid: MAOIs • May ↑ impairment in thinking and motor skills caused by alcohol, other CNS depressants • May ↑ the effects of: Retrovir • May ↓ the effects of: Videx, Zerit • The following can ↑ effects of methadone: Biaxin, Diflucan, erythromycin, Flagyl, grapefruit juice, marijuana, Nizoral, Norvir, quinidine, Serzone, Sporanox, SSRIs (for example, Luvox, Prozac), Tagamet, verapamil • The following may ↓ effects of methadone: barbiturates, Dilantin, Rifadin, Sustiva, Tegretol, Viramune
ORLAAM	Trouble breathing, heart palpitations, dizziness, fainting, seizures, clammy skin	Often decrease with time: anxiety, constipation, insomnia, sweating, weakness	• Avoid if: heart disease; sales have been suspended in Europe due to life-threatening heart arrhythmias • Need an EKG before beginning ORLAAM • Take 3x/wk; can be fatal if taken every day	Feeling "wired," reduced concentration, drowsiness, dizziness	• Avoid: MAOIs, pain medications (for example, Darvon) • Avoid the following drugs, which can ↑ heart toxicity of ORLAAM: heart arrhythmia drugs (for example, Betapace, Cordarone, Norpace, Pronestyl, quinidine, Rythmol, Tambocor, Tikosyn, Tonocard), Allegra, antipsychotics (especially Geodon, Haldol, Mellaril, Orap, Risperdal, Serentil), Anzemet, Asendin, Biaxin, Cerubidine, doxorubicin, erythromycin, Lorelco, Lozol, Ludiomil, pentamidine, Propulsid, Raxar, Sandostatin, Seldane, TCAs, Tequin, Zagam

(continued)

TABLE 11.2. (*continued*)

Brand name	Report right away	Discuss at next visit	Important cautions, tests	Symptoms of toxicity	Interactions with other drugs
ORLAAM (*cont.*)			• Elderly, impaired liver: may need reduced dose		• May ↑ impairment in thinking and motor skills caused by alcohol, other CNS depressants • The following may ↓ effects of ORLAAM: barbiturates, Dilantin, Rifadin, Sustiva, Tegretol, Viramune • The following may ↑ effects of ORLAAM: Biaxin, Diflucan, erythromycin, Flagyl, grapefruit juice, marijuana, Nizoral, Serzone, Sporanox, SSRIs
Antabuse	*Symptoms of alcohol reaction:* vomiting, severe headache, trouble breathing, severe weakness, sweating *Symptoms of hepatitis (rare):* abdominal pain, yellow eyes or skin, fatigue, weakness, nausea, vomiting, appetite loss Seizures (rare)	Often ↓ with time: drowsiness, impotence, headache, skin rash, metallic taste in mouth	• Avoid if: severe heart disease • Use caution if: diabetes, thyroid disease, epilepsy, stroke, kidney, or liver disease • Obtain baseline physical exam, cardiogram, blood and urine tests, and repeat every 6 months	—	• Do not use alcohol, including medications, cough syrup, mouthwash, or toiletries containing alcohol! • May ↑ impairment in thinking and motor skills caused by CNS depressants • May ↑ effects of: anticoagulants (for example, dicumarol, warfarin), benzodiazepines (for example, Valium), cocaine, Dilantin, Flagyl, Isoniazid, Parafon Forte, theophylline • Use with TCAs may cause delirium
Nicotine replacement (all forms)	Severe headache, fainting, weak pulse, vomiting, dizziness	Headache, ↑ appetite, constipation, diarrhea, painful menses, flushing, insomnia, irritability *Gum:* belching, jaw ache, mouth irritation *Patch:* Rash, itching *Nasal spray:* nasal irritation or congestion, sneeze, cough *Oral inhaler:* Cough, mouth/throat irritation	• Check with doctor if: heart disease or irregular heartbeat, diabetes, high blood pressure, or pregnant • Watch for: high blood pressure, especially if using nicotine replacement therapy with Zyban • Do not use gum if smoking	Nausea, vomiting, abdominal pain, diarrhea, headache, weakness; larger overdose can cause fainting, low blood pressure, seizures	• Smoking cessation, with or without nicotine replacement, may ↓ the effects of: Isuprel, phenylephrine (for example, Neo-Synephrine) • Smoking cessation, with or without nicotine replacement, may ↑ the effects of: benzodiazepines, beta blockers (for example, Inderal), caffeine, Darvon, insulin, Minipress, Serax, Talwin, TCAs, theophylline, Tylenol
Zyban	see Table 6.2, Wellbutrin, page 80				

Boldface italic = more common (10% or more of patients); ↑ = increase; ↓ = decrease

146

TABLE 11.3. Indications, Advantages, and Risks of Drugs Used to Treat Substance Abuse

a FDA approved b non-FDA approved ++ strongly yes + yes	Patch	Nicorette	Nasal spray	Inhaler	Zyban	Antabuse	Methadone	ORLAAM	ReVia
Used for:									
Prevent opioid relapse							a	a	a
Prevent alcohol dependence						a			a
Reduce self-harm in mentally retarded									b
Smoking cessation	a	a	a	a	a				b
Depression					a				
Advantages:									
Easy to use	+								
Few drug interactions	+	+	+	+					+
Nonprescription	+	+							
Risks and drawbacks:									
Weight gain	+	+	+	+					
Seizures					+				

CHAPTER 12

─────

Nondrug Physical Treatments

I could fill pages with all the physical treatments mental patients have tried over the centuries. Physicians have squeezed, prodded, and electrified patients' bodies and heads in an effort to relieve melancholia or drive out "demons." The claims made for many of the treatments offered even in our own lifetimes have been mainly testimonial in nature, often glowing but unsubstantiated recommendations from patients or clinicians. In the past two generations, mental health clinicians have increasingly relied on the results found in double-blind studies, which reduce to a handful the number of effective nondrug physical treatments. The first three I describe have been well studied and proven effective; the rest seem promising but haven't yet been studied enough for a clear recommendation.

PHYSICAL TREATMENTS KNOWN TO BE EFFECTIVE

Bright Light Therapy (Phototherapy)

As a metaphor, depression is dark and gloomy, so treating it with light seems like a bright idea. If you have winter depression (also called winter blues and, more formally, seasonal affective disorder), bright light therapy (BLT) can work as well as Prozac. A very bright light shining on you for an hour or two each day can relieve depressive symptoms, especially if your depression is not too severe and if one of your symptoms is excessive sleep. It has also been used to reduce the depression some women experience before their menstrual periods, to decrease bingeing in bulimia nervosa, and to improve sleep and reduce agitation in patients with dementia. Even if you have a nonseasonal major depression, some clinicians would recommend BLT, though proof of effectiveness outside winter depression is scanty.

Sal, whose story appears on page 221, had had a seasonal depression each fall for the past 3 years. When his doctor gave him a choice—medication or BLT—Sal chose the bright light. First thing each morning, he studied in front of his light box

148

for an hour and a half. The light was so bright that, when he glanced directly at it, he quickly had to look away. In just a few days he felt less depressed; within 10 days he was sleeping normally and had regained his normal energy and interest in sports. Although he felt a little restless for the first couple of weeks, he noticed nothing else he could call a side effect of treatment. The following year, beginning in late October, Sal started using his light box each morning. That winter, he didn't develop depression at all.

Most of these products use light from cool, white fluorescent tubes in a box that stands on your desk or table. They emit an impressive amount of light, up to 10,000 lux—that's 20 times brighter than typical indoor lighting. The light entering your eyes causes changes in your brain's chemistry, relieving the depression. That's why you have to let the light fall right on your face. Although bright light can be helpful no matter what time of day you use it, recent reports suggest that it works best first thing in the morning. Most people use the light box for 30–90 minutes at a time— your doctor will advise you depending on the brightness of your box and the depth of your depression.

Side effects are few, though you could experience jumpiness, nausea, or headache. Some patients have also reported disturbed sleep. If you have certain eye problems, such as cataracts, glaucoma, or retinal detachment, you should consult your ophthalmologist before you use BLT to be sure it won't damage your vision. There don't appear to be any age limitations on who can use BLT; even children have been helped by it.

You can buy a light box for as little as $200. It will last for years, though you'll probably have to replace a bulb from time to time. I've listed some sources in Appendix A. Even though these devices are available without prescription and are generally safe, let me stress the importance of using them only under the care of a qualified clinician. That's the only way to be sure you are getting important information about diagnosis, length of treatment, side effects, and treatment alternatives. If your doctor isn't comfortable with the use of light therapy, the local medical or psychiatric society may be able to recommend someone who is.

Electroconvulsive Therapy

Electroconvulsive therapy (ECT) is a method of relieving mental symptoms— mainly, severe depression—by passing a small electric current through the brain. This current produces a generalized seizure that lasts half a minute or so, followed by a short period of sleep. The entire procedure is done under general anesthesia and takes only a few minutes. Although it has sometimes been called electro*shock* therapy, this is an error: sparks never fly, and the only shock is the feeling you might experience on first hearing the suggestion.

Of the possible treatments for mental illness, ECT is both the most effective and the most controversial. I know people who wouldn't consider using it; frankly, I can understand how frightened they might feel at undergoing a series of convulsive seizures while they are unconscious. In the past, this fear has been deserved, to some extent. For one thing, when introduced in the 1940s, ECT was rather primitive. Though standard procedure now, patients often did not receive anesthesia or muscle relaxant; the result was terror and, sometimes, broken bones. No wonder, then, this treatment has been pilloried in films such as *One Flew Over the Cuckoo's Nest* and vilified by Scientology and other groups that, on philosophical or religious grounds, would like to see it banned forever.

Some who object to ECT are former mental patients who think it has harmed them or that it was used to control their behavior. It is true that years ago, when we knew far less about mental illness than we do today, ECT was tried for many different conditions. For example, it was prescribed for schizophrenia, where it often confused but rarely improved the patients. Some clinicians probably did use it for behavior control. Today, ethical clinicians agree that ECT should be used only to treat those conditions for which it has been proven effective and that it should never be administered solely for the purpose of controlling behavior.

At least 100 careful studies in the past 30 years provide evidence that over 70% of severely depressed patients respond to ECT, and that it often works even when psychotherapy and many different drugs have failed. It is also clear that ECT can treat other mental disorders, although these studies have been less numerous. A doctor might recommend ECT for:

- Severe depression that doesn't respond well to medications, or if the drugs cause serious side effects
- Urgent symptoms, such as plans to commit suicide, deep melancholia, psychosis, or dangerous weight loss from refusing to eat (ECT is less effective in atypical depression)
- Mania that medications can't handle
- Schizoaffective disorder (symptoms of both psychosis and mood disorder that occur together)
- Catatonic or schizophrenic symptoms that haven't responded to other treatments.

ECT can also improve symptoms of Parkinson's disease, though it wouldn't be used for this without one of the other indications I've mentioned. For patients whose main problem is a personality disorder, obsessive–compulsive disorder, any other anxiety disorder, or somatization disorder, ECT doesn't work well and can even interfere with more helpful forms of therapy.

No one knows for sure just why ECT works. There are many theories, most of them surely wrong. For example, it doesn't work because patients fear the procedure, or because they get attention from doctors or family. The response has nothing to do with lack of oxygen to the brain or damage to neurons or other parts of the brain (which don't occur). ECT probably works for the same reasons drugs do: it causes changes in brain chemistry. Exactly how this happens hasn't yet been worked out, but the improvement is no less real. Although the complicated nature of ECT means that there have been relatively few studies in which patients are given sham (fake) treatments as a test of effectiveness, a 1985 British study did demonstrate that real ECT produced improvement far in excess of fake treatments.

Occasionally, I've seen a patient recover completely after just three or four ECTs, but the usual course is six to 12 treatments, given two or three times a week. More than 12 usually add nothing positive. To prevent relapse, your doctor will prescribe follow-up treatment with an antidepressant medication (different from those already tried). If you are one of those few people who respond to nothing but ECT, you may need a maintenance treatment every 2 to 4 weeks to prevent a recurrence of symptoms.

Because I believe you should know exactly what takes place, I'm going to give a pretty complete description of the procedure, as experienced by Brian, whose story appears on pages 204–205.

The day he was admitted to the hospital, Brian had a thorough evaluation, including a history and physical examination, laboratory tests, and a cardiogram. Because he was over 60, he also had a chest X-ray. All exams and tests proved normal. Just after lunch, when Brian's wife was present, his psychiatrist reviewed the treatment's advantages and drawbacks. Brian learned that, for his illness, other treatments could be used, but that over the years many studies had found that ECT had the best chance of eliminating the depression quickly and surely. Time was of the essence, given his serious thoughts about suicide. Although drugs might help, it could take weeks to find the right combination and dose.

His doctor also discussed the drawbacks of using ECT (see page 152). Depressed and upset as he was, Brian was still able to understand this explanation and gave informed consent to the procedure. His wife also understood and consented. To ensure that the diagnosis was correct, that the prescription for ECT was reasonable, and that he was mentally competent to give informed consent, in the late afternoon a second psychiatrist spent an hour interviewing Brian and going over his history.

The following morning, Brian lay on a table in the procedure room, while an anesthetist inserted a tube for an intravenous drip into his right arm and attached electrodes to his chest and head for cardiogram and electroencephalogram monitoring. A blood pressure cuff was attached to his left arm, and a pulse oximeter on a finger would continuously read the oxygen level in his bloodstream. The anesthetist next inserted a rubber bite block into Brian's mouth to prevent broken teeth and tongue lacerations when his jaw muscles contracted.

Now he received a series of medications: oxygen through a face mask, followed by an injection of atropine to stabilize heartbeat and prevent excessive mouth secretions. To induce sleep, he was then given a barbiturate (Brevital) that would last just a few minutes. Next, Anectine given through the IV paralyzed his muscles to lessen the force of the seizure; this would reduce muscle soreness and the risk of fractures in his spinal column, arms, and legs.

While he was asleep, electrodes were strapped to the right side of his head. Then, for just an instant, a current was passed through the electrodes. The resulting seizure made his body's muscles contract, visibly but not violently. For a couple of minutes after it began, his heart rate and blood pressure nearly doubled. After a little over half a minute, the seizure stopped spontaneously. For several minutes, the anesthetist pumped oxygen through the face mask into Brian's lungs until the Anectine wore off and he could breathe on his own. After sleeping for half an hour in a recovery room, he awakened. At first, he wasn't sure where he was, but the nurse reminded him that he had had a treatment and gave him a Motrin for his headache. Within a few minutes, alert but still a little confused, he was escorted to the dining room for breakfast.

Although no one keeps very accurate records, a conservative estimate of 25,000 Americans receive ECT each year. Despite sometimes unfavorable press, in surveys of those who have actually had ECT, four out of five patients report that they would accept it again, if needed. However, if this is a first time for you, you may want further reassurance. For example, what standards does a hospital use to decide which physicians can prescribe and administer ECT?

The assessment of medical competence stands on three legs: education, training, and experience. By completing medical school and a residency in psychiatry, your doctor will have received education in the science and art of ECT—when to use it, how to give it, what side effects to watch for. Continuing medical education (at medical conventions or through independent study) provides updates on recent changes in technique and equipment. The training aspect comes from observing while a practicing clinician administers ECT to some patients, then being observed by an expert while giving treatments. Finally, there is the issue of experience—the number of treatments your doctor has personally given. This evaluation can be a little tricky. There must be enough to stay current and expert, but not so many as to suggest a "treatment mill" approach, where everyone gets the same treatment. Somewhere in the neighborhood of 5–20 patients per year is about right.

Modern hospitals grant specialized privileges only to those clinicians who fulfill these three requirements for competence, and they require renewal of privileges every couple of years. You should feel free to ask your doctor about these three aspects of medical competence. The answers you receive will help you feel confident that you are in the hands of an expert who knows when—and when not—to prescribe and administer this treatment.

Drawbacks

Just since 1990, more than 25 studies have addressed issues relevant to safety. To jump right to the bottom line, ECT is one of the safest treatments available. You cannot overdose; complications are few and rare. However, there are some concerns and potential risks that you would need to discuss very carefully with your clinician before agreeing to this treatment.

As you would learn from the discussion with your doctor about informed consent, anesthesia for any reason carries a small risk of death: of those given general anesthesia for any reason, about 1 in 25,000 don't wake up. However, repeated studies have demonstrated that ECT itself doesn't add any risk beyond this figure. As you might imagine, brain tumors, recent heart attacks, and strokes increase the risk, but even they don't absolutely rule out ECT. Although your heart rate increases during the treatment, this isn't dangerous. Rarely, a serious complication arises during treatment, which is one reason that most treatments are done in a hospital, where a heart specialist could respond, if necessary.

Nearly everyone experiences some temporary memory loss. If you received ECT throughout a 3-week hospitalization, later you might not remember much about this hospitalization. However, you would still be able to remember what had happened before hospitalization and to form new memories after your last treatment. To keep memory loss to a minimum, your doctor would probably place the electrodes only on one side of your head. This is called unilateral ECT, and it is what most people treated for major depression will receive. If you were being treated for mania, however, you would probably have to use bilateral treatments—unilateral treatments often just aren't strong enough to break through the manic mood. With experience, some depressed patients are found to require bilateral treatments.

Loss of memory is so common that some people worry about brain damage. Let me be candid: there is no way I can promise you this could never happen. What I can say is that over the past 60 years, researchers have never found clear evidence that brain damage occurs. Studies using an X-ray technique called *magnetic resonance imaging* (MRI) show no apparent structural damage to the brain after ECT. Some years ago there was a report in England of an elderly woman who, over the course of many years of depression, had had a total of 1,250 ECTs—yet her brain showed no evidence of brain damage when she eventually died of unrelated causes. Of course, this extreme example is only a testimonial of sorts, but it does demonstrate that the human brain can survive over a hundred times the number of treatments that a typical patient receives.

Sore muscles and headache are minor ECT side effects. Occasionally, someone will awaken from the treatment so severely confused and disoriented that agitation occurs. This may require calming with Valium, but it is not dangerous and soon passes. Some medications can raise your seizure threshold, which means that it would take more electricity to produce the convulsion needed for the antidepressant effect. These medicines include (predictably enough) mood stabilizers, benzodiazepines, and barbiturates.

Neurosurgery in Mental Patients

Each year, perhaps two dozen patients with either severe depression or obsessive–compulsive disorder respond so poorly to treatment that they undergo neurosurgical procedures. Psychosurgery is rarely used in this country—or worldwide, for that matter. In fact, only one center in the United States currently performs this brain operation, which is used only with extremely well-informed consent of patients (at least one relative must also consent) who have had severe and incapacitating illness lasting for an average of 5 years or more. The patient must have had multiple trials with numerous forms of therapy, including various medications, psychotherapy, and electroconvulsive therapy.

This treatment is far too specialized to discuss at length in a general book such as this one. Readers who need further information should investigate the resource listed in Appendix A.

LESS WELL-ESTABLISHED PHYSICAL TREATMENTS

Each of the four treatments I discuss has received some investigation, though not the amount of scrutiny needed to elevate it to the pantheon of mainstream therapy. None of these approaches entails serious dangers or side effects; I have listed them in decreasing order of strongest evidence for effectiveness—so far.

Exercise

It's no news that exercise is good for you—it tones up muscles (which, in older people, makes them less likely to fall), it increases the blood supply to your heart to help stave off heart attack, and it reduces weight to avert diabetes. Clinicians and researchers have found that exercise can help limit the pain, physical limitations, anxiety, and depression in fibromyalgia. In fact, you may be surprised at the positive effects exercise can also have on your mental health. The best evidence—over 80 controlled studies—finds that exercise can significantly improve depression. One recent review of the field concluded that exercise may be as effective for depression as psychotherapy. Some studies have also suggested that exercise can help people with autism, binge eating, cigarette smoking, insomnia, and even dementia.

Just about any sort of exercise will do: walking around the neighborhood, raking leaves, vigorous sports, or working out at a gym. It doesn't take much—as little as three times per week, 20–60 minutes of moderate effort each session. The findings of benefit are independent of sex and age, as long as the exercise is regular. Exercise is also cheap, convenient (you can do it on your own), and compatible with other forms of treatment, including medications and psychotherapy. Side effects are largely positive, and it is almost impossible to overdose.

Sleep Deprivation

Trouble sleeping is almost routine in mood disorders, so it may seem perverse that going with little or no sleep can actually relieve depression. However, numerous studies over the past decade have found that going sleepless, or even getting by on 4 hours, for a night can greatly improve mood in moderately severe depression. This simple procedure would seem to be an attractive approach to the treatment of depression—it is quick, cheap, and relatively painless—but the depressive symptoms usually return after a night's normal sleep! This distressing fact has recently prompted an intensive search for ways to prolong the effect. One solution has been to add bright light therapy; another is to add an antidepressant or lithium. So far, however, no one has hit upon a technique that makes sleep deprivation a mainstay of treatment.

Because the technique isn't reliable, clinicians don't use it routinely. However, if you aren't helped by standard treatment methods, or if you need extremely rapid mood elevation—for instance, should you have serious plans for suicide—your doctor might suggest sleep deprivation. However, it can worsen the condition of a person who is both depressed and psychotic, and like most of the antidepressant medications, it has been known to cause mania or hypomania in those with bipolar depression.

Repetitive Transcranial Magnetic Stimulation

If you've heard about repetitive transcranial magnetic stimulation (rTMS), you haven't heard much. It is still an experimental technique to treat mood disorders, but it could turn out to have broader application in mental health treatment. It started as a tool to explore functioning at the surface of the brain, but because its powerful magnetic fields can cause neurons to discharge, it was quickly explored as a possible treatment. Although it is an electrical event, unlike ECT it doesn't require anesthesia, produce a seizure, or cause memory loss. It requires multiple sessions a week for several weeks, though the energy used is about one-millionth of that required for ECT. It is painless, well-accepted by patients, and relatively safe (a very few patients have had seizures after rTMS; many more report mild headache). The apparatus does create a terrific racket that requires patient and therapist to wear earplugs.

Does rTMS make a difference? Early indications are that it may be able to relieve depression in some patients, perhaps even substitute for ECT in some seriously depressed patients. It has also been reported to reduce hallucinations in some patients with schizophrenia. But it is still experimental, has not received FDA approval, and is offered only in a few medical centers. If you have the opportunity to try rTMS, it will probably be because your doctor is familiar with a center that has the apparatus and is doing research on this technique. If not, I've provided a contact point in Appendix A. Whenever you pursue a treatment that is still in its experimental stage, remember that the path of mental health is littered with treatments that were, at first, embraced enthusiastically by patient and clinician alike but later proved worthless.

Acupuncture

Followers of this ancient Chinese treatment method believe that energy (or life force, called *chi*) circulates throughout the body. *Chi* must be kept in balance from one side to the other, bottom to top, outside to inside, and it must freely circulate throughout the body. When *chi* is blocked, symptoms result. Treatment reestablishes the balance by stimulating certain points on the body by various means, including the insertion of slender needles, pressure, ultrasound, temperature change, and even vacuum. Because the ear is alleged to be a sort of crossroads of this circulating energy, stainless steel staples are sometimes placed there.

In the West, acupuncture has been used most often to manage the chronic pain of arthritis, backache, and migraine. Some alcoholism or addiction counselors recommend it for withdrawal or to reduce the craving for alcohol or other drugs (methamphetamine, cocaine). Some studies have shown that it may actually help drug users stay in treatment and have fewer arrests (though the results for smoking cessation are pretty unencouraging). Although some clinicians also recommend acupuncture for depression or schizophrenia, there is no substantial evidence that it is useful in these disorders.

I know that millions of patients worldwide have received acupuncture and swear by it, but for most mental disorders the data simply aren't there. If you've tried it for a substance use disorder and it helps, fine. But for most conditions, I'd stick to the proven therapies discussed in this and other chapters.

TABLE 12.1. Indications, Advantages, and Risks
of Physical Treatments

+++ excellent evidence ++ good evidence + some anecdotes	Bright light therapy	Electroconvulsive therapy	Neurosurgery	Exercise	Sleep deprivation	Repetitive transcranial magnetic stimulation	Acupuncture
FDA-approved or used for:							
Major depression	+	+++	++	+++	++	+	
Mania		+++					
Seasonal mood disorder	+++						
Premenstrual depression					+		
Obsessive–compulsive disorder			++				
Substance dependence							+
Dementia				++			
Jet lag	++						
Advantages:							
Extremely rapid onset of benefit					++		
Few side effects	+			+		+	+
Augments antidepressants					+		
Risks and drawbacks:							
Temporary memory loss		++					
Risk of seizures			+				
Personality change			+				

157

CHAPTER 13

Psychotherapy

Those who study mental health outcomes agree that at least four out of five psychotherapy patients do well. This astonishing success rate can be attributed to a number of factors, among them that even serious mental illnesses such as depression and anxiety may improve without treatment, and that the desire to improve motivates many patients to work hard in therapy. Perhaps most significant for improving your chances, though, is that the quality and variety of psychotherapy options have risen considerably over the past half century. In the next two chapters I provide information that can push your chances of success even beyond the 80% mark.

When you saw the title of this chapter, did you envision yourself lying on a couch and talking while a doctor sits behind you unseen, taking notes? That form of psychotherapy represents only a tiny fraction of all the techniques mental health clinicians use. In fact, psychotherapy is really any verbal method used to improve mental health. Take away all the drugs and physical treatments covered in previous chapters, and psychotherapy is everything that's left. The clinician may talk with you, or just let you talk; one style involves asking you to do certain things to modify your behavior, either in the office or as homework. (I use two chapters to discuss talking therapy and behavior modification, though the distinction isn't always sharp.) Whatever form of psychotherapy you choose, you will be more than a passive consumer of treatment. In a sense, you and your therapist will operate as full partners in your recovery.

To a degree, all techniques share a number of features:

- Two parties talk with one another.
- The therapist is sympathetic to the patient's problems.
- The therapist provides explanations about the cause and remedy . . .
- . . . and offers hope for a positive outcome.

Psychotherapy is both mystical and familiar. Its mysticism stems from the popular image of the silent therapist exploring our minds, reading our innermost secrets from signs no one else can see. In reality, a simple sort of psychotherapy is a familiar ritual that takes place every day in our homes, at work, and on the street. It is provided not just by professionals but by all manner of people—including you. Consider the following scenario:

You're ready to leave work one evening, when you notice the light still on in Jack's office, so you stop in. Jack is staring into space, his brow furrowed. "What's up?" you ask.

Jack sighs and unburdens himself. "I really blew that presentation today," he says. "I had the slides in backward, I stuttered—I got my tongue so twisted when I tried to answer questions, everyone in the room was smiling behind their hands. I gotta get a different kind of job."

"Let's talk about that," you say. You toss your overcoat onto the desk and sit down. "I could see you were struggling. We all felt bad for you."

Jack doesn't respond, so you continue. "Look, you have two advanced degrees, and you're the best designer in this office. But how much training have you had in making presentations?"

Jack shakes his head and stammers something, then falls silent again. You say, "I don't know anything about design, but I've attended a couple of seminars on making presentations. Let me coach you for the next one—you'll provide the content, of course, but I'll listen to you practice a few times."

Jack sits up. Together you start to work out how you will coach him in the fine art of making an effective presentation.

Although your interaction with Jack may sound like simple counseling (page 175), it has all the characteristics of psychotherapy mentioned above. Two people are talking about a problem of great concern to one of them. By tossing down your coat and taking a seat (at quitting time), you clearly demonstrate sympathetic concern. You don't deny there is a problem—Jack would have recognized that empty reassurance. Instead, you listen to his point of view, offer a believable explanation of the cause of his problem (he hasn't been trained in giving presentations), and bolster his ego by pointing out that he is well regarded as a designer. Together you plan a remedy, promoting hopeful optimism for the future.

The most fundamental elements of psychotherapy can be present in any social relationship that embodies encouragement, kindness, and support. We get "psychotherapy" of a sort from all manner of people—bosses and bartenders, clergy and cops—encounters from which we gain insights into ourselves that help us better navigate a course through life. But if all of psychotherapy were as easy as Jack's example, there would be no need for professional therapists.

Professional psychotherapy gets you a lot more than compassion, advice, and an available ear. A trained therapist melds a complex variety of attributes—education, experience, interpersonal sensitivity, style, and objectivity. Your therapist's lack of personal involvement with you is essential to find the best solution for you and not one that benefits someone else. A good therapist also has the experience to recognize patterns and trace connections in your life that you didn't dream existed—for example, that how you and your grown children relate is influenced by your shared experience of a divorce when they were teenagers. Also key is the manner in which the experienced therapist helps you understand these relationships—not force-feeding but guiding you to your own conclusions in a journey of self-discovery. A professional therapist is also sensitively attuned to your emotions, perhaps even before you recognize them yourself, helping you understand how you respond to anxiety (perhaps by eating?) or that you avoid situations that make you sad. These skills combine to help you understand and cope with your identified problem.

SELECTING A TYPE OF PSYCHOTHERAPY

Of course, people have various responses to the prospect of psychotherapy. For some, it seems as routine as having their teeth cleaned; others may view it more like a weekly extraction. If you don't like the idea of sharing your innermost secrets with a stranger who asks awkward, disquieting questions, or if the typical weekly visits sound too frequent and the expense too great, I urge you to read to the end of these two chapters before rejecting the whole enterprise. You may find that understanding what's involved puts you more at ease. Certainly, you should weigh the pros and cons of psychotherapy versus other effective treatments. That way, you can enter treatment only after rationally deciding that it is the best course. In my experience, many people who are initially uncomfortable with the idea quickly become enthusiasts, once therapy begins to show benefits. Of course, a lot depends on the fit between professional and patient, so look hard for a therapist who seems just right for you (see Chapter 3).

In this chapter I can describe only a few of the many forms of psychotherapy that have been devised over the years. Some are minor modifications of established treatments; others are innovative. With hundreds of available techniques, how do you decide which one might be right for you? How can you know whether it works at all?—psychotherapy doesn't even have the advantage of FDA approval. Fortunately, through the years many research groups have been hard at work trying to determine what works, and when.

In the late 20th century, at least four double-blind studies of depressed patients found that, for mildly to moderately depressed individuals, cognitive-behavioral therapy (CBT) and antidepressants were about equally effective, and each was better than placebo. Other studies have found that interpersonal psychotherapy (IPT) is about the equivalent of CBT. Similar studies have been done for many other mental disorders. Very recently, evidence from brain scanning techniques has revealed that, similar to medication, psychotherapy actually corrects abnormalities in how the brain functions.

Psychotherapists tend to have a particular theoretical orientation and base what they do on that theory. This is fine as long as the treatment fits you and your problem, but what if it doesn't? If you needed surgery to reset a broken arm, would you ask a general surgeon to open you up "to see what you can find"? New drugs aren't designed for everyone who enters a doctor's office—rather, they target a specific disease such as meningitis, schizophrenia, or diabetes. The type of psychotherapy you seek out should depend largely on the nature of your problem.

Specific Psychiatric Diagnoses

Many mental disorders may require individualized attention (usually one clinician, one patient), at least during the initial phases of psychotherapy. This should be a treatment type that has a proven track record with your particular disorder. For example, looking at Table 14.1, depression, phobias, and eating disorders should respond well to CBT or IPT. Phobias may do well with either CBT or a behavior modification therapy (discussed in Chapter 14). If yours is an especially sensitive topic (such as sexual issues) or if you have trouble speaking in front of others, you might also need individual care, rather than group therapy.

Personality Issues and Style of Living

Personality styles and actual personality disorders (pages 262–263) respond poorly to medication or other physical therapy, but they do respond to psychotherapy. Although psychoanalytic psychotherapy has been advocated for just this type of situation, less intensive methods may be equally effective at far less cost in terms of time or money.

Other Problems

Millions of people are beset by problems that may not be due to a specific mental illness. They may have any one of the thousands of problems of living that plague us as a species. Here is a small sampling:

- Ruth wants to move to Arizona to be near her boyfriend, yet she feels pulled to remain in New Jersey where her children live.
- Dorothy feels caught between anger and love for her husband, who has AIDS.
- Armand feels a vague sense of failure even though his dot-com venture is still afloat.
- Bill has finished college, but he can't decide what he wants to do with his life.
- Maria is so stretched by her job, her husband, and her kids, she doesn't even know how she could find time to see a therapist.
- Amanda's fourth marriage just soured, and she feels crushed by yet another failure.

- Toby has been ordered by the court to seek counseling for anger management.
- Tracy has a terminal illness, and she needs to say good-bye.

Any of these problems could be a clue to one of the diagnosable mental conditions I discuss at length in Part III, but very often they are just—problems. As useful as a diagnosis can be, many people seeking treatment don't have a mental disorder. For those who are "only" unhappy, confused, dissatisfied, or overanxious, medications and other physical therapies are unlikely to help, but psychotherapy is likely to help a great deal. Just talking with someone who has no personal stake can give you perspective on your situation. Even if it doesn't produce a solution to the exact problem, it may provide you with new ways of thinking, feeling, and behaving that will move you on toward your own solution. However, for reasons I've stated repeatedly, first get a good diagnostic evaluation.

Education and Support

Education and support for specific illnesses and problems are often handled in groups dedicated to their care. Leaderless groups on the AA model provide mutual moral support and shared practical information on illnesses such as substance abuse and overeating, and in support groups for families whose relatives have illnesses such as schizophrenia or bipolar disorder.

THE PSYCHOTHERAPIES

In these two chapters, I discuss the most popular, best studied, and most-used types of psychotherapy. Each is a verbal way of getting you to look at or feel different about your problems, your feelings, or yourself. Regardless of which method you use, you need to have a clear understanding with your clinician about your shared expectations regarding duration and outcome.

Cognitive-Behavioral Therapy

Cognitive-behavioral therapy (CBT) is a brief form of highly structured psychotherapy that seeks to improve mental health through reeducation. (By its name, it is obviously also a behavioral treatment, but its main focus is on the cognitive side; years ago, it was simply called cognitive therapy.) CBT is based on the belief that how we interpret our experiences affects the way we feel and behave. Cognitive distortions, which are mistaken beliefs we develop in response to experiences, are associated with mental disorders, though no claim is made that the distortions actually cause the disorders. By correcting this distorted thinking, CBT seeks to decrease symptoms, prevent relapse, improve compliance with medication, and address social problems such as anger management or family or marriage problems.

If you are depressed, for example, you may believe that you are helpless, incompetent, unlovable, or some other unfavorable evaluation. You will tend to interpret your everyday experiences in light of this negative frame, and the future will look bleak indeed. Focusing on current problems, a cognitive therapist would teach you to identify negative thoughts that come to you automatically, such as "I'm such a failure" or "I can't possibly finish this task." The therapist then helps you identify evidence that these ideas are illogical and invalid, and formulate alternative thoughts. If depression has mired you in inactivity, you might need some behavioral tasks just to get moving again. You would probably be assigned homework, such as keeping a record of your negative thinking.

Of all the illnesses for which CBT is used, major depression is the most frequent—it may be as helpful as antidepressants in treating an acute depression. Some studies find it even more effective than antidepressants in preventing relapse. It can help "double depression" (long-standing dysthymia complicated by acute depression—see Chapter 15) and depression that's a part of medical disorders such as multiple sclerosis. It is effective in anxiety disorders such as panic disorder and obsessive–compulsive disorder; if started immediately after trauma occurs, it may even help prevent posttraumatic stress disorder.

Like other psychotherapies, CBT is less useful for people who are severely delusional or who have trouble thinking (as with Alzheimer's dementia). It can be given in group settings for patients with similar problems, such as depression or anxiety disorders. CBT can even be effective for substance dependence and chronic suicidal behavior. A complicated variation, called "dialectical behavior therapy," has been devised for patients with borderline personality disorder.

To address the serious problem of recurring substance abuse, relapse prevention therapy (RPT) was developed based on CBT principles. In this commonsense approach, the therapist is both active and directive in helping patients explore the factors that encourage ongoing abuse and develop strategies for self-control. Within a few weeks, patients learn skills that generalize to other areas of their lives. Though developed for alcohol users, it has been especially successful for those with cocaine dependence.

CBT works best—usually within a few weeks—if you are flexible enough to see how your symptoms are connected to your automatic thoughts and motivated enough to change both behavior and thinking. Here is how a CBT therapist worked with Ariel, whose husband had left her "for his telephone repair lady." Ariel had begun to blame herself for spending too little time on her marriage. A note from her son's third-grade teacher that he wasn't paying attention in class seemed evidence that she was also inadequate as a mother. For more than a month, Ariel had felt "in a fog" most of the time. She had lost interest in caring for her young children, and she couldn't concentrate on her job as a legal secretary. She had used all of her sick leave and worried that she would soon be unemployed.

The therapist started by explaining that depressed people have three main patterns of negative thinking: a negative view of self, negative interpretations of experiences, and a negative view of the future. In their sessions, Ariel and her therapist tested the logic of her assumptions, and through questioning, eventually identified Ariel's core, dysfunctional beliefs—among them, she felt that she had accomplished nothing with her life and wasn't worth anything to her family or to herself. Ariel was also asked to keep a diary of her automatic thoughts. She would record the thought, the event that preceded it, her mood at the time, and the behavior that resulted from the thought. In each session, she and her therapist reviewed the diary to assess her progress. At first, keeping up her diary added to her exhaustion, but she knew that she must persevere in order to improve. Based on her progress, they planned the next week's homework.

Ariel's diary revealed how she interpreted her experiences in the worst possible way. If she dropped a plate in the kitchen, she would think, "I'm the world's biggest klutz." When she discovered she hadn't paid her telephone bill on time, she concluded, "I'm incompetent to run a household." The most frequent of these automatic thoughts seemed to be "I'm a horrible mother," so she was asked to gather evidence that could challenge it. Here's what she found: in a week she had had two meetings with teachers and had driven her son to soccer practice each of three afternoons. Her children were both healthy and getting good grades. A friend had even said she wished her son was more like Ariel's. Ariel concluded that a realistic response, when she had her automatic thoughts, could be "I must be doing something right." In subsequent sessions, they subjected her other automatic thoughts to similar analyses.

Ariel had so much to do that her task list overwhelmed her. "I can never get this done," she thought (automatically). Because she felt overwhelmed, she frequently just sat. "I felt so guilty, I could hardly move a muscle," she confessed during one session. She and her therapist attacked her inertia with graded task assignments. They divided each of her household tasks into small components. "Clean the house" became a list of the different rooms, with individual jobs listed for each room; she could then decide which job to do first. Each day, Ariel performed a certain number of these tasks, recording the outcome. As she met with success in the following weeks, they gradually increased the number and difficulty of tasks.

After 6 weeks, Ariel had improved enough to resume working part time. Though she saw the therapist less frequently, she continued with her CBT exercises. By the end of 3 months, she proudly noted that her recovery was nearly complete: "This program has been a terrific struggle, but it got me well, and I didn't have to take medicine."

There is one risk with CBT: for specific disorders, it has been so well-described and thoroughly programmed—there are manuals describing how to do it, step by step—that even an inexperienced therapist can use it. Although this could work just fine for you, a therapist with a lot of CBT experience may be better able to steer you away from common pitfalls. On the other hand, standardization also has made CBT suitable for self-help with less severe problems, such as managing mild anxiety, anger, or moodiness.

Interpersonal Psychotherapy

Based on our strong need for attachments to other human beings, interpersonal psychotherapy (IPT) is intended for people who have trouble getting along with others or whose lives are in transition. The focus is on current life events and social interactions that may contribute to a mental illness or condition. Sometimes called "coaching for real life," IPT emphasizes how patients seek and change dysfunctional relationships to prevent future problems.

At once optimistic and realistic, your IPT therapist would probably find that your emotional problem has one or more of four possible interpersonal underpinnings: grief (a severe bereavement); interpersonal role disputes (such as fighting with a spouse, arguing with a boss or coworker); role transitions (such as the beginning or end of a romance or career); and interpersonal deficits (such as the chronic isolation that results from difficulty relating to others). You would learn that your problems don't occur in a vacuum but have a social context. For example, people who are depressed don't handle their social roles well, thereby inviting further complications. Treatment focuses on your current social situation and unfolds in three phases:

Phase I. The first two or three sessions establish a framework for treatment, which begins with education about your mental condition—it is not due to laziness or moral laxity but to an illness that is every bit as medical as an infection or a broken leg. You and your therapist make a contract for a specific number of sessions, during which treatment will focus on the here and now.

Phase II. Most sessions revolve around the treatment itself. The treatment strategy will depend on the therapist's perception of the underpinnings of the illness: for grief, facilitate mourning; for role dispute, explore the nature of the dispute and find options to resolve it; for role transition, learn to recognize and evaluate the positive and negative aspects of the change; for interpersonal deficit, define and attempt to develop the social skills needed. The therapist begins each session by asking how you've felt overall, since your previous meeting. If you answer, "Not so well," you will discuss the events that might be responsible. To facilitate the analysis of what might have gone wrong, you will be prompted for specific examples of your interactions with others, recalling exact wording whenever possible. Role playing may help you find new ways of expressing yourself.

Phase III. In the final sessions, the therapist will review your achievements and acknowledge the gains you've made, and warn you about the symptoms that could mean recurring depression. Although you would deserve the credit for success, the reverse doesn't hold true: if you haven't improved by the end of your contract, it is seen as a failure of the method, not of your efforts. You would then discuss other treatment options.

Even if you are depressed, you may find the informal and relaxed style of IPT acceptable, even enjoyable. IPT was developed for use in mild to moderate major depression, but it has also been used for patients with depression of long standing (dysthymic disorder) or who are depressed in the context of being HIV-positive. It has been used for women who have postpartum depression and who are breast-feeding and therefore don't want to take drugs, and it has been used for other problems such as bulimia nervosa and social phobia.

The therapeutic optimism for using IPT with depressed patients is based on solid research data. For example, a study of 250 depressed outpatients treated with IPT, CBT, imipramine, or placebo found that the two psychotherapies were about equally effective (though not quite as effective as medication). Two 2001 studies found that IPT and antidepressant medication produced similar metabolic changes in the brain. For more severe depressions, IPT was better than CBT. However, IPT is not intended for delusional depression, and it has not been of benefit in treating people for substance abuse. In practice, therapists will sometimes use elements of both CBT and IPT, or begin with one and later shift to the other.

Psychoanalysis and Psychoanalytic Psychotherapy

Sometimes called insight-oriented or uncovering therapy, psychoanalysis stems from the analytic theories and techniques Sigmund Freud described nearly a hundred years ago. Two basic concepts underlie psychoanalytic theory: (1) our personalities and behavior are molded largely by our childhood experiences, and (2) symptoms are caused by conflict between our unconscious thoughts.

For example, suppose that as a small child you learned from your parents that sex outside of wedlock and for purposes other than procreation is wicked and "dirty." Though you may not even consciously remember these lessons, they continue to affect your feelings and behavior, preventing you from enjoying a normal physical relationship as an adult. A planned romantic weekend with a lover might provoke depression, anxiety attacks, even physical pain, and you wouldn't understand why. You might conclude that the problem was with your lover, whereas the actual root of your conflict is churning inside you.

The tenets of psychoanalysis hold that symptoms emerge from the collision between your normal adult desires and our "duty" as we learned it (usually from our parents) in childhood. It won't be corrected until we recognize and resolve in our own mind the origins of the conflict. Wouldn't it be terrific if you could just go to a doctor who would point out the conflict, and your symptoms would magically disappear? Unhappily, it doesn't work that way. Rather, here is a rough approximation of the process, which still uses many of Freud's original techniques:

Usually lying on a couch, you would tell the therapist (who sits behind you) everything that comes to mind, holding nothing back. The analyst, largely quiet and unseen, might ask clarifying questions or confront you about apparent contradictions, but otherwise doesn't direct your thinking. Through dreams, fantasies, and slips of the tongue, the long-forgotten lessons emerge, and you begin to recognize the connections between them and your current problems. To assist this process, the analyst might make interpretations (that is, explain the unconscious meaning behind behaviors, feelings, or thoughts). Usually, interpretations are presented as a possibility, not a fact, and are open for discussion.

In the course of any treatment, it is normal to form an attachment to the therapist that reflects how you felt about your parents or other persons important in your earlier life. This attachment is called *transference* (you transfer the love and anger your felt for your parent to the analyst). Transference is usually both positive and negative; exploring it can be a powerful means of reconstructing your view of the world and substituting new, more appropriate behaviors. Analysts traditionally are quiet and neutral; if they told you much about their own lives, it would be harder for you to transfer to them the feelings you had for your parent.

Much of the material you dredge up takes time to accept because it is unpleasant, so the analytic process is gradual. Sometimes you might reject what comes up outright, in which case your analyst might conclude that you were resisting. By continuing to discuss this material, you gradually accept it. As you achieve this insight, you will be on the road to recovery.

Psychoanalytic (or psychodynamic) psychotherapy uses some of the same techniques but in a much tighter time frame; think of it as "psychoanalysis *lite*." There are usually fewer sessions and no couch—you talk to the therapist face-to-face. Therapists use many of the same techniques developed by psychoanalysis, including interpretation, confrontation, and clarification; to shorten treatment, some focus strictly on recent events. When transference feelings develop, the therapist will deal with them quickly so they don't dominate the therapy. The therapist also offers a supportive atmosphere of empathy, advice, and praise that you wouldn't experience in traditional psychoanalysis. Your goal is to develop insight into your own character and to change the way you relate to other people by resolving your unconscious conflicts.

In an era when no treatment for mental disorders was much improvement over the passing of time, psychoanalysis was embraced without proof of efficacy. Even today, hardly any of its tenets are provable by science. In particular, there are few studies proving that it relieves any specific mental disorder. My assessment? Although it is not appropriate for most of the conditions covered in this book, I believe psychoanalysis can help some people whose longstanding problems result from the way they have learned to interact with other people—for example Tina, who so needs to be the center of attention that she drives away those who might become her friends, or Tom, whose fearful timidity prevents him from advancing in his company. The paradox is that a person's basic mental health must be fairly stable overall to withstand the self-revelations of classical analysis. It also requires the investment of much time and capital; insurance doesn't usually cover the cost of psychoanalysis, which can top $20,000 a year.

Supportive Psychotherapy

You'll probably never be offered it, as such, and you're unlikely to ask for it by name. However, if you spend more than about 2 minutes with your health care provider, you'll get some degree of supportive therapy. This nonspecific treatment embodies psychotherapy's general qualities mentioned at the beginning of this chapter. You receive understanding, support, and hope for the future. The therapist may suggest new activities (hobbies, join a group to enhance social contacts), a move to new quarters, or a change of habits, such as those that relate to work or study. You'll probably get a lot of praise for abstaining from harmful activities such as drinking, smoking, or excessive eating.

Supportive therapy has been an important part of health care for centuries. Today it remains appropriate for monitoring progress with long-term medication (for example, a patient with schizophrenia or bipolar disease); short-term counseling of the bereaved (ministers do a lot of this); care of those who know that they are dying; and assistance in changing life roles, such as a divorce. It can help people endure tough situations, after more specific problem-solving techniques have been employed.

However, because it has no known, specific effect on any mental disorder, supportive psychotherapy is not appropriate as sole treatment for the conditions described in this book. It should be used only as an adjunct, or when more proven treatments such as CBT or IPT are not an option. If your clinician says, "Come back in a week and we'll talk about your problem," you need to learn what the long-term game plan is and whether a more specific psychotherapy is planned. It is easy to fall into a comfortable routine of seeing the doctor for regular appointments, sometimes for years, without any clear expectations.

Group Therapy

This branch of psychotherapy grew out of an observation that the group itself has the ability to heal in several ways. First, there is a sense of acceptance and belonging ("We are all in the same boat"). Second, the group promotes interpersonal relationships that may be lacking in the lives of some members. Third, although it can be difficult to disclose private or embarrassing details of one's life, once that barrier has been passed, the sense of shame is often lifted.

Contrary to the image put forward in films and television sitcoms, groups rarely comprise random patients with widely divergent problems and personalities. To be effective, members need the bond of common experience. Groups may be formed for the following purposes:

- **Supporting a particular patient population.** Examples abound for mood disorders, alcoholism, AIDS, obesity, and schizophrenia. Other groups support those who are undergoing stressful life events or personal relationships, including widows, caregiving spouses, people struggling with homosexuality, and families of alcoholics.

- **Promoting personality change.** How many people have you ever met who thought they had deficient personalities? Character pathology is not something the patient is aware of; the group can help bring it home and reduce resistance to change. The desired end is to enhance an individual's productivity and sociability. Of course, it takes a long time for any therapy to alter character structure, but the group process is sometimes more efficient than traditional psychotherapy.
- **Reducing symptoms.** Many groups try to help members control cigarette smoking, binge eating, or compulsive gambling.
- **Restoring previous levels of functioning**. Groups of hospital inpatients or day treatment patients sometimes meet to learn grooming, cooking, and financial management.

Many types of psychotherapy can be pursued in groups, including analytical, cognitive-behavioral, and supportive. The usual group includes five to eight members and fosters free discussion. Individual patient's difficulties with problem solving or relationships are demonstrated in the group format, where members can recognize and respond to them. Members discuss and even constructively criticize the statements and actions of others. Group therapy is an efficient way to deliver health care. In the right hands it can be highly effective, producing change that might otherwise take far longer. Even for patients with terminal cancer, it can improve mood and the tolerance of pain.

Although a group can be established and run by just about anyone, it is vital that your leader be trained in group therapy. Merely possessing a degree in medicine or psychology isn't enough by itself. Group leaders serve several important functions. They set boundaries that ensure safety of members, protect members' identities to ensure confidentiality, and prevent the group from becoming a social club.

For over a dozen years, the Bipolar Group has met every second month in the doctor's office. Most of the dozen members have had hospitalizations for mania and therefore have strong motivation to take their medication and come regularly to sessions. "I really look forward to the group," offered Tina. "It's fun, efficient, and inexpensive as compared to individual therapy. I usually feel that I've learned something from the experiences—often, mistakes—of the other patients."

Before each session begins, blood is drawn from those who need mood stabilizer levels checked. Meetings generally begin with a brief educational talk by the group leader (a psychiatrist) on some relevant subject—symptoms of depression or mania, the influence of diet on medication levels, the risk of illness in close relatives. Afterward, the leader monitors the general discussion closely to ensure that more verbal members don't freeze out the timid. The only refreshments served are coffee and tea.

After an hour, the psychiatrist meets briefly with each member to discuss medication, that day's blood level, and other private matters.

"Last session," Tina continued, "I was shocked to hear about the medical problems Jorge had had when he combined Capoten and lithium. My internist had just given me a prescription for lisinopril, which is a lot like Capoten."

Family Therapy

In the sense that it involves several people, family therapy is much like group therapy. However, it is also more complicated—families have many competing yet intersecting interests, which is not the case for people who are unrelated and don't live together. There may not even be a patient as such—the whole family is often "the patient." When one individual does have a diagnosable mental illness, that person is usually present, except in the case of young children. Then parents may meet privately with the therapist to discuss progress.

Although many family constellations are possible, family therapy is probably most often used when children live with their parents. The group can include grandparents and other relatives as well as parents and children, even outside people such as teachers or caseworkers, if they are important to the family's functioning. Often a child starts out as the identified patient, then therapy is expanded once it becomes evident that the child's behavior is symptomatic of larger family issues. However, don't assume that because you have been referred for family therapy that yours is a "dysfunctional family." Many normal families need help in coping with a crisis such as death or divorce or in supporting a member who has a serious mental illness.

With a focus on current problems, a family therapist may act as a teacher who provides facts about a specific illness or helps parents recognize the power of positively reinforcing behavior. Another role is as a healer who suggests more effective ways of communicating. While remaining impartial overall, an experienced therapist may occasionally take the part of an individual who clearly needs support. The varied techniques boil down to steps you would take either during the treatment session (such as training for better communication or problem solving) or homework tasks designed to improve parenting skills or enhance communication. Based on an initial clinical assessment, you might select one or more of several goals: to reduce symptoms; to enhance the resourcefulness of individuals in your family and the family as a whole; to enhance an individual's capacity for attachment, cohesion, or intimacy; to increase the family's ability to interact with outsiders (such as social support systems).

Family therapy often is not a complete treatment by itself but is used to enhance the management of a member's mood or anxiety disorder, anorexia nervosa, substance dependence, or schizophrenia. Although family therapy doesn't always work, an analysis of 19 studies showed that just over 75% of those who received it did better than those who received other treatment or no treatment at all. However, family therapy is unlikely to work when members refuse to divulge essential information, when members aren't committed to making the family unit work, or if there is ongoing violence within the family.

Jason's family began coming to therapy sessions at the request of his psychiatrist, who thought that the constant family uproar could be contributing to the relapses of his schizophrenia (page 265). The entire family attended every session—Jason, both parents, John (his mother's live-in boyfriend), Julia (Jason's older sister) and her live-in girlfriend. Within 10 minutes, they were all arguing about who was at fault for almost making them late. The only person who didn't participate was Jason, who sat silently, his gaze lowered, hands clenched in his lap. After restoring order, the therapist observed that the family's presence and spirited discussion showed how eager they all were to contribute to Jason's care. They then committed to a series of 10 weekly sessions, beginning with a home visit the therapist would make to learn more about the environment to which Jason would shortly be returning.

The next session was an educational workshop, in which they listened to basic information about schizophrenia—how to identify early symptoms, how medication is used, and what side effects could be expected. From a list the family made of problems they could work on as a group, they decided to start with their frequent shouting matches. The following week, the therapist taught them how to make positive requests and avoid excessive criticism. Still later, they explored the elements of problem solving: identifying the problem, listing alternatives, selecting one, implementing the choice, and reviewing the outcome. By the time Jason returned home, they had agreed that they had made their home "less a place where someone could be wounded by friendly fire."

Even when the family identifies an individual as the problem, the therapist may recognize the family as the real patient. The Breier family (Mom and her 10-year-old daughter, Rose; Dad and his 12-year-old son, Billy) came in because Billy was "antisocial" (in Mom's view) and "depressed" (in Dad's). During introductions Billy announced, "This is the last you'll hear from me." "Fine," said the therapist, and invited everyone else to tell their stories. After a half-hour discussion that centered mainly on his behavior, Billy became increasingly agitated and finally burst out, "You're all just looking for someone to blame." Mom and Dad both opened their mouths to remonstrate, but the therapist jumped in with praise for Billy's "acute" observation. That first session ran 10 minutes overtime as Billy told his side of the story.

Here was the dynamic that emerged: Mom had been physically abused by her first husband, Rose's father. She had protected Rose, but they had become so enmeshed that now she couldn't let her second husband assume a parenting function toward Rose. However, she felt comfortable disciplining Billy, who had taken to tormenting Rose verbally, defying her and stealing money from his father. Husband had withdrawn from wife, and Rose took her mother's side by ignoring Billy.

During their second session they were encouraged to speak directly with one another about their perceptions of how the family was working. The therapist noted that Mom and Rose clung to each other and didn't talk much at all with Dad and Billy. Billy was now an active participant, siding with his father as he discussed his feelings of isolation. The suggestion that they play roles was rejected unanimously. The therapist praised the family for acting as a unit and said that later they could try this method for learning to appreciate one another's points of view. At the end of the hour, homework was assigned: Mom and Dad were to leave both children with her parents and go away for the weekend.

The following week, Mom and Dad met privately with the therapist. They sat together on the couch and seemed more affectionate. They were encouraged to spend private time talking about their own feelings for one another ("What drew you together in the first place?") as well as the children. Mom intellectually accepted the idea that she and Dad had to unite regarding child rearing, and that they should let Billy and Rose settle their own differences, interfering only when war threatened.

Within two months, the Briers reported that they were functioning far better as a unit. Billy and Rose played amicably together most of the time, and Dad and Mom, now largely sharing the parenting of both children, had taken another long weekend together.

Couple Therapy

Couple (or marital) therapy rests on the premise that the problem is not with one individual but with how two people interact. The couple can be married or living together, same or opposite sex, but both must be seriously involved in their long-term relationship. A couple may seek treatment when both members want to improve their relationship or when one has lost commitment and wants out. That's why therapists define success as either reducing marital discord or helping the couple recognize that the problems are insoluble—at which point, the therapy may strive to make the best split possible. Sexual therapy is a special form used to help people adjust to one another's sexual needs. Examples of sexual therapy would include a man who has trouble maintaining an erection or a woman who experiences severe pain with intercourse. Sometimes, couple therapy eventually includes children or other family members.

If you and your partner seek couple therapy, the therapist will probably begin by evaluating your shared goals and values, your concern for the other's well-being, your ability to tolerate your differences, and how you share the decision making. The initial interview may take place across three sessions—one with both of you, and a separate session with each. This time-consuming process is necessary to learn how the two of you interact and to explore the problems you each perceive but perhaps choose not to discuss in front of the other.

Although there are many theories and styles of couple therapy, three have been studied enough to demonstrate effectiveness. In most studies, treatment is far more likely than a comparison situation involving no treatment—usually, couples on a waiting list—to produce a successful outcome. No one has yet proved that one type of couple therapy works better than another, or what types of problem (or couple) might respond best to a given therapy. Indeed, many therapists use a combination of the methods discussed here. Some studies suggest that younger couples may have somewhat better outcomes than older ones; and most clinicians would agree that therapy is unlikely to succeed in the face of either physical abuse or chronic infidelity.

To portray the dominant methods used today, we'll discuss Donald and Jean's relationship. Both had told the therapist privately that they were in love and deeply committed to their marriage. Nevertheless, within a few months of their wedding (a second marriage for each), they had settled into a routine of fairly constant bickering. Jean had left her home of 20 years to live with Donald in a distant city, where she felt she didn't fit in. Further, they had the burden of his alimony payments and his 9-year-old son, Ronnie, who was distinctly chilly toward her. Donald felt that she was too passive and didn't express her needs clearly. "If she wants to go to dinner, she should say so," he grumbled, "instead of just observing that a new restaurant has opened in the mall."

Jean had married for the first time to escape living with either of her parents. Her father had been dictatorial and demanding; her mother had responded to his bullying with whining and hysterics. They had separated when Jean was still in school. With her father gone, Jean no longer had a source of support for her education. In fact, she had to emotionally support her mother, who coped with the divorce by forcing Jean to choose between her two parents.

Throughout his childhood, Donald had also endured his parents' emotional strife. His mother stoically refused to be drawn in by his father's ill temper. Donald had always promised himself that he would never shout and argue, as his father did. Instead, whenever his first wife berated him as unsuccessful, he had responded with silence. After several years of this unsatisfying pattern of relating, he had escaped into an idealized relationship with Jean, whom he had known since college.

During their first session together, Donald worried that Jean rejected Ronnie when he stayed with them on alternate weekends. Jean countered that she felt unsupported in her need to visit the friends she had left behind when she moved. "And he makes me arrange our social life," Jean complained, "despite the fact that it's *his* city." "You never made it clear that you resented it," Donald shouted. "I hate you," she sobbed. "Is that plain enough?"

Behavioral Marital Therapy

With over 20 careful studies demonstrating its benefits, behavioral marital therapy is by far the most evaluated form of couple therapy. The therapist takes an active role in focusing on three vital areas of the current relationship.

1. **Behavior exchange**—couples learn to strike bargains whereby both members gain something of what they want, and later show appropriate recognition.
2. **Communication skills**—the partners learn to listen actively to one another and express themselves while neither accusing nor blaming.
3. **Problem solving**—partners learn to identify problems, create a list of possible solutions, negotiate over the best choice, then implement and evaluate it.

Often, cognitive therapy approaches are incorporated into the matrix of the therapy. The behavioral approach usually takes place over just a few months.

A behavioral marital therapist would assign Donald and Jean homework tasks to help them obtain more satisfaction from their relationship. For example, to address Jean's need for more responsiveness from Donald, every Monday evening they were asked to talk about their perceptions of the marriage and their plans for the coming weekend. In return, once a week Jean would ask to be taken out to dinner. During the course of their therapy, they would practice talking in measured tones, phrasing their comments so as to avoid blame and anger. Next, they might begin work on improving Jean's relationship with Ronnie.

Insight-Oriented Therapy

This technique assumes that unconscious forces determine behavior, even extending to the selection of a mate: we tend to choose a person whom we believe will compensate for some part of us that seems to be missing. We feel unhappy if our partner fails to fill this void or in some way mirrors earlier relationships we had with our parents or a former spouse or lover. Bringing these feelings to light and correcting them could take a year or more.

An insight-oriented therapist might focus on Jean's reaction to Donald's emotional distance, which reminded her subconsciously of how she had feared abandonment when she was a student. Donald, in turn, feared that his relationship with Jean had begun to go the same way as his first marriage—she, nagging, and he, retreating into silent resentment. He didn't realize that, on one level, he would prefer a mate who was serene and cool, like his mother. The therapist would help each recognize and express these feelings and realize how their emotional needs fit those of the other.

Emotionally Focused Therapy

Increasingly, research demonstrates the value of emotionally focused therapy (EFT), which is based on the theory that people have inborn needs for security and trust (attachment). It acknowledges that members of a couple need one another and, in fact, have interdependent needs for emotional support—for feeling protected and special. When a couple comes for treatment, usually one partner is so emotionally distant that the other, feeling insecure, nags or lashes out in anger. The other partner defends too vigorously or withdraws further. The therapist seeks to improve communication and increase awareness of feelings. It is important to hear not just the words but the emotional content of what is being said— "listening with your heart," some therapists call it. Similar in some ways to insight-oriented therapy, EFT is briefer and focuses on issues of dependency, insecurity, and vulnerability.

Donald and Jean's EFT therapist would recognize the emotional content of their strife. When Jean said, "I hate you," she was feeling fearful that she would be abandoned. Once Donald understood that, he could more readily support her need for security. At the same time, the couple would explore Donald's vulnerability concerning his son and his need for support as he tried to reestablish his relationship with the boy.

Counseling

People often wonder how psychotherapy differs from counseling. Counseling is really just an all-purpose term for a process that involves giving advice and information. These are also elements of psychotherapy, but most psychotherapy has a better-defined agenda and is directed toward a diagnosed mental disorder or the resolution of symptoms. Counseling tends to be briefer, uses methods that are less technical, and seeks to resolve acute problems or crises. It requires far less education and, in most cases, no certification at all—anyone who can hang a shingle can start charging for counseling sessions.

Psychotherapy Combined with Drug Therapy

In contemporary mental health care, drugs and psychotherapy are often used together. The emphasis may vary—more medication for one condition, greater reliance on psychotherapy for another. Especially for severe or longstanding mood and anxiety disorders, scientific studies have repeatedly shown that the combination of psychotherapy and medication often works better than either modality by itself. The question sometimes arises, should one therapist or two provide the different therapies? Of course, that will depend largely on the therapist. A psychiatrist who is well trained and experienced in both medication and psychotherapy could provide both ends of the treatment, perhaps as effectively and certainly more efficiently than two different providers. (It worked for Tony Soprano.) However, in many health care settings, a psychiatrist handles the medicine and a psychologist or other professional handles the psychotherapy. In such a case it is vitally important that your two clinicians coordinate your health care by conferring frequently.

STAYING ON TRACK IN THERAPY

Once into the routine of psychotherapy, it is easy to make it a regular part of your week without giving a lot of thought to its effectiveness. Perhaps the mere act of going makes you feel better for a few hours, though all the reasons for starting in the first place remain. Don't let the fact that you like your therapist deter you from taking the occasional hard look at your progress.

Let's say you've been in therapy for several months. Ask yourself, "How am I now, compared with when therapy began?" Pick a number of target symptoms, such as sleep, appetite, panic attacks, or the frequency of arguments with relatives or coworkers; be sure to include the problems that made you seek therapy in the first place. For each symptom, score a plus (meaning progress toward meeting your goals), a minus, or "no change." Don't ignore other changes that weren't part of the reason for starting treatment—improved work output, perhaps, or a warmer relationship with a neighbor. Try to involve your spouse or a close friend in this evaluation process, but ask for a truthful evaluation: "Be frank with me, and *please* don't be afraid to say 'You're worse than ever' or 'You haven't changed a bit,' if that's the case."

In addition, take an objective look at your therapeutic relationship. Do you feel like a collaborator in your own treatment, working jointly toward goals you agree upon? I'd hope you could describe your therapist as warm, supportive, and open to your ideas; "cold, uninterested, and inattentive" would be cause for serious concern. At the same time, your therapist should be willing to express constructive views that are contrary to your own. One characteristic you definitely want to avoid in a mental health clinician is a "yes person," which might only reinforce some of the personality traits you need to change. More than mere absolution, you want guidance. On a more subjective level, I'd expect you to feel angry sometimes (it's a natural response when confronting your own behavior and emotions); you may also sometimes feel foolish. But thoughts such as "I'd like to quit!" or "What am I doing here?" would weigh heavily on the negative side of the balance.

Now consider your own evaluations and those of your spouse or close friend. If the evaluations don't appear mainly on the plus side of the ledger, you and your therapist have fodder for much discussion to sort out what is wrong and how to put it to rights. What does your therapist hope to accomplish in the next few sessions? How will this goal be evaluated? Ask for a plan, which may involve changing the focus of your treatment. (Ordinarily, you should expect to see some improvement in symptoms within the first 4 months of treatment.) If you decide to pursue the same course a little longer, how much time are you prepared to spend? A few weeks might be reasonable; many months would not. If you can't agree on a plan, you may need a second opinion.

As you navigate this psychotherapeutic sea, you should keep in view additional landmarks that constitute a sort of code of conduct for therapists:

- A responsible therapist keeps the relationship professional. Not everyone calls patients by their last name (e.g., Mr., Mrs., Ms. Wilcox), but I find it is a useful and constant reminder of the nature of the relationship. Of course, there must be no social interactions outside of office hours.
- A responsible therapist treats you with respect. Although sometimes you might leave your session feeling upset or even angry, it shouldn't be the norm. If you do become angry, your therapist shouldn't respond in kind but should help you examine your anger to learn about yourself and your relationships with others.
- Your therapist shouldn't just tolerate your questions but welcome them and provide you with answers that are factual and thoughtful, not automatic or glib.
- Your therapist shouldn't make decisions for you but facilitate your own decision-making process.
- Your therapist should create a roadmap of your treatment, which you will update at intervals, so that both of you are fully aware of where you are going, how you plan to get there, and how soon you will arrive.
- Your therapist must be willing to examine your plans objectively and point out possible downsides. Contrary to what a person who has never been in therapy might believe, you don't go to a therapist just for validation but for the opportunity to grow.

CHAPTER 14

Behavior Modification

When Jeff appeared for therapy, he was nearly crying because he couldn't pass his driver's license exam. He drove perfectly well (he said) and he had aced the written, but each time he went out for a road test, he became petrified with fright. "The examiner would make little marks on my record as we drove—he almost seemed to grow horns and a tail," Jeff commented. "I don't like to take drugs, and I can't afford the time for psychotherapy—there must be something that can help me."

In fact, a whole field of treatment is devoted to problems like Jeff's. Behavior modification therapy is based on theories of how all animals, humans included, learn to fear and avoid certain objects or situations. This type of psychotherapy focuses on what can be observed, rather than on the more speculative workings of the mind. Theories of behavior emerged during the early part of the 20th century, when scientists discovered that they could produce fear by a procedure called "conditioning." In effect, they were teaching the habit of fear. These experiments revealed two kinds of conditioning: classical and operant. The first type has had more immediate consequences for treating mental illness, so we'll talk about it first.

CLASSICAL CONDITIONING: OF DOGS AND RATS

Early in the 20th century, the Russian physiologist Ivan Pavlov performed his well-known experiments with dogs. When any dog is fed, of course it salivates. Immediately before feeding his dogs, Pavlov rang a bell. After a few days, the sound of the bell reminded the dogs of dinner, and they would salivate, food or no food. They had come to associate the sound of the bell with food. (This is the same principle that advertisers exploit to link smoking with sexiness and alcohol with good times.) This type of learning was described so long ago that for decades it has become known as "classical conditioning."

In 1920, American psychologist J. B. Watson reported how he had trained 11-month-old Albert to fear a white rat by making a loud noise behind him when the rat approached. Watson later reported that Albert also showed fear of other white furry things—evidence of what is now called "stimulus generalization." For obvious ethical reasons, such an experiment could never be conducted today!

Through the years, many clinicians have felt that, with variations, classical conditioning can help explain anxiety disorders such as phobias, panic attacks, and posttraumatic stress disorder (PTSD). For example, let's say that throughout their ordeal, several hostages in an attempted bank robbery sit next to a loudly ticking clock. Afterward, one man feels panicky whenever he hears a clock ticking, or even a finger tapping or a metronome. Of course, this reaction requires more than the traumatic incident, perhaps experiences in the man's past or something in his genetic makeup, otherwise all the hostages would have similar reactions.

Nonetheless, Pavlov's experiments set a lot of clinicians to thinking: if fear could be created by coupling a noxious stimulus (a loud sound) with something that is not inherently frightening (the white rat), why not use the reverse as treatment? This question has motivated countless clinicians and researchers during the last half of the 20th century, yielding several valuable treatments.

REDUCING FEAR THROUGH BEHAVIOR MODIFICATION

Perhaps the main reason your phobia persists is that you keep avoiding what you are afraid of; you never have the chance to learn how harmless it is. If you exposed yourself to the stimulus for long enough, you might learn that it poses no real danger.

Exposure

The quickest way to break the association your mind makes between the phobic stimulus and your feeling of fear is to face the feared object boldly and squarely. This technique exposes you, through a number of treatment sessions, to small doses of whatever frightens you; it is especially effective for simple phobias such as a fear of animals or being enclosed in an elevator. To get you going, you might start out in the company of your therapist or someone else you trust, who can rescue you from any real danger or if you become too frightened to continue.

Suppose you are afraid of dogs, even small puppies. Every time you encounter one, your heart pounds and you try to put a lot of distance between you and it—preferably including a wall. You consult a behavior modification therapist, who explains the technique and its rationale, outlines some of your likely reactions, and on the first day of treatment brings into the room a small, quiet dog on a leash. Although it is friendly, you want to bolt, but your therapist urges you to stay. "Just touch him on the head," says your therapist. "Too hard? OK, touch me while I touch him on the head." Your terror builds for what seems like hours, but when you look at your watch, only 20 minutes have elapsed. Finally, you begin to calm down as you realize that you aren't being harmed. The next session is a repeat of the previous one, though it doesn't seem as stressful. As you advance through more sessions (and meet new dogs), you become less and less fearful, until you can encounter a strange dog in the park without panic. Forever afterward, though you may never want to own one, you should find that you tolerate dogs pretty well. "Flooding" is a form of exposure that involves sudden immersion, in which you try to resolve your fear in a single, long session. It isn't used much anymore because most people find it so traumatic.

Systematic Desensitization

Confronting your anxiety directly isn't practical in some situations such as fear of taking tests, PTSD, and some social phobias such as fear of public speaking. (And just try to get someone who fears flying near an airport.) Instead of sudden immersion, you might try a toe-in-the-water approach. This more cautious method is called "systematic desensitization" because it gradually reduces your fears by exposing you to them in your imagination. Relaxation (pages 184–185) aids desensitization by reducing anxiety and improving the effectiveness of your imagination.

You and your therapist would begin by making a list of activities related to the fear and ranking them from least anxiety-provoking to most. Then you would repeatedly visualize these scenes, calming yourself between presentations by visualizing a pleasant scene. Gradually, over a number of sessions, you become able to tolerate once anxiety-provoking scenes. The remarkable feature of all this is that as you learn to tolerate the imaginary scenes, you find you can confront your actual fears.

Jeff identified a dozen scenes that caused him anxiety. When arranged in ascending order, they included awakening on the day of his driver's examination, eating breakfast, driving to the exam with his father, waiting for the examiner, seeing the examiner walking toward him, getting into the car with the examiner, and driving with the examiner, who was marking a test paper.

Jeff first focused on the relaxing scene he had chosen—lying in a field of daisies, looking up at fluffy clouds overhead. When his anxiety was at its lowest—rated as a 1 out of 5—he signaled by raising a finger. The therapist asked him to visualize the scene in which he was getting dressed before leaving for the test. His anxiety level shot to 5, so he retreated to the daisies. Back and forth he went, several times, until he was able to visualize that first scene at an anxiety level of 1 or 2. Then he moved on to the second scene. It took six hour-long sessions, gradually moving up his list, before he could visualize himself driving with an examiner (wearing horns and tail) who was marking Jeff's test paper. Shortly afterward, he took the actual test one more time and passed.

Behavior modification isn't a way for someone else to control you. Rather, it helps you better control your own behavior and feelings. Researchers have found that exposure and desensitization are about equally effective, though exposure works better for agoraphobia. Note that you don't have to eliminate the anxiety—reducing it so it doesn't disable you is good enough.

AN ANXIETY SCALE

You'll need a way to communicate the degree of anxiety you are experiencing. Your therapist may suggest something different, but a good method is a simple 5-point scale. If you are using such a scale during relaxation therapy, you can even indicate how anxious you are feeling just by raising the fingers of one hand, as Jeff did.

1 = no anxiety at all ("right on edge of sleep")
2 = some anxiety
3 = severe enough to interfere with the current task
4 = still worse, though not the worst
5 = as severe as you ever imagine

Exposure and Response Prevention

Another technique that uncouples anxiety from its source is exposure and response prevention (ERP), which is especially useful in treating obsessional thoughts that are accompanied by rituals. Suppose an obsession about dirt compels you to wash your hands each time you touch something that could be contaminated—doorknobs and shopping cart handles are typical examples. A behavior modification therapist might ask you to sit on the floor and contaminate yourself on purpose for an hour or so at a time. You wouldn't be allowed to wash your hands, and you could take a shower (10-minute limit!) only every other day.

Such treatment may seem heartless, but it is based on a learning theory model that handwashing actually encourages your fear of dirt. Here's how: washing reduces anxiety rapidly, before you have a chance to learn that no disaster happens when you touch something that has been handled by others and don't wash immediately. When prevented from washing during treatment, of course your anxiety initially increases, but eventually (perhaps after half an hour) it will begin to decline. Your clinician will probably stay with you at first; later, you can do it on your own.

To bring obsessions under control may require up to 15 sessions of ERP that are 90 minutes long. This may seem like forever, but long exposure to anxiety-provoking stimuli produces the best results. You will also progress faster if you practice on your own by imagining the consequences you fear—this will help you learn to think about the imagined consequences without feeling terrified. After all the sessions, you should follow up with your therapist from time to time (in person or on the telephone) to maintain your gains. The majority of OCD patients find that their obsessional thoughts and the urge to perform rituals decline in strength and frequency. At follow-up 2½ years after treatment, 75% of patients in 16 studies were still maintaining the gains they'd achieved in therapy.

Thought Stopping

If you have obsessions without rituals, a behavior technique called "thought stopping" may help. A mental equivalent of response prevention, it works like this: When obsessional thoughts come to you unbidden, anxiety about them fills your thoughts. A thought-stopping exercise can break through these distressing thoughts. One variation is to say "Stop!" either silently or aloud. Another is to visualize your therapist banging a fist on the desk and shouting, "Stop!" Still a third is to wear a rubber band around your wrist; when the distressing thought begins, snap the rubber band, breathe slowly, and begin to think of something pleasant. Each time your distressing thought occurs, quickly start one of these procedures, before panic can set in. Follow your procedure consistently, so as to break the habit cleanly and prevent new anxious thoughts from developing.

Stimulus Control

Sometimes you can limit unwanted behavior by changing the type or timing of the stimulus. For example, if you are a binge eater, clearing the table of food as soon as you've finished your meal removes the temptation to go on eating. Here's another example: Because he cannot understand what he is being asked to do, your demented father often lashes out in frustration. Speaking slowly and clearly may improve his understanding, reducing both his frustration and his aggression.

Guided Mastery

Whereas other behavioral techniques aim to rid you of fear, guided mastery focuses on improving your ability to function, frightened or not. A therapist or friend accompanies you as you face the object of your phobia, offering advice and encouragement of this sort: "You're scared, but with determination and effort, you're going to lick this thing." The technique has proven successful with a variety of specific phobias and agoraphobia.

Suppose your fear of driving over a bridge causes you to take a roundabout route to and from work. Your therapist might help you find someone who had a similar fear, though perhaps not as severe as yours, whom you could ride with and observe driving over the bridge. This process of observing the driver would serve as a model for coping with the threat. Then that person might ride with you as you drive, nearer and nearer to small, less threatening bridges, reminding you when to turn, to keep your eyes directly in front of you, to breathe normally through your nose, to keep on going. If you fail, a briefer trip over a yet smaller bridge could be tried. In discussing the task, your therapist would emphasize that you failed not because you are incompetent but because you initially selected a task that was too hard. Once successful with bridges across streams or culverts, you would move on to ever bigger threats, until you mastered the bridge that thwarted your drive to work.

Habit Reversal

If you have a habit such as a tic, stuttering, or hairpulling that interferes with your social or personal life, your behavior therapist might suggest habit reversal training. Your therapist would first make sure that you could recognize when you were experiencing the habit, and that you could find a different behavior to counteract it. If you had trichotillomania (pathological hairpulling), you might be taught to recognize the tension you typically feel prior to pulling out a strand of hair. Then you would learn to substitute something else, such as clenching your fist. For stuttering, you might be instructed to change your pattern of breathing before you speak and during the time that you are talking.

OPERANT CONDITIONING

In classical conditioning, the response is simple and involuntary (remember the examples of the salivating dog and fearful Albert). In operant conditioning, the response is complex and voluntary, and it comes about as the result of actions taken by those who interact closely with the subject. As children and as adults, we frequently encounter positive reinforcers in the form of attention, food, money, and praise; negative reinforcers common for children are time-outs or a whack on the bottom.

Behaviorists believe that we learn our more complex behaviors through operant conditioning. Here is an example. Mother and 2-year-old Bert are at the supermarket. Feeling out of sorts, Bert whimpers, so Mother quiets him with a fig bar. The next day, in the drugstore, Bert feels just fine, but he remembers the fig bar and tries his whimper. Dad dispenses a piece of candy, and Bert quiets down. As time goes by, Bert learns that whenever he wants something, the first thing to try is whining. Fig bars, candy, and other rewards reinforce his behavior; we say that he has been conditioned to whine.

Although reinforcement can be either positive (reward) or negative (punishment), positive reinforcement is by far the more powerful in shaping behavior. In fact, punishment may only perpetuate many unwanted behaviors, because the child or adolescent might prefer a scolding, say, to no attention at all. Years of clinical research have determined that the best way to get rid of unwanted behavior is to ig-nore it—unreinforced, the child's attention will usually turn to something else.

When unwanted behaviors are too intrusive or too harmful to ignore, a good ap-proach is to restrict access to something the person wants—watching TV, dessert at supper, and the like. This form of punishment works well partly because it motivates the individual with the prospect of reward for the wanted behavior the next time. This is why the time-out is the time-honored method for dealing with unruly behav-ior in children (and hockey players). Operant conditioning is occasionally used to manage mentally retarded adults who intentionally injure themselves, often because they have learned it helps them avoid tasks they dislike. Organizations like AA use operant conditioning to manage addictions by rewarding sobriety with group ap-proval. Patients with eating disorders, including overeating, bulimia, and anorexia nervosa, can benefit from similar applications of behavior modification therapy.

An example: When Camilla (page 288) was admitted to the hospital at age 15 with anorexia nervosa, she had lost about a third of her normal body weight and was on the verge of collapse. Even then, she thought she looked "fat," and every day she asked to go to the gym to work out. Her doctor proposed the following bargain: each day, she would be weighed first thing after getting out of bed. If she had gained a pound, she could work out; if she had gained less than a pound, she must remain on the ward that day. Placing the bargain squarely on the issue of objective weight gain avoided arguments about how much she was eating and whether she was regurgitat-ing it. Within a few weeks, Camilla had gained enough weight to be discharged from the hospital.

RELAXATION TRAINING

One effect of anxiety is that muscles all over the body tense up. This causes vari-ous unpleasant sensations—pain, stiffness, even headache. Of course, it would be wonderful if you could put an end to it by telling yourself (or your loved one) "Don't be tense," but such a direct approach often yields just the opposite. How-ever, your therapist may suggest that you train yourself to recognize tense muscles and bring your responses under voluntary control. The instructions would go something like this:

"Sit quietly in a comfortable chair, feet flat on the floor, hands in your lap. Stretch your legs as far as they will go, then relax and stretch again. Move your toes upward, hold them, then turn them downward, hold, and relax. Repeat. Next, work on your calves, then your thighs. Tense them up tightly, hold, and relax. Now notice how relaxed your legs feel, how calm you are becoming. Then move on to your hands and arms, repeating the above steps." You would progressively relax your ab-domen, chest, hands, and arms, finishing up with your shoulders, neck, and head.

A related exercise is regular or paced breathing. It can sometimes help correct the panic-driven habit of breathing too deeply or too rapidly, resulting in a heaving chest and even worse panic. Patients are instructed to practice breathing from the abdomen (diaphragmatic breathing), inhaling slowly through the nose, then exhaling slowly, at a rate of about 8–12 times per minute. (Lying face down when you first practice helps—it forces you to breathe from the abdomen.) You would use this technique to help you cope as you imagine the scenes that make you anxious or panicky.

Applied relaxation is a multi-step technique that takes several sessions to implement. It is based on the observation that a phobic stimulus causes people to tense up and develop negative thoughts (for example, "I'm afraid I'm going to faint"). The thoughts increase the tension, which in turn makes the thoughts worse. Applied relaxation breaks through this cycle: first you learn to recognize the early signals of anxiety, then use relaxation methods to abort the cycle. The entire process might take half an hour, and you would practice it once or twice a day for several weeks. The techniques can be learned in a group, from audio tapes—or, for that matter, by reading about them in a book.

Of course, we feel better about almost any situation if we are rested and relaxed. A few controlled studies have found that relaxation training also helps relieve the distress of a number of conditions, mental and physical. For example, it appears to be effective in panic attacks, though less so than cognitive therapy. Some studies find that relaxation is about as good as benzodiazepines in treating anxiety. Besides its role in desensitization therapy, relaxation is useful for migraine, tension headache, insomnia, and mild hypertension.

EDUCATION AND TRAINING

The topics of education and training may seem a little odd here, but behaviorists consider education an important tool for treating mental disorders. Simply explaining the meaning of some disorders (somatization disorder is a good example) can help patients and families understand that although the symptoms are not their fault, they can take steps to improve their situation. It is hard to modify extremely angry behavior, but education as to the nature of anger can sometimes help people monitor this emotion and modify their responses. If you have a relative with a hair-trigger temper, learning not to respond to an outburst with anger of your own can prevent escalation that might otherwise lead to violence.

Social Skills Training

This special educational model can help people who need to improve their personal interactions. For example, those who have trouble making their needs known or developing romantic relationships can have their social behavior evaluated, probably by a videotape made while holding a conversation. More effective behaviors can then be taught by modeling, role playing, didactics, and video feedback.

Suppose you have been too severely depressed to cope with your boss's demands. The videotape shows that you don't make eye contact when talking with the person who is role playing your boss; your posture is slumped and defeated, your voice is a monotone, and you stammer as you struggle to put into words what you want to say. Your group leader might then encourage you to look your "boss" in the eye and speak out as you make a statement that you have written out in advance. Other problem behaviors to address include what and how much you say and how long you wait to say it. Improving your assertiveness can assist you in a variety of tasks that range from setting limits on pushy family or friends to resisting sales schemes to getting fair treatment at work.

Social skills training is especially helpful for patients who are socially hampered by schizophrenia, social phobias, borderline personality disorder, autism, and mental retardation. These individuals learn to be appropriately assertive without excessive aggression (for example, to request privacy without flying into a rage); to enhance their appearance with better grooming; to receive (and give) compliments; to recognize and accommodate emotions in others; to find alternative solutions to problems; to develop recreational and leisure skills.

BEHAVIOR TECHNIQUES TO AVOID

Some techniques just haven't held up to scientific scrutiny. I recommend that you avoid them in favor of the more reliable methods already mentioned.

- **Biofeedback**, in which a machine continuously reports your pulse, respiration rate, or the electrical conductivity of your skin, has been used for years to manage disorders that are believed to result from stress, including headache and high blood pressure. It probably does help control some physical conditions such as urinary incontinence and jaw pain, but it hasn't been proven to add anything to relaxation training other than expense. Nonetheless, it continues to be offered as a treatment for depression, anxiety disorders, failing memory, and many other problems.
- **Aversion therapy** (such as a painful electric shock or a medication that produces nausea) was used years ago in an attempt to condition people to change undesirable behaviors (substance use and homosexuality were two prominent targets). Obvious ethical issues aside, it is clear now that, at best, aversion techniques work no better than less unpleasant treatments. Often it doesn't work at all.
- **Mass practice**—having a person do something over and over again until boredom sets in—once seemed an effective remedy for phobias, but there is no evidence that it produces sustained improvement.

• **Energy therapy** and **thought field therapy** are touted in popular literature and on the Internet. They purport to treat phobias and a variety of other conditions in the briefest of time periods by channeling energy flow associated with painful thoughts. This is accomplished by tapping on various body parts that introduce "vibrational energy into energy meridians." No scientific studies confirm that these methods are better than placebo.

• **Eye movement desensitization and reprocessing** (EMDR) is widely used to treat PTSD. In this type of treatment, you would focus your attention on the body sensations, feelings, and negative thoughts you associate with some past traumatic event. At the same time, your therapist would move a finger back and forth about twice each second, for up to half a minute, while you followed the motion with your eyes. You would report any changes in how you feel. Then you would be asked to focus on more positive thoughts while you perform the same eye movements. Although the procedure seems to help, recent evidence suggests that the effective component is exposure to the traumatic event; the eye movements themselves may not be relevant. The future of this treatment remains in doubt.

• **Hypnosis** is a state of consciousness best described as highly focused attention, to the exclusion of other stimuli. (Contrary to popular belief, it has nothing to do with sleep.) Hypnotherapy has been advocated for treatment of a variety of physical and mental disorders, including depression, bereavement, overeating, insomnia, anxiety disorders, and the addictions. On the web you can even find it touted for bipolar disorder, OCD, and Alzheimer's; its widely reported abuse in recovered memory cases has provoked legal action. Despite the enthusiasm of its adherents, scientific evidence for the medical benefits of hypnosis is thin, with one exception: pain. Double-blind studies have found that hypnotherapy helps reduce the need for medication in patients experiencing pain from disease or surgical procedures. However, hypnosis is not a proven remedy for the conditions described in this book, and it can actually cause harm in dissociative disorders. If you've used it and it helps, fine, but there are better, proven approaches.

TABLE 14.1. Indications, Advantages, and Risks of Psychotherapy and Behavior Modification Therapy

a well-established efficacy b some evidence c supplementary therapy Used for:	Cognitive-behavioral therapy	Interpersonal therapy	Psychoanalysis	Psychoanalytic psychotherapy	Group therapy	Family therapy	Couple/family therapy	Exposure	Systematic desensitization	Exposure/response prevention	Thought stopping	Stimulus control	Guided mastery	Habit reversal	Operant conditioning	Relaxation training	Social skills training	Relapse prevention
Agoraphobia	a							a								b		
Alcohol abuse					b													
Anorexia nervosa	b					b									a			
Bipolar disorder	b				c	c												
Body dysmorphic disorder	b																	
Bulimia nervosa	a	b														b		
Chronic fatigue	a																	
Cocaine use																		b
Dementia													c					
Dysthymic disorder	b	b																
Generalized anxiety disorder	a																	
Hairpulling														b				
Heroin use						b												
Insomnia												b				b		
Major depression	a	a			c	c												
Marital discord							a											
Mental retardation																		c
Obsessive–compulsive disorder	a							a	b									
Pain management															b			
Panic disorder	a															c		
Personality disorder	b	b	b	b	b													c
Posttraumatic stress disorder	a								b	b								
Schizophrenia	c	b			c	c											c	
Smoking cessation	b				b							b						
Social phobia	a	b						a	b							c	c	
Somatization disorder		b			b													
Specific phobia	b								a	b			b			b		
Stuttering															b			
Tic															b			

PART THREE

MENTAL DISORDERS

According to a 2001 survey, only about one in five clinically depressed or anxious Americans has ever received treatment. Some people just don't realize they have a mental health disorder; they need information on symptoms and diagnosis. Others self-treat with prayer, rest, or health-counter remedies; they need scientific data on the course and management of their conditions. All of this is the sort of information Part III provides for the disorders that cause about 95% of mental health consultations.*

After a clinician has diagnosed your disorder (or that of your relative) and proposed treatment, you may want to review information in Part III to make sure you understand the illness and what it entails:

Do the symptoms mentioned there describe what you are experiencing, or do you still have some question about your diagnosis?

What can you expect in the coming months and years?

Does what is known about the cause of your disorder prompt you to alter your environment or to warn relatives that they could be affected, too?

Are there proven treatments other than those your doctor recommends that you should consider?

Asking these questions will help you form a fruitful partnership with your mental health care providers and build toward a successful outcome. Of course, some men-

---

*If you or a family member has been diagnosed with a disorder not included in this book, you might consult a librarian for standard psychiatry texts and other books or articles that can help you, or browse the Internet for information.

tal disorders respond more readily to treatment than others, but we can offer relief and hope for all.

If you haven't yet learned what is wrong, the following chapters may suggest possible diagnoses. However, only a qualified mental health professional can eliminate the myriad possibilities to pinpoint what is wrong. You may have more than one disorder, as many people do. Certainly, your experience of any disorder will be unique to some extent, so don't expect to find your "twin" in the pages of this book. Consider Part III a jumping-off point to proper diagnosis, effective communication with your mental health care providers, and, above all, treatment that will ease your symptoms and help you reclaim your life.

CHAPTER 15

Depression

Depression is more than just feeling sad; it is a profound gloom that seems never to end, a feeling that you are all alone in your misery. Severe depression invades the mind and chases away all other thoughts. Often, there are also physical symptoms, such as weeping, troubled sleep, and loss of appetite and weight. People experience depression in many ways, from mild moodiness to the "Black Dog" of Winston Churchill, who suffered from depression throughout his life. However, with modern treatment it doesn't have to linger or even cause serious inconvenience. And if you are one of those whose depression tends to recur, you can enlist the help of a variety of medications and other treatment programs to keep you well. In this chapter and the next, we explore each of these themes to help you understand why mental health professionals so often speak of the "good news" about depression.

A lot of people need this good news. Up to 25% of adult women and 12% of men will experience clinical depression—one serious enough to require treatment—at some time during their lives. No one really understands the cause of the sex difference, though a cynic might suggest that it is because men and women live with one another. Depression usually begins in a person's 20s or 30s, but no one is immune—children, adolescents, and senior citizens are also at risk. Depression directly costs upward of $12 billion each year in the United States alone, with indirect costs such as lost wages in excess of $30 billion each year.

Unfortunately, many people still go untreated or receive inadequate treatment for depression, perhaps partly because depression is so poorly understood, both by those who have it and by those around them. Over the years a whole family of myths has sprung up to explain depression. These myths have been debunked by research, and I can confidently report some of the things that depression is *not*. For example, if you have depression you are not just imagining it, not is it just "anger turned inward" (as Freud famously stated), nor are you merely reacting to misfortune—in fact, you've probably received bad news numerous times in your life without becoming depressed. Depression is not punishment for sin, it doesn't mean you have a weak character, and you can't "just pull yourself out of it." What's true about depression is that it isn't your fault. Depression is an illness, every bit as much as diabetes or a broken leg. It seems different because so very little about it is visible—you might as well try to view a broken heart.

SOME DEPRESSIVE SYMPTOMS

If you have a clinical depression, you will probably experience a number of symptoms. Some are almost guaranteed, whereas others are less common. Though you probably won't have them all, these are the typical symptoms of mild to moderate depression:

- **Depressed mood.** You feel sad or some equivalent—mournful, blue, despondent, anguished, "down"—or other people think you look depressed. You may cry a lot; time passes slowly and everything looks gray. Clinical depression isn't just a brief "I've had a bad day at work" sort of feeling. It sticks with you most of the time for at least a couple of weeks, and it usually lasts for months.
- **Loss of interest or pleasure in your usual activities.** Life is boring and you care less about things you used to like, such as hobbies, reading, watching TV, or even having sex.
- **Problems with appetite and weight.** When loss of interest extends to food, your appetite declines and your weight drops. However, some depressed people eat so much *more* than usual that they gain weight.
- **Problems with sleep.** You struggle to fall asleep or awaken throughout the night or too early in the morning; you feel tired and grouchy during the day. Some depressed people sleep too much, which clinicians call "hypersomnia."
- **Fatigue.** Even if you sleep well, depression can wear you down until you are too tired to perform everyday tasks.
- **Change in activity level.** Many depressed people become restless, sometimes so agitated that they cannot sit still (pacing, pulling hair, wringing hands). Depression slows others down; some do little more than sit slumped in a chair and stare at the wall. Your own activity level could change in either direction and to almost any degree.
- **Low self-esteem.** In a depressed state, you may feel nearly worthless. Guilt feelings could make you feel your life has been a failure, that you have let everyone down. You might wish that you had been a better person or done things differently.
- **Poor concentration.** When all of your thoughts are painful, it is hard to keep your mind on your responsibilities and other important matters. Even trivial decisions could seem impossibly complicated. One patient said that focusing on a thought was like trying to grasp a piece of soap that kept squirting away.

A severe depression can bring additional symptoms that demand immediate attention:

- **Thoughts of death.** Brooding about death (it can be either a fear or a wish) occasionally can escalate to suicidal ideas or even attempts.
- **Psychosis.** At the extremely severe end of the spectrum, some people experience hallucinations (for example, hearing voices shouting that they are evil or witnessing scenes of torture). Guilt feelings can grow to the point that people believe they deserve to suffer for their sins; I've known patients who believed that they had died and gone to hell. Ideas or beliefs so obviously false are called "delusions."
- **Hopelessness.** At the bottom, you may conclude that you are condemned forever to your own personal corner in hell, that things will never improve.

But you would be wrong. Even without treatment, depressive disease naturally tends to linger for months and then melt away. The problem is, without treatment a lot of damage can be done to your life while you wait for the symptoms to subside. In fact, unless your symptoms are very mild, you should probably seek help—now. Early evaluation and treatment can protect you from the dire consequences of severe depression on jobs, personal relationships, and even your very survival.

HOW SERIOUS IS YOUR DEPRESSION?

For treatment purposes, it is important for a clinician to determine the severity of your depression. Here's a guide to how clinicians think:

- **Mild.** You'll have just a handful of the symptoms I've listed above, and they won't bother you much—you'll still sleep pretty well, and you'll maintain your weight within a few pounds. You'll continue with your work (or school) and family life, but you should nonetheless consider mental health care: depression starts small but can grow fast.
- **Moderate.** You'll accumulate more symptoms, which will begin to take over your life. Sleep fails, so you're tired during the day. You lose weight. Your guilt feelings occupy your thoughts. If you do go to work, you don't get much done; maybe you fight with fellow workers, or avoid them. The future seems bleak and you begin to have gloomy thoughts about death. You need help soon—you're on the cusp of a severe depression.
- **Severe.** Still more symptoms, increasingly extreme. Unreasonable guilt feelings deepen; sleep is a nightmare; appetite has gone; you're on

sick leave from work. You might begin to plan suicide. Perhaps you even have hallucinations or delusions. You must seek help now.

Although I've emphasized the progressive nature of depression, only a small percentage of mild or moderate depressions ever become really severe. The problem is, you only know how bad things will get once your episode is over.

WHAT CAUSES DEPRESSION?

An enormous amount of research has explored the many theories about what causes depression. Here is an overview of the important current thinking.

Heredity

We have known for decades that relatives of depressed people have an increased risk of depression themselves, but is this because mood disorders are inherited, or because something else in the family environment promotes its development? Powerful evidence comes from studying co-twins of depressed patients. Identical twins bear exactly the same genetic information, whereas fraternal twins come from two fertilized eggs and are no more similar genetically than any nontwin brothers or sisters. If heredity were not an important factor in depression, we would expect all co-twins of depressed people to have depression at about the same rates. The finding that identical twins of depressed people have over twice the chance of depression as fraternal twins strongly supports a genetic role. Overall, heredity can explain half to two-thirds of the risk of depression.

Cognitive Theory

According to this model, depressed people think of themselves in negative terms: they feel worthless and helpless, define everything bad that happens as proof of their incompetence, and regard the future as hopeless. An example of this sort of thinking is given in the treatment of Ariel (page 163). The cognitive model has inspired much innovative psychotherapy directed at specific disorders.

Other Psychological Explanations

The history of mental health is littered with psychological explanations of depression.

1. Early psychoanalysts thought that depression occurs when your mind turns angry feelings into sad ones—an interesting idea that is totally unsupported

by facts. In fact, many depressed people feel extreme anger that remits as they recover.

2. Another theory is that a perceived decline in your influence, status, or values provokes depression—but does this loss of self-esteem cause the depression or is it the reverse? Also, many people with apparently high self-esteem (Winston Churchill, Abraham Lincoln, and many others) have become depressed.

3. Some clinicians believe that losing a parent or other important figure in childhood predisposes an individual to experience depression as an adult, perhaps in response to the death of a spouse or the other parent. There are problems with this theory, too. Just after their loss, only about 30% of the widowed report symptoms of clinical depression, and the vast majority of clinically depressed patients have not been recently bereaved.

Depression as a Learned Response

Suppose that depression were learned from past experiences where you were helpless to avoid unpleasant situations. A child who has repeatedly failed (or has *perceived* personal failure) at attempts to master motor skills, scholastic subjects, or a musical instrument, for example, might be at increased risk for depression later in life. This interesting idea, based on experiments done with dogs and rats, has not been tested adequately with humans, but it seems unlikely that it will ever explain even a substantial minority of human depressions.

Brain Chemistry

Deficiencies or imbalances in a variety of neurotransmitters (chemicals that allow neurons in the brain to communicate with one another) have been suggested as the mechanism whereby depression occurs. So far, most of the evidence for the role of brain chemistry has been indirect, though the hypothesis has led to many effective treatments. Another virtue of the hypothesis is that it is compatible with other theories—brain chemistry can explain the final common path for depressions resulting from any of the above causes.

None of these theories can account for every depression. The best clinicians will consider many explanations when evaluating a patient. Sometimes, several factors contribute to the development of individual instances of depression.

IS DEPRESSION EVER NORMAL?

After a really major loss, outright depression seems perfectly normal. Of course, we naturally feel down when bad things happen. A promotion lost or a romance gone awry might cause any of us to feel bad. Suppose you lost your job and couldn't find another. As the months rolled on, you'd begin to feel more and more dejected. Increasingly you'd feel you couldn't provide for your family. After 6 months of rejection, you might feel unable to pound the pavement any longer, looking for work.

Although it could seem that the sole cause of your depression was job loss, a clinician might uncover the fact that your mother had repeatedly been hospitalized for depression when you were a child, suggesting that genetics were as much a part of the cause as psychological factors. And when an antidepressant proved effective in treatment, biochemical factors would seem implicated, too.

As I've tried to suggest, the line between clinical depression and "normal" depression isn't always clear-cut. If you feel down for just a few days and have few symptoms, most clinicians would probably regard you as normal and not in need of treatment. But depression that interferes with your life for long stretches of time is not normal. When low moods drag out for weeks or longer, when symptoms worsen and their number increases, clinicians make the diagnosis of clinical depression and propose treatment. Until your mood improves, it is important not to make major life changes such as getting married or divorced, buying or selling a house, starting or quitting a job, or having a baby. Such changes not only don't cure the depression, but the results may eventually even be cause for regret.

It is normal that most people who have suffered bereavement feel terribly sad, but only about a third of them have many symptoms of major depression. Most don't need mental health treatment—acute grief runs its course as those left behind adapt to a new existence and resume normal life, sometimes assisted by friends or groups such as the AARP Widowed Persons Service (see Appendix A). If depression lasts past 2–3 months, most clinicians would treat for major depression, perhaps emphasizing a specific psychotherapy such as CBT.

DEPRESSIVE DISORDERS

When diagnosing clinical depression, your doctor will carefully consider several subtypes. Such care is important because accurate diagnosis will enable more effective treatment. Here are brief descriptions with references to later expanded discussions. Note that the first five are all variants of major depression.

- **Major depressive disorder.** In this, the most common type of depression, you would have five or more of the symptoms mentioned on page 192. Ranging anywhere from mild to extremely severe, major depression usually lasts under a year (page 197).
- **Atypical depression.** In this variant, instead of insomnia and loss of appetite and weight, you sleep and eat too much. It is a little uncommon, which is

why it is called "atypical"—the symptoms are different from those most people have (page 202).

- **Psychotic depression.** In addition to extremely severe symptoms of major depression, patients develop delusions or hallucinations, sometimes both (page 204).
- **Recurrent depression.** About a third of patients have only one episode of major depression—ever. The rest will have two or more episodes, which will sometimes return frequently (page 205).
- **Bipolar depression.** In addition to typical depressive symptoms, these patients have periods of mania, the emotional opposite of depression—they feel excessively and unreasonably happy, are extremely "hyper" and overactive, and display very poor judgment (page 219).
- **Seasonal affective disorder.** These people regularly have major depression in the fall or winter; in the spring or summer they feel normal, or even better (page 221).
- **Dysthymia.** If you've had just a few depressive symptoms for several years (page 192), you may have dysthymia. This condition is always mild (no suicidal ideas or psychosis), and it may last so long that people just assume it's your personality—"gloomy," "negative," "pessimistic," and the like (page 207).
- **Depression due to medical illness or substance abuse.** The same symptoms as those of major depression can be caused by many medical illnesses or the heavy abuse of substances, especially alcohol (page 208).

Major Depressive Disorder

The official term for the most frequent type of depressive illness is "major depressive disorder," which is a wordy way of saying you have a depression with quite a few symptoms. Here is a fairly typical case.

"It was the insomnia that got my attention," Suzanne said to her doctor. "I've always slept like I was drugged, so when I kept waking up at 3 A.M., something had to be wrong." Recently she had become increasingly listless and had lost interest in the things she usually enjoyed. "I used to have a passion for bridge; now it seems so trivial. I don't seem to have much energy for anything; I just sit, staring out the window. I feel like I've lost my life."

After a medical checkup revealed she was physically healthy (and that she had never used alcohol or drugs), Suzanne was referred to a psychiatrist, to whom she repeated her story. "I've never felt like this before," she said, fighting back tears. "I don't even want to talk on the phone with my friends, never mind see them." Though her weight hadn't varied, she had little appetite; she had stopped cooking, a favorite hobby, and now relied on fast food and TV dinners. Jack, her husband, wondered if she needed a change: perhaps she was just lonely (they lived far out in the desert, and she didn't drive). However, being with people didn't help her shake off the feeling of constant fatigue. She said she'd never before felt so miserable and often found herself crying "over nothing."

For about 5 months, she said, the stress of her job—working at home for a dot-com marketing firm—had been getting to her, so she cut back to part time. "And I've been so irritable with Jack, I'm lucky he didn't just leave me." Instead, he had urged her to seek help, had even made the call for her. "I haven't even had the energy to dial the phone."

The Diagnosis of Major Depressive Disorder

If you are depressed, like Suzanne, you will experience a mood change. You'll probably say you feel depressed, down, blue, or something similar, and almost always you'll experience it as a change from your normal self, not just a worsening of how you usually feel. A few people don't recognize just how unhappy they are; they may only identify a loss of pleasure or interest in activities they used to enjoy. An occasional patient (usually someone older) will think the problem is something physical, like a severe headache or abdominal pain. Clinicians call this "masked depression," and it can require a lot of probing to reveal the real problem.

In addition to low mood, Suzanne reported other typical depressive symptoms: low energy, trouble sleeping, poor appetite, and loss of interest in her usual activities. Her thoughts had become gloomy (she felt she had accomplished nothing with her life), though she wasn't so seriously ill that she had psychotic symptoms or thoughts about dying.

It's the collection of these symptoms appearing together in the same time frame (called a "syndrome") that indicates clinical depression and the need for treatment. Suzanne's doctor also noted that this was her first episode of depression, that she had no substance abuse or medical disorder that could explain her symptoms, and that she hadn't been depressed long enough for dysthymia. All of the information indicated a single episode of major depressive disorder.

Treating Major Depression

With rare exception, treating your episode of major depression won't immediately eliminate it, but it will improve your symptoms so that you feel well. Then the episode eventually goes away completely, and you will no longer need treatment. (It is a little like a person with diabetes who must take insulin to compensate for something missing. However, with depression, the treatment isn't forever, just a few months, and it isn't necessarily medication.)

The brevity of Suzanne's symptom list helped her doctor decide what treatment she should try. She was started on Celexa (page 66) at 20 mg/day. For the first few days she noticed dry mouth and a headache, but neither bothered her enough to prompt a special call to her doctor. As instructed, she did call after a week, but when she could only report that her mood was no better, she was told to double her dose. Within another 10 days her mood was brighter, and when seen in the office 3 weeks later, she was again working full time. To guard against relapse she took the medicine for another 6 months, then gradually reduced it to zero. A year later, off medicine, she was feeling well—and had even learned to drive on the freeway.

Clinicians tend to think of treatment in terms of three phases—an acute phase (the first few days or weeks when you still have symptoms), a maintenance phase (keeping the symptoms at bay until the current episode ends), and, for many people, prevention of future episodes.

Acute Phase. The choice of treatment will depend largely on four factors: its availability, the severity of your symptoms, any treatment that helped you previously, and your own preferences. If your depression is mild to moderate (see sidebar on pages 193–194), the options include psychotherapy, such as cognitive-behavioral therapy (page 162), and medication. Either approach can be very effective; your doctor will help you sort through the pros and cons of each. For example, some people simply don't like the prospect of taking medicine; others see no sense in psychotherapy. Your insurance coverage, available time, or other commitments may also influence the treatment you try, but your own wishes should be the deciding factor.

For several reasons, many clinicians would advise combining medication with psychotherapy to treat a more severe depression. First, your disorder already troubles you a lot, and it could worsen rapidly. You need effective treatment quickly. Second, because you don't know how effective any treatment will be until you try it, using two approaches hedges your bets. Third, people seen frequently in psychotherapy tend to have their questions answered and their doubts assuaged, ensuring that they will take their medicine faithfully and remain in treatment. Combined therapy may be especially important if you have interpersonal or social problems such as disputes with family, friends, or coworkers.

For a severe depression, there is something additional to consider—where is the best place to be treated? Anyone whose depression involves hallucinations or delusions may behave too unpredictably to be safe at home, even if accompanied by responsible adults 24 hours a day. Such a person belongs in the hospital until the psychosis has cleared. Suicidal ideas also suggest hospitalization. Your doctor would want to learn just how serious these ideas were and judge how likely you were to make a suicide attempt. If you had thought about suicide only to reject it, and you otherwise seemed stable enough to remain at home, perhaps you wouldn't need hospitalization. But you would need to see your doctor frequently, perhaps twice a week, until you were out of the woods. If you had made plans to kill yourself, or if you also had severe guilt feelings, marked loss of weight, or other symptoms that seemed especially grave, your doctor would probably insist on hospitalization for a few days, until your safety could be assured.

Someone who is both depressed and psychotic would also be given an antipsychotic medication such as Zyprexa or Risperdal (Chapter 9); an alternative would be to begin a series of electroconvulsive treatments (page 149). Because ECT is the most reliable treatment we have for very severe depression, I would probably urge you to think seriously about it early in the course of your treatment. It is the best way I know to assure a good outcome for the most severe symptoms.

Suzanne's depression was on the mild side of moderate, so she didn't need hospitalization. Because she lived far away from any psychiatrist and had to depend on others for transportation, frequent office visits and psychotherapy were impractical. Instead she was asked to telephone once a week; if her symptoms had been a little more severe, she would have called in at least twice a week. If ever she forgot, her doctor would probably have contacted her.

When Suzanne elected to try medication, her doctor starter her on Celexa. Balancing effectiveness against side-effect profiles, the best first choice for a mild to moderate depression is usually Effexor, Wellbutrin, or one of the SSRIs (such as Celexa). If you couldn't take an SSRI (perhaps due to side effects or because they hadn't worked previously), you might be given one of the older tricyclic drugs, probably one with relatively few side effects, such as Norpramin or Pamolar. With most drugs, your doctor would try to limit side effects by asking you to start with a relatively modest dose and increase it gradually, so as not to overshoot. After a couple of weeks or so, you would reassess the situation together: Had you begun to respond to the medication? Did you have side effects? To what extent? You could be advised to increase the dose. In another week or two, you would assess again. Had you accomplished your goal? If not, a further increase in the dose or a change to another drug might be needed.

If your depression is being treated with psychotherapy alone, don't settle for a nonspecific "supportive" psychotherapy. You need treatment with proven ability to relieve depression, such as either cognitive-behavioral therapy or interpersonal psychotherapy, which may be as effective as medication in mild depressions. Psychoanalysis and psychoanalytic psychotherapy are too slow, too expensive, and too unsure to use as the main treatment for depression.

For most depressions, you'll probably be asked to return for a second visit a week or two later to assess your progress. In second and subsequent visits, you will want to accomplish the following:

- **Report any improvement in your target symptoms.** When the problems you most want your treatment to fix, such as sleep disturbance or poor concentration, begin to recede, improvement is on its way.
- **Assess side effects.** Have any of the side effects you've been warned about appeared? Are they serious enough to require a dose adjustment? Have any other side effects cropped up?
- **Address the effects of stressors.** Family problems, marital discord, illness of

friends, and many other stressful events can complicate your life while you are battling your disease. Depression can create havoc with your personal and interpersonal worlds, so you may have a lot to talk about.

- **Assure family education and support.** Relatives should know as much as possible about your illness, including medications and their side effects. They can also watch for evidence of relapse—usually the same symptoms that brought you into treatment in the first place.
- **Plan for future visits.** How frequent do your psychotherapy visits need to be? If your psychotherapist doesn't also prescribe your medicines, these clinicians should communicate frequently.

Mental health treatment is like a stool whose three legs are biology (medicine and physical treatment), psychology, and society. Take away a leg and the stool tips, and you could fall off. Of course, not everyone requires the same amount of support from each leg. If you have "only" depression, you might rely on medication to see you through. Complicating interpersonal problems could require psychotherapy, whereas job, legal, housing, or other social problems might necessitate social support for you and your family. In general, the more complicated your circumstances, the more care your doctor will take to ensure that your treatment is supported on three strong legs.

When you are acutely depressed, you shouldn't make any big decisions or major life changes. You might be tempted, for example, to seek relief from depression in the high of a marriage proposal or to distance yourself from a spouse you think is making you depressed. Remember that big decisions can have big consequences, and the merit of your decisions may look quite different to you once you are no longer depressed. In most cases, this will require from 3 to 6 weeks, once you begin treatment.

Medical conditions can influence treatment. A variety of heart, kidney, and liver disorders could narrow the choice of medicine (see Table 6.2). All medications carry some risk of fetal deformity, so if you are pregnant, I'd recommend them only if you have no reasonable alternative. If you are pregnant and mildly to moderately depressed, you could try a specific psychotherapy, such as CBT. If you are seriously depressed, your doctor might suggest ECT.

Maintenance Phase. Once your depressive symptoms remit, you enter the maintenance phase of treatment, a period that could last half a year or more. You will need this period of observation and care because no treatment for depression actually cures it the way penicillin cures pneumonia. Even though medicine, psychotherapy, or some form of physical treatment can wipe out the symptoms, your depression is still rumbling along; you just can't feel it. Stop treatment, and you could become ill again—until you reach the end of that episode.

During this maintenance phase, you probably won't want to change anything if your improvement continues, and your doctor would surely advise against it. But what if you start to lose ground? Your first step should be to get in touch with your clinician right away; don't wait until your next appointment. You may need something as simple as a small increase in medication—this worked for over half the patients in one study who, after initial improvement, had developed symptoms again. Or you may need to change medications or start psychotherapy. The main point is that you must continue contact with your clinician at regular intervals—perhaps once a month, if you are doing very well, more often if not—until you are completely free of depression.

Plan to continue therapy for about 6–9 months for a first episode, a little less for subsequent episodes, which tend to be briefer. I've known many patients who, during the maintenance phase, have noticed a sudden change in how they felt ("It was like someone threw a switch"). From that moment on, they "knew" that they were no longer ill. With this unusual, though hardly rare, experience, you can stop treatment. However, most patients cross no such dramatic bar; perhaps 9 months after depression begins, you will probably be asked to try to taper your medication. Tapering means reducing the dose of medicine to see if you can get by with a smaller amount, or increasing the intervals between psychotherapy sessions. If all goes well, further stepwise reductions are in order. There are two reasons you should always taper treatment rather than discontinue it abruptly: (1) If your symptoms reappear, they'll be mild and you can deal with them before they become troublesome, and (2) you'll minimize the discomfort of discontinuation side effects, quite common with the antidepressants and some other medications.

Prevention Phase. In the final treatment phase, you would focus on preventing further episodes of depression. I say "would" because this phase applies mainly if you've had a previous episode of depression. If this is your only episode, you don't know whether you ever will have another. Your doctor will consider a number of factors to help determine your risk of recurrence. It will be a greater risk if you have a family history of bipolar disease or if you've ever had manic symptoms yourself (pages 215–216). If either is the case, your physician will want you to consider prophylactic medication, especially if your episodes have featured serious symptoms, or if they have been close together—months apart rather than many years.

Medication is the only intervention known to prevent future depressive episodes (page 206). You should inform your family and close friends about your mood disorder and the symptoms to watch for. Some patients don't realize when they are becoming ill; their close associates are often in a better position to recognize the recurrent symptoms. Should you ever have a future need, your "early warning network" of family and friends can help you get treatment quickly.

Atypical Depression

Atypical depression means a type of major depression in which certain symptoms (notably, appetite and sleep) are different from what is usual. An example is the best way to illustrate atypical depression. Though everyone always said that she was the ideal mother-in-law, after her son's divorce Alice began to blame herself. She brooded that she had spent too much time worrying about herself and not enough time making her son's wife feel welcome in the family. Now, for more than a month, she had felt "all fuzzy" most of the time, "like I needed to clean off my glasses, but I wear contacts," she explained to her doctor. She had begun to neglect her younger children (two teenagers) and "couldn't care less" at her job, a florist's assistant. "I'd plop the flowers into a glass of water, and if they didn't arrange themselves, that was just too bad," she said. She had used all of her sick leave, and she wondered how long it would be before she was let go. Each day, she felt steadily worse as evening drew near.

Alice admitted that despite lack of appetite, she was eating a lot and had gained about 10 pounds. Though she slept at least an extra hour each night, she felt constantly tired and listless. She spent much of her time crying or accusing herself of being "a terrible mom" and volunteered that her own divorce several years earlier had been all her fault. She told her doctor that she felt she had accomplished nothing with her life and had lost whatever worth she had once had to her family. Alice had recently thought about driving her car off a mountainside road near her home. However, she perked up and felt "almost normal" whenever she was with her best friend, Marge.

Symptoms and Diagnosis of Atypical Depression

Here are three of the main symptoms that make a depression atypical:

1. Whereas the typical depressed patient has a poor appetite and loses weight, Alice ate so much that she gained weight. If she'd had diabetes or high blood pressure, weight gain could have endangered her physical health.
2. The typical depressed patient complains of insomnia, but Alice slept more than usual. (Depressed teenagers and young adults often have hypersomnia.)
3. Depressed people often observe that they feel no better if something good happens to them, but Alice felt almost normal in Marge's company. People with atypical symptoms also sometimes complain that their arms and legs feel heavy, as if weights were tied to them, and even when they are not depressed they may be unusually sensitive to rejection.

Treating Atypical Depression

As with other major depressions, atypical depression responds rapidly to appropriate therapy; even untreated, it will eventually remit. However, Alice had quite a few depressive symptoms, two of which were alarming: the worsening feelings of guilt (though she was not psychotic—she recognized that they were exaggerated) and her thoughts about driving off a cliff. Although she continued to work, her functioning

there was impaired. For her moderately severe symptoms, she was offered both medication and psychotherapy; she started CBT with a psychologist at once.

Alice's doctor started her on 20 mg/day of Zoloft, one of the SSRIs, which often
works well. After 2 weeks of treatment she had improved a little, so it was increased
to 40 mg. Two weeks later, still stalled at "slightly improved," she stopped Zoloft.
For a 2-week washout period she took no medicine at all. The ongoing CBT helped
her through the transition. Then she began Nardil, an MAOI (page 72), with instructions to follow the special diet carefully. A month later she cheerfully reported that
she felt "lots better" and was back at work arranging flowers.

As for social support, Alice needed help in caring for her children until her
mood disorder improved. Although she lived apart from her husband, a social
worker could explore the possibility that he might take the children for a few weeks.
Failing that, family services should be involved, through her county health department or perhaps a religious organization. Marge might also be a resource. Overall,
Alice presents a good example of depression that requires all three legs of the "therapeutic stool."

Psychotic Depression

About 15% of people with major depression become worse and worse, until they
lose touch with reality. They may hear the voices of dead people (hallucinations) or
believe that they have died or are being persecuted by Satan (delusions). We
recognize these symptoms as psychosis, but they seem all too real to these patients.
Because they can react impulsively to delusional thoughts or hallucinated voices,
immediate action is necessary to prevent unpredictable, destructive behaviors,
including suicide.

Brian's wife, Joyce, worked quickly when she found him cleaning the shotgun
he hadn't picked up in years. For weeks, Joyce had been trying unsuccessfully to
persuade her 55-year-old husband to see a therapist. Nearly 3 months earlier, Brian's
mood had darkened and the chores on his almond farm seemed a burden. Mornings
seemed the worst to him—"Another damn day to get through," he would mutter on
his way outdoors. She couldn't even get him to eat his favorite foods, and she looked
on in dismay as he buckled his belt a couple of notches smaller. Although he complained of feeling tired all the time, he would awaken at 2 or 3 in the morning.
When Joyce was awakened by his tossing and turning and asked what was wrong, he
would say he was worried about being in debt. "Of course, we owed a few hundred
dollars on our VISA card," Joyce later told the doctor, "but we pay it off every
month. We own the farm, and there's my paycheck. But Brian insists we're poverty-
stricken, that we'll have to sell out."

As time passed, Brian spoke less and less. When he did talk, he apologized for
all the pain he had caused. Joyce had no idea what he was referring to. Then he began to ruminate about his health. He thought he was going to have a stroke, then

that his heart would stop. Joyce described how he'd get up, feel his pulse, pace around the room, lie down, put his feet up above his head, do anything he could to keep his heart going. He'd ask to have his blood pressure taken several times an hour. "I pointed out that he'd had a checkup last month, but it didn't help."

When Brian brought out the shotgun, Joyce called the doctor, who admitted him to a hospital. By this time, he was barely moving and speaking so slowly that it could take minutes to convey a single thought. When asked whether he planned to use his shotgun on himself, he slowly nodded his head.

Symptoms and Diagnosis of Psychotic Depression

Brian had many severe depressive symptoms, including loss of pleasure in his usual activities, undeserved feelings of guilt, feeling worse in the morning than in the evening, activity level that was severely slowed down, marked insomnia, and a profound loss of appetite and weight. Particularly striking were his delusions: despite good physical and financial health, he remained convinced that he was poverty-stricken and about to have a stroke or heart attack. When delusions or hallucinations do occur, they are not some separate disease but depressive symptoms that require special treatment.

Treating Psychotic Depression

With the right treatment and enough time, even psychotically depressed patients will improve. Brian's psychosis and plans for suicide demanded hospitalization for the sake of safety—no clinician can predict what someone who is psychotic and depressed will do next. Brian's doctor recommended electroconvulsive therapy (ECT; see page 151 for a full account of his treatment). Three weeks later, he went home, recovered. This may seem like a miraculous recovery, but it is not unusual. Nonetheless, patients who fear ECT can instead use an antidepressant and an antipsychotic drug together (neither drug alone is likely to relieve all symptoms). The antidepressant could be one of the newer generation of drugs, though TCAs sometimes work better. However, their side effects and toxicity make TCAs more dangerous, especially for someone who is psychotic or suicidal. When first admitted to the hospital, Brian was probably too ill to get much out of an organized psychotherapy program. However, his doctor would be careful to see him each day and repeatedly assure him (and Joyce) that he would recover.

Recurrent Depression

About a third of patients with major depression will have only one episode—which is plenty, they will assure you. However, the rest will have repeated episodes, sometimes recurring throughout their lives. Although multiple episodes of depression might seem pretty serious, once the problem has been recognized, they are usually managed readily.

Symptoms and Diagnosis of Recurrent Depression

This will be quick. The symptoms are the same as for any episode of major depressive disorder, though they are often severe (profound guilt, suicidal ideas). Most patients recover completely between episodes.

Treating Recurrent Depression

Treating an individual episode is the same as we have discussed previously. Future episodes of depression can often be prevented with antidepressant medications or specific psychotherapy (such as cognitive-behavioral therapy or interpersonal psychotherapy). The final decision is up to you and your family, but your physician can help you evaluate the following factors to determine whether you should protect yourself against another episode.

- Were your symptoms especially severe? You should strongly consider doing whatever is necessary to prevent a recurrence of psychosis or suicidal ideas.
- Have you had three or more previous episodes? Multiple episodes predict greater likelihood of future ones. If you've had only two episodes, but they were serious, your doctor will probably suggest prophylaxis.
- Do your episodes occur every 2–3 years, or even more frequently? If so, you could spend nearly half your future life fighting depression unless you accept prophylactic treatment.
- Were the episodes especially long-lasting or difficult to control? Needing several pounds of cure also argues for the ounce of prevention.
- Was your life badly disrupted? Even a moderately severe depression can lead to divorce or loss of job.
- Do you have a family history of bipolar disease (page 216)? You could be at risk for future episodes of both mania and depression.

If you accept prophylactic treatment, you'll probably continue the same treatment that was effective in the first place. If the treatment is psychotherapy, it could be gradually reduced in frequency, perhaps to once every 3–4 weeks. If medication, it should probably be continued at the same dose (lower doses will often allow breakthrough depression), though clinical appointments can usually be reduced to every 2–3 months. If you have a family history of bipolar disease, a mood stabilizer such as Depakote or lithium would make a lot of sense. If you are pregnant now and previously had a postpartum depression, you might want to start psychotherapy now or take medication after you deliver. Regardless of which form of protection you and your doctor select, use faithfully whatever works best for you; prevention truly lies in your own hands.

Despite long-term protection, you could experience breakthrough symptoms, which would usually prompt your clinician to increase the frequency or amount of your current therapy. However, you might need to take further measures, as discussed under treatment-resistant depression (page 209). Finally, I've had any number of patients ask, "Will I need treatment forever?" I usually reply that *forever* is a long time, and the vast majority of depressions don't require treatment nearly that long. However, if you are one of those with frequent or severe recurrences, long-term treatment will seem a breeze compared to the whirlwind of depressive disease. If you decide to discontinue maintenance therapy, taper very slowly so that you can catch and remedy symptoms of returning depression before they become disabling.

Dysthymia

If you had dysthymia (the formal name is "dysthymic disorder"), you would feel depressed most of the time. Compared with major depression, you would have fewer symptoms and they would be less severe (neither suicidal ideas nor psychosis), but your mood would still be low enough to cause interpersonal or work-related problems. You might have felt this way most of your life since adolescence; many dysthymic patients have told me, "I've always been depressed." Many people go for years without realizing that chronic low mood isn't normal. Some only seek help when they also develop a major depression, which happens frequently. Once the major depression is over, they usually return to their "normal" state of dysthymia—unless it is recognized and treated.

Recognizing it is no mean feat, because dysthymia often seems to be a part of the person. Ira discovered his dysthymia when he and Carol sought marriage counseling. "I knew he was a quiet, private sort of person, even before we got married," she explained. "But he won't even go on vacations with us. Most of the time, I feel like a single parent!"

Ira admitted that he had always felt lonely and isolated. "I've never been self-confident, but she sure hasn't helped matters any. According to her, I've never done anything right with the kids—couldn't even change a diaper properly. It seemed easier just not to be involved." He had always felt inferior to others; any form of rejection could devastate him for days. Carol added that he was reluctant to make decisions and that he always complained of feeling tired. His sleep and appetite had always been adequate and he never had suicidal ideas. "I've never been worse, but I've never been much better, either. It didn't even make much difference when I won ten grand in the lottery."

Symptoms and Diagnosis of Dysthymia

Ira's low self-esteem, difficulty making decisions, and gloomy demeanor are typical depressive symptoms (page 192), but there weren't enough for major depressive disorder. Also, they had lasted far longer than most major depressions; his symptoms seemed almost normal to him. If it weren't for the marriage counseling, he might never have received appropriate treatment.

Treating Dysthymia

Ira's counselor referred him to a psychiatrist, who started him on Paxil. If this SSRI drug was ineffective, it would be rational next to choose just about any other antidepressant, including MAOIs. Just as in major depression, specific psychotherapy (cognitive-behavioral therapy or interpersonal psychotherapy) can often either supplement or replace medication. Because dysthymia is often a chronic condition, prolonged treatment may be needed to prevent recurrence.

Regardless of the specific treatment, be prepared for consequences. As Ira and Carol discovered, successful treatment can change the way people feel about themselves. Within 2 weeks, Ira was much better, to the point that he tried to take charge of all the family decisions. It quickly became apparent that he needed psychological help in adjusting to his newfound confidence. He and Carol continued their couple therapy, which eventually helped the family learn to live in a relationship where no one was depressed, passive, or dependent.

Dysthymia is not a dramatic condition. Perhaps that's why it tends to go unrecognized and undertreated, despite affecting about 3% of all adults. However, it can cause a great deal of problems for patients and families. If you have dysthymia, stick with therapy until you improve. Don't be satisfied with "a little better!"

Depression Due to Medical Illness or Substance Use

Many medical conditions can mimic major depression or its variants. The causes include such common disorders as thyroid disease, menopause, migraine, premenstrual syndrome, sleep apnea, and stroke. I could list over 40 such conditions, some of which verge on the exotic—tick-borne Lyme disease, for example. Though it is unusual for these conditions to cause depression, that makes them dangerous—if they routinely produced depression, mental health clinicians would think of them automatically. Instead, it is often only when antidepressants and psychotherapy don't work, or perhaps more serious symptoms of the medical condition appear that we tumble to the correct diagnosis.

On the other hand, depression due to substance abuse is probably a lot more common than most people realize. Alcohol-related disease probably causes more depression than all other drugs combined, but barbiturates, cocaine, heroin, or even nicotine withdrawal can occasionally be the culprit.

Depressions caused by either medical disease or substance use don't need specific treatment, but they do require special care with diagnosis. That's why your clinician must know all your habits, all the facts; something as hidden as closet drinking or as small as a tick bite could provide the clue to the right diagnosis.

A special kind of medically related depression develops in 10–15% of women within a few months of giving birth. The symptoms are apparently related to rapidly falling hormone levels that occur after the expulsion of the placenta; estrogens, taken either orally or by transdermal patch, can sometimes relieve depressive symptoms. Standard antidepressant therapy should also be pursued, though this depressive syndrome should not be confused with the milder and much more common "baby blues," which develops within the first few days after giving birth and remits spontaneously within a week or 10 days.

TREATMENT-RESISTANT DEPRESSION

This isn't a distinct type of depression, just one that treatment appears not to redress. I say *appears* because the biggest two causes of treatment resistance have nothing to do with the effectiveness of your medication or psychotherapy. Most "resistance" is caused by treatment that is inadequate or for the wrong diagnosis.

A few years back I ran into Jon, a friend of many years. He had always been a quiet sort, but that day he seemed a little sadder than usual. "I finally went to see about my mood," he said, "and my GP started me on Prozac. It really seemed like it was going to help, I felt so much better."

"Why is that a problem?" I wanted to know.

"It's stopped working. I'm back to the way I used to feel, though I'm still taking the same dose—10 mg."

Now, Jon must weigh twice what I do, so I told him that 10 mg was a pretty modest dose for any adult. I suggested that he might ask his doctor about taking more. When I saw him again a few weeks later, he had doubled the dose and felt great. And he's been fine ever since.

Jon was getting the right medicine but at the wrong dose—his doctor was too cautious by half. No medication can work well if you take too little, whether for major depression or dysthymia, as was probably the case with my friend. The same might be said for someone who is being seen too infrequently in psychotherapy or by the wrong therapist.

Jon's situation was easily diagnosed in a few minutes of casual conversation, but not all "resistant" depressions yield so readily. Take Earl's experience, for example. For several months he had been treated for depression. His partners in an accountancy firm had voted him out for erratic behavior and lack of due diligence in the practice of his profession. After he and his wife separated, he began treatment with a clinician who first tried an antidepressant, then a mood stabilizer. Nothing worked.

In consultation, I reviewed his history for something his clinicians were missing, and came up dry. Then one evening his wife called and said that he was sounding very depressed, and could I go see him?

When I arrived, Earl was lying on his bed, propped up on pillows with a bottle of whiskey in one hand and his 12-gauge shotgun in the other. The gun was pointed at me but seemed intended for him. It was then that I realized he hadn't been strictly candid about his drinking. Several months, some Antabuse, and a generous helping of Alcoholics Anonymous later, Earl was sober and no longer depressed.

Drugs and other physical methods of treatment are just plain wrong for some depressions. Earl's "treatment resistance" was due to a mistaken diagnosis that led away from management of his drinking problem. I could tell similar stories about patients with other diagnoses—among them, eating disorders and borderline and other personality disorders. Miserable patients and frustrated clinicians result from trying to treat the wrong diagnosis in the mental health field, where the balance between art and science hasn't yet tipped quite far enough.

All of that said, there are still many patients with correctly diagnosed depression who haven't responded to the usual treatments. If this describes you, the following suggestions could point the way to the right treatment. All steps are important, though their order will depend on how you and your doctor judge your needs.

1. Are you receiving enough treatment? If several weeks have yielded little or no effect from your antidepressant, a higher dose of the same medication may be the best next step—especially if you've felt no side effects. If psychotherapy every 2 weeks isn't helping, perhaps you should step it up to a weekly basis.

2. Have you been at it long enough? Although antidepressants can require 6–8 weeks for full effect, in 2–3 weeks you should at least *begin* to feel better. If a month on a normally adequate dose hasn't even begun to produce change, you probably won't have much success with that drug. It's time to move on to something else.

3. Clinical depression is probably more than a single illness. Furthermore, all human beings have individual metabolism and chemical makeup. That's why some patients who don't respond to one treatment will do better with another. Although professional opinions vary, if you haven't done well with your first drug choice, I'd change to a drug in a different class of antidepressants.

4. Add psychotherapy, or increase its frequency, or change its focus or type. If you aren't using cognitive-behavioral therapy or interpersonal psychotherapy, strongly consider changing to one of these modern, effective treatments.

5. Blood level checks can sometimes help. Your metabolism or other factors may be reducing the amount of medication that actually gets into your system.

6. Try an MAOI—they sometimes work when nothing else does.

7. Beyond this point, resistant depressions usually get treated with increasingly complicated collections of medicine. For example, you can augment an antidepressant that has helped some by adding another drug. This strategy is far more efficient,

and possibly safer, than repeatedly stopping one and starting another antidepressant. Lithium plus an antidepressant (TCA, SSRI, or MAOI) is one of the most effective combinations. Other drugs you can add include another mood stabilizer, thyroid hormone, and a central nervous system stimulant such as dextroamphetamine. You could also combine Pamolar or Norpramin with an SSRI such as Celexa. A small 2001 study suggested Prozac plus Zyprexa.

8. By this time a consultant should have thoroughly reviewed your history, physical condition, mental state exam, and previous treatment to see whether another treatment might be effective or that another diagnosis is more likely.

9. Although ECT is often the last treatment option people want to consider, it remains the most effective for severe depression.

By no means is this the end of the road, but it is about as far as I can go in this book. Here is my parting shot: because diagnosis and treatment have improved so much over the past quarter century, "chronic" depression is now really unusual. Don't be satisfied with less than a good improvement.

RECOMMENDATIONS

Here are some of the many factors you and your doctor will have to consider when deciding what treatment to choose:

- **Target symptoms.** If you are agitated or have insomnia, SSRIs should be avoided and a sedating drug, such as Remeron or Serzone, or a TCA, such as Elavil, considered. If you have atypical symptoms, such as excessive sleepiness and increased appetite, either SSRIs or MAOIs may work well for you. Symptoms that appear mainly in the winter suggest bright light therapy.
- **Severity.** If your condition is mild or moderate, consider one of the psychotherapies or a newer medication such as Celexa or Zoloft (they have fewer side effects and drug–drug interactions). If you are more severely depressed, you may respond better to a TCA or Effexor. For a really severe depression (symptoms of psychosis, profound weight loss, or severe risk of suicide), I wouldn't risk delay—I'd go right to ECT.
- **Side effects and interactions.** If you are troubled by sexual dysfunction, either as a symptom of depression or as a side effect of another antidepressant, you might try Serzone or Remeron. Wellbutrin doesn't usually cause weight gain, sexual dysfunction, sedation, or anticholinergic effects such as dry mouth and constipation, and it may be less likely to cause mania. Bright light has few side effects, and the psychotherapies have almost none at all. If you take a lot of other medications, consider Effexor or Remeron, which interact with few other drugs.
- **Associated diagnoses.** If you have depression plus another psychiatric disor-

der (such as obsessive–compulsive disorder or bulimia), treating the other disorder will often address the depression, too. If you abuse substances, take dead aim at that problem first. If you have both depression and an anxiety disorder, consider Paxil or Zoloft but not Wellbutrin. If you need to use an antipsychotic agent, avoid the SSRIs and try a TCA.

- **Previous episodes.** Doctors are fond of saying, "Past behavior is the best predictor of future behavior." If a previous episode of depression responded well to a given treatment, that's what I would start with for a new episode.
- **Compliance.** If you've had trouble complying with treatment, be sure to see your doctor weekly.

And here are some other thoughts on treatment that bear repeating:

- If you have had depressions prior to this episode, you are likely to have another episode later, which strongly suggests that you should use long-term prophylactic treatment.
- It may make sense to use several treatments. Although not all depressions will require both a medication and psychotherapy, combining treatments may improve your rate and degree of recovery.
- For a first episode of depression, the scales tip most favorably toward one of the newer drugs, such as an SSRI or Effexor.
- Sleep deprivation would be reasonable to try if your doctor suggests it and you haven't had much luck with traditional treatment for depression. You would probably use it with lithium or an antidepressant medication.
- I feel that an experimental treatment such as repetitive transcranial magnetic stimulation (page 155) is justifiable if other treatments haven't worked or if your condition is not urgent and you can afford the time and effort.
- Considering the losses that the elderly often must endure, people sometimes think of depression in older people as being understandable; treatable depression may go unnoticed. If you are a depressed older patient, your doctor may suggest a psychomotor stimulant such as Ritalin in a low dose to improve mood, energy, and interest.

HOW TO TALK TO A DEPRESSED PERSON

What Not to Say

There are hundreds of things a depressed person doesn't want to hear, because they seem unbelievable, insincere, or impossible. Such statements are often made by caring people who have no conception of what a depressed patient is going through. In no particular order, I've listed a few of the more common statements.

"Nobody promised you life would be fair."
"If you'd just try, you could pull yourself out of it."
"Hey, everyone feels down once in a while."
"Lots of people have worse problems than you do."
"You have so much to be thankful for."
"Go shopping. That always helps me when I feel down."
"Depression, happiness—it's all choices you make."
"I know just how you feel—I have a bad day now and then myself."
"What you need is a [job] [romance] [new car] [hobby]."
"Just snap out of it."

What a Depressed Person Might Need to Hear

On the other hand, here are some sentiments a depressed person might find entirely appropriate, even helpful, to the healing process. Of course, you should say only what you really feel and make no promises that you don't intend to keep.

"Your doctor says that you'll get over this and be well. And I believe your doctor."
"I've known others who have been depressed, and they got well."
"I can't imagine feeling the way you do, but I can feel how much you are hurting."
"Call me anytime—I'll come over."
"It's OK to [cry] [be depressed] [feel angry], I'll still care."
"I'll see this through with you."
"You are so important in my life."
"I know you can't help the way you feel, and it won't change the way I feel about you."
"When we get through this, we'll still be together."
"I love you."

TER 16

Mania and Mood Swings

About 25% of all people who have episodes of depression will also have the opposite experience—periods of feeling high, hyper, euphoric, and the like. Formally called "bipolar mood disorder," this illness has two main features.

1. As you would expect, there are mood swings to both poles, from depression to mania. The depressions are very similar to those of major depressive disorder (page 197), but eventually there will be a period of abnormal high.
2. Although there may also be long periods of normal mood, without treatment patients with bipolar disorder tend to cycle up and down for many years.

About 2 of every 100 adults have bipolar illness, and if you are reading this chapter because you are wondering if your mood swings are abnormal, the mood disorder that you are most likely to have is bipolar disorder. There are, however, other bipolar mood disorders that are discussed later in this chapter.

Although half of those with bipolar illness can be treated as outpatients, the rest have typical manias that often require hospitalization. We used to call this more severe disorder "manic–depressive disease," but most clinicians today use the term "bipolar I." If you have bipolar I disease and don't get effective treatment, you could lose many years of active, effective life to your illness. Several factors can contribute to such an outcome:

- It sometimes takes years to get the right diagnosis. Remarkably, even with modern criteria and all the publicity these disorders have received during the past 40 years, some patients are still misdiagnosed as having schizophrenia or some other psychosis.
- At any given time, about a third of bipolar patients are not receiving the care they need—some because they feel they don't need treatment between

episodes, some because they don't believe they are ill, even though they are in the middle of an acute episode.

- In addition to the mood swings, it is extremely common for bipolar patients to have other mental problems. When a person has two or more illnesses simultaneously, clinicians say that the conditions are "comorbid." In bipolar disorder, the most common comorbid condition is substance abuse, especially alcoholism.

Bipolar disease tends to begin in the late teens or early 20s, earlier than major depression. It can even start in childhood, and it is seriously underdiagnosed in children. It affects males and females about equally and is no respecter of race, culture, or economic status. I've known it to affect entertainers, factory workers, politicians, and psychiatrists.

Like clinical depression, bipolar disease runs in families and is strongly genetic. If you have a parent, brother, or sister who has had manias, your risk of bipolar disease is greater than that of most people, though the chances are still 80–90% that you won't develop this disease. However, if you've had a depression already and have relatives with mania, your risk of eventually developing mania or hypomania (a milder form) is high enough that you should warn your family and friends to watch for symptoms of mania or renewed depression in you.

SYMPTOMS OF MANIA

As with depression, there is always a change of mood, which usually lasts a week or more. Certain other symptoms will also occur, at various levels of severity.

- **Mood.** The mood of a person in the midst of a manic episode usually seems high, excited, euphoric, or excessively joyful. If mood is only moderately elevated, it can be quite infectious—when you are around someone who is manic (as long as that person isn't *too* high), you feel good yourself. Occasionally, a person will be cross or irritable; many people have told me that they feel pretty uncomfortable when they are manic. Some patients don't always recognize the mood change, but those around them do.
- **Increased activity level.** Everything about manic people tends to be speeded up—they move fast and are constantly busy. Sitting still can seem almost intolerable to them; they make many plans and may start a dozen projects that they never finish.
- **Talkativeness.** Speech is rapid (sometimes it is called "pressured speech"). Manic people tend to talk a great deal, about nearly anything, sometimes for hours on end. They can be so difficult to interrupt that you don't really converse with them—you just listen.

- **Racing thoughts.** So many thoughts occur during a manic phase that even their rapid speech cannot keep up as they jump from one idea to another.
- **Distractibility.** Small diversions—noises outside, a moth at a light bulb—can divert them to a whole new stream of thought.
- **Reduced need for sleep.** They may not sleep much, but often they don't describe this as a problem—why sleep when there is so much to be done?
- **Inflated self-esteem.** Manic people typically feel important and overconfident, describe their accomplishments in glowing terms, and ignore their failings.
- **Psychosis.** Some manic patients become so grandiose as to be delusional. They may believe that they have super powers or that they are celebrities or religious figures.
- **Impulsiveness and bad judgment.** Manic patients typically purchase things they don't need or sign contracts they can't comply with; some have sex indiscriminately. Their actions can create extreme danger for them and those around them.
- **Lack of insight.** Typically, manic patients don't comprehend that they are ill. If you try to explain, they won't believe you. ("How could I be sick?—I feel terrific!")

If you haven't experienced mania personally, you can barely imagine the extent to which such symptoms can interfere with work, school, and personal relationships. Even with modern treatments, some people with bipolar disorders do not fare well. Their acute mania gradually disappears, replaced by chronic grandiose delusions. Alienated from their families, they become less and less likely to get competent mental health care.

BIPOLAR I DISORDER

"Bipolar I" is the term clinicians use for patients who have full-blown manias, as just described. If you fall into this category, you'll probably also have at least one major depressive episode during your lifetime. Occasionally, someone will have only manias, though most clinicians will tell you that, given enough time, all manic patients will eventually have a depression. Some bipolar patients have mixed states, in which they experience a combination of manic and depressive symptoms. On average, bipolar I patients have 8–10 episodes, beginning in their late teens or early 20s and returning off and on throughout life. However, I have known a few patients who had only depressions until quite late in life, when they developed mania for the first time.

When I first met Mercedes on a locked inpatient ward, she claimed that she had been "infiltrated by the devil" and offered to dance at a strip joint in town. During our first interview, she couldn't sit still, talked incessantly, and would only occasionally focus on our conversation. She shouted that she had never felt better in her life and drifted into discussions of paranormal experiences. She was channeling for the spirit of Sylvia Plath and thought I was Barbra Streisand.

I later learned that Mercedes had been first hospitalized at the age of 24, when one day she abruptly abandoned her work station and her shoes, climbed atop her desk, and began to sing and dance. When her supervisor and coworkers tried to talk her down, she fought back. Within an hour, singing ecstatically and reciting poetry, she was transported by paramedics to a psychiatric ward. After treatment with the antipsychotic Thorazine (see Chapter 9), she recovered completely and remained well without any medication for several months. Then she briefly became excited and overactive again before plunging into a severe depression. Although she was briefly diagnosed with schizophrenia, her highs and lows of mood were so typical of bipolar disease that she was soon started on lithium, a mood stabilizer (see Chapter 7). She had remained well until just a couple of weeks before I met her.

Mercedes's current symptoms were typical of a "classical" mania: markedly elevated mood, hyperactivity, talkativeness, distractibility, and poor judgment. She was also grandiose and psychotic. Typically, mania builds up over a week or two. Its social consequences are so dire that it is almost never left to run its natural course, which is to last perhaps 3 months, then spontaneously resolve into either a depression or a normal mood. Even knowing nothing about her symptoms, most clinicians would strongly suspect bipolar I disorder based solely on the course of her illness—episodes of mania and depression separated by periods of normal mood. Mistakes in diagnosis (Mercedes was briefly considered schizophrenic) probably occur less often now than they did half a century ago, which is a great blessing. The consequences of delay in treatment can be devastating in terms of anguish sustained, money spent, and even lives lost. Though people rarely kill themselves while acutely manic, suicide is a tragic potential outcome once a person falls into severe depression.

Treating Mania

Once started on lithium, Mercedes remained well for 9 years. For decades, lithium has been the standard treatment for acute mania, but for some patients it isn't enough—and adding another drug may be necessary. Suppose that after several weeks you have responded only partly to lithium. Your doctor would probably suggest adding a mood stabilizer, such as Depakote or Tegretol. If that didn't work, you might try a different mood stabilizer—poor response to one does not predict poor response to the others. At this point, a very new one (see Chapter 7) might be of value—Lamictal (it has been used and studied the most), Topamax, or Neurontin. Any of these newer drugs by itself can also be effective in treating mania.

If agitated or psychotic, you would most likely be given a benzodiazepine such as Klonopin or Ativan (Chapter 8) to manage the severe insomnia, agitation, or panic that often accompany mania. If you didn't respond well to the benzodiazepine, one of the newer antipsychotic medications such as Zyprexa (Chapter 9) might be the next step. Once used routinely, the older antipsychotics (Thorazine, Haldol) are still sometimes needed, but their potential for serious side effects has dropped them into a backup role. For the rare patient whose mania doesn't respond adequately to any medication, ECT will probably normalize mood.

Preventing Future Episodes

You can take important steps yourself to prevent further episodes of either mania or depression. First, take your medication faithfully—treatment noncompliance often leads to a recurrence of bipolar disorder. Attending a mood disorders clinic (page 169) every month or two may remind you of the problems you had when you were ill and help motivate you to stick with treatment. Also, there is something about meeting with a group of other people who have had similar problems that usually helps people feel better about their illness.

Because relapse is likely within half a year of a first mania, you should probably begin maintenance therapy right after your first manic episode. Of course, you could wait to see whether you will be one of those lucky enough to avoid a relapse, but do you really want to take that kind of chance? You'll especially want to prevent a recurrence if you are young, when you need to get through school, start a job, and raise your family. Manias tend to be more common in younger people, depressions in older, and mania is by far the more disruptive of the mood swings.

Which drug is likely to help you the most? If you have had relatively few episodes and they are typical of mania—euphoric (not irritable) mood, history of mood disorder in relatives, no current substance abuse—lithium still works the best. It's less effective for patients who have had many prior episodes, who cycle rapidly, who function poorly between episodes, who have a personality disorder (pages 262–263), or who abuse alcohol or street drugs. If you are one of these, your doctor will probably recommend Depakote or Tegretol.

For some, lithium's effectiveness improves with continuing use, but others become resistant to it after a time. (There is some evidence that if you stop lithium for any reason, it may be less effective when you restart.) If lithium doesn't stabilize your mood adequately, adding Tegretol or Depakote often helps, and most patients seem to tolerate these drug combinations well. If you are among the few who continue to have mood cycles despite these measures, the newer mood stabilizing drugs (Lamictal, Topamax, and Neurontin) may help, just as they can for acute mania.

The recurrence of Mercedes's mania that brought her into my care came about shortly after she had started a "sea salt" fad diet, which required her to eat a lot of table salt. Her lithium level, never very high, had fallen almost to zero, and she became increasingly hyperactive, euphoric, and extraordinarily interested in sex. She then thought that lithium made her feel depressed, so she stopped taking it altogether, leading to even more symptoms. We quickly restarted her lithium, and within 2 weeks she had improved enough to return home. I explained that her increased salt intake had caused her kidneys to excrete other salts, including lithium, so that her lithium level dropped and her mood swung up and out of control. Ever since, she has avoided fad diets and has continued to take her lithium, with no recurrence of either mania or depression in over 20 years.

Mercedes's story shows how important it is to let your doctor know about medical illnesses, medications that other physicians might prescribe, and changes in your diet. Although she didn't drink alcohol, many mania patients do abuse it. Maybe they are trying to treat their illness, maybe just trying to enhance the high feeling; I usually suspect the former. In any event, alcohol and other substance use can confuse the picture and even fool experienced clinicians.

Treating Bipolar Depression

If you've had a mania and now you're depressed, you'll need treatment that is a little different from a depressed person who has never had manias. For one thing, many antidepressants can cause a sudden switch from depression to mania, so you should always be on a mood stabilizer. In fact, you may be able to avoid antidepressants altogether by using just a mood stabilizer (lithium, Tegretol, or Depakote, or one of the newer ones mentioned above)—they can often produce a good antidepressant effect without risking a switch into mania. If you need more treatment than this, you could either add a second mood stabilizer or an antidepressant (either Wellbutrin or an SSRI may minimize the risk of a switch to mania). You will probably be advised to taper the antidepressant soon after your depression lifts. Total sleep deprivation for a night (page 154) combined with lithium has relieved some bipolar depressions, though the effect may not last.

RAPIDLY CYCLING MOOD DISORDERS

The average bipolar patient will have fewer than a dozen lifetime episodes, up or down. However, about one in five bipolar patients cycle rapidly, which means that they have at least four episodes of typical depression or mania during the course of a year. Some far exceed even this. For unknown reasons, rapid cycling is especially common in women. If you cycle rapidly, you may have found that traditional antidepressants can cause you to switch into a manic phase or that lithium doesn't stabilize you adequately. Depakote or Lamictal may then be a good choice, even if you are one of those rare persons whose mood swings up or down every 48 hours. Topamax and Neurontin have helped some, and combinations of mood stabilizers may work when a single drug doesn't. The bottom line is, even when multiple treatments fail, other approaches may help. Stick with it.

HYPOMANIA AND OTHER BIPOLAR DISORDERS

Some people have upward mood swings far less severe than the mania discussed above. For this "moderate" sort of mania, clinicians use the term hypomania (*hypo* means *less than*). Hypomanic symptoms aren't as extreme as those of full mania. For example, you may talk loudly and quite a lot, but your train of thought can be interrupted; your increased activity is generally goal-directed and quite possibly productive. You retain insight that something is different or wrong, and you don't have hallucinations or delusions or require hospitalization.

With hypomania, you could have one of two additional diagnoses:

- **Bipolar II disorder.** This designation means that you would have hypomanias and major depressions.
- **Cyclothymic disorder.** Here you would never have severe depression but would alternate between mild depression and hypomania.

Taken together, the hypomanias of bipolar II and cyclothymic disorder are more common than bipolar I (and during some episodes, bipolar I patients may have hypomania), but mania and hypomania are treated about the same. It is only the urgency that is different. However, because they are not so severely ill, people with hypomania sometimes don't bother seeking treatment. Instead, in reaction to swings of mood, they disrupt their lives by moving house, changing jobs, or falling in or out of love. If a major depressive episode develops and is treated, even clinicians may not recognize the need for mood stabilization because the patient seems to have "returned to normal."

For over 10 years, Holly had had mild mood swings once or twice a year. When she was down, she was quietly unhappy and lethargic, had little use for people, and irritated her relatives. After a few months as a recluse, her mood would brighten to a steady, infectious euphoria. Over the next several months, her energy and enthusiasm allowed her to accomplish a great deal ("You can, when you get up at 4 A.M.," she pointed out). She and her husband would go to a lot of parties, and she wrote poetry. When she was 42, her husband finally persuaded her to seek a mental health evaluation. She was surprised to learn that she had a disorder with a name. "I never thought much about it," she commented. "I always assumed it was just the way I was, that there was nothing for it."

What she found for it was lithium, which stabilized her moods. For a time she thought of herself as "productive but dull," but as the months went by she discovered that she was just as creative as ever because she was so much better disciplined. Her daughters told her how much better they could relate to her, now that they no longer had to wonder "where Mom would be from one day to the next."

SEASONAL AFFECTIVE DISORDER

Some people have a particular seasonal pattern to their mood disorder—they feel depressed in the fall or winter and become normal or hypomanic in the spring or summer. In tropical regions, the pattern may be reversed. Although seasonal affective disorder (SAD) is somewhat more likely to occur in the far north, factors such as genetics and climate (heat and humidity in the tropics) may play roles. The diagnosis has special implications for treatment. Another name for it is seasonal mood disorder.

Sal was a junior on a college athletic scholarship when he requested treatment for depression. For 3 years, he had become depressed each autumn. His interest in school, even in playing football, would drop off. He ate less and had trouble maintaining his playing weight, and he complained of insomnia. "I might as well be setting an alarm," he told his doctor. "My eyes click open and there I am, worrying about the next game, or passing chemistry, or whatever." In the spring, it was a different matter. When he went out for baseball, he seemed to explode with enthusiasm. He batted .400 and played in every game. He said that he had loads of energy and felt like "another Babe Ruth."

The symptoms of Sal's fall–winter depression included insomnia, low mood, reduced appetite, loss of interest, and ruminations. Although Sal was by no means incapacitated throughout autumn, his performance was minor league compared to the spring. Springtime hypomania is common, and full remission in the summer is the rule. Note that Sal was not delusional—he only said that he felt like another Babe Ruth, not that he *was* the Bambino.

Although medications (especially the SSRIs) may help patients with SAD, bright light therapy (BLT) is the treatment to try first. This is what Sal did (the report of his BLT is given on page 148). For rapid cycling, you are especially likely to respond if you have atypical symptoms (sleeping too much, increased appetite, feeling worse in the evening). Although it often works quickly, it can take several weeks for light therapy to take effect, so you should begin treatment as soon as symptoms appear. Depending on how severe your seasonal mood swings are, your doctor may also suggest a mood stabilizer for protection.

MOOD SWINGS DUE TO A MEDICAL DISORDER

Medical diseases and substance abuse can cause manic-like symptoms, as depicted in the riveting 1994 film *The Madness of King George*. When he was 27 years old, George III, King of England during the American Revolution, became depressed. He was so melancholic that for several weeks he complained of fatigue and insomnia, and he lost weight. After a month or so, he recovered spontaneously and remained well for the next 23 years.

When he was 50, King George experienced his first psychosis. In the fall of that year he suffered a bout of abdominal pain and fell into low spirits for 4 days, then suddenly became high-spirited and agitated. He spoke rapidly and with intensity, sometimes becoming hoarse from hours of nonstop talking. At times he merely jumped from one subject to another; at others, his speech was incoherent.

He was irritable and so easily offended that Charlotte, his wife, became alarmed and afraid of him. When he was finally, forcibly placed under care, he became markedly hyperactive and lost weight. At times he was abusive, swearing at and even physically fighting with those who tried to restrain him. He slept little, had trouble concentrating, and often appeared worse in the evenings. He thought that London had been submerged in a deluge and ordered his royal yacht to pick up survivors. He sometimes appeared to be depressed, and once he begged his attendants to kill him. He would refuse to take his medications and throw them away.

Although the King's symptoms sound very much like those of mania, he probably suffered from porphyria, an abnormality of the metabolism of blood protein. Blue urine and abdominal pain are among its symptoms. Mood swings can be caused by other medical conditions, including hyperthyroidism, steroid treatment, brain tumors, syphilis, and AIDS. In old age, manic symptoms can be caused by underlying neurological problems such as stroke. Of course, treatment depends on the nature of the underlying disease, which is why anyone with a mood disorder needs a complete physical evaluation as well as competent mental health care.

DO YOU REALLY HAVE MOOD SWINGS?

Some believe that psychiatrists diagnose bipolar disorder too frequently and prescribe mood stabilizers too freely. Mistakes in diagnosis can occur if a clinician thinks someone has an unstable mood due to bipolar disease, when it is really irritability brought on by drug use, personality disorder, even the ups and downs of normal adolescence. Limits on hospital stay or insurance reimbursement may cause clinicians to make a diagnosis too quickly. Then mood stabilizers can end up being used to treat mere moodiness.

What might this warning mean for you? If you are being treated for relatively mild mood swings and several attempts at therapy haven't helped, consider asking for a consultation. Your diagnosis, not your treatment, could be the problem. You may be asked to keep a life chart calendar and rate your moods to help you and your doctor decide whether you really belong in the bipolar ball park.

RECOMMENDATIONS

- Chart your illness to identify a possible trigger—it could be the season or distressing life events—and what seems to help.
- Educate your family to watch for early symptoms of depression or mania, which may be evident to others before they are to you.
- For full-blown bipolar I disease, either Depakote or lithium is a good place to start—both are powerful mood stabilizers. Lithium is inexpensive, excellent for typical mania, and has even been proven effective at preventing suicide; Depakote works faster and has fewer side effects.
- Because of their side effects, antipsychotic agents should be used only for especially resistant manias. If you need something for agitation in addition to the mood stabilizer, use benzodiazepines first; try novel antipsychotics if necessary.
- Prevention is better than any treatment. It is especially important to begin prophylactic medication early (and stay on it) if you have rapid cycling, multiple episodes, or especially severe episodes.
- If you have a relatively mild seasonal affective disorder, try bright light therapy. If you have moderate or severe winter depression, I'd combine bright light with an SSRI.
- For rapid cycling (four or more changes from high to low mood, or the reverse, in a year), try Depakote first; if it doesn't work, try Tegretol.
- In searching for the right treatment, augment rather than substitute. For example, if you are already taking lithium and have depressive breakthroughs, you might try adding thyroid hormone or Tegretol. Some clinicians report fewer relapses with lithium plus Depakote.

CHAPTER 17

Anxiety and Panic

Because it takes so many different forms, anxiety is hard to define. It has emotional, mental, physical, and behavioral effects, some of which you would instantly connect with being anxious and others that you might not associate with anxiety at all. Have you ever felt an uneasy sense of apprehension that you couldn't quite put your finger on? At the same time, you might have lost some of your ability to concentrate and felt nagged by a sense of unreality. You may have had heart palpitations or felt a tightness in your chest. Maybe you couldn't swallow, or your mouth was dry. You might have hyperventilated or felt nauseated. If the anxiety lasted for an extended period, you could have lost interest in sex. Anxiety can be felt as irritability or fear, which could make you lash out. You might feel a strong urge to run or a peculiar inertia that roots you to the spot. Anxiety can also take the form of chronic worry, as if you were trying to control the future by worrying about it.

We have all felt some of these symptoms of anxiety at one time or another, perhaps before a test or public performance or when confronting an unpleasant task or person. As a natural, normal reaction to a perceived threat, anxiety is useful when it is short-lived and relatively mild. It signals us to watch for possible danger, sharpens our senses to help us prepare for upcoming tests or performances, and reminds us to stay on the right side of the law, moral codes, and our relatives. Problems arise when anxiety becomes too intense or lasts too long. Instead of spurring us to run the race of our life or ace an exam, it muddies our thinking and robs us of focus and alertness. Some recent studies have suggested that chronic anxiety may increase the risk of developing heart disease.

Anxiety is a little like food: sometimes it is a struggle to judge how much is too much. Clinicians use a variety of scales and inventories to evaluate anxiety, and you can find self-rating scales on the Internet (see Appendix A). However, they all boil down to an assessment that your worries, tension, fears, and concern about the future somehow interfere with your life.

Over the past several decades, we've learned an enormous amount about the biological underpinnings of the anxiety disorders. We now know that they are the most common of all mental disorders, conservatively estimated at about a 20% lifetime risk for all adults. All are found more often in women than men, a finding that has scientists worldwide scratching their heads. Most seem to run in families and have some genetic basis, but heredity alone can't explain them: life's events and circumstances also play powerful roles. Treatment is extremely effective and getting better. If you have an anxiety disorder, you can expect to get better with psychotherapy, medications, or their combination.

I discuss half a dozen anxiety disorders in this book; there are others less well-identified or less frequently encountered. All have in common one or more of the following features:

- **Anxiety**—an uneasy state of apprehension that exceeds any actual threat you may be facing
- **Panic**—acute anxiety accompanied by bodily symptoms such as racing heart, trouble with breathing, and uncontrollable trembling
- **Phobia**—anxiety where you can pinpoint the cause
- **Stress**—which causes anxiety (or fear)

Panic and generalized anxiety, which often occur without a specific focus, may be symptoms of separate disorders or symptoms of other anxiety disorders. I discuss them first (this chapter). Chapter 18 covers phobias, which have a specific focus and include the following types: specific phobias (fear of relatively tangible objects and situations such as snakes and thunderstorms; page 237), agoraphobia (fear of being away from home or in some other place from which escape seems difficult; page 240), and social phobia (fear of such situations as speaking, eating, or writing in public; page 241). Chapter 19 discusses posttraumatic stress disorder, the classic reaction to stress. Chapter 20 covers obsessive–compulsive disorder, in which anxiety or the effort to counter it causes obsessions and compulsions.

SYMPTOMS OF PANIC ATTACK

A panic attack involves riveting anxiety that creates a characteristic pattern of incapacitating physical symptoms. Everyday "panic" ("I panicked when I thought I'd locked my keys in the car") pales by comparison. True panic attacks can so flood the intellect that we cannot focus our attention, even on extremely important things.

Isaac told his doctor about his first panic attack nearly 21 years earlier, when he was only 16. During an algebra test, his heart had pounded so hard he couldn't concentrate on the paper in front of him. He asked to be excused and stumbled out of the classroom. A few moments later, the teacher found him sitting on the bathroom floor, breathing heavily and clutching his chest. After a hurried trip to his family doctor, he was pronounced well, but ever since he had experienced episodic attacks of feeling acutely frightened and disoriented.

Beginning abruptly and without warning, Isaac's panic attacks rapidly swell to a terrifying climax. His heart pumps so fast that he can't even count the beats and he feels like all the breath has been sucked out of him. Sometimes a pain begins on the left side of his chest and surges like a tidal wave, spilling into his abdomen and pelvis. At first his vision blurs, then narrows until he loses nearly all of his peripheral vision.

Isaac's attacks have occurred in a variety of circumstances—at the theater, on his job as a city planner, while driving to visit his mother. Once he even had one as he and his wife were making love. He may go for several months without much trouble at all, then experience attacks daily for weeks on end. Nearly every time it happens he thinks, "I'm about to draw my last breath." He can sometimes abort his attacks by breathing into a small paper bag, but he feels desperate to find something that will get rid of them permanently.

Isaac's symptoms include trouble breathing, chest pain, heart palpitations, and multiple problems with his vision; other people complain of dizziness or faintness, sweating, numbness or tingling of their hands, hot and cold flashes, or feelings of unreality. During a typical panic attack, patients will experience several of these symptoms and have a foreboding sense that some disaster is imminent. Some attacks are set off by a stressful event, such as seeing a spider or hearing the sound of gunfire. Clinicians call such attacks "cued." Uncued attacks come "out of the blue" without any known precipitant. Some people have both types of attack.

Typical panic attacks usually start suddenly and rapidly build to a peak. The entire episode is usually over in less than half an hour, though it can seem a lot longer if you're afraid that you are going crazy or your heart's about to explode. It isn't at all unusual for severe panic attacks to cause repeated trips to an urgent care center or emergency room.

If you were suddenly attacked by a dog or you realized your 2-year-old was missing from the backyard, it would be perfectly normal to feel the same physiological symptoms I've just described. However, repeated panic attacks, cued or uncued, interfere with one's life. For example, some people persistently believe that they have heart disease, or experience the side effects of medications more intensely than normal. When severe, social and interpersonal lives are interrupted—a student may find it impossible to move out of the parental home, or a spouse may become so distressed that a divorce results. At a minimum, the breathlessness and weakness can force you to lie down or otherwise interrupt your normal routine.

As with most "mental" symptoms, the first step is to make sure that no medical illness can account for them. Contrary to your worst fears, a dire physical cause will hardly ever be the case. Only rarely will panic attacks be caused by thyroid disease, infections such as pneumonia and Lyme disease, low blood sugar, certain types of heart disease, chronic lung problems such as emphysema, mitral valve prolapse, or a rare, adrenalin-producing tumor called "pheochromocytoma." Most of these diseases can be detected by history, physical examination, or simple testing procedures. A medical cause of anxiety attacks is somewhat more likely if attacks begin after the age of 30, if they have begun only recently, or if there are unusual symptoms such as trouble walking, an altered level of consciousness, or loss of bladder control. Attacks can also occur with the excessive use of drugs, including amphetamines, marijuana, and caffeine.

Anyone who has ever experienced a panic attack will definitely feel something is wrong, but one attack doesn't mean that you are going to have more. With a lifetime prevalence of around 10%, many young people have a few panic episodes without ever developing a lasting pattern of repeated attacks.

PANIC DISORDER

If you have repeated panic attacks, your most likely mental diagnosis is panic disorder, which just means a series of panic attacks that no other physical or emotional illness can explain. In panic disorder, attacks may happen only occasionally or many times a week; it isn't unusual to awaken at night with them. They may come in waves—daily for weeks, then nothing for months. Of course, the prospect of more attacks occurring any time, unexpected and unexplained, is enough to worry anyone. Small wonder that people will do nearly anything to avoid them.

Panic disorder has been known by other names for over a hundred years, but only in the last few decades has it been called by its current name. No one knows why women are twice as susceptible as men. Panic disorder runs in families and is at least partly genetic, though many clinicians also believe that we learn to have panic attacks through behavioral conditioning. Still others implicate loss of parents in childhood and loss of important adult relationships as possible psychodynamic causes, but no one really knows for sure. We do know that no racial or ethnic group is immune, that panic disorder usually begins in the late teens or 20s, and that it is more common than you might expect, affecting perhaps 3% of all adults.

What's less common is panic disorder that occurs by itself—most patients have at least one other mental disorder, such as agoraphobia (fear of being in a situation from which you cannot escape) and major depression (which strikes over half). Some people try to control the panic by overusing alcohol or drugs, prescribed or otherwise. If you find it alarming to think that a visit to the doctor could uncover a laundry list of possible disorders, remember that the more you know, the more focused and effective your treatment will likely be. Be sure to tell your doctor about any substance use or other medical problem, no matter how inconsequential it seems.

Although most seek treatment soon after the first attack—panic is just too uncomfortable to tolerate—left untreated, many people follow an up-and-down pattern of symptoms over the years. Frequent attacks for weeks on end may yield to a period of months when they experience essentially no attacks at all. When their symptoms are severe, they may avoid leaving home (agoraphobia) or treat themselves with tranquilizers or alcohol. Of course, all of this can lead to increasingly serious work and social problems.

Treating Panic Attacks and Panic Disorder

Here's why the folk remedy of breathing into a paper bag helps the isolated panic attack: when you are anxious, you tend to breathe more rapidly than your lungs require for gas exchange to take place (oxygen *in*, carbon dioxide *out*). In fact, hyperventilation forces your carbon dioxide level so low that you feel lightheaded or faint, and you may notice tingling or numbness of your mouth, hands, or feet. Bag breathing forces you to rebreathe some of your carbon dioxide, which gradually rises to normal, and your symptoms fade away. Reassurance from your family doctor that your heart and lungs are normal could be all the treatment you need to prevent further attacks.

For actual panic disorder, the treatment your clinician recommends will depend on the severity of your attacks and the presence of other mental conditions—depression, for example. The good news is that treatment is almost always outpatient, and patients almost always improve.

Isaac's doctor approached his panic disorder from several angles, beginning with some education. Isaac felt reassured when he learned that he didn't have a serious physical disease. It also helped to know that panic disorder was a well-known condition that thousands of others had successfully conquered, that he could learn to control the condition that had controlled him for so long. First he was instructed to avoid using nicotine and caffeine, which can worsen panic attacks. Next he was sent to a behaviorist who taught him paced breathing (page 184), then to cognitive-behavioral therapy (page 162). Among other things, he learned to change the irrational thought "I will die" to "Oh, well, I've got those palpitations again."

Isaac also started taking an antidepressant, the SSRI Celexa (page 66), at the very low dose of 5 mg/day. After the first week, he began to increase it by 5 mg/day each week, until he eventually got to 20 mg/day. Several weeks after beginning his treatment, Isaac noticed that he hadn't had a panic attack for days. This wouldn't have been especially noteworthy—he had sometimes gone for weeks at a time without one—but always before, they had seemed to tail off gradually. This time, as he told his therapist, it was as if they had "packed their bags one night and sneaked away."

Most physicians would probably do as Isaac's doctor and recommend an SSRI, because they work well for panic disorder and produce relatively few side effects. If the first SSRI failed, Isaac and his doctor could try a different SSRI, Effexor, or a tricyclic antidepressant such as Norpramin. If he hadn't fully responded, they might have added a beta blocker, such as Inderal, to the SSRI. Monoamine oxidase inhibitors would usually be reserved for those who don't respond to other drugs. Many panic disorder patients are quite sensitive to the side effects of antidepressants—not uncommonly, they cause an initial increase in agitation. That's why Isaac started with a dose less than half that used for depression. This period of hypersensitivity usually lasts a week or 2, after which the dose can be increased slowly until symptoms remit. As with so many other mental disorders, the most frequent cause of nonresponse is taking too little medication.

You'd do well to avoid a variety of other medicines that have been used to treat panic disorder. The risk of tardive dyskinesia (page 118) completely eliminates high-dose antipsychotics. The antianxiety agent BuSpar is ineffective in treating panic. Of the benzodiazepines (Chapter 8), only Xanax has good evidence for effectiveness at reasonable doses. I'd recommend it, except that some people have trouble stopping it. If you must control your symptoms very rapidly (say, you're about to lose your job or you are virtually housebound), then, of course, use a benzodiazepine briefly—but only until the crisis passes.

Even when drugs block panic symptoms, patients often continue to experience anticipatory anxiety (fear of having another anxiety attack) and avoidance behavior. That's why Isaac's doctor also recommended psychotherapy—it could help him control his symptoms right away and later assist him to discontinue medications. Cognitive-behavioral therapy (CBT; page 162) specifically targeted at panic symptoms is at least as effective as medication, and the effect may last longer. Breathing retraining (page 184) to control hyperventilation that occurs with panic attacks is one behavioral component. Patients who don't respond to CBT can consider other forms of psychotherapy, including dynamic psychotherapy for some.

It will probably take several weeks to show improvement, though medication may reduce your symptoms in the first couple of weeks. If you don't see some improvement within 2 months, your doctor will need to reassess the treatment plan. The acute phase of treatment should last about 12 weeks. By the end of this time, you should be experiencing far fewer panic attacks, and those remaining should be much less intense. You could choose either CBT or medication, especially if your symptoms are relatively mild. Combination therapy may be especially indicated if your symptoms are severe, if you have agoraphobia, or if you want the greatest assurance of success. Your doctor may recommend that you start with both and taper medication later in the course of treatment.

Once improved, no one knows for sure just how long treatment should last, so Isaac and his doctor will probably try to discontinue the antidepressant after 12–18 months. If he relapses, which isn't uncommon, they will simply restart medication. Well over half those who complete treatment are well or very much improved. Only about a quarter still have severe symptoms and may require ongoing treatment trials with other therapies. The prognosis is often better if symptoms have been present for just a short time—another excellent reason to begin treatment as soon as the diagnosis has been made.

STRESS AND ITS MANAGEMENT

The relationship between anxiety and stress is complex: stress can cause anxiety (and other ills, both physical and mental), but anxiety is also a symptom of stress. There is powerful scientific evidence for some of these causal relationships, such as when a hard workout immediately precedes a heart attack or job loss leads to depression and anxiety. However, environmental factors can modulate the effect of stress. For example, losing a job may be felt more keenly by someone with no money in the bank.

These intertwining relationships between stress and mental illness provide one motivation to reduce stress in our lives; many people without diagnosable mental disorders are made miserable by the effects of stress.

Prevention

Of course, we may have little control over many of life's most stressful events—death of a relative, separation or divorce, severe illness, being fired, and pregnancy. Even so, there are steps you can take to help reduce the toll stress takes on your health and happiness.

- Make a list of your pressing tasks and start working down the list, beginning with the most important. Having the source of stress enumerated in black and white can help you gain a sense of control over your burdens.
- For each problem, be sure to include all your choices, even if your only alternative is "do nothing." The feeling of no options creates a sense of helplessness and anxiety.
- Interrupt your routine with something you don't have to do—listening to music, reading for pleasure, taking a shower or warm bath, talking with friends. Giving yourself time-outs to pursue a pleasurable activity is a reward that can quickly recharge your batteries.
- Keep regular hours. Nothing stresses the system like "pulling an all-nighter."
- Spend time outdoors. Daylight improves mood, fresh air is bracing, and communing with nature (even in its urban form) helps maintain perspective.
- Eat several small, well-balanced meals each day. Avoid eating at your desk and discussing work at mealtime.

- With their obvious effects on stress and anxiety, do I even have to mention smoking and excessive caffeine?
- Exercise for at least an hour each week.

Treatment

If your best efforts at prevention fail (as they do nearly all of us from time to time), here are some suggestions for helping to keep a lid on your anxiety.

- You'll feel perkier if you are well-hydrated, so drink plenty of liquid (but don't rev your motor unnecessarily: keep alcohol, coffee, and tea to a minimum).
- Practice regular breathing exercises, but avoid hyperventilating.
- Practice time management. In simple terms this means: (1) list your tasks, (2) prioritize them, putting the most important ones first, (3) estimate the time needed for each (add about 10% to each as a cushion), (4) search your calendar for blocks of time for each task, (5) match your tasks to the block available (maximizes efficiency).
- For a few moments, think about something pleasurable you have done lately or would like to do.
- Nothing helps you through tough times like knowing what to do; establish routines (but plan for change).
- Ventilate your frustrations to anyone who will listen, but share your triumphs with someone you love.

GENERALIZED ANXIETY DISORDER

Lyman complained that he kept falling asleep at work. He had first been bothered by daytime sleepiness the year before, when he was still in college. Struggling to finish his senior thesis in psychology, he would stay up writing and revising until nearly midnight. Even then, he would lie awake for several hours, the tension mounting. "I just couldn't seem to turn off the worrying," he later told his therapist. A year earlier, he had two important things to worry about—finishing his thesis and finding a job. Though he had managed to accomplish both, that hadn't stopped the worrying. "Now I'm worried about keeping my job, paying the rent, saving for retirement, and the economy. Last year seems like the good old days."

The worry caused him to feel tense. Most days he noticed the knotted muscles in his neck; at its worst, he felt so agitated that he literally could not sit still. He had tried positive thinking and meditation, but when his mind seized on one of his worries, he found it nearly impossible to concentrate on anything else.

If you are a chronic worrier, at some point you've probably been called a worrywart and advised to "loosen up." If only it were that simple! It is especially hard if your worries have a particular pattern that clinicians call "generalized anxiety disorder" (GAD). This term has been used as a diagnosis for only about a generation, so a lot of research remains to be done. There are three important elements in making this diagnosis—two that must be present, and one that must not.

- **Worry about a lot of things.** If you are a typical patient with GAD, your worries cover a great deal of ground—your job performance, school grades, your children's health, your relationship with a lover, finances—even down to such mundane matters as leaky windows and dry rot in your house. Most of these worries will be personal, though some people fret about world hunger and the risk of earthquakes. These worries are hard to control and extremely durable, typically persisting despite abundant evidence that they won't come true. A healthy bank balance and stable job are no shield against worry about poverty. The pattern of worrying typically lasts for years, though the dominant focus may change from time to time.
- **Physical symptoms.** GAD is always accompanied by physical symptoms that include restlessness, fatigue, difficulty concentrating, irritability, muscle tension, and trouble sleeping. Of these, the increased muscle tension is probably the most specific, but you would undoubtedly be bothered by several physical symptoms.
- **No specific focus.** The third characteristic is the one that must *not* be present; your worries must not occur solely in the context of another mental disorder. If you do have another anxiety disorder, as is often the case, your GAD worries will go far beyond those normally associated with it. For example, if you also have a phobia, you will worry about many problems in addition to whether you could stand the sight of a spider or eat in public; if you have panic disorder, your GAD worries will be in addition to the possibility that you might have a future panic attack. In GAD, the problem isn't what you worry about but the worry itself.

In addition to the sheer number of their concerns, people with GAD tend to worry much of the time; they sometimes feel that's all they ever "accomplish." You may have noted that your worries keep you awake until long after bedtime or awaken you in the middle of the night. However, they probably haven't restricted you from normal activities such as work, school, or a social life, though you may worry about how well you do them and whether you can keep it up.

Around 5% of the general population has GAD. It often begins in childhood or adolescence, though it typically isn't diagnosed until much later. Like most other anxiety disorders, it is no respecter of race or gender, though women are more susceptible than men. (Some report more GAD symptoms before their menstrual periods.) It runs in families, and it may get worse when the person is under stress. Patients with GAD often have major depression, in addition, with substance abuse sometimes an associated problem.

Of course, worrying and anxiety don't always mean a diagnosis of GAD. In fact, most of us probably worry excessively at some time or other, often related to a specific situation: Your mother is sick in the hospital—will she pull through? What with the downturn in the economy, is your job stable? We can worry about weddings or dinner parties, school examinations or dental appointments, and yet be perfectly normal. Such worries are expected, as long as they don't take over our lives, produce physical symptoms, and cause such distress that we cannot function well in our jobs and personal relationships.

Treating Generalized Anxiety Disorder

Some clinicians still aren't sure whether GAD is a genuine clinical entity—perhaps it only indicates a basic trait of anxiety. However, *patients* usually realize that their worries are excessive, and they very much want to combat them. The problem is, there just hasn't been enough research done yet to determine which treatment approach works best—drugs or psychotherapy. Of course, you can use either independently, but if your anxiety and distress are severe, your clinician may suggest both approaches.

Treatment is likely to be a long-term proposition, so I'd start with an approach that could create permanent change. Two psychotherapeutic formats have been about equally successful: applied relaxation (page 184) and cognitive-behavioral therapy (CBT; page 162). Several studies have found that even after these treatments have been completed, patients maintain their gains for many months.

If your symptoms are serious enough to produce intolerable physical or mental symptoms or to interfere with your normal activities, your therapist will probably recommend drug therapy in addition to the behavior modification program. Antidepressants (Chapter 6) have been shown to help the most, and the best studied has been Effexor XR, the only one currently FDA-approved for GAD. If Effexor is ineffective or too expensive, other antidepressants, including the TCAs, may also serve. Medication is usually temporary, but relapses are common after stopping, so your doctor will want to reevaluate your needs every 6 months or so.

If you need more antianxiety ammunition than the antidepressants can muster, consider BuSpar first (page 99). It produces less sedation than the benzodiazepines, enhancing your ability to cope without dulling your senses. Also, one study found that patients maintained their improvement better with BuSpar than with benzodiazepines. However, BuSpar won't start working for at least a couple of weeks, so if you can't wait, use a benzodiazepine in addition. All benzodiazepines (Chapter 8) are about equally effective, but limit their use to a few weeks—after an extended period of use, many patients find them hard to discontinue.

People who have GAD also often have depression, which is usually the more pressing problem, so you'll probably be advised to treat it first. The antidepressant will often be effective for both conditions. If you also have a substance use disorder, you must address it forthrightly, either first or at the same time as the GAD. You will need to find a clinician who is comfortable with and experienced in treating patients who have two major mental disorders, one of them substance abuse.

Lyman began treatment with a form of CBT in which he was encouraged to practice progressive relaxation (page 184) and to restructure the negative thoughts he was constantly having. Although he initially refused medication, after several weeks with little progress, he finally asked for something "to take the edge off." He had tried an antidepressant a couple of years earlier and didn't like the way it made him feel, so this time he started on BuSpar 5 mg three times a day and gradually increased the dose to 40 mg. Several weeks later he reported that he was feeling calmer and more confident. He now approached the CBT and progressive relaxation with renewed zest; within 2 months he could joke, "Now I mainly worry that my improvement won't last!"

To be candid, Lyman's experience may have been somewhat better than that of many patients. GAD has not yet been well studied, so we cannot confidently predict outcome. Untreated, it will almost surely either last and last or, more likely, continue with exacerbations and remissions (though half or more of affected people have only mild or moderate symptoms). With treatment, some symptoms may linger, especially if they are severe. Even if your case is difficult to treat, with medication, psychotherapy, or the combination, you should improve.

RECOMMENDATIONS

For Panic Disorder

- Try CBT first, to see if it works for you. I think it is better to gain personal control over your symptoms than to depend on medications.
- Practice slow (not deep) breathing.
- If you need medication, first try an SSRI, beginning at a very low dose and working up.
- If the SSRI doesn't work, try another SSRI or an MAOI such as Nardil. Wellbutrin and Desyrel probably *won't* work.
- Avoid benzodiazepines, especially Xanax, if you can. If you must use them, try to limit your use in terms of both dose and time.

For Generalized Anxiety Disorder

- For relatively mild symptoms, use applied relaxation or CBT.
- If you need medication, Effexor XR has the best proven track record, though other antidepressants are also effective. For more severe cases, try combined treatment with CBT and Effexor.

- If you need further antianxiety medication and you can wait 2–3 weeks for the effect, try BuSpar.
- Try to avoid benzodiazepines. However, if you do need one and it works for you, see whether you can get by with it on an as-needed (as opposed to regular) basis. Nearly every patient I have ever encountered who has used benzodiazepines has used them responsibly, without abuse. I've had far more patients who try to take too little medicine than who try to take too much.

CHAPTER 18

Phobias

A phobia is a fear of some situation or thing that far exceeds any real threat. Fear is normal if a poisonous spider suddenly appears on your pillow. If you encounter a "Daddy Long Legs" on a basement wall, however, it isn't normal to have a panic attack and refuse ever again to enter that basement. Feeling anxious if you were trapped alone in an underground cavern would be reasonable, but a full-blown panic attack whenever you must drive across a bridge would not. Shyness and stage fright plague many of us, but some people feel so uncomfortable in social situations that they dread leaving home, meeting anyone new, or talking to anyone but close relatives. When imagination makes something benign seem so ominous that fear significantly restricts their behavior, people are diagnosed as having one of three types of phobia: specific, social, and agoraphobia.

Phobias often begin in childhood or the teen years and almost always start by the age of 25. A fairly strong hereditary component has been identified for the phobias, but many experts today will tell you that they probably come about when something acts as a trigger in a person with genetic vulnerability. Several circumstances can pull that trigger: you could directly experience something that subsequently causes you to be afraid (being terrified and alone in a thunderstorm when you are young, for example); you could see someone else react fearfully to storms; you could even become phobic by hearing about someone who has been struck by lightning. The intensity of your reaction may be influenced by how close you are physically to the feared object and how hard it is to get out of the way.

Phobias are different from panic disorder and GAD in that the threat is something you can identify, such as snakes, thunderstorms, using a public urinal, speaking in public, or going shopping. When confronted with the feared stimulus, people may respond with a panic attack, though it could also be just a feeling of intense anxiety or dread, without the physical symptoms typical of panic attacks. Many years ago, before there was effective treatment for phobias, about all mental health professionals could do was to pretty them up with fancy Greek or Latin names. There are over 250 of these, hardly any of which are used anymore. Besides agoraphobia, the two that you may still encounter are acrophobia (fear of heights) and claustrophobia (being closed in).

SPECIFIC PHOBIA

These are the fears most people understand by the term "phobia"—when someone needs comfort during a thunderstorm or dissolves into tears upon spying a mouse. Anticipating harm, embarrassment, or other dire consequences, the person becomes frightened the moment the feared thing appears, perhaps even when it creeps into consciousness. Some people are afraid of more than one object; for example, composer Richard Rogers feared almost anything having to do with travel, including bridges, elevators, and tunnels.

Andrea's fear of flying started on a return flight from a European meeting. The plane was buffeted by high winds, and during the landing she had "a clear vision" that they would be caught in a wind shear and crash. Although she continued to fly, her misery grew with every business trip. She would start to worry several days before she was due to fly. She felt terribly anxious; her heart "banged along something fierce" and sometimes skipped beats. Whenever she stopped to think about an upcoming trip, she had trouble breathing and felt "weak, dizzy, and out of control." Terrifying thoughts about crashing or being hijacked kept her from concentrating on her work.

Her anxious thoughts would come in waves and increase over several days until they peaked on the day of her trip. She had never failed to complete a flight, but it required an almost superhuman force of will. A couple of years earlier, she had taken a course in which she was encouraged to meditate and visualize successful flying, but it never made much difference. She had also tried several medications and self-hypnosis, but she remained fearful. "I know it's way out of proportion," she said, "but job or no job, I don't think I can survive this way."

Like other phobias, fear of flying presents a spectrum of distress. Some people feel only mildly nervous or take Valium; others call themselves "white-knuckle flyers" who will travel by plane only as a last resort. Even then, it may only interfere with vacation plans—after all, you can always go by car and avoid visiting other continents. A few refuse to fly for any reason, creating problems at work or in their personal or social lives. Andrea seems to have been headed in that direction.

Fear of flying is a fairly common type of what are called "situation phobias"; other examples include riding in elevators and driving across bridges. Besides situations, people sometimes fear three other classes of things: animals, conditions of the natural environment (thunderstorms, heights, water); and injury or blood (needles, visits to the dentist). A few other phobias are harder to classify—the fear of getting sick, for example, or, in children, fear of clowns or other characters who wear costumes. Many people have more than one phobia, usually of the same type, such as snakes and spiders.

Many people don't fear the thing itself but the imagined outcome. Andrea feared that the plane would crash with her on it. Those who fear heights visualize a fall; those with spider phobia worry they'll be bitten. One woman who feared crossing bridges worried that an earthquake would strike while she was on a bridge and that she would be plunged into the river below. These fears are not only excessive but unreasonable (logic doesn't resolve them) and lasting (they persist).

Specific phobias are common, affecting perhaps 10% of us at one time or another (women are more likely to have any type of phobia). Animal phobias typically begin in childhood, but most others begin in adolescence or early adulthood. They are more likely to occur in people who have witnessed trauma, been confronted by an animal, been warned repeatedly to beware of certain things, or been trapped in situations such as a small room. Some phobias begin suddenly; others begin gradually and increase in intensity. Unless treated, most are likely to continue indefinitely.

Treating Specific Phobias

Many people successfully cope with a specific phobia by just ignoring it. That isn't hard to do if it is mild enough, but then, most clinicians probably wouldn't dignify it with the term "phobia." Living someplace where you won't encounter the stimulus is another coping strategy. For example, city dwellers don't meet many snakes (of the slithering type), and if you live in the West you'll not often have to endure a thunderstorm. Indeed, most patients seek treatment because of something else entirely—another anxiety disorder, major depression, or substance use problem, all of which can occur with phobias.

However, certain situational phobias demand resolution. Suppose, for example, you lived or worked in a skyscraper and were afraid to ride an elevator above the second floor. The most efficient (though most anxiety-provoking) treatment would be direct exposure, also called exposure *in vivo* (in life), which puts you in direct contact with your fear. Your therapist might start out by walking with you to an elevator in a three-story building and just stand there, talking with you for whatever time it took for your anticipatory anxiety to subside. Next, you might both step inside, with the door open. Riding to the second floor would be the next logical advance, then to the third floor, pausing at each step long enough to allow your fear to climax and subside. Many sessions might be necessary before you could comfortably take elevator trips alone to the top of tall buildings, but once attained, your mastery would probably be permanent.

Direct exposure is also useful for fears of driving, crossing bridges, and other specific phobias. It isn't practical for thunderstorms, which are hard to schedule, but cognitive-behavioral therapy and other techniques can be used, depending on the feared stimulus, your willingness, and your therapist's judgment. Andrea got her treatment for fear of flying through systematic desensitization, much as did Jeff (page 180).

Other than managing associated panic attacks, drugs are hardly ever a useful main treatment for specific phobias. However, your doctor may suggest a low-dose benzodiazepine or a beta blocker (Chapter 8) to reduce anxiety right at the start of your exposure treatments.

A DEADLY FEAR

Any phobia can have serious consequences, but fear of needles has occasionally proven lethal. Its physical danger stems from the fact that it affects a person's physiology in ways not found in any other phobia.

When most people must confront something they fear, their adrenal glands start pumping out adrenaline, which raises heart rate and blood pressure. This is the classic "fight or flight" preparation our bodies use to respond to threats. However, when people with needle phobia encounter needles, heart rate slows and blood vessels in their arms and legs relax. As a result, blood pressure falls, they sweat and become pale, nauseated, and lightheaded; sometimes they faint. Fainting is the body's mechanism to fight low blood pressure—in a horizontal position, your brain gets as much chance at the blood and oxygen supply as your feet. Occasionally, such a patient can die: the loss of blood pressure leads to a heart attack or a fatal arrhythmia.

Fainting as a response to medical care clearly requires treatment. A number of approaches to needle phobia are currently used. If the case is relatively mild, lying down with legs elevated when having an injection or blood drawn may prevent fainting; breathing slowly to prevent hyperventilation may also help. Some people find relief in antianxiety drugs taken before a procedure. Rubbing a local anesthetic cream onto the spot a few minutes before the needle penetrates can reduce the pain and allay anticipatory anxiety. Iontophoresis (a $400 gizmo that draws a local anesthetic into the skin, allowing painless penetration) has worked very well for some patients. Although some people are helped by systematic desensitization, it should only be done in or near a doctor's office, where medical help is quickly available.

No one knows just why some people respond so strongly to the prospect of a needle stick. Its physiological underpinnings and the fact that it seems to run strongly in families suggest that this diagnosis should be completely separate from other specific phobias. The outcome can be dire: the medical literature reports death in a score of patients, and 5% or more of Americans avoid essential care because of it. In this case, there is more to fear than fear itself.

AGORAPHOBIA

The *agora* is a Greek marketplace, but agoraphobia has come to mean far more than just a fear of going shopping. The 10 million or more adult Americans with this condition are afraid of being in places from which escape seems difficult or embarrassing, or where help might not be available if anxiety symptoms develop. Examples include malls, crowds, theaters, and travel away from home—much as it affected Winfield, a 31-year-old accountant.

Winfield's first panic attack had occurred about 5 years earlier when he was flying to Europe on vacation. They had just cleared the U.S. coastline when he suddenly felt he was about to suffocate. His chest hurt, his heart pounded, and he thought he was on the verge of "a true, personal disaster." His head seemed to bob and spin, and his hands trembled so that he couldn't eat his meal. The woman next to him kept pulling away "like she thought I was crazy," but a man sitting behind him suggested that he breathe into a paper bag. He survived the trip with an air sickness bag cupped around his nose and mouth.

When he arrived in Paris, he felt overwhelming anxiety whenever he left his hotel room, which was where he remained for most of a week, venturing out only for meals and a quick trip to the Eiffel Tower. After he returned home he had no recurrences for several months until one evening at a concert he realized that he was sitting in the middle of the second row: it would be difficult to get out if he wanted to. Once again, "everything seemed to be closing in" around him and he expected that he might die or lose his mind. He consulted his general physician, who said his health was good and minimized the problem.

Lately his attacks have occurred frequently, especially if he is in a crowded place like a shopping mall or a football stadium. Just the thought of attending an event like a football game is enough to cause intense anxiety, so he avoids crowded places and spends most of his time at home. He telecommutes to work, but he cannot even go for a drive without experiencing severe anxiety. When he must shop for groceries, he asks his brother or a close friend or neighbor to go with him.

Symptoms and Diagnosis of Agoraphobia

Patients with agoraphobia typically fear being in a place unaccompanied by someone familiar or where escape might be difficult or embarrassing, as from tunnels, bridges, buses, or waiting in line at supermarkets. Winfield had terrible anxiety when he was away from home; when he had to go out, he either found a companion or forced himself to endure, despite severe anxiety. People who are severely ill can become essentially housebound, though they may be able to travel with a trusted companion. The fear seems irrational, even to them, and they may think they are going crazy.

As with Winfield, many patients have panic attacks with their agoraphobia. In fact, that's probably how it often starts. When away from home, you have a panic attack that is subsequently forgotten. However, through a process of generalization, you begin to fear other situations that involve being away from home. Although conventional wisdom holds that agoraphobia is pretty uncommon by itself, it may be more common without panic than we once thought—possibly 3% of the general population. Perhaps only those with panic come in for treatment; those with only agoraphobia stay home.

Treating Agoraphobia

Even if you have typical symptoms of agoraphobia, right away your clinician will want to learn whether you also have another disorder. Panic disorder is present in at least half of people with agoraphobia, and depression and other anxiety disorders are also common. In their quest for relief, many people also turn to the use of drugs or alcohol.

Winfield's physician prescribed Effexor (page 67) for his panic attacks. Within a few weeks they had subsided a lot, but he still remained nearly housebound, fearing another attack if he went out. At that point he was referred to a therapist, who urged him to join a group of patients with agoraphobia for direct exposure treatment (page 179). They made lists of what bothered them the most and ranked the items in order of increasing anxiety. Then they went out in small groups to face their fears.

After the first couple of sessions, one group member reported such marked improvement that he dropped out, but the others continued for 12 weeks. By the end of their sessions, most had improved. In addition to the group therapy sessions, Winfield went out each day by himself, even though it initially caused him to feel shaky and frightened all over again. His panic attacks had already yielded to the medication, and by the end he could go shopping alone and attend theatrical performances once again.

Most people who are treated with exposure therapy improve a lot—they experience reduced anxiety, improved morale, and greater ability to form relationships and pursue work and leisure interests. However, anyone who cannot use the exposure approach may derive help from other treatments, including cognitive-behavioral therapy, assertiveness training, meditation, and relaxation.

SOCIAL PHOBIA

Gordon got into treatment when he was 24 because he had become clinically depressed. On Paxil, his mood improved dramatically; that was when he noticed that he had started blushing again. He had first noticed his problem years ago in a speech class. He was supposed to make a 5-minute speech about his favorite hobby, which was stamp collecting. The very thought of getting up in front of the class dried his tongue like a flannel cloth, so that he felt he couldn't utter a word.

His muscles twitched and he shook so hard he felt glued to his chair. "Even if I could have spoken, I couldn't have physically gotten up to make a speech," he told his doctor. He was supposed to debate a few days later, but terribly self-conscious, he stayed in bed that day. He did well on all the tests but earned only a C-minus in the class because he hadn't given any speeches. "The grade was a gift," Gordon agreed.

As the months went along, Gordon had found that other social situations caused him terrible anxiety. A simple, formal introduction made him blush or stammer. He stopped attending football games, because he knew he'd have to use a urinal when other men were waiting in line behind him. Although he had once envisioned a business career, he eventually took a job writing ad copy so he could work in a cubicle and not meet people. He was especially leery of his boss; though he admitted that she was "a very nice person," Gordon always tried to be out of the office when she came around. If he ever met someone he knew from work, he'd avoid eye contact so he wouldn't get trapped into making small talk, which always left him feeling flustered. He was attracted to women but didn't date—the thought of asking a woman out made him feel weak in the knees. "I know this is stupid, but I'm afraid I'll look like a nerd."

Symptoms and Diagnosis of Social Phobia

One person feels she has disgraced herself in a business meeting; another is intentionally late for a new course in school rather than introduce himself to classmates; a third can't go to a party for fear of appearing an idiot on the dance floor. Like Gordon, people with social phobia often feel as though all eyes are trained on them to detect their smallest mistakes. They experience their distress most acutely with strangers, though for some no social situation seems safe. One woman likened her social phobia to wearing a sheer dress that barely concealed her nakedness yet offered no warmth or protection from the gaze of others. These experiences cause far more distress and disability than garden-variety shyness, which would not be diagnosed as social phobia unless it impaired the individual's life or caused a great deal of distress.

Fear of public speaking ("mike fright") is the most common social phobia; other situations include meeting people, eating in restaurants, using a telephone or public restroom, even writing when in full view of other people. The common thread is that you fear you will do something that will prove acutely embarrassing. The feared situation causes intense anxiety, which can grow into a full-blown panic attack. Of course, the anxiety symptoms only lead to further embarrassment. You know that your fears are irrational, and you hate the low self-esteem you feel after a social encounter.

The anxiety of social phobia attaches itself to three points of your behavior. Of course, there is the activity itself, but just its anticipation can generate automatic thoughts ("I'll look like a complete idiot") that breed fear. If you have social phobia, you harshly judge your own social performances and view others in the same situation as being more capable than you. The result is poor performance, or at least the perception that you perform poorly. And that generates the third point of behavior, avoidance to reduce the anxiety. If you cannot avoid the activity entirely, you may try to blend in with the crowd, so as not to stand out. If you do speak up, it is only with much anxiety, and later on you typically worry about what you said and how you looked.

Because both social phobia and agoraphobia are associated with places where people meet, you may wonder how to distinguish them. (Even therapists sometimes mix them up.) Being with people is what bothers the person with social phobia. Those with agoraphobia aren't afraid of people; they just want to avoid places that have a lot of them.

Social phobia is the third most common mental illness, behind major depression and alcohol dependence. It tends to begin in adolescence or young adulthood. It usually develops slowly, but occasionally it starts abruptly following an embarrassing social event. As with the other phobias, no one knows exactly what sets it off, though it often runs in families. Some patients and their clinicians prefer the term "social anxiety disorder" (an older name for it) and may even become huffy at the suggestion it is anything like a regular phobia. Social phobia patients also tend to have other fears: about half have agoraphobia, 60% have specific phobias. About one in five abuses alcohol (some may drink to combat the anxiety), and like Gordon, one in six has major depression.

Some people with social phobia get along rather well overall because they fear only specific social situations. However, they experience severe anticipatory anxiety when they must confront that special fear. Those who fear most social situations and feel comfortable only with close friends and family are said to have "generalized social phobia"; for them, phobic avoidance becomes a way of life. Untreated, they are more likely to remain isolated and unmarried, perhaps depressed and alcoholic, with limited capacity for work and interpersonal relationships. Still others drink to reduce their discomfort. Social phobia tends to become chronic unless treated effectively.

Treating Social Phobia

Becoming depressed was luckier than Gordon realized, because it got him into treatment—way under half of those with social phobia ever seek treatment. On Paxil, which is the only antidepressant that is also FDA-approved for treating social anxiety, his depression had largely remitted and he felt less panicky at the thought of group cognitive-behavioral therapy (CBT), the psychotherapy most often used. Group therapy for this disorder is logical, because the anxiety can be addressed in a social context, where it naturally occurs. (However, right at the outset, the group leader acknowledged that some patients need greater privacy when working on their social skills.) The group can model behavior for the individual and provide support as well as feedback about some of the automatic, erroneous thinking (contradicting, for example, the belief that the signs of anxiety must be obvious to everyone). Gordon learned to substitute the response "I'd feel nervous, but I could still ask a question" for "I'd look like a nerd." To become more comfortable in social situations, he and the other group members did some role playing and practiced initiating conversations and making small talk.

Some members joined Toastmasters, and all were encouraged to consolidate their gains with homework—for example, giving toasts at dinner or reading stories to friends. Between therapy sessions, they were told to practice on their own what they had learned during role playing. The group leader said that real-life practice is essential to the treatment, but that if someone didn't complete a homework assignment, it just meant that the assignment was too advanced and needed to be adjusted. Gordon felt especially successful when he invited a woman in his group out for lunch.

The treatment strategy your clinician recommends will depend on the severity and extent of the social phobia, as well as the presence of other disorders. If you fear many different social encounters, your doctor will probably recommend pulling out all the stops and using both a drug treatment and psychotherapy, though you may need to work on just one at a time.

Medication is often an important part of recovery. For many people, the SSRIs (Chapter 6) work just fine for social phobia. Though double-blind studies have shown that monoamine oxidase inhibitors (MAOIs) are the most effective medication, their potential for side effects and the diet they require usually put them out of the running for first choice. For those who do use, say, Nardil at up to 90 mg/day, the response rate is over 50%, though it may take 6 weeks or longer to reach full benefit. Serzone, Effexor, and Neurontin are also sometimes used. Some people need medication long-term; others, just long enough to get started with CBT. In either case, the drugs don't *cause* improvement, they only enable it.

If you are one of the countless people whose only difficulty is performing in public or giving a speech, a beta blocking agent (page 99) such as Inderal can prove very useful. Even professional speakers and performers use these drugs to reduce the fluttery feeling of performance anxiety. Though there is little risk that such use will interfere with your performance, avoid hidden surprises by trying it out a few days *before* the chips are down. If you use Inderal, you'll need to repeat the dose after 2–4 hours for continuing effectiveness. If your problem in such circumstances is nausea or fear of vomiting, your physician might prescribe Zofran (ondansetron), which works to prevent vomiting.

Using one or more of the available treatments, the vast majority of those with social phobia will improve. Their anxiety may not be completely eliminated, but it should be reduced to a manageable level. Onset after age 11, advanced education, and absence of other psychiatric conditions all favor a good outcome.

RECOMMENDATIONS

The treatment of all phobias has these steps in common:

- Determine whether there are other disorders (especially of mood, anxiety, and substance use).
- If panic attacks accompany the fear, treat them as discussed in Chapter 17.

For Specific Phobia

- Repeated, direct exposure to the feared stimulus is the most efficient method of getting over it.
- If direct exposure isn't practical, systematic desensitization also works well.
- Other than for associated panic attacks, drugs are usually of little value.

For Agoraphobia

- The best form of behavior modification therapy is repeated exposure to the circumstance you fear. Go repeatedly to the mall (or wherever), and dispense with your companion as soon as possible.
- Other psychotherapies that are potentially useful include CBT and assertiveness training.
- Other than to manage associated panic attacks, drugs are not generally indicated.

For Social Phobia

- Approach severe or generalized social phobia with CBT (often done in groups), social skills training, and exposure to the feared situations.
- Antidepressants are often indicated; SSRIs have the fewest side effects, but MAOIs are somewhat more often effective.
- Performance anxiety can often be combated with a beta blocker such as Inderal, taken 30 minutes before your performance or speech.

CHAPTER 19

Posttraumatic Stress Disorder

If you've ever been in a minor car accident, you've probably had some of these physical reactions. Afterward, your heart beats fast, you feel too weak to stand, you can hardly breathe. Later, perhaps for days or weeks, the squeal of tires or honk of a horn brings it all back to you. Just for an instant, you feel some of the same anxiety you had after your accident, and you'd rather be just about anywhere but on the road. Some people who survive severe trauma develop symptoms that last much, much longer—perhaps even a lifetime—and their symptoms are far worse than the aftermath of your car wreck. This is the syndrome that clinicians call posttraumatic stress disorder (PTSD).

As far back as the American Civil War, similar symptoms were identified in combat soldiers. Earlier names included "shell shock" and "battle fatigue." Now we know that some of the same symptoms develop in those who have survived other natural or man-made disasters. These include airplane crashes, abductions, floods, rape, and terrorist hostage-taking situations. Recently, PTSD has been identified in some patients who have just suffered a heart attack.

The range of circumstances in which PTSD can develop is even wider than I've stated. You wouldn't have to be hurt or even threatened to develop symptoms—watching as someone else dies or is maimed in an accident or attack can provide the traumatic stimulus. Just hearing about something awful, such as a life-threatening illness in someone you know, could also be traumatic. However, the more direct your exposure to a threat, the more likely you are to develop symptoms. In all, perhaps 5% of men and 10% of women have at some time had PTSD.

Aretta was admitted to a VA hospital several months after she had been discharged from the army. While she was on duty at a military base in Germany, a master sergeant had raped her in the mess hall storeroom. Throughout the ordeal, he had clenched a knife in his fist. Afterward, he threatened to kill her if she reported him.

From then on, whenever she was assigned to KP in the mess hall, she tried to avoid the storeroom. If she had to enter it, she invariably cried, her heart beat fast, and her hands shook. She went to sick-call several mornings because of a panicky feeling that her heart would beat "right out of my chest," and she couldn't breathe. Then she discovered that she was pregnant. Though closely questioned, she would never reveal the name of the sergeant who had raped her.

Her pregnancy earned her a general discharge under honorable conditions "for the convenience of the government." Though she begged them, the military physicians had refused to perform an abortion. Once she returned to her hometown to live, she paid for the procedure out of her separation pay. The abortion left her feeling empty and "more guilty than I ever thought possible."

Although Aretta had been told she could have her civilian job back, she never even telephoned her former boss. She returned to her parents' house, where she spent most of the time alone in her bedroom. She reported that she "just sat," because she couldn't really keep her mind on anything, even reading. She wouldn't talk to a friend who had enlisted with her, and she wouldn't watch a comedy about the army on TV. On the rare occasions she helped her mother in the kitchen, she refused to use a knife; it made her think about the afternoon she was raped.

Aretta felt depressed and guilty ("though in my saner moments, I don't believe I led him on"). She often had flashbacks, during which she felt the same fear and horror as on that day; sometimes she seemed to be going through the rape all over again. It usually took her hours to fall asleep; several times she awakened screaming with a nightmare about being trapped in a sealed box.

SYMPTOMS AND DIAGNOSIS OF POSTTRAUMATIC STRESS DISORDER

As with any mental disorder, the symptoms of PTSD vary enormously from one person to another, but four elements will always be present, to one degree or another. Here is how Aretta experienced them:

- A wrenching experience, which would traumatize anyone, caused her to feel threatened, fearful, and helpless.
- After some delay (symptoms often don't begin immediately), she began to relive her experience. She had bad dreams and flashbacks, and she trembled whenever she entered the storeroom. (Some people even hallucinate.)
- Aretta tried to avoid anything that reminded her of her experience, including talking with army friends and even using a knife. (Some people develop amnesia about parts of their experience.)
- Severe insomnia and her difficulty focusing attention on reading repeatedly showed that her body was in a state of unusually high arousal. (Other people startle easily or maintain an abnormally high degree of vigilance.)

Many patients with PTSD feel guilty: "I should have done something to prevent it" may seem irrational, but this attitude affects even combat survivors, who feel guilt and shame that they lived when friends did not. Like Aretta, many patients are also depressed; this symptom is often important in determining what treatment to use.

PTSD—WHY ME?

Why does trauma cause PTSD symptoms in some people but not in others? There are two sorts of reason, one relating to the trauma, the other to the person. Greater injury or threat to life both increase the risk of PTSD. Nearly a quarter of those who survive heavy combat will have symptoms, as will two-thirds of former prisoners of war. Exposure to continuous or repeated trauma increases risk—which is why many schools limited videotape showings of the collapse of the World Trade Center in New York City. PTSD symptoms are less likely to follow forest fires, floods, and other natural disasters.

On a personal level, your risk of PTSD increases with the degree of fear, helplessness, or horror you experience. The presence of a mood disorder or another anxiety disorder also increases the risk of PTSD. Women are at greater risk than men, as are those who suffer a sense of loss of support within their families or in the community. In the case of rape, history of childhood sexual abuse may increase risk of PTSD symptoms. Older adults are less likely than younger ones to develop symptoms, and advanced education may provide some protection. Although not yet well studied, there are hints that genetics could play an important role.

TREATING POSTTRAUMATIC STRESS DISORDER

Even without treatment, about half of PTSD patients recover within a few months, and many others experience relatively mild symptoms. Only about 10% of those who develop PTSD remain ill for many years. Of these, some have symptoms that wax and wane, and only a few seem to become worse and worse. However, if your symptoms have lasted for months or years, you should consider the many options you have for treatment.

The first issue to consider is that PTSD symptoms are a conditioned response. This means that they are involuntary behaviors you have learned during the course of your traumatic experience—a sight, sound, or even smell that reminds you of the event brings on terror and other emotions you originally experienced during combat or some other awful experience. The good news is, you can "unlearn" it with psychotherapy or a behavioral technique.

The current choice of many clinicians is a form of exposure therapy that forces you to confront, possibly in real life but more often through imagery, the events or thoughts that remind you of the event. Aretta's therapist asked her to describe the rape, as if it was occurring at that moment, and to report what she could see in her mind's eye. It took a bit of persuasion before she'd even try, and her first attempt made her cry for the rest of that session. The following day, she felt a little more comfortable, and after a few trials revealed that nothing bad would happen, her anxiety began to recede. To speed things along, her therapist encouraged her to practice confronting her fears just this way when she was alone. You may need quite a few sessions of exposure therapy before you can bear to face some of the situations that set off your symptoms.

Exposure may be too traumatic for some causes of PTSD, such as combat or concentration camp experiences. Cognitive-behavioral therapy (CBT) is probably just about as effective at teaching new ways to respond to something that frightens you. You write down your irrational beliefs and thoughts and figure out more helpful responses, based on a rational interpretation of the events that you devise with your therapist. Regardless of whether you are treated with behavior modification or psychotherapy, you should continue it (with homework) for at least 6 months to solidify your gains. Eventually, you will come to believe that your symptoms are not due to personal weakness but a reaction to severe stress.

If you need medication, as most patients do, especially early in treatment, antidepressants (Chapter 6) are a good first choice because they attack most of the anxiety symptoms as well as the depression that so often accompanies this disorder. Aretta started on Zoloft (it and Paxil are the only antidepressants FDA-approved for treating PTSD). Once she got to 100 mg/day, her mood symptoms and eventually her insomnia improved. However, any of the other SSRIs would probably have worked as well. Some studies suggest that the monoamine oxidase inhibitors (Nardil, Parnate) work especially well for the insomnia and recurring thoughts, dreams, and memories. If you are especially troubled by flashbacks, nightmares, or symptoms of hyperarousal (poor concentration, easy startling), a beta blocker (page 99) such as Inderal could help. If you need still more help, your physician may want you to try a mood stabilizer (Chapter 7); Lamictal has been found to help PTSD symptoms in civilian and military patients. Whatever drug you finally settle on, experience with many patients indicates that you will probably need it for at least a year.

If you've just experienced a traumatic event, an even better approach would be to prevent PTSD from developing. One preventive attempt is through debriefing, in which the incident is reviewed immediately and in detail, with deep probing about the emotions and thoughts experienced during the event. By providing information about common emotional reactions to trauma and stressing the importance of talking about the incident, this approach is supposed to help you heal. Unhappily, careful scientific studies have now shown that one-shot debriefing doesn't prevent PTSD and actually makes some people feel worse. Taking antianxiety drugs just after a severe automobile accident or other trauma doesn't seem to prevent PTSD, either. However, some evidence suggests that starting CBT soon after the trauma may help prevent the onset of PTSD.

Another caution concerns the issue of compensation. One tradition of our litigious society is that, when bad things happen, someone must pay, especially if that someone has deep pockets. Such litigation is likely to be hard-fought and prolonged, and the outcome may depend on how seriously damaged the injured party was. If it appears that you must demonstrate continuing disability to prevail in court, you run the risk of unwittingly prolonging your disability. Balancing your need for recovery with your desire for compensation can pose a real dilemma—one that you should discuss frankly with your therapist.

RECOMMENDATIONS

- Because PTSD results from something that is done to you, it makes intuitive sense to deal with it using techniques that help you regain control over your own body and thinking. Start with exposure therapy or CBT.
- Most people will need an antidepressant. The SSRIs are probably the best first choice for most patients, though MAOIs and TCAs have worked very well for some. Avoid benzodiazepines.
- Whatever therapy you use, stick with it and attend sessions regularly. If you feel no better after several weeks, discuss other options with your clinician.
- Try not to regard yourself as a victim. As soon as possible, return to your normal daily life. To every extent possible, avoid disability payments and other forms of compensation. The dividends they pay in the short run can be vastly overwhelmed by a tax on your future capacity for normal life.
- Right after a severe trauma, such as an automobile accident or sexual attack, avoid debriefing procedures, which have been shown to carry the potential for greater disability. However, starting CBT early may help prevent onset of PTSD symptoms.
- Eye movement desensitization and reprocessing (EMDR) was developed expressly for use with PTSD patients. Although it has been used extensively and with some success, especially among combat casualties, it is probably less effective than cognitive therapy.

CHAPTER 20

Obsessive–Compulsive Disorder

Judy and Peter Digby went for marriage counseling ("divorce counseling," Peter called it) because they fought constantly about their 17-year-old daughter. They agreed on one point: Paulette's problem was tearing the family apart. It started a year earlier when one of her jobs was taking out the garbage. She wore gloves to do this because she had seen a TV show about where bacteria live. Putting on rubber gloves whenever she removed the lid gradually developed into a complicated routine for removing the gloves without touching the outsides of them with her fingers.

She also spent a lot of time in the bathroom. Whenever her mother asked what she was doing, she'd say "nothing," but once she forgot to lock the door. Judy peeked in and saw her scrubbing her hands, even though she had just showered. That evening, Judy confronted her about the 10 trips she had made to the bathroom that day. Paulette cried, "I don't like it, I just can't help it. I just always feel so yucky."

That was several months earlier. Now she washed half an hour at a time, at least a dozen times a day. Otherwise, she wore three pairs of gloves. When she slept, she wore only one ("I might get up and touch something"). She even had special gloves for washing the other gloves.

Every couple of days, Paulette cleaned the kitchen, starting with the sink and stove, working her way through the cupboards, and finishing up under the sink. For the last several months her mother had helped her, scouring the already sparkling floor on her hands and knees. ("She seemed so frantic," Judy explained, "I had to do something.") From her volunteer job at the hospital, Judy had brought home scrub booties, which the whole family had to wear indoors. Paulette had also taped all the doorknobs so that none of the latches in the house worked—she could push or pull the doors open with her wrist. At about that time, two events coincided: her sister Candy, fed up with the home climate, moved out to live with her boyfriend; and

Peter stopped cooperating with his wife's need to "protect" their daughter by joining in her extreme behavior. His wife only redoubled her efforts, which made him even angrier at his daughter. "She's dragged the whole family down," he grumbled. "She makes a production out of what normal people take for granted."

SYMPTOMS AND DIAGNOSIS OF OBSESSIVE–COMPULSIVE DISORDER

In everyday conversation we may casually talk about being "obsessed" with a thought or idea or describe someone's behavior as being "compulsive." What we mean is that the person pursues an idea excessively or insists that something be done a particular way; we're talking about simple exaggerations of normal thinking and behavior. Clinical obsessions are unwanted mental events that shove their way into consciousness, interrupting the normal course of thought; compulsions are mental acts or repetitive behavior that someone feels the powerful urge to perform, usually to decrease the anxiety caused by an obsession. Together, they constitute obsessive–compulsive disorder (OCD), which affects 1–2% of the general population. Paulette couldn't control her thoughts about contamination, and she couldn't resist performing the rituals that momentarily reduced her anxiety about germs. Her story shows the danger of OCD: obsessions and compulsions that absorbed her life, split her parents, and drove away her sister.

Paulette's condition developed so gradually that it took months for her family to seek professional help. At the onset, the problem often seems innocuous, and relatives may try to ease the person's fears, as Paulette's mother did, hoping to erase the rituals. We now know that the more the person performs compulsive rituals, the worse the OCD becomes. Fortunately, several different approaches to treatment can reduce or even eliminate obsessions and compulsions and allow patients to resume normal living.

Paulette was obsessed with dirt; other common versions involve thoughts (for example, distressing ideas about sex; numbers that are believed to be unlucky), pictures or images of dreaded actions (such as compulsively disrobing in public), fears (perhaps of a disease like AIDS or hepatitis), mental acrobatics (for example, visually dividing a line exactly in two), and impulses (for example, feeling compelled to scream in church or the supermarket checkout line). These mental events are often violent, disgusting, sacrilegious, sexual, or senseless.

Paulette's drive for cleanliness is one of the most common types of compulsion, but counting and checking things (such as locks, gas and electric appliances) also occur frequently. Some people have no obsessions at all, just compulsions that they must perform according to set rules. For example, Joseph felt that he could only get into bed at night by following an agonizing procedure—step in and out of his slippers three times (later, three times three, then three times three times three); smooth out his bedspread, turn it down to a 45-degree angle three times, put his pajamas on bottoms first, then tops, remove them, and repeat three times. If he was interrupted or began to doubt whether he had fulfilled all the prescribed steps, he had to start all over again.

The obsessional ideas can generate an enormous amount of anxiety, and attempts to resist compulsions can lead to tension that is relieved only by giving in to the rituals. A few people have what's known as obsessional slowness, in which they will take hours to complete a simple household chore. Others have mental compulsions (such as ritualized praying) that is not externally apparent. A very few have obsessions without compulsions.

OCD sufferers often devote much time to what most of us would regard as the infrastructure of our lives. They usually realize how peculiar their obsessive thoughts and compulsive rituals must seem, and feel embarrassed. That's partly why OCD was once thought to be rare—shame and the fear that they are going crazy make people hide their guilty secrets even from best friends and physicians. Now we know that it is actually fairly common, affecting about one in 50 people at some time during their lives. It is somewhat more common among women than men, though boys tend to outnumber girls (it begins earlier in boys). In both sexes, it usually begins in the teens or early 20s, though it can affect children of 10 or even younger.

From mounting evidence, we now know that OCD has strong biological roots. Although the genetics aren't thoroughly worked out, several studies have found that OCD in a relative increases a person's risk for the disease fivefold. There is also a familial link to Tourette's disorder (the uncontrollable and disconcerting tendency to have motor tics and blurt out obscenities). A type of brain X-ray, called "positron emission tomography" (PET scan), has found abnormal metabolism at sites deep within the brains of people who are having obsessions; these brain abnormalities resolve with effective treatment. In recent years, childhood OCD has developed apparently as an immune reaction to streptococcal infections. Whatever the initial starting point, biologists have uncovered considerable evidence implicating the neurotransmitter called serotonin, the same chemical whose action is normalized by SSRI drugs such as Luvox and Anafranil—which are effective in treating OCD.

TREATING OBSESSIVE–COMPULSIVE DISORDER

Paulette did not abuse substances or have other anxiety disorders or major depression that would complicate her treatment. In an effort to jump-start her recovery effort and ensure success, her physician recommended using both psychotherapy and drugs. They began with the SSRI Luvox (page 66) at 50 mg/day and increased it by 50 mg every 4 or 5 days. At 200 mg/day, she felt a little less stressed and was referred to a therapist for exposure and response prevention treatment (ERP; page 181).

Paulette was told that she would improve faster if she intentionally "contaminated" herself by touching germ-laden objects; she reluctantly surrendered her gloves and spent an hour each day rubbing her hands in a bucket of dirt. That was how the exposure part of her treatment began. The response prevention part allowed her to wash her hands only four times a day. "The anxiety was really terrible at first," she later admitted. "Mom had to sit with me for the first hour or so each day. After a few days, though, I lightened up."

ERP works best for patients who are highly motivated and have both obsessions and compulsions. If Paulette had been unable to tolerate the anxiety of ERP, CBT would have been an alternative, though perhaps less effective, intervention. If she had had only obsessions, she would probably have been offered the thought stopping method (page 182). There is no evidence that dynamic psychotherapy is of much use; this lack of evidence parallels most clinicians' abandonment, in recent years, of "inner conflicts" as a cause of OCD. Paulette was grateful for her therapist's consistent reassurance—an example of supportive psychotherapy (page 168) at its finest.

Certain antidepressant medications increase serotonin transmission in the central nervous system, but high doses (or, perhaps, a long duration of treatment) are needed to be effective. Luvox has been specifically approved by the FDA for OCD, though Prozac and Zoloft have also proven effective. You may need to try more than one drug until you improve. Anafranil, starting at 25 mg/day and increasing to an average of 200–250/day, is effective but is beset with side effects and has a slow response time. If you need more help than a single drug can provide, your doctor may recommend augmenting an SSRI with Anafranil, a TCA. You could also be helped by adding an antipsychotic agent, either a newer one like Zyprexa or Risperdal, or one of the older ones (but watch closely for tardive dyskinesia).

For several reasons, families should be included in the overall treatment plan. Relatives need education so that they can stop blaming themselves and the patient for behavior they cannot control. It is also vital that those who live with a person who has OCD learn to stop accommodating the compulsions. Paulette's family had to stop using gloves and decontaminating the house—stop-gap measures that reduced Paulette's anxieties short-term but ultimately worsened the problem.

Although it only rarely comes to this, neurosurgery remains a possibility for those rare patients who are incapacitated by OCD and who respond to nothing else. Only a dozen or so such operations are performed each year in this country, with relatively minor complications. About a third of patients who have such surgery function better.

Let me be completely candid: severe OCD can be difficult to treat successfully. Although medication or psychotherapy alone may help some people with milder symptoms, if you are like many patients, you and your family should gird yourselves for a long campaign. People with OCD generally have more trouble achieving a satisfactory response if they have been ill for a long time or were quite young when it started; if they've been hospitalized or more or less continuously ill (no remissions) since it started; if they have washing rituals; or if they have a personality disorder. Even for those who continue to have some symptoms, the outlook for sufferers of OCD is far brighter than it was just a couple of decades ago—given their persistence, hard work, and enough emotional support. That was the experience of Paulette and her parents—who are still married.

OBSESSED WITH PERFECTION

Stunning and statuesque, at age 23 Tamara was consulting her third plastic surgeon about her nose. The others hadn't thought they could improve on what nature had given her, but Tamara was unconvinced—and distressed. "It's ugly and misshapen," she insisted as she scrutinized herself in her hand mirror. She had lost several boyfriends over her preoccupation with her nose, which she had lately tried to conceal by wearing her long hair draped across half her face.

Tamara had body dysmorphic disorder (BDD), a condition you may not have heard of, though it was first described over 100 years ago. Even mental health professionals often don't know a lot about it, though as many as 1 or 2% of adults, and many children, may be affected. These men and women (who are about equally represented) are haunted by their appearance. Where others see beauty, or perhaps the slightest hint of a flaw, they perceive only disaster. Theirs is an obsession with the impression of imperfection. Most often, they worry about the appearance of skin, hair, or nose, but hardly any body part is immune: ankles, arms, even one teenager's pubic bone. People with BDD may spend much of the day in embarrassed, painful brooding about their deformities.

Almost all have impaired social lives, and over 80% of patients with BDD also have trouble on the job or at school. Half are hospitalized at some time; nearly a third become housebound. If they do go out, like Tamara, they may try to conceal their features with clothing or bandages. Most check their appearance compulsively in mirrors and compare themselves mentally to those they meet. To smooth away the tiny bumps and blemishes only they can see, they may pick or scrape away at their skin until they cause actual pitting and scarring. Most of them have had major depression, and nearly one-fourth have made a suicide attempt; a few succeed. In the effort to repair their fancied deficits, many patients with BDD, like Tamara, consult plastic surgeons or other physicians, and too often they are obliged. Usually, they are dissatisfied with the outcome of surgery; even those who think they have been improved often shift critical attention to another body part.

No one knows what causes BDD, though it probably involves a problem with the transmission of signals in the brain by serotonin—or so the response to drugs that inhibit serotonin reuptake would suggest. Although the repeated double-blind studies that would provide definitive evidence have not yet been done, so far it appears that drugs like Luvox, given in high enough doses and for a long enough time (typically, 12–16 weeks), will help around two-thirds of patients with BDD. Anafranil (TCA) can also help, and for patients who need even more assistance, the combination of Luvox plus Anafranil, cautiously administered, may work well. Some clinicians find that BuSpar (60–90 mg/day) augments the antidepressant effect.

ERP helps reduce the anxiety and unwanted behaviors. Patients like Tamara must be persuaded to throw away their cover-ups and discard their magnifying mirrors. Low-wattage light bulbs in the bathroom may help remove their focus from their appearance. However, patients with severe BDD will probably also need long-term "thought repair" through CBT: identifying automatic and unrealistic thoughts and core beliefs, challenging them, and replacing them with more useful thinking. Tamara learned to tell herself that her thoughts about her nose were just part of her BDD, "and I feel pretty good about that."

She had a right to be proud. A complex illness that continues to perplex patients and professionals alike, BDD falls into what mental health clinicians have come to call the OCD spectrum of disorders. Some of the others are Tourette's disorder, anorexia nervosa and bulimia, and kleptomania, each of which features obsessional thinking and ritualized behaviors.

RECOMMENDATIONS

- Psychotherapy, such as ERP, may remedy a mild case of OCD; CBT is a good second choice.
- Patients with complicated, longstanding, or moderate to severe OCD should consider using both drugs and psychotherapy.
- If your doctor recommends drug therapy, the best place to start is with an SSRI such as Luvox. If that doesn't work, try another SSRI or Anafranil.

CHAPTER 21

Somatization Disorder

Norma had been seeing doctors all her adult life. "It's been almost a life-style," she told me during our first interview, when she was 33, "and none of them could tell me what was wrong."

The first medical problem she could remember occurred the summer she was 15. She had been scheduled to transfer to a new school that fall, and for a couple of weeks in late August she had felt a little sick to her stomach. Labor Day night she was rushed to the hospital with a terrible pain in her lower abdomen. Ultrasound and a CT scan revealed nothing, but not wishing to miss an infected appendix, the doctor operated anyway. Her appendix had been normal, after all, and Norma was in class a week later.

"But *I* wasn't normal," she told me. "That was only the start of being sick. Later that year I missed the junior prom because I hurt so bad with my periods. The doctor said I'd get over it, but I still go to bed with them, 3 days a month. I feel like a freak."

She hadn't been able to graduate from high school because she developed severe diarrhea two months before graduation. She was prescribed Lomotil and "had every test in the book. They thought it might be a parasite, but they could never find anything wrong. The doctor said I was fine. That's what they've always said, all my life. Do you know how scary that is?"

As it happened, I did know. I had encountered dozens of patients with histories of multiple, unexplained physical symptoms, and I was beginning to wonder whether Norma might have somatization disorder (SD). Patients with SD have physical symptoms but no evidence of physical disease, yet they aren't just making up their symptoms. If you think about it, most of us have any number of twinges, aches, and pains whose meaning we ponder—are we sick, or are they just part of the business of growing up or growing older? For the most part, we ignore them and they go away, but patients with SD cope with their symptoms by seeking repeated medical tests, procedures, and operations. Because SD mimics physical disease, it can elude detection; I'd need much more information before I could determine Norma's diagnosis. "Go on," I encouraged her.

Out of school, she had obtained a job as a receptionist. Bright and capable, she taught herself how to type and was soon working as a secretary. Within a couple of years she had married, had a baby, returned to work (her choice)—and continued having symptoms. Not that she was sick all the time—for weeks or months she might feel pretty well, but intermittently new symptoms would send her back to the doctor. Her medicine cabinet held Darvon for migraine, Advil for joint pain (though her blood tests and X-rays did not indicate arthritis), and Midol (later, codeine) for menstrual pain. She began missing work, and medical bills piled up. At times she felt too fatigued even to care for her child; when her husband left her, taking their son, she was "too tired to fight it."

SYMPTOMS AND DIAGNOSIS OF SOMATIZATION DISORDER

SD symptoms are many and varied. By one count, 60 or more are possible, though no one has them all. Typically dating from their teen years, the many symptoms of SD patients have impaired their ability to work, attend school, or relate to other people, or have caused them to seek medical treatment. The diagnosis of SD is determined by the presence of many symptoms that have not responded to the usual treatments and that extend across different areas and functions of the body (such a broad pattern of symptoms argues against organic illness). To establish Norma's diagnosis, I'd need to learn how serious each new symptom was, how it had affected her life, whether she saw a doctor for it, took medicine, or had an operation. If the doctor had found a medical cause, I wouldn't count that symptom toward a diagnosis of SD.

For convenience, the criteria for SD are arranged into four categories of symptoms: Pain symptoms, gastrointestinal distress, sexual and reproductive problems, and (false) neurological symptoms. A patient must have qualifying symptoms in each group—eight or more in all, though the typical patient has far more than eight. Here is how I evaluated Norma:

Pain symptoms (four are required in this group). I already knew about the abdominal pain she'd had as a teenager and her menstrual pain. As recently as the year before, Norma had been to the doctor because of muscle spasms in her hands and wrists. She wondered if she was developing carpal tunnel syndrome, but a neurologist could find no evidence of it. In time, the spasms went away. Several years earlier an episode of severe chest pain had sent her to the emergency room. Her EKG was normal, and the doctor reassured her that "nothing was wrong." Other patients with SD may complain of backache, headache, and pain related to bodily functions such as urination or sexual intercourse.

Gastrointestinal symptoms (two or more are required). I knew about the diarrhea during Norma's senior year; a few years back she had also suffered a prolonged bout of severe nausea and vomiting. It had lasted several weeks—far too long to be food poisoning, as she had feared—but again her doctor could find no physical cause. For several weeks she took Mylanta to reduce the nausea; finally, it disappeared.

Sexual and reproductive symptoms. A patient with SD will have at least one problem in this category, such as excessive menstrual bleeding, markedly irregular menstrual periods, lack of interest in sex, vomiting throughout pregnancy, or trouble maintaining an erection or having an orgasm. Norma had vomited through all 9 months of her only pregnancy ("Worst case my OB had ever seen," she told me). Afterward, her menstrual periods had been so irregular and heavy that, when she was only 26, she'd had a hysterectomy. And she had never been much interested in sex and had never experienced an orgasm.

False neurological symptoms. Every patient with SD must have at least one symptom that resembles a neurological disease but with no apparent neurological pathology. These experiences, almost always temporary, include problems such as seizures, loss of consciousness, blindness, deafness, amnesia, difficulty swallowing, and poor balance or coordination. When she was 21, Norma had consulted her doctor because of her unsteady, staggering gait, but a neurologist had found nothing wrong. Without treatment, her walking had returned to normal in a few days.

I requested copies of her old medical records and was soon poring over several volumes of notations, hospital summaries, doctor's scrawled notes, dictated letters to other physicians, and laboratory studies. They confirmed what I had suspected almost from the first—an extraordinary history of mysterious illnesses, multiple evaluations and referrals to specialists, and a great deal of treatment that had done her little good. Norma had somatization disorder—which is what I told her when she appeared for her next appointment.

She took it well. Some patients are upset at even the idea of seeing a psychiatrist. "I'm not crazy," they might say when a referring doctor suggests it. "Why should I pay to let a shrink tell me it's all in my head, when I know how much I hurt?" If Norma had objected to my conclusions, I'd have pointed out that she'd had trouble for years, nothing had worked well, and perhaps it was time to try something else. However, as is more often the case, she had been through so much already that she was willing to explore anything that offered the chance of improvement. "But," she said, "just what *do* I have wrong?"

WHAT IS SOMATIZATION DISORDER?

I view the symptoms of somatization disorder as a response to stress. Under tension, some people develop mental or emotional symptoms such as anxiety or depression; symptoms of patients with SD involve the body (*soma* is Greek for *body*). If you have

SD, you suffer the same sorts of conflicts, doubts, and concerns that worry everybody else, but your constitution translates them into physical symptoms. Let me re-emphasize that the exact symptoms are not what's important; the features of this disease aren't as predictable as with, say, pneumonia, where nearly everybody has chest pain, cough, fever, and shortness of breath. Rather, clinicians recognize SD by the fact that symptoms affect many areas of the body, change from time to time, and don't respond well to the usual physical treatments.

SD has mystified patients and clinicians alike for hundreds of years. Even today, it is one of the most puzzling, alarming, frustrating, and anxiety-provoking conditions known to medicine. In fact, I believe that patients with SD often suffer far more than do those with more recognizable diseases who know what is wrong and can turn to a physician for a prognosis and treatment plan. Because the true diagnosis goes unrecognized, patients with SD often go from one doctor to another, seeking relief. SD affects about 1% of adults, mainly women, though I've known a few men who have had it; any religious or ethnic background is possible. Although they have more hospitalizations and far greater medical expenses than the average person, their life expectancy is about normal.

The cause of SD is still in dispute. Studies long ago found that it runs in families—which could mean, as two older theories speculated, that children learn to somatize by imitating the behavior of adults, or that somatization may develop in response to abuse at home. Although each of these theories has some scientific support, scientists have begun to find biological underpinnings to the disorder. For example, genetic studies have found evidence for hereditary influences. It has also been noted that patients with SD have trouble filtering out irrelevant stimuli that most people would ignore, such as minor aches or pains, and may have trouble adapting to ongoing annoyances, such as a dripping faucet or buzzing fly. These traits may relate to evidence of subtly altered functioning in the front parts of the brain.

Even though no one is exactly sure what does cause SD, I can tell you two things that don't. First, it isn't the patient's fault. My experience with dozens of patients has told me that they don't like being sick and hate the consequences of this disorder. I also know that they aren't faking their symptoms. I am sure of this because patients like Norma aren't trying to collect insurance or disability fraudulently or to avoid responsibilities (or jail), as would be the case with a malingerer—someone who consciously makes up symptoms. Sure, she had temporarily avoided the stress of a new school, but later she missed the prom. And the divorce, the loss of her job, the loss of custody of her son had been far greater blows. I believe that by their symptoms, patients with SD are trying to communicate, even as weeping speaks of sadness and trembling betrays fear or anxiety.

People with SD often have other mental disorders, especially depression, panic attacks, sometimes even hallucinations, or the abuse of alcohol. Although many have attempted it, few actually complete suicide. Norma had been treated with Prozac and other antidepressant drugs. None of them helped her longer than a few days, which is pretty typical of SD. Physical treatments aren't usually any more effective for emotional disorders than they are for medical illnesses.

TREATING SOMATIZATION DISORDER

The first thing these patients need is as much information as possible. If you have SD, you know how much in the dark you have felt for many years. Clear, unambiguous information about what's wrong will help you and your family understand why you have had these problems, what the future holds, and how best to cope. The good news is that you have a real disorder with real symptoms, about which a great deal is known.

In the past, you and your medical team may have tried to treat the symptoms directly. The results were less than satisfactory because you hadn't addressed the root causes. It would be the same as if you treated pneumonia with cough medicine but no antibiotic. Several studies have found that either cognitive-behavioral therapy or interpersonal psychotherapy can help you learn to cope with stressors so that they don't produce physical symptoms. Studies show that, if you join a group of patients with SD, you might be able to learn a great deal from others who have had (and are conquering) the sort of problems you have.

It is important that you find a clinician you like, who seems to listen, to care, to understand—one who doesn't promise an immediate cure. Of course, it should be someone who has had experience treating SD. Although this sounds like a tall order, it may be easier than you think. Primary care practitioners are in an excellent position to evaluate any new physical symptoms you might develop, and many are interested in just this sort of problem. Your care provider (it could be a physician's assistant or nurse practitioner) might refer complicating mental disorders, such as substance abuse or severe depression, to a mental health specialist. Of course, a psychiatrist could fill the role of main care provider, referring any new physical problems to an internist for evaluation. To avoid excessive medication and mixed messages about health, it is vital that one person have overall charge of your care.

As psychotherapy begins to improve your ability to handle stress, you will probably depend less on medication. Even other mental problems, such as depression and panic disorder, may respond better to psychotherapy than to drugs. Another important effort will be to involve your relatives, who must come to understand that you are neither malingering nor just imagining your symptoms. I believe it is important that relatives hear from your clinician that SD causes overwhelming distress and disrupts lives just as much as would a heart attack, broken bones, or cancer.

Over the next 18 months, Norma shed most of her medications and obtained joint custody of her son. She got a secretarial job at a company that competed with her former employer; within months she was running a branch office. Although she still had symptoms from time to time, she learned to regard them as signals of stress that needed attention.

"SOUNDS LIKE A PERSONALITY DISORDER"

Many clinicians believe that somatization disorder is so similar to a personality disorder that it may actually *be* one. Then what, exactly, is a personality disorder? Here is an extremely brief summary of a subject that can fill bookshelves.

All of us have a mixture of personality traits—the consistent ways, present at least since adolescence, in which we tend to feel, think, and behave. There are roughly five categories of traits: openness (for example, how original, curious, and imaginative we are), agreeableness (the degree to which we are appreciative, generous, and kind), conscientiousness (the degree to which we are efficient, reliable, thorough), neuroticism (the degree to which we are anxious, tense, unstable), and extraversion (the degree to which we are energetic, outgoing, assertive).

Partly inborn, partly absorbed from early childhood, your combination of personality traits can enormously influence those around you, affecting your happiness and general effectiveness. Consider Tom, who blusters and threatens whenever he feels angry or frustrated. Because of his size (he was the star center of his college football team) and his booming voice, he usually gets his way. But he wonders why he has so few close friends and why his two ex-wives constantly bad-mouth him. When certain personality traits come to dominate many aspects of our lives (relationships with coworkers, relatives, and friends) and cause distress for us or those around us, clinicians sometimes diagnose a personality disorder.

There are various "official" personality disorders; you have probably encountered some in people you know. People with somatization disorder are often quite dramatic as they describe their illness and its consequences; they may be described as overly emotional, vague, and attention-seeking. Paranoid personalities tend to be suspicious and quick to take offense; narcissistic personalities are self-important with a sense of entitlement that may cause them to take advantage of others. Those with avoidant personality disorder may be so timid and easily wounded that they hesitate to become involved with others; dependent personalities have trouble making their own decisions. An impulsive person who often shows intense bursts of inappropriate anger, feels empty or bored, and has trouble maintaining stable relationships with others is sometimes referred to as borderline; and people who habitually display lack of remorse for their irresponsible, criminal behavior may be termed antisocial. We have identified illnesses with more and more subtle definitional distinctions; well-known clinicians have even seriously suggested that there are "thousands" of different personality disorders. A given person may have a "freestanding" personality disorder or one that is associated with other mental disorders (and even other personality disorders).

Tom might benefit from, say, interpersonal psychotherapy, though in order to change his aggressive style of dealing with others he would have to commit to a prolonged effort. Studies have shown that "remaking character" may require 18 months or longer.

RECOMMENDATIONS

- If your symptoms and life story seem to fit SD, you need a thoughtful diagnosis by a careful clinician who can evaluate all your history and symptoms. A good place to start could be a medical school psychiatry department, which may have a faculty member who is expert in the diagnosis of SD.
- With the diagnosis in hand, you may be referred to another clinician for therapy. A family physician, trained in the management of both mental and physical illnesses, might be best able to evaluate any further physical symptoms. A psychiatrist who uses behavior treatment and works closely with your internist or family doctor could also provide the kind of care you need.

CHAPTER 22

Psychosis and Schizophrenia

Have you ever had a dream in which you were being watched, perhaps followed; everyone knew something you didn't, and you could hear the voices of dead relatives or friends? Then you've had a taste of what it is like to be psychotic—except that if you're psychotic, it's all still happening when you wake up. Psychosis is a horrible, alienating experience that mystifies and terrifies everyone it touches, especially the patient.

The word *psychosis* means *out of contact with reality,* and it implies a number of possible symptoms. A psychotic person may hallucinate (hear or see things that aren't there) or have delusions (believe things that are not true, such as being persecuted by the FBI). Psychosis can also mean a class of illness that includes schizophrenia and other, less well-known disorders. It can occur in depression, mania, dementia, substance abuse, and a variety of medical conditions. As you'll see, the treatment for psychosis depends strongly on its cause.

SCHIZOPHRENIA

The best-known chronic type of psychosis is schizophrenia. For convenience, everyone speaks of it as a single disease, but it is really a group of diseases with many common symptoms. Known for many centuries, it is far from rare today—about 1% of all adults have schizophrenia—and it is found in every culture on earth. It affects men and women about equally, though for reasons still unknown, males tend to develop it earlier than females. It is encountered more often in disadvantaged social and economic groups, probably because so many of these patients cannot take good care of themselves and drift into poverty. In the United States schizophrenia remains one of our most important public health problems, by some estimates costing as much as all cancers combined. In recent decades, improved treatment has enabled the release of many chronically hospitalized patients. However, follow-up care has lagged so far behind that many patients stop taking their medicines and relapse, often living on the streets, committing minor crimes and misdemeanors, and becoming wards of the criminal justice system. In larger cities, up to half the homeless have some form of psychosis, most often schizophrenia.

Symptoms and Diagnosis of Schizophrenia

If you know someone who is showing symptoms of psychosis, keep in mind that schizophrenia is a real possibility—but not the only one. I will use the case of Jason, who does have typical schizophrenia, to point out some of the symptoms that can be found in various psychoses.

When he was 17, Jason's parents and two other adults took him to the hospital because he had been hearing the voice of his Spanish teacher—late at night, when he was alone. Her voice seemed entirely real to him, and she told him (in Spanish) that he had been selected to be sacrificed. He had heard the voice, with increasing frequency, for nearly a year, and he was becoming more and more frightened. His mother could hear him pacing his room at night, but when she asked what was wrong, he just shrugged and silently turned away. The day he was admitted, she had entered his room to straighten up and found it "completely destroyed." The shelves were bare; all their contents had been piled in front of the wardrobe door. His clothes had been dumped from the dresser and shredded with the scissors he had then used to inflict dozens of tiny wounds on his forearms.

Jason had been a very sensitive, friendless little boy who had never shown the slightest interest in girls. Instead, he developed such a passion for moths and butterflies that by the age of 13, he had collected several hundred varieties. Before becoming so ill, he had often studied the wonderful collection at the natural history museum. He even thought that he had discovered a new variety of *Papilio polyxenes*, the black swallowtail butterfly. However, he hadn't chased a butterfly in weeks, and his only scientific activity had been talking into his portable tape recorder.

His family life had been marked by the divorce of his parents several years earlier. Each of his parents had subsequent lovers (his mother's current boyfriend lived in their home), and his father also continued to live at home. An aunt had had a breakdown when she was in college and never recovered; she lived with her parents until she died, an eccentric and lonely woman.

Jason's doctor started him on Haldol, which quieted the hallucinated voices and calmed his agitation, but a few weeks after leaving the hospital he stopped taking it. He told his mother that it made him feel "wired" and he didn't need it anyway; he wasn't sick. For several weeks he just seemed anxious and irritable, then he gradually became aware that his telephone conversations were being "intercepted." He thought that the museum curator was trying to steal his *P. polyxenes*.

On his second hospital admission, the doctor asked whether he could be mistaken about the curator. Jason just gazed out the window. This time his appearance showed neglect. His jeans were stiff with dirt, and he needed a wash himself. He sat sullenly, arms folded across his chest. Later, his mother brought in his little tape recorder. On it, Jason's voice said this: "I think I have developed a new construction of a *P. polyxenes*. This construction is built largely on a *podel* that mitigates its life force." When asked about the word *podel*, he said that it was a model of a *P. polyxenes*.

Jason's example illustrates most of the types of psychotic symptoms that are typical of people with psychosis, especially schizophrenia: (1) hallucinations, (2) delusions, (3) disorganized speech, (4) disorganized behavior, (5) negative symptoms.

1. Hallucinations are any sensation that the person only imagines. They can involve any of the five senses, but hallucinated sounds are the most common in schizophrenia. Jason heard the voice of his Spanish teacher, and as is typical in schizophrenia, this voice seemed entirely real to him. Some patients hear the voices as though they were coming from far away; some hear them close by or just outside the room; still others hear them in their heads. Often, patients recognize the voices, but sometimes they are of strangers. There may be one voice or many that often ridicule, threaten, or command.

2. Delusions are false ideas or thoughts that a person believes, no matter how improbable. Many types of delusions are possible, such as believing that you can read minds, that the television is sending you encoded messages, or that electrodes have been secretly implanted in your brain. The most common delusions in schizophrenia are those of persecution (someone is following, spying upon, or trying to harm you); Jason thought that the curator had stolen his butterfly. All sorts of real events and conditions can get pulled into these delusions. I once treated a woman who had ankle swelling due to kidney disease. She thought that water was being pulled downward into her legs by gravity machines installed in her basement by Nazis (she'd been ill a long time, and this happened many years ago). Whatever the content of the delusional belief, the person cannot be persuaded that it is false.

3. Jason had two negative symptoms: lack of motivation (he just sat around, with no interest in accomplishing anything) and blunted affect (his emotional state was flat and showed little change). Another negative symptom is talking very little, even when the situation calls for more extended speech. These symptoms are "negative" because they suggest that something is missing from the patient, not added to, as is the case with hallucinations or delusions.

4. Jason's tape-recorded speech was disorganized, stilted, and contained made-up words. It had meaning for him, but another person would be hard-pressed to understand him. Sometimes called "loose associations," disorganized speech moves from one idea to another without an obvious thread.

5. Jason didn't have any behavior that I would call disorganized, but psychotic

patients occasionally do. They may grimace, maintain postures for many minutes, or perform rituals that have meaning only for them.

Patients with schizophrenia may also respond inappropriately to other people's emotions—laughing at someone else's grief, for example, or giggling without obvious cause. Hygiene may deteriorate badly, heavy cigarette smoking is the rule, and patients may abuse substances (some clinicians think that alcohol and drugs may serve as home remedies for hallucinations). Patients typically deny that they are ill, even when it seems obvious to everyone else, and often refuse to take medicine.

Violent behavior is an especially serious consequence—but please don't conclude that patients with schizophrenia are usually violent; in fact, intentionally harming another person is rare. It can happen, however, as in the case of Sam Berkowitz, the serial killer who, as "Son of Sam," terrorized New York City women in the 1970s. Another example was the patient who killed Tamara Tarasoff, a student at the University of California. (A subsequent lawsuit led to the *Tarasoff* ruling, which requires mental health workers to protect people from threats a mental patient may make against them, either by reporting to the police or by other means.) Patients with schizophrenia often become suicidal; however, about 10–15% eventually take their own lives. The risk of either tragic outcome—suicide or violence against others—is only one reason to provide careful diagnosis and competent treatment for psychotic individuals.

In a number of ways, Jason was typical of patients with schizophrenia.

1. Before he became ill, he was an isolated, quiet young man with few friends. This personality type (clinicians call it "schizoid") occurs in about 25% of patients with schizophrenia. However, most people with schizoid personalities do *not* develop schizophrenia.
2. The onset of schizophrenia is usually gradual. Careful clinicians won't make the diagnosis unless a patient has had symptoms for at least 6 months, as was the case with Jason.
3. By far the majority of patients are young (teens and 20s) when they first fall ill.
4. Although most relatives of patients with schizophrenia do not have a mental illness, schizophrenia has a strong genetic component. Most clinicians would suspect that Jason's aunt, who remained mentally ill for many years, had schizophrenia and would therefore feel even more confident of Jason's diagnosis.
5. Jason had no apparent medical illnesses or problems with substance abuse that could account for his psychotic symptoms.

The main psychotic symptoms will determine which subtype of schizophrenia the patient is experiencing:

- **Catatonic.** Abnormalities of motion are prominent. These include frozen postures (holding uncomfortable poses, sometimes for hours at a time) and pronounced negativism (such as Jason's tendency to turn away whenever his mother spoke to him).
- **Disorganized.** These patients think and speak illogically, such as Jason's made-up word, *podel*. Facial expressions and mood tend to be stiff or unchanging, though some patients may laugh or giggle inappropriately. Behavior may be bizarre and not understandable—carrying around collections of paper cups, gesturing in ways that no one can understand, and so forth.
- **Paranoid.** Persecutory delusions (such as Jason's fear of the curator stealing his butterfly) characterize people with paranoid schizophrenia, who may seem pretty normal unless a topic related to their delusional ideas comes up. Paranoid schizophrenia often begins later than the other subtypes—typically, when the patient is 30 or older.
- **Undifferentiated.** This term is used when the patient has features of two or three subtypes, like Jason. This is the type most commonly diagnosed today; a strong minority of patients has paranoid subtype, whereas the number of disorganized and catatonic types is small.

Still another type of chronic psychosis is schizoaffective disorder, a term that would apply to patients who have about equal parts mood and psychotic symptoms. Quite frankly, the term has been used so variously over the years as to be almost meaningless today. If your relative receives this diagnosis, treatment will depend on whether the symptoms are closer to schizophrenia or a mood disorder.

What could possibly cause a disease comprising such varied symptoms? Most researchers believe that schizophrenia is a collection of disorders with a variety of causes. In many cases, more than one cause may well be necessary. I've already alluded to the genetic aspects: dozens of studies have shown, beyond doubt, that what we inherit can account for half or more of the risk of developing schizophrenia. However, there is additional evidence implicating other factors as diverse as viruses (more people with schizophrenia are born during the winter months) and birth complications. Each of these mechanisms probably influences a patient's thinking through changes in brain chemistry. Although other neurotransmitters may also be involved, dopamine almost certainly plays an important role (we believe this because all antipsychotic medications affect dopamine receptors within portions of the brain that are thought to produce the symptoms of psychosis). Finally, the brains of many patients with schizophrenia contain anatomical abnormalities, of which the best studied is a reduction of brain tissue leading to dilatation of the ventricles, the fluid-containing spaces in the brain.

With so many threads in the tapestry left untied, it is clear that we are still far from completing our picture of what causes schizophrenia. Although chaotic, high-volume family life (like Jason's) is undoubtedly stressful and may contribute to symptom relapse, we can completely discredit old psychological theories that as recently as a generation ago blamed families (especially mothers) for producing psychosis by inducing stress. The balance of the evidence has even caused some researchers to claim that schizophrenia is actually a neurological disorder.

WHEN IS SCHIZOPHRENIA NOT SCHIZOPHRENIA?

I've known many patients who were diagnosed with schizophrenia at one time but who turned out to have another illness entirely. This error can still happen today, partly because psychosis is a confusing condition that can take many forms, partly because clinicians sometimes don't give enough thought to the diagnostic process. The error is extremely serious because an incorrect diagnosis of schizophrenia can delay appropriate care and promote lengthy, unnecessary, and even dangerous treatment.

Accurate diagnosis depends on knowing not just the symptoms but the patient's lifetime course of illness. In schizophrenia, the course is almost always chronic, which means that once illness strikes, most patients do not resume their former level of functioning, even though substantial improvement can occur. Contrast this prognosis with that of a psychosis caused by substance use or a physical disease, which often remits completely once the underlying illness has been treated successfully. And people with psychotic bipolar mood disorder, another common type of psychosis, usually recover completely.

A number of features might suggest that your relative doesn't have schizophrenia, after all: abrupt onset, mood symptoms (mania or depression), a strong family history of mood disorder, brief course (symptoms present less than 6 months), good social adjustment prior to becoming ill (reliable student or worker with stable personal relationships); upsetting emotional factors (such as death of a parent) that might cause psychosis; and symptoms beginning after age 30. Even when the diagnosis of schizophrenia is correct, a patient with some of these features may respond to mood stabilizers.

Treating Schizophrenia

Even 50 years ago, schizophrenia was considered very difficult to treat and had a gloomy prognosis; often patients with this diagnosis spent years in mental hospitals. Now, with effective treatments that can return them to their lives, jobs, and families, their outlook is much brighter. Many patients work, though sometimes at jobs less complex than their education and training prepared them for. Although most do need long-term treatment, they are far less likely to require chronic institutional care.

Throughout this book you will read about the psychotherapy alternatives for patients who don't want to take drugs. Schizophrenia is an important exception. Although psychotherapy helps manage schizophrenia, *it is not effective as a sole treatment*; medication plays an indispensable role. Moreover, it is important to begin drug therapy at once: considerable data suggest that effective medication early in the course of the illness, with consistent follow-up care, reduces the likelihood of relapse and limits social decline—possibly because early treatment averts changes in brain structure.

Previous experience is one of the most important factors to consider in choosing one of the growing list of available drugs. A drug with few side effects that has worked well in the past (and that the patient will take) should perform well again. Usually, I avoid the older antipsychotic agents in favor of newer ones (Chapter 9). They have fewer immediate side effects, so patients are more likely to continue to take the drug, and they are far less likely to have longer-term side effects, especially tardive dyskinesia (TD). The newer drugs are also more likely to improve disorganized thinking and other negative symptoms.

The treatment of all four schizophrenia subtypes is about the same. A doctor might recommend starting with Zyprexa, 5 or 10 mg once a day, then increase it gradually, at weekly intervals, until the target symptoms begin to disappear. If Zyprexa isn't effective, Risperdal or Seroquel might work just fine; as a first approach to therapy, I'd try each of these drugs. For the first month or two, someone who is psychotic and acutely agitated may also need Ativan or Klonopin to calm down. Clozaril has the longest track record of success in patients who are especially difficult to treat, but it occasionally reduces the number of white blood cells, which are vital for fighting off infections. That's why Clozaril should be reserved for patients with greatest need—those who simply don't respond well to other treatments.

If an older antipsychotic is needed, doses below the equivalent of 300 mg/day of Thorazine will probably be ineffective, and doses above 1000 mg/day aren't likely to improve response. If your relative has been taking an older drug for many months, the doctor may suggest changing to a newer agent, again to reduce the risk of TD. When making any change, the usual practice of gradually tapering off the current drug should be followed.

How well patients accept any drug depends a lot on their comfort, so side effects must be corrected quickly. This is especially the case with the older antipsychotics, but even the newer ones cause weight gain and other minor discomforts. Every 6 months, the doctor will check to see whether patients show any symptoms of TD. Other movement disorders, such as akathisia or parkinsonism (page 117), can be dealt with fairly simply by adding an antiparkinson agent (for example, Artane).

Some patients simply don't take medications well. Sometimes these are people who are terribly forgetful, but more often it is someone who resents being controlled by others or who thinks that medicines are harmful or unnecessary. If your relative has repeatedly rejected medication, the answer may be Haldol or Prolixin, given by injection once or twice a month. As of this writing, the newer antipsychotic drugs are still not available as long-term injections.

In the maintenance phase of treatment (once the patient has stabilized and has no hallucinations or delusions), the doctor, patient, and family will share two goals: reduce medicine to the absolute minimum needed to prevent recurrence and watch carefully for symptoms of relapse. In some cases, such as with a first episode, the doctor may agree to scale back the medicine very gradually, perhaps by about 20% every 6 months. If symptoms resurface, it will be easy enough to increase the dose again, before they can become severe. Occasionally, drug treatment can be stopped completely; then it is important to watch carefully for recurring symptoms.

Several forms of psychotherapy may augment the effects of medication. Cognitive-behavioral therapy can help reduce the severity of delusions and other symptoms. Family therapy can help prevent relapse, especially when relatives are overly involved with, and critical of, the patient. Social skills training seeks to improve patients' adaptation to the environment, thereby reducing stress.

If your relative responds poorly to conventional treatment, the doctor will probably want to consider several steps. First is to be sure that your relative is really taking the prescribed medications (blood level checks can help determine this). Other steps include: using Clozaril, if it hasn't been tried yet; Risperdal plus Clozaril; adding lithium, Tegretol, or Depakote; adding an antidepressant, if your relative has been troubled by depression; trying electroconvulsive therapy, especially for catatonic symptoms. Consultation with another clinician may identify other measures to try.

Family and Social Issues

One of your biggest hurdles may be to understand just how difficult some patients find it to communicate with those they love. They don't want to be difficult, but illness has reduced their trust and empathy. They don't refuse their medicine because they enjoy being ill but because they are afraid of swallowing something they think could harm them. One way to learn about these behaviors is to meet in a group with others who have relatives with this disease. I've suggested some resources in Appendix A.

You already know some of the challenges that face patients and their families. What you may not realize is how profoundly your collaboration with clinicians can affect the outcome of treatment. An example is taking medication, which many patients go to great lengths to avoid. You can watch to be sure they don't spit it out or hide it between cheek and teeth. You may have to ask for a liquid form, which is hard to pretend to swallow. You might also ask the doctor about long-acting, injectable forms of Prolixin or Haldol—it is far easier to get someone to a clinic for an injection once a month than to assure the swallowing of medicine every day.

There may be forms for the patient to sign, stating that the doctor has explained all the possible risks of treatment. The forms are meant to forestall lawsuits that could result if a serious side effect such as tardive dyskinesia results from treatment. Signing release forms is really only a formality, but you can use the occasion as an excuse to ask all about side effects, until you truly understand the pros and cons of treatment.

You could have to face hospitalization for your relative. Many acutely disturbed patients need inpatient care at first to protect them from their own actions, to ensure that they get a fair start on medication, or to shield them from stress. However, patients with schizophrenia can become so ill that they refuse all suggestions from their doctors, including voluntary hospitalization. The question of administering treatment against a patient's will is a thorny one for everyone. Concerns about involuntary hospitalization and treatment spring from legitimate historical concerns that patients' civil rights have been ignored while forcing them to accept potentially harmful treatments. With the cards now stacked steeply in the other direction, legal issues sometimes end up trumping medical needs. Every clinician can tell stories of patients, released from treatment by a judge, whose health subsequently deteriorated. There is no perfect solution to this dilemma, though you may be able to avert it by persuading your relative to accept treatment voluntarily. If not, work with the clinician to ensure the best possible solution, given the mental health laws and regulations where you live, and to reduce the stress and embarrassment of commitment.

The acute phase of illness is an excellent time to participate in family education sessions. (Multiple family groups are an effective and efficient way to expand your social resources.) Whether in large groups or individual sessions for your family alone, you will learn about symptoms, early relapse, medication use and side effects, problem solving, and communication skills—for example, how to request cooperation without alienating the patient. This information can help decrease the stress for you and your family; you may even help prevent relapse. (An example based on the ongoing treatment of Jason is given in Chapter 13.) Your relative may also benefit from case management (in which a social worker periodically visits to assure good continuity of care) or supported housing (should you become unable to provide shelter). These resources are most likely to be available at larger mental health care centers.

You and your family should be ever alert for evidence of renewed psychosis. Usually, symptoms will be similar to those of previous episodes—feeling nervous or tense, pacing, trouble sleeping, loss of appetite, problems with memory or concentration, social withdrawal, or neglect of hygiene or appearance. Any recurrence of symptoms should prompt an immediate call to the doctor: many studies have shown that rapid intervention can reduce the need for rehospitalization. Fortunately, in the 21st century it is unusual for a patient to require chronic hospitalization.

DELUSIONAL DISORDER

In schizophrenia, the patient has several psychotic symptoms, such as hallucinations *and* delusions. In the much less common delusional disorder, the patient has one psychotic symptom—delusions. These delusions can be of several types, the more common of which are:

- Persecutory—the patient feels in some way intentionally cheated, drugged, followed, slandered, or otherwise mistreated.
- Grandiose—the patient has a special talent or identity, such as being a rock star or Jesus.
- Erotomanic—someone, such as a television actor, is in love with the patient.

These delusions are not bizarre—that is, they are ideas or events that could conceivably happen, as opposed to extravagant beliefs such as being abducted and probed by Martians. Except when they talk about the content of the delusion, these patients usually seem quite normal.

Delusional disorder is more common in women than men, and the patients are often widowed and middle-aged or older. Orville was in the nursery business with his father, then ran it alone for several decades after his father died. He was nearing 65 himself when he became convinced that his neighbor was stealing precious orchids from him. He had repeatedly called the sheriff to complain and was outraged at the lack of results. He was finally committed, against his will, to the county mental health unit, when he sent the neighbor (courtesy copy to the sheriff) a typewritten note threatening to "use my .44" if his greenhouse wasn't left alone. His son told the caseworker that Orville didn't have any precious orchids, only some cymbidiums that he had nursed back to life when the local KMart tossed them out after Christmas. He had no hallucinations or other symptoms of schizophrenia. Twice in the last couple of years he had been taken to a private psychiatric hospital, but each time he had refused medication and left, against advice.

If they can be persuaded to take medicine, most patients greatly improve, especially if treatment begins without delay. Over the past few years, the traditional neuroleptic drug most recommended for delusional disorder has been Orap, which is probably effective. However, the need for medication may be permanent, so a newer antipsychotic should be tried first. If antipsychotics don't work, some people appear to respond to an SSRI. Psychotherapy alone is of no value, but the family's involvement is at least as important as in schizophrenia.

PSYCHOSIS DUE TO MEDICAL DISEASE OR SUBSTANCE ABUSE

When Helen was 24, a serious automobile accident required her to undergo several blood transfusions. She didn't learn until 10 years later that she had contracted hepatitis C. She took the prescribed interferon for several weeks. One day she complained to her doctor that she felt tired and grouchy and that she heard talking when no one was around. The voice was that of her ex-husband, telling her to stop the interferon because it was causing her to lose her hair. Laboratory testing showed that Helen's thyroid gland had almost stopped working, probably an effect of the interferon; a low thyroid hormone level occasionally causes psychosis. With replacement thyroid hormone therapy, her hallucinations vanished and she successfully completed the treatment for hepatitis. Helen's experience suggests that in any psychosis, it is important to rule out a medical cause.

Although a variety of drugs (street and prescription) can cause psychosis, alcohol is by far the most common. An example: Danny had been a heavy drinker for at least 20 years, consuming over a pint of bourbon a day. He stopped drinking abruptly when he developed a case of the "stomach flu." Within a few days he began to hear the sound of chanting, and he wondered whether someone had put a transmitter into his ear. By the time he finally sought mental health care, he could hardly concentrate—the voices yelled things like "Don't tell them about your drinking!" and "Why don't you just kill yourself?" He was so terrified that he admitted himself to a locked psychiatric ward. Despite an admitting diagnosis of schizophrenia, within 2 weeks the voices melted away without medications and a consultant rediagnosed his condition as an alcohol-induced psychosis.

A mistaken diagnosis could have complicated Danny's life and future treatment for years to come. In each of these cases the best approach was not to address the psychosis directly but to treat the underlying disorder.

RECOMMENDATIONS

With only a few exceptions, antipsychotic drugs should be avoided unless there is a diagnosis of psychosis, as defined in this chapter.

- For a first episode of schizophrenia, treatment should probably start with one of the newer antipsychotic agents. I'd begin with Zyprexa, due to its overall effectiveness, lack of interaction with other drugs, and low incidence of serious side effects. If it doesn't work, try another newer antipsychotic.
- Patients should use an older drug only if (1) already well established on it without major side effects, (2) newer drugs haven't worked, or (3) a long-acting injectable drug (Prolixin or Haldol) is needed. Watch carefully for evi-

dence of tardive dyskinesia or another movement disorder. The physician should do a special survey of symptoms (called the Abnormal Involuntary Movement Scales, or AIMS) every 6 months.

- Because of potentially lethal side effects, Clozaril is a last-choice medication—even according to its manufacturer. Use it only for someone who has not responded well to other drugs, and read up on early symptoms of low white blood cell count.
- For psychosis that responds only partially to the antipsychotic, adding lithium, Depakote, Tegretol, or an antidepressant may yield greater improvement.
- Group therapy, cognitive-behavioral therapy, or social skills training may augment the drug therapy.
- I'd strongly recommend family education and, quite possibly, family therapy designed to assist your ill relative.

CHAPTER 23

Alzheimer's and Other Dementias

When you think about retirement, for yourself or a parent, what do you envision? Traveling abroad? Pursuing hobbies? Starting a small business? Moving to the Sunbelt? Whatever your dreams, I'll bet they don't include dementia, yet that is the nightmare that will confront many of us as we age.

Dementia is more than a problem with memory. The term actually means that someone has at least partly lost the ability to think. (You can see the distinction from a mentally retarded person, whose level of functioning is low from the start.) The older a person gets, the more likely dementia becomes. Of those who are 65 or above, "only" about 5% have dementia, but it affects nearly 25% of those who are 85 or over. Do the math: if you live long enough, you will probably encounter dementia—in yourself or in a relative. Most people who read this will not be the demented patient, so I've addressed my comments to family members like Sylvia—or you.

Sylvia started worrying about her mother when Edith turned 75. Edith had always been a little absentminded, but now she was becoming downright forgetful— 3 weeks in a row she had forgotten to place her regular Friday night telephone call. Each time, she seemed surprised when Sylvia called to see if she was all right.

When she finally took a week off work for a visit, Sylvia discovered that Edith had also neglected the marketing and housecleaning. The sink was full and the refrigerator was nearly empty, and dust smothered everything. Edith's speech and physical appearance seemed the same, but clearly something was wrong. By the end of the week, a neurologist gave them the answer: early Alzheimer's dementia. Sylvia was taken aback. Her mother, always independent and strong, had become sluggish and passive. Indeed, Edith received the news with hardly a blink of her eyes; she only asked where they were going to have lunch. Sylvia took an extra week off work and moved her mother across the state and into her own home. A paid companion came to stay during the day, when Sylvia was away at work.

This arrangement worked well for several months. Her new doctor prescribed Aricept (page 130), which Edith took faithfully each day. She seemed to brighten up and enjoyed reading and watching TV. At supper she would cheerfully talk about the good times they'd had when Sylvia was a little girl. However, she slowly lost ground. Several times when she tried to cook for herself, the companion had had to turn off a burner she had used and abandoned.

SYMPTOMS AND DIAGNOSIS OF DEMENTIA

All demented people have trouble with memory—amnesia—that usually comes on gradually. At first they may forget only more recent events. Edith forgot that she regularly phoned her daughter; others may have having trouble figuring out just why they are in a certain location. Unfamiliar surroundings perplex them; travel is a challenge. Because they know that they are not functioning well, they may seem depressed, irritable, or anxious; they may appear to suffer a change in personality. Occasionally, people who are still alert enough to realize that their faculties are declining will feel so depressed they attempt suicide.

Moderately demented people will find it hard to concentrate. They tend to withdraw from social interactions and have trouble attending to their everyday personal needs. Even with great effort they may be unable to recall events that happened just a few minutes earlier. Typically exercising poor judgment, such a person may wander far from home or become agitated, even striking out with aggression. Normal social inhibitions may be lost, releasing inappropriate jokes or other rude behavior. Sleeping during the day may become commonplace, perhaps because it is less frightening to awaken when it is still light and the surroundings are familiar. When dark falls, agitation may begin, a condition known as "sundowning." Not infrequently, the person hallucinates and becomes delusional. Is it any wonder that many demented patients become belligerent and refuse to cooperate with their caregivers?

Severely demented people remember less and less, until they forget even the names and faces of spouses and children. In the final stages, patients may become so disoriented that they lose even the sense of who they are—they cannot recognize their own reflection in a mirror.

Alzheimer's is usually a downhill slide that takes several years, whereas the decline of patients with a vascular dementia (where brain tissue is destroyed when a blood clot blocks its oxygen supply) is a sudden drop. A few months after Edith moved in with her daughter, a stroke left her limping and unable to remember words. Now her memory was worse than ever, and that was when her depression began. If she talked at all, it was to complain to the companion about how useless and lonely she felt. She slept poorly and ate very little. She cried and said she was a burden.

When she next saw her neurologist, Edith's left hand lay useless in her lap. She answered questions in a syllable or two. Sometimes she had trouble finding the words she wanted—she said "writing thing" when she meant to say "pencil." Asked to identify a magazine, she thought for a moment and called it "this papers." She agreed that she felt depressed and said that she hoped she would die soon.

Edith's story shows how the thinking of people with dementia is affected in ways other than amnesia:

- Even before her stroke, Edith couldn't care for herself—the house was dirty and she hadn't stocked adequate food. Clinicians call this inability to accomplish things a "loss of executive functioning."
- Later on, she could not think of the word *pencil*; this and other problems in using language are called "aphasia" ("without speech").
- Edith couldn't identify a magazine; some patients cannot even recognize ordinary objects such as a keychain or wristwatch; this inability is called "agnosia" ("without knowledge").
- Finally, still others will have trouble doing things, such as copying a simple design; clinicians call this sort of problem "apraxia" ("without action").

CAUSES OF DEMENTIA

The most common form of dementia is Alzheimer's, which used to be called "senile dementia" or just plain "senility." However, dementia can be caused by many other diseases, such as Edith's stroke (vascular dementia). It isn't unusual for a person's dementia to have more than one cause. There are many possible causes, some of which can be treated so as to slow, or even reverse, their progression. That is why the doctor will consider other possibilities before making a diagnosis, even if the symptoms look like Alzheimer's disease. An important example is major depression, which can so reduce interest and initiative that an elderly person may just sit and stare, seemingly incapable of answering questions or holding a conversation. This condition, called "pseudodementia," is reversible with treatment for depression. Other potentially treatable causes of dementia include tumor, trauma, infection, hydrocephalus, various vitamin deficiencies, Parkinson's disease, Wilson's disease (an abnormality of copper metabolism), multiple sclerosis, and toxicity from alcohol and other substances. Though not currently treatable, dementia due to variant Creutzfeld-Jakob disease, the human form of bovine spongiform encephalitis (mad cow disease), has been much in the news in the past few years.

Who among us will become demented? Although we cannot predict accurately (would we ever want to?), there are a number of known risk factors. Of course, for Alzheimer's the main risk factor is advancing age, but a history of Alzheimer's in close relatives or head trauma when young adds to the likelihood. On the other hand, several factors may work to protect against it, including red wine (consumed in moderation!), anti-inflammatory drugs (for example, Motrin), and estrogen replacement therapy used by many women after menopause. There is even evidence that advanced education helps to preserve the ability to think, a scientific verification of the adage "use it or lose it." Sometimes Alzheimer's dementia begins as young as 50 or 55; this type has a strong genetic link but is quite rare. The risk of vascular dementia is increased by conditions that cause stroke: hypertension, diabetes, sickle cell disease, and heart disease. Most of the risk factors for vascular disease can be treated effectively, but they must be treated before a stroke occurs: afterward, the pound of cure is worth practically nothing.

The outlook for Alzheimer's dementia is usually a steady, progressive decline, though some patients will stabilize, only later to resume their downhill course. (With vascular dementia, the decline is stepwise, corresponding to additional, small strokes.) If the cause can be eliminated or controlled, the course of a correctable dementia may be arrested indefinitely, though functions already lost may never return.

TREATING DEMENTIA

Even though there are few cures, many steps can lessen the effects of dementia on those who suffer from it—both patients and relatives—and to provide comfort for the demented person. From the first, make sure your relative gets to know the clinician who will be providing health care. If the clinician's face and voice become familiar now, they won't seem so frightening later on, when the disease has progressed.

The clinician may suggest a few specific psychotherapies that have been found useful in Alzheimer's dementia.

1. At home you can do reality orientation (repeatedly reorienting the patient to time and place), which promotes a better understanding of surroundings, perhaps leading to better self-esteem and sense of control. Persistent reality orientation measures can sometimes lead to anger, frustration, and depression, so discuss your plans with your clinician and watch carefully for problems.
2. In reminiscence therapy, the patient quietly reviews life events. In a typical weekly group meeting, participants are encouraged to talk about past events, often assisted by aids such as photos, music, objects, and videos of the past.
3. Individual psychotherapy may help some early-stage patients cope with the helplessness they feel as they face their impending loss.

Intellectual stimulation is vitally important to maintain orientation and socialization in a demented person. Encourage as much music, TV, reading, crafts, and just plain talking as your relative can manage. Occupational therapy may help to maintain the ability to provide self-care and to enjoy leisure activities. Physical exercise can preserve or even improve balance and overall functioning. Perhaps the most important therapy of all is your familiar touching, hand-holding, hugging, and kissing that convey the comfort and security of love.

Should the patient be told the diagnosis, as Edith was? Years ago, clinicians routinely withheld this sort of information from patients—and often, even from families. The rationale may have been to shield their patients, but I wonder if these old-time clinicians were really trying to protect themselves from the pain of confrontation. Modern-day surveys reveal that although most people wouldn't want their loved ones told, they themselves would want to be told if they had such a diagnosis! It seems that our urge to protect sometimes overwhelms our sense of duty to inform. I believe that patients have the right to this information, which creates a duty for clinicians to deliver it as supportively as possible. When still mildly impaired, people can express their wishes about such vital matters as wills and health care options.

Drug Therapy

A few years back, this section would have been brief indeed, because there were no medications that could directly affect a demented patient's ability to think. Now there are several, with more on the way. Each of the antidementia drugs—Aricept, Exelon, and Cognex—can help some dementia patients think better and function more effectively for a few months, at least. Of the drugs available today, I'd choose Aricept first: it can have a modest effect on both the thinking and behavior of patients whose dementia is still mild to moderate, and its side effects are relatively mild. However, none of them actually prevents the ultimate deterioration. Another possibility for slowing the effects of Alzheimer's disease is to use one of the off-label (that is, not FDA-approved) or over-the-counter (OTC) drugs currently available. These include vitamin E, ginkgo biloba, estrogen, and Eldepryl. (I discuss these in Chapter 10.)

For a vascular dementia, diet, medication, exercise, and control of diabetes and weight are all vitally important to prevent further strokes. The doctor will also want to make sure that blood pressure is brought under reasonable control, though not reduced too far—people with vascular dementia need extra steam to maintain the ability to think and remember.

If your relative has developed psychosis or agitation, the doctor has probably already prescribed an antipsychotic medication (Chapter 9). The first choice should be one of the newer drugs, such as Zyprexa or Risperdal. The reasons: good effectiveness and far less chance of serious side effects. Another choice: a new mood stabilizer, Neurontin, sometimes reduces the aggression and agitation of dementia.

An Alzheimer's patient who develops major depression usually should be treated first with an SSRI because of mild side effects. For example, Zoloft or Celexa may help improve mood (according to some clinicians), reduce agitation, and even slow the rate of decline in activities of daily living.

Family Matters

Of the 4 million demented Americans, over half live at home. This puts the burden of care squarely on relatives, often an elderly spouse. The caregiver has a number of important responsibilities that can help assure the relative's comfort and enjoyment of life. In fact, the steps taken by the caregiver are probably the most important resource the patient will ever have.

Report to the Clinician

The doctor needs to know about changes in mood, thinking, or behavior. Has the patient been falling? Wandering? Weeping? Have other health problems surfaced? If changes occur suddenly, don't wait for the next appointment to report them. Be sure to mention the use of food supplements or OTC drugs, such as ginkgo biloba or vitamin E—these could cause side effects of their own or interact with medications the doctor has prescribed. If your relative has more than one medical provider, make sure they communicate frequently, even putting them in touch with one another right away, if need be; transmitting medical information between professionals is a job that you shouldn't undertake. While you are at it, be sure to tell the doctor if *you* are experiencing symptoms of depression or anxiety—about a third of spouse caregivers do.

Provide for Home Safety

"Elder-proof" your home to make safe the bedroom and other areas your demented relative uses. To prevent burns, turn down the temperature on the water heater. Falls are a constant threat for weak, unsteady people with brittle bones. Remove or tack down loose throw rugs and other objects that can catch the toe of a shoe or slipper, and remove clutter and sharp objects that could cause injury in a fall. A low bed will also help prevent falls. A trip to the bathroom at bedtime can help reduce the need for late-night bathroom visits. You also might want to consider an in-room radio monitor, to ensure that you can always be within earshot. However, monitors do reduce privacy and may introduce some new problems while dealing with old ones.

Enhance Orientation

Especially when dementia is still mild, have clocks and calendars within easy view. Keep furniture and decorations constant. To someone who desperately clings to every shred of the familiar, change is frightening and frustrating. A label sewed into clothing bearing name and phone number can help, especially for someone who tends to wander. And nightlights in the bedroom and hallways can help maintain orientation at a time when diminished alertness and sensory input can undermine your demented relative's stability.

Maximize Self-Care

Small changes can improve your relative's sense of mastery and enhance physical capability. For example, snaps, buttons, and zippers signal defeat daily for many people; Velcro closures for clothing and shoes simplify the dressing process and reinforce self-esteem. Don't try to do too many things at once, or when the person is tired or unwell. Encourage someone who is only mildly demented to maintain to-do lists and to follow through—but be prepared to take over if frustration sets in.

Provide for everyday needs, such as assistance with personal hygiene, transportation, and communication. Older people need recreation and exercise—car rides, movies, and walks in the park are good for the spirits and for the body. Some older people lose their gag reflex, which puts them at risk for choking; many such patients have come to grief when given foods that require careful chewing, such as nuts, raw vegetables, and popcorn. Reduced noise, bright lights in the evening, companion animals, and activities such as gardening have all been reported to reduce agitation or aggression.

Legal Issues

Clinicians are duty-bound to provide the medical care they believe patients would want when fully competent. You should have an honest, forthright discussion about the future with all of your relatives as they age, to learn their wishes for health care alternatives. Hard as it may be to talk about, you'll thank yourself later if you must serve as a proxy for a loved one, advising clinicians about which treatments to use or avoid. I've worked with many families where this discussion did not take place, and I know how confused and guilty relatives can feel. If you've had such discussions in your family, you can feel confident that the information you are giving is just what your relative would have chosen.

Even better, encourage preparation of a living will. All 50 states accept living wills, which are sometimes called "advance directives." These legal documents clearly state what treatments people would prefer—or reject—at the end of life, should they become unable to communicate their wishes personally. For example, would your relative want tube feeding, a respirator, or other measures of artificial life support? What about IVs or a cardiac monitor? A living will helps both physician and family by identifying the patient's preferences, rather than forcing you to make decisions when you are under stress or when various relatives recall the patient's wishes differently. Hospitals and nursing care facilities have living will forms that you can use, but don't wait until admission to a facility. Have a full, frank discussion, get advice from the physician, and help your relative complete a declaration before the need arises. In my experience, it is best to have all close family members (spouse, siblings, children) present when discussing health care priorities. It could be much easier to obtain consensus now than at the end of life.

A "durable power of attorney" allows people to appoint someone to make medical decisions for them, should they become unable to do so. The substitute decision maker is ordinarily a spouse or child—someone who knows the person's moral or religious convictions and is prepared to act as the patient would wish. The durability of this power of attorney lies in its permanence, even if your relative becomes incompetent. The statutes concerning living wills and durable powers of attorney differ from one state to another. Your attorney can help with these documents; there are also books and websites that can give you more information.

It is also a good idea to have a family member become a cosigner on bank accounts and safe deposit boxes. It will greatly reduce the legal red tape when your relative becomes unable to participate in the management of personal affairs and must surrender charge cards and checkbooks.

Driving

What about driving a car? I know elderly people with failing memories who, for the sake of their own self-esteem, are allowed to drive on relatively deserted country roads with a "co-driver" beside them. I understand wanting to help them feel they can still do some of the things they used to, but for their safety and that of others, I believe that driving is a bad idea. Even mildly demented people are likely to make judgment errors when driving, and the risk of accidents will be even greater if the person has trouble seeing or other medical problems.

Family Education and Support

To handle all of these responsibilities, you will undoubtedly need help. A number of agencies and groups can provide therapy or support for caregivers, day care for patients, or family education. Check with your county mental health department or with the Alzheimer's Association for these resources. A nearby medical school may have a geriatric psychiatry division that can assist with diagnosis and management. You may also want to use Meals on Wheels, in-home health care and homemaker services, and assistance with general legal services. Online chat groups offer support, information, and experiences.

Respite Care

A valuable step for all concerned is to find and use any available respite care. That is a place where your relative can spend a few days—both a vacation from you and for you—to give everyone in your family time to recharge their batteries. Respite care can reduce caregiver stress and improve quality of life for patients; it can sometimes even delay the need for institutional care. VA, the largest provider of dementia services in the United States, offers excellent respite care. You can also check with the

Alzheimer's Association, church groups, and local community mental health agencies for other resources.

Medical Decisions

In your capacity as health care proxy, you may need to authorize hospitalization, operations, drug treatment, or nursing home admission. If agitation or psychosis provokes a psychiatric hospitalization, avoid admission to a regular psychiatry unit. Elderly Alzheimer's patients are too frail and vulnerable for care on the same mental ward that houses psychotic younger adults.

Need for Placement

The time a demented person remains at home can be prolonged by attendance at a clinic that provides full services, including general physician, psychologist, neurologist, nurse, and social worker. Nevertheless, as the disease advances you may reach the point where home care is no longer feasible. It is understandable that you might have feelings of guilt and anxiety about nursing home placement, but the reality is, sometimes the health and safety needs of a demented relative can become too great for relatives to cope with. Your clinician can help with this decision, but it also needs the input of other family members. No one relative should have to shoulder the responsibility for such an important decision.

It is also a decision that needs plenty of advance preparation, preferably several months, before you actually make the move. That way, your social worker or case worker can help locate the best placement possible. Its selection will depend on many factors, including your relative's finances, how close the facility is to you, adequacy of staff, cleanliness, possibly a religious affiliation. To the greatest extent possible, involve your relative by making trial visits to meet the staff, see the room, and become comfortable with the facility. After the move, there will still be the need for contact with family and friends, gifts of small personal items, and food from home (as allowed by diet and consideration for roommates).

At the End

Approaching death strains the fabric of any family. If your relative is not already in a nursing home, I'd strongly recommend that you enlist hospice services. Hospice is an organization that helps patients who are terminally ill and no longer responsive to attempts at cure. The goal of hospice is neither to prolong life nor to hasten death but to provide comfort, dignity, and support in the home during the final days of life. Hospice services can also be delivered in a nursing home; the services are available throughout all 50 states, in some 2,500 facilities nationwide.

However, you may have to decide what steps to take either to prolong life or to relieve suffering. From personal experience with many elderly patients and their relatives, I know how hard it is to make a reasoned, logical decision about a long-loved parent, spouse, or sibling when you are grieving and frightened about the very near future. Here is where the frank discussions you've had earlier will give you the comfort of knowing that you are carrying out the wishes of the person you are bidding good-bye.

RECOMMENDATIONS

- Before accepting a diagnosis of Alzheimer's dementia, check with your doctor to make sure treatable causes of dementia have been considered and ruled out.
- With its once-a-day dosing and low side effect profile, Aricept would be the first prescription drug I'd try. Use the highest dose tolerable, up to the maximum recommended. However, if your relative is already taking Exelon or Cognex and it is working, don't waste precious time by changing to something else. All of them can work for a limited time, and none of them alters the course. I'd start Cognex only if the other drugs don't work or cause side effects.
- Any woman who is postmenopausal should discuss with her physician the advantages (and possible disadvantages) of hormone replacement therapy, which can prevent bone loss from osteoporosis as well as its probable effects on dementia. A woman who already has Alzheimer's dementia probably has nothing to lose by taking estrogen.
- Try vitamin E, 2000 IU a day. It is unlikely to have toxic symptoms, and it could delay the progression of Alzheimer's decline by as long as half a year or more. If your relative is using ginkgo biloba and feel it helps, continue. If it hasn't made any difference after 3 months, it can be discontinued.
- Multiple medications or alternative remedies might be warranted, but they should be authorized by a doctor who knows about possible interactions and side effects.
- Try to find day treatment, in-home care, and homemaker help; join an Alzheimer's support group.
- Be sure that your doctor recognizes and vigorously treats depression, especially if your relative is severely depressed or suicidal.
- At the end, consider hospice services, whose staff know things that physicians don't, and whose profession it is to help your loved one make a peaceful, dignified exit.

COMMUNICATING WITH A DEMENTED PERSON

You can take (or avoid) many steps that will improve your interactions with a demented relative. Here are just a few of them:

- **Stay calm.** Your own quiet demeanor is the best response if your relative becomes upset. If you have trouble making yourself understood, speak slowly, not loudly (which only suggests that you are upset).
- **Explain yourself and the situation.** If your relative seems upset or balks at a request, the cause may be a lack of understanding what is wanted. The more reminders and cues you can give, the more reassurance and security you will convey. However, you will have to repeat your words more often than for someone who has no problems with memory and thinking.
- **Keep it simple.** Demented patients respond better to one request at a time, clearly expressed in just a few words. Avoid complex tasks that might lead to frustration. Deal first with the most pressing problem or one that can be solved easily (this gives everyone a boost).
- **Avoid confrontation.** No one wins an argument with a demented person. Deal with problematic behaviors by modifying requests to reduce frustration and the opportunity for demands on your family. Often, you can find a way around an impasse, such as by scheduling baths when a home health aide is there to help.
- **Look beyond the words to the meaning.** Demented people may become unable to express their concerns exactly in words. Try to figure out other ways to determine meaning—by pointing, using pictures cut from magazines, asking multiple-choice or yes/no questions ("Do you need to use the toilet?" "Do you want a drink?")
- **Practice the art of persuasion.** Sometimes it is difficult to deal directly with rapidly changing moods and behaviors. You might approach your requests obliquely, with the promise of a small treat right afterward ("Let's take a walk to get your cookie"). It can also help to break a request down into tiny parts. ("Undo the buttons; get out of the sleeves; now the shoes.") This can get around resistance caused by confusion or the fear of looking incompetent. In many such situations, your greatest asset will be your own ingenuity in devising acceptable ways to meld personal care needs with your relative's desires.
- **Lower your expectations.** Learn to accept a new norm of declining abilities and to celebrate the small triumphs of living.

CHAPTER 24

─────────────

Eating and Sleeping Disorders

Problems with eating and sleeping, two activities essential to life itself, have undoubtedly been around as long as there have been people. Some of these problems will yield to common sense, but others require science and the assistance of experts.

PROBLEMS WITH APPETITE

Eating too much and eating too little are the twin scourges that plague a healthy diet, yet at some point nearly everyone has done one or the other. Carried to extremes, either can be deadly. The publicity surrounding celebrities such as Jane Fonda, Lynn Redgrave, and Princess Diana has raised our interest in, and concern about, anorexia and bulimia nervosa. It has not, however, debunked all the myths surrounding these disorders. For the record, eating disorders can affect men; intelligent, educated people can have them; and you *can* starve yourself to death, as proven by Karen Carpenter, the Grammy-winning singer who died in 1983 when she was only 33. The descent into ill heath, threat of death, and strange attitudes and behaviors that characterize the eating disorders place them among the most heartbreaking mental conditions that patients and families can suffer. Of course, problems with appetite and weight loss can stem from medical problems, such as brain tumors and various intestinal diseases, but these patients don't have the fear of fat and the overconcern with body image typical of those with eating disorders.

Anorexia Nervosa

If you want to lose weight and you live in the United States or another Western culture, you are like the majority of your fellow citizens. If you are underweight for

287

your height and still think you should lose weight, you may have anorexia nervosa, a condition in which people lose weight, and perspective, on how they ought to look. Anorexia affects primarily young women (but it can start as early as the age of 10), whose concern with body image takes over their lives. Even as weight plummets far below healthy norms, they fear being fat and starve themselves into smaller and smaller clothing sizes. When given a normal meal, they may toy with their food or, if they do eat, run to the bathroom afterwards to throw it all up. To control weight, some exercise vigorously, others use laxatives or diuretics. So intensely do these young people desire thinness that some would give anything, including their lives, to achieve it.

Camilla's eating problems began when she was a sophomore in high school. During gym class she noticed that she seemed fatter than most of the other girls. (Even today she thinks there was some basis for this belief—she remembers being teased about "love handles.") Whatever the truth of her perception, she resolved never again to risk being called fat. She joined the Health Club, an unofficial organization of girls at her school who exchanged diet tips and supported one another's weight loss efforts.

Camilla became one of their most successful members. Through strict dieting and prodigious exercise, she had whittled herself down to 97 pounds from her highest-ever weight of 135 (she stood only 5-feet 3-inches tall). Even then, she thought the love handles still showed, so she began using laxatives and diuretics supplied by a club member. Although she managed to shed another 5 pounds, her mirror told her that she still looked fat. By this time she was consuming what she now estimates at about only 400 calories a day. Even some of that she would throw up; she had learned the trick of vomiting at will.

As she slid from slender to gaunt, her parents watched with mounting horror, and the "family food fights," as her older sister Becky called them, increased in frequency. Her mother tried to reason with her, but Camilla could see no logic but her own: to diet was completely normal for someone as overweight as she. "Fat!" her father exploded. "What are you looking in, a funhouse mirror?" First he demanded that she eat and physically tried to put food into her mouth; when she let it dribble down her chin, he angrily told her she could no longer date. When her mother tried to intercede and protect her, they fell to bickering. "They had no idea how awful it is to feel fat," Camilla told a doctor later. "And all the commotion at mealtime just shot my appetite." When her weight dipped to 87 pounds, her periods stopped and her skin took on a pasty, yellowish hue. Finally, her parents had her admitted to the hospital.

People like Camilla fear being fat and believe that they look overweight and grotesque. This greatly distorted self-perception is why they refuse to maintain a minimum normal body weight and will do just about anything to lose even more weight. When slender, they may feel they look disgusting; when emaciated, they may feel attractive. Those who have been sexually active may lose interest in sex. As the result of starvation, many medical problems can develop, ranging from heart disease to hormonal and intestinal disturbances.

Problems with maturation and control are among the alleged causes of this disease—perhaps, as Camilla hinted, refusal to eat is an area where young people feel they can overrule the control of their parents. Noting that anorexia is less common outside Western societies, many observers speculate that a cultural desire to be slender influences its expression. That may explain why the incidence appears to have mushroomed in the last half century. Because people often deny their symptoms, exact prevalence is uncertain, but estimates range up to 1% in young women. It is much less common in males. In both sexes, relatives tend to have the disease—but does this mean an underlying genetic causation or a learning process (imitating the eating habits of others)? No one knows for sure, though many researchers believe that there is a hereditary tendency, and there is little evidence that either anorexia or bulimia is a learned behavior.

Treating Anorexia Nervosa

Although anorexia may eventually remit even without treatment, 5% of patients die from the complications of starvation and many more suffer from severe social and medical complications. That is why early recognition and vigorous treatment are so important. Camilla was furious at being forcibly hospitalized, and she vowed that she would never cooperate with treatment. Her clinicians told her they understood her feelings, but she was so underweight that she was in danger of dying. She would have to remain in bed until she gained a pound. Only then could she have more freedom.

Wearing only a hospital gown, she was weighed first thing each morning. For the first 2 hours after breakfast an aide stayed with her to make sure she didn't vomit up what she had eaten. After a week in her room, she finally gained a pound and was allowed into the day room during her free time. She and her parents also began family therapy.

Education and treatment had their effect: Camilla was discharged weighing a healthy 117 pounds. Her periods, absent for nearly a year, had begun once again, and she was able to resume school. To protect her from further influences of the Health Club, Camilla's parents moved to another community at the opposite end of the county.

Anorexia is often the cause for emergency treatment—far too many patients die of their disease, as starvation causes muscle and heart protein to be broken down to supply energy. If suicidal depression or severe emaciation ensue, the doctor may recommend round-the-clock medical observation and care in a hospital setting. I urge you to cooperate with whatever steps are necessary in your state or jurisdiction, even if this means involuntary commitment (which research has shown to be about as effective as voluntary treatment). I realize that you will feel uncomfortable with this, and that your relative might complain of violated human rights and even threaten to "disown" you. I sympathize with these views, but I believe that the first priority is to preserve life; in all likelihood, once health has been restored, the patient will thank the family and doctor who placed health and safety first.

In most cases, however, outpatient treatment is sufficient. It is especially likely to help someone who has been ill for less than 6 months, who does not binge and then vomit, and whose family is cooperative and supportive. Family therapy seems to work well for patients who are under the age of 18, but it may even hinder improvement for older patients with anorexia—no one is really sure just why this is. Group therapy with others who have similar eating problems affords the opportunity to learn about the role of nutrition and appropriate exercise in overall health. There is some evidence that psychoanalytic psychotherapy may further stabilize patients whose weight has returned to near normal.

Only once she actually gained weight was Camilla allowed to have privileges. This is a form of behavior modification therapy that has been shown to work very well for inpatients. Drug therapy doesn't seem to help much, though antidepressants may decrease bingeing and purging. Periactin (cyproheptadine) at doses up to 28 mg/day sometimes helps increase weight.

Bulimia Nervosa

A generation ago, bulimia nervosa had barely made it into the diagnostic manuals; today it is known to affect over 1% of the young adult population, about twice the prevalence of anorexia. During an eating binge, the person will consume enormous amounts of food—usually starches and sweets, though I once knew a woman who would peel and eat a stick of butter—then compensate by vomiting, exercising, or using laxatives or diuretics. Patients with bulimia also often abuse alcohol or other substances. About half of patients with anorexia go on to develop symptoms of bulimia.

A few years after her treatment, Camilla became bulimic. Eventually she entered outpatient treatment, where she met Laura, who had grown up with parents who were "always fighting the Battle of the Bulge, just like me." They had been careful with Laura's diet, so that she was never overweight and always conscious of what she ate. After college, she had lived with a roommate and clerked at Starbuck's, until her job disappeared in the economic downturn. With little to occupy herself, Laura abandoned her regular eating habits and began gorging on large quantities of food, almost always consumed when she was alone. At the movies she might eat a "family-size" tub of popcorn and a giant cola drink; at home, she would devour a quart of frozen yogurt during a rerun of *Law and Order*. To avert weight gain, she would usually throw up most of what she had eaten. Recently, these episodes had occurred two or three times a week and had extended beyond snack time to her meals—whenever she took the trouble to prepare one. "I've put away as much as a 1-pound package of cooked spaghetti and two cans of sauce. I don't binge every day, but once I start, I can't stop. I feel like a human garbage can," she told her therapist.

Both anorexia and bulimia occur mainly in women; despite their similarities (vomiting, exercise, or use of laxatives to control weight), there are noteworthy differences. Patients with bulimia tend to be a few years older, and they can better conceal the shame of their disease because their weight is usually normal. Patients with anorexia starve themselves to become ever thinner; patients with bulimia eat huge quantities in binges. Whereas patients with anorexia have distorted self-images, those with bulimia are only *concerned* about their image. Bulimia also has medical consequences, though they are generally less severe than with anorexia. Dehydration, salt imbalances in the body, heart damage, and even sudden death can occur, but more common are dental erosion (from frequent contact with stomach acid) and salivary gland enlargement.

Treating Bulimia Nervosa

Most patients with bulimia don't seek help; Laura only sought care when her roommate threatened to end their relationship. As with most patients, she didn't need hospitalization. Although she denied feeling especially depressed, she was given Paxil, which helped reduce the number and length of her binges. (When taken at doses appropriate for depression, all antidepressants appear to reduce binge eating.)

Because most patients with bulimia relapse if treated with drugs alone, Laura's therapist also started her on cognitive-behavioral therapy (CBT). In contrast to anorexia, in which no single treatment has been very successful, many studies have shown that CBT is the treatment of choice for bulimia, though it may require up to 20 sessions over 6 months. Interpersonal therapy can also help, but it too must usually be given over many weeks. Family therapy doesn't appear to be especially useful, possibly because most patients with bulimia no longer live with their parents.

EARLY RECOGNITION AND MANAGEMENT OF EATING DISORDERS

Anorexia can seem so ordinary when it first begins. Its catalyst might be a friend's innocent remark or a magazine ad. When the diet starts, it may be no different from those many teenagers pursue today. How, then, can you recognize when normal dieting or other eating behaviors are getting out of hand? And what can you do about it? Here are a few guideposts.

An eating disorder may be developing in someone who:

- Prefers to eat alone or skips meals.
- Continues dieting once at or below normal weight.
- Cooks but doesn't eat the food prepared.
- Rushes to the bathroom just after meals.

- Frequently uses laxatives.
- Exercises compulsively.
- Pushes food around on the plate.
- Collects recipes or hoards food.
- Shows certain physical symptoms, such as thin hair, fragile nails, absent menses, marked fluctuations in weight (up to 20 pounds a week), enlarged parotid (salivary) glands from repeated vomiting, feeling cold.

How to respond to someone who may have an early eating disorder:

- Seek professional help from an experienced specialist.
- Don't be publicly confrontational or demanding; rather, ask for the person's viewpoint, listen, accept, be supportive.
- Watch for other emotional problems such as depression, use of drugs or alcohol.
- Be persistent yet patient. Even though your suggestions are rejected, you may have planted a seed. Give it time to sprout.
- If your relative is actually overweight, don't deny it. Instead, go together to obtain medical consultation about a sensible diet.
- Don't argue about diagnosis or make eating a battleground; eating disorders are often at least partly about control. Instead, focus on feelings and relationships.
- Avoid critical talk about the appearance of any person; emphasize health and fitness, not shape. Praise deeds and personal qualities other than looks.
- Seek family therapy to deal with interpersonal problems and encourage communication.
- If you are following a diet, try to de-emphasize it. Lead by example.
- If symptoms include very rapid weight loss, depression, other medical complications, or especially, suicidal thinking, seek further treatment *at once.*

PROBLEMS WITH SLEEPING

Your problem with sleep most likely falls into one of these categories: sleeping too little, sleeping too much, or sleeping at the wrong times.

Sleeping Too Little

If you have insomnia, you are in excellent company. To one degree or another, it affects perhaps 60 million Americans. For many, it is a serious problem—they feel ill and function poorly. However, half of these sufferers probably have a much less serious problem than they think. And many of the others have a specific problem that can be addressed to help improve sleep. The following information should help you figure out which group you belong to and what you and your physician can do about it. First, let's broadly outline the causes of insomnia.

- **Mental disorders.** Insomnia can result from a variety of disorders, discussed earlier in this book: major depression, dysthymia, mania, schizophrenia, posttraumatic stress disorder, and substance abuse. In any such case, treating the underlying cause will usually relieve the insomnia.
- **Medical illnesses.** Because of pain, difficulty breathing, or other symptoms, many physical illnesses can interfere with restful sleep. Obvious examples include arthritis, congestive heart failure, menopause—even something as simple as a persistent cough; a complete list would go on for pages. In addition, certain drugs prescribed to treat medical or mental disorders can also cause insomnia.
- **Your environment.** This includes anything nearby that keeps you from sleeping, such as car horns and alarms, blaring TV, noisy children, fighting neighbors, a bed partner who snores, and sunlight streaming through your bedroom window.
- **Your habits.** Daytime napping is probably the most common example of a habit that can interfere with restful sleep at night, though the excessive use of caffeine runs a close second. Going straight to bed after a late night out, without time to unwind, can also leave you staring at the ceiling. Even reading or eating in bed can create an association in your mind between bed and activities other than sleeping. Other interfering habits include smoking, exercising late in the day, and late-evening food or liquid, including alcohol.
- **Sleep apnea.** If you have sleep apnea (it means "without breath"), during the time you are asleep your throat periodically closes up and you stop breathing. Each episode can last for many seconds, up to 2 minutes in extreme cases, during which your blood oxygen may drop and you may become restless, kicking at your covers or bed partner. You may awaken frequently throughout the night and feel tired and irritable in the morning and sleepy during the rest of the day. The condition is especially common in middle-aged men who are overweight and snore. The diagnosis can be obvious, if your partner tells you that your snoring is sometimes interrupted by long pauses of half a minute or more. Sometimes polysomnography— simultaneous recording during sleep of various body functions, including brain waves, breathing, eye movements, and temperature—is necessary to make the diagnosis.

If the description fits, you need a careful medical evaluation right away. Although hardly any sleep disorders are what you'd call life-threatening, sleep apnea is an important exception. When severe, it can contribute to death from cardiovascular disease. In a mild case, the treatment could be as simple (!) as losing weight or sleeping on your side. Avoiding alcohol, tobacco, and sleeping pills is also important. If you need more, something called "continuous positive airway pressure" is the most effective treatment: a small electric motor delivers air to a nose mask you wear all night, preventing closure of your pharynx so that sleep apnea cannot occur.

Treating Insomnia

Many causes of insomnia suggest their own remedies. When the cause isn't obvious, the vast majority of people turn to sleeping pills—probably because a prescription is easy to get and easy to take, and it usually works just great for a few days. However, other approaches can do the job better, last longer, and have far fewer unwanted effects. By the time you finish reading this section, I hope you will resolve to make sleeping pills your last resort, not your first.

Your doctor will want to rule out all medical and mental disorders, which together cause the greatest number of insomnia cases. If your insomnia is chronic or recurrent, you'll probably need to keep a sleep diary. For several weeks, note the time you got to bed, how long before you fell asleep, the number of times you awakened, the time of final awakening in the morning, how refreshing your sleep was, and whether you used caffeine or alcohol, ate or exercised just before bed. A 2- to 3-week record of your observations should clarify the extent of your problem. For example, you may find that you've simply been caught in an unworkable cycle of daytime napping and nighttime wakefulness. The remedy would be good "sleep hygiene," a term that encompasses many commonsense steps you can take to improve your sleep (see sidebar).

Use medicine only if other measures fail. Each night, try to go to sleep without using a sleeping medication; the new ones work so fast that you don't have to take them early, in anticipation of need. If you do use a sleeping pill, a newer one such as Sonata or Ambien (Chapter 8) will provide brisk onset of sleep with the least risk of morning hangover. In addition, clinicians have recently found that cognitive-behavioral therapy (page 162) can produce substantial, permanent improvement for people with persistent insomnia.

Sleeping Too Much

Excessive sleep can be related to atypical major depression or dysthymia, and it can also have physical causes. However, about five people out of 100 sleep excessively with no identifiable cause; this is called "primary hypersomnia." Despite a normal amount of sleep at night, they feel sleepy during the day. Because they aren't alert, they don't function well at work or at school. The first line of treatment is good sleep hygiene; if more help is needed, a physician may cautiously prescribe a stimulant medication such as Ritalin.

Sleeping at the Wrong Times

Circadian Rhythm Disorders

The amount you sleep may be perfectly normal, but if your body needs to do it when you are supposed to be working or studying, you've got problems. Your sleep schedule is governed within your brain by a cycle that normally takes a shade over 24 hours to complete. The period lengthens during adolescence, which is why teens tend to stay up late at night, then sleep till noon. As life goes on, it shortens again, causing older people to fall asleep in their chairs in the evening. This 24-hour sleep–wake cycle is called the circadian ("around one day") rhythm, and it is normally recalibrated each morning by the influences of daylight, your morning's activities, and caffeine. The rather complicated machinery presents a smorgasbord of opportunities for things to go wrong.

Jet lag is probably the most familiar example of a circadian rhythm sleep disorder. After flying thousands of miles across continents or an ocean, you feel tired and cranky. Then, just when you should be pursuing important business or leisure activities, the overpowering need to sleep suddenly yanks your eyelids shut. This is because your internal clock is still set for the time at your point of departure. Most people find it easier to adjust when the cycle is lengthened, which happens when you are traveling east to west, with the sun. That's logical: it is far easier to force yourself to stay awake than it is to shorten your cycle by forcing yourself to go to sleep. People who work rotating shifts are also thrown into a sort of stationary jet lag every time they change to a new shift and must start sleeping at a different time of the day.

Both jet lag and shift work sleep disorders are self-limited—after a few days, you'll readjust without intervention—but another related sleep problem could become chronic. Burl first noticed it when he was 14 and, as a freshman in high school, had to get up at 6 A.M. because his school was on double shifts that year. He found that he slept so soundly in the morning that his alarm clock was useless—he just kept hitting the snooze button. Finally, he positioned a clock radio on the other side of his room so that he had to get up to stop the racket. By then he had missed so many early classes that his parents had been called in for a conference with his counselor. As sleepy as he was in the morning, Burl was wide awake at night; he found that he could do his best studying from midnight to 2 A.M. This pattern pursued him through high school and college, and continued to impair his performance as he entered the workforce.

Burl was eventually diagnosed with delayed sleep phase syndrome (DSPS). For reasons as yet unknown, the circadian clocks of these people run long and don't get reset each morning. They become drowsy a little later each night and need to sleep progressively later each morning to compensate, and end up physiologically unable to perform their responsibilities. DSPS usually begins in childhood or the teen years; up to 7% of adolescents have it. How often it persists into adulthood is as yet unknown, though it appears to be rather common.

DSPS, jet lag, and shift work sleep disorders can be treated with bright light or the hormone melatonin. Burl was asked to avoid bright light in the evening and to take 5 mg of melatonin not long before bed. Within a few days he was sleeping on a more "normal" schedule and awakening in time for work. His physician explained that the treatment regimen had "entrained his circadian rhythm" so that it ran closer to the normal 24 hours. When you travel, taking melatonin between 10 P.M. and midnight at your destination should help you adjust more quickly to the time zone change. (Also avoid alcoholic beverages and other substances that interfere with normal sleep.) If you cross more than six time zones, avoid morning light if you've flown east, and avoid late afternoon light if you've flown west. For fewer time zones, reverse the timing for daylight exposure.

Narcolepsy

When we dream, most of our muscles become paralyzed. This is normal; we don't notice it because we are safely asleep. In narcolepsy, a person will suddenly fall asleep at inappropriate times, perhaps while working or even driving. Often there are also attacks of cataplexy—sudden episodes of paralysis that even cause some to fall down. Stimulants such as Ritalin, starting with 5-mg doses and increasing gradually, can reduce the intensity of the sleep attacks but not the cataplexy, which can sometimes be helped by a TCA such as Tofranil. If you are among the .1% of adults with narcolepsy, you may find that planned daytime naps (as brief as 15 minutes, though some require a 2-hour siesta in the afternoon) help prevent unexpected attacks. Many people have worked out nap breaks with their employers in lieu of coffee breaks.

"SLEEP HYGIENE" MEANS GOOD SLEEP HABITS

I've outlined the commonsense behavioral measures your clinician may suggest to help you get a good night's rest.

- Search your bedroom for anything that interferes with sleep. Bright sunlight tends to reset your biological clock to awaken you early, so make sure your curtains or shades adequately darken the room. This is especially important during the summer months (or any season, if you work rotating shifts). Just moving your bed to a different wall may make a difference. Soundproofing or double-glazed windows can muffle disturbing sounds.
- Don't use your bed for activities other than sleep and sex.
- Avoid daytime naps; they will reduce your need for sleep at bedtime.
- If you worry when in bed, choose an earlier time to think about your problems. Try to determine one positive action you can take when you

awaken, then tell yourself that you've "done your worrying bit" for that day.

- Don't work yourself up with bedtime exercise. Regular exercise is good for you, but do it earlier in the day.
- A light snack may calm a growling stomach, but don't eat heavily at bedtime. Neither should you drink a lot of fluids, which will only necessitate trips to the bathroom when you'd rather be sleeping.
- Go to bed and get up at the same time every day; marked variation can desynchronize your internal clock.
- Watching the clock when you are trying to fall asleep can make you worry about the time; avoid looking at it until morning.
- Keep the same sleep schedule on weekends or vacations. Even a couple of hours spent sleeping in on Saturday and Sunday can give you a little taste of jet lag every Monday.
- Maintain a regular prebed routine. Nothing succeeds like boredom at putting you to sleep quickly.
- Practice relaxation techniques (page 184), which can help you gain control over muscle groups that you've been tensing up all along, without realizing it.
- Tossing and turning makes you feel victimized, and you'll begin to associate bedtime with failure. Some people actually dread going to bed because they fear they won't sleep. So if you aren't asleep after 20 or 30 minutes, get up and do something useful, but quiet, such as reading. Go back to bed when you feel sleepy. For a few days you'll be drowsy during the day (so what's new?), but later on it will help you fall asleep more quickly.
- Regardless of when you fall asleep, get up at the same time each morning. You need regular habits more than a given amount of sleep. Plan to spend a minimum of 5 hours in bed each night at first; you can increase it gradually as you learn to sleep more efficiently.
- When you awaken in the morning, get right up. Lounging in bed is incompatible with good sleep habits.
- If you are an older person, you may be spending too much time in bed. As people age, they need less sleep.

RECOMMENDATIONS

For Eating Disorders

- Anorexia will respond best to a combination of behavior modification therapy and, for younger patients, family therapy. Begin as soon as the diagnosis is made.
- Bulimia tends to respond best to a combination of antidepressant therapy (to

decrease bingeing) and psychotherapy, especially cognitive-behavioral therapy or interpersonal therapy.

For Sleep Disorders

- First, identify and treat any medical or mental health diagnosis that could be causing problems with sleeping.
- Investigate any history compatible with sleep apnea at once. Using continuous positive airway pressure will relieve most cases.
- Insomnia with no discernible cause should be approached first by use of good sleep hygiene.
- Cognitive-behavioral therapy may be useful for chronic insomnia that is not caused by physical or other mental health conditions.
- If you feel you must use over-the-counter sleeping pills (I realize that many people will), please limit them to a very few nights. They can actually change the way you sleep, and you can become so used to them that you won't sleep without them. You already have insomnia; you don't need drug dependence, too.
- If you suffer inordinately from jet lag and you must fly several thousand miles, try melatonin and bright light treatment.
- If your doctor recommends medication and you primarily have trouble getting to sleep, a rapidly acting drug (for example, Ambien or Sonata) has little risk of hangover.
- If you awaken throughout the night or too early in the morning, Halcion may work better, though you risk daytime drowsiness.
- If you and your doctor decide that long-term sleep therapy is indicated, use Ambien or Sonata and reassess your progress every 2 or 3 months. When you stop, taper gradually to avoid rebound insomnia.

CHAPTER 25

Substance Abuse

Substance abuse, ranging from tobacco to alcohol to heroin, is one of the most challenging problems a person can face. When does benign use become misuse, and when does misuse turn into abuse and dependence? How do concerned friends or relatives persuade users to address the problem? How do users transform a glimmering of worry into the motivation to change—and the follow-through to make change stick? How does one find the best kind of help—and professionals who can best deliver it? In substance abuse, just getting to the point of seeking treatment can be a major achievement.

Despite huge investments of resources into understanding causes and devising effective treatments, substance abuse is a growing struggle in our society. In fact, headlines in early 2001 cited substance abuse as the number-one health problem in the United States. Let me get this point off my chest right away: although some people believe that abusers of alcohol and other substances are just morally lax, careful study reveals that substance abuse is no different from any other medical disease. Like many other diseases, substance abuse disorders run in families, have distinct symptoms and courses, respond predictably to certain treatments and have well-defined, predictable outcomes, if not treated.

Some people in the early stages of substance abuse stop spontaneously or with a nudge from someone who is concerned. If they keep using and don't seek help, many medical complications and emotional and behavioral sequels are possible: disorders of mood, anxiety, sleep, and sex, as well as psychosis, dementia, and delirium. Although clinicians without much specialized mental health training often provide services for patients with substance abuse problems, you will probably consult a psychiatrist or psychologist if you or your relative has a serious problem with any of the drugs I cover here. They are the professionals who have the most training, experience, and resources to help you and your loved ones.

In this chapter I review the symptoms of substance abuse, explain how different drugs affect emotions, cognition, and behavior, and cover many aspects of treatment, both in general and for specific addictions. Here are the types of substance I discuss:

- **Drugs that slow you down.** Sometimes called depressants, these substances slow brain and body functioning to a snail's pace. They include alcohol, sedatives such as barbiturates, and antianxiety drugs such as Valium.
- **Drugs that speed you up.** Amphetamines and cocaine are stimulants that cause brain and body to work faster—for awhile.
- **Drugs that distort perception.** These substances produce hallucinations and include LSD and other hallucinogens, PCP (known on the street as "angel dust"), marijuana, and those that are inhaled (such as model airplane cement).
- **Nicotine.** This highly addictive substance keeps smokers coming back for more.
- **Opioids.** Heroin and its relatives are the most familiar paradigm for addictive substances.

THE DIFFERENCE BETWEEN USING AND ABUSING

At one time or another, nearly everyone overuses something—DSM-IV even lists several caffeine-related disorders, yet no one proposes limiting traffic in coffee. According to the National Household Survey on Drug Abuse, in 1999 about 40 million Americans age 12 or over reported using an illicit drug at least once, and 7 million had used one or more within the last 30 days. Just using a drug, even an illegal one, doesn't automatically mean that you will have a diagnosable substance use disorder. For that to happen, problems must result.

Let's put a human face on the situation with the Monaghan family. Del Monaghan, a 45-year-old salesman, tried marijuana a few times in college and once became so intoxicated on vodka that he had to stop every block or so, at 4 A.M. on a Sunday morning, to make sure the street ahead was truly deserted so that he could continue to drive home. The following day, as his headache subsided, guilt and fear made him resolve never again to put himself in that position. To this day, he'll drink a beer or two, but never three, when he attends a ball game, and he has exactly two cups of coffee each morning.

Del worries about his daughter Eva, 21. Last year in college, Eva got two tickets for driving while intoxicated, and several times she has been too hung-over to attend class. She and her mother spent Christmas vacation fighting about her drinking, but she refused to seek treatment. She even stayed sober for 2 weeks, just to prove that she didn't "have to have it." Remembering his own youthful misadventures, Del couldn't bring himself to confront Eva about her behavior.

Del's concern was fed by memories of his own father, Stanley Monaghan, a proud, self-made man who hadn't finished high school but had used his experience as a produce buyer to become a grocery importer. By the time he was 40 Stanley was both wealthy and drinking heavily, often going through a fifth of bourbon in a day, yet hardly slurring his words. Within a few years he had neglected his business and was drinking his way through the family savings. Threatened with divorce, Stanley consulted physicians and joined AA, but nothing worked. When he entered a hospital for "the cure," the sudden cessation of drinking caused such severe shakiness and nausea that he checked out immediately and returned to the bottle. One time, he had put his head on Del's shoulder and cried, "I'm a hopeless alcoholic, nothing without a drink!" The following winter he froze to death in an alleyway behind the liquor store.

Even Stanley identified himself as an alcoholic. Despite attempts at treatment, he depended on alcohol as a lame man does his crutch. In fact, *dependence* is what clinicians now call such a severe degree of reliance on any substance. In simplest terms, a person who is dependent on something needs it to function. We sometimes speak of two kinds of dependence, physiological and psychological. Tolerance and withdrawal, two symptoms that indicate physiological dependence, are especially typical of alcohol and heroin use. Drinking large amounts of alcohol without appearing drunk indicated that Stanley had tolerance: he needed increasing doses to produce the same intoxicating effect. Withdrawal occurs when the cells of body and brain become so used to a substance that they complain if the dose is reduced. Each substance has its own characteristic withdrawal symptoms (Table 25.1), including Stanley's shakiness and nausea. However, you don't have to have physiological symptoms to be dependent.

"Psychological dependence" means loss of the ability to control substance use, as when Stanley spent much of his time drinking, neglected his work and family, and repeatedly tried to quit. Another indicator of lost control is using far more than intended, which occurs especially with cocaine. In general, the more problems a person has from substance use, the more severe the dependence.

Dependence is the state we usually mean by "addiction," a term many experts now reject because it is imprecise—we also use it for people who just like to do something, such as eating chocolates or reading mysteries. The severity of dependence varies with the individual, the length of use, and the substance itself. People dependent on heroin tend to have most of these symptoms, and those dependent on marijuana tend to have fewer; the severity of cocaine or alcohol dependence can be all over the map. The vast majority of these people are not criminals or homeless derelicts. They are employed, normal-looking, have families who care about them, and in most other ways are responsible citizens.

Although you probably wouldn't consider Eva dependent (she even quit for 2 weeks to demonstrate her control), drinking had created social and legal problems for her. She'd had fights at home and missed classes, and she'd had a couple of citations for driving while intoxicated. Other symptoms that don't come up to the stan-

TABLE 25.1. Symptoms of Intoxication and Withdrawal

Substance	The attraction	Behavioral/emotional changes during intoxication	Physical/cognitive changes during intoxication	Withdrawal symptoms
Alcohol, sedatives/ antianxiety drugs	Reduced inhibitions (including sexual), improved sociability, brightened mood	Inappropriate sexuality or aggression, labile mood, impaired judgment, impaired job or social functioning	Slurred speech, poor coordination, unsteady walking, nystagmus,[1] poor memory, loss of concentration, stupor or coma	Sweating, rapid heartbeat, tremor, sleeplessness, nausea or vomiting, brief hallucinations, increased activity, anxiety, seizures
Amphetamines, cocaine	Elevated mood, increased talkativeness and sociability, alertness, self-confidence, relief from fatigue; some claim improved sexual performance; some inject or inhale cocaine for sudden rush of intense pleasure	Euphoria, blunted mood, extreme vigilance, interpersonal sensitivity, anger, anxiety, tension, changes in sociability, stereotyped behaviors,[2] impaired judgment, poor job or social functioning	Dilated pupils, rise or fall in blood pressure or heart rate, chills, sweating, nausea, vomiting, weight loss, agitation, weakness, depressed breathing, chest pain, irregular heartbeat	Unhappy mood, fatigue, unpleasant dreams, excessive sleepiness or sleeplessness, increased appetite, speeded-up or slowed-down activity
Hallucinogens (LSD, designer drugs)	Mild euphoria, sensory distortions	Depression or anxiety, ideas of reference,[3] persecutory ideas, fears of insanity, poor judgment, impaired job or social functioning	Perceptual changes, dilated pupils, rapid pulse, sweating, irregular heartbeat, blurred vision, tremors, poor concentration	None, though flashbacks (hallucinations that persist after the drug is out of the system) can occur
Inhalants	Giddiness, stimulation, loss of inhibitions, an illusion of strength; they are cheap and legal (hence, available), which appeals to children	Apathy, assaultive behavior, belligerence, poor judgment, impaired school, job, or social functioning	Dizziness, nystagmus,[1] poor concentration, slurred speech, unsteady walking, lethargy, slowed reflexes, slowed psychomotor activity, tremors, muscle weakness, blurred or double vision, stupor or coma, euphoria	None
Marijuana	Relaxed sense of well-being, reduced inhibitions similar to alcohol, dreamy fantasies	Motor performance deficits, anxiety, euphoria, impaired judgment, social withdrawal, sensation that time has slowed down	Red eyes, increased appetite, dry mouth, rapid heart rate	None
Nicotine	Initially, glamour, social acceptance; later, relief of withdrawal symptoms	None	None	Unhappiness or depression, insomnia, anger, irritability, anxiety, trouble concentrating, restlessness, slowed heartbeat, increased appetite or weight

TABLE 25.1. (*continued*)

Substance	The attraction	Behavioral/emotional changes during intoxication	Physical/cognitive changes during intoxication	Withdrawal symptoms
Opioids (e.g., heroin)	Euphoria, reduced concern for the present, indifference to pain	Euphoria leading to apathy, depression, or anxiety; activity level up or down; poor judgment, impaired job or social functioning	Constricted pupils, sleepiness, slurred speech, poor memory or loss of concentration	Unhappiness, nausea, vomiting, muscle aches, tearing, runny nose, dilated pupils, sweating, erect hairs, diarrhea, yawning, fever, sleeplessness
PCP	Euphoria, hallucinations, "disconnectedness"	Assaultive behavior, belligerence, impulsiveness, agitation, unpredictability, poor judgment, impaired job or social functioning	Nystagmus,[1] numbness, trouble walking, trouble speaking, rigid muscles, abnormally acute hearing, coma, seizures	None

[1]A back-and-forth flicking of the eyes.
[2]Behaviors that are not goal-directed.
[3]Such as a television program being directed specifically at the individual.

dard of dependence might include using substances when it is physically dangerous to do so (driving, operating heavy machinery). Some mental health clinicians use "abuse" in a technical sense to mean a person who isn't dependent but who uses a substance enough to cause social or legal problems; they would say that Eva is an abusive drinker. There is evidence that, whereas a few abusers (like Eva) progress to become dependent, most do not. However, I wonder how important these technical distinctions seem if you worry that you or a relative might have a problem with substance use. Call them what you will, nearly anyone would agree that both Stanley and his granddaughter had problems. In the balance of this chapter, I ignore these technical matters and focus on the information you need to recognize and combat substance abuse.

WHY DO PEOPLE MISUSE SUBSTANCES?

One of my professors years ago liked to say that the cause of alcoholism was alcohol. That is true, to a degree: a person who's never had a drink cannot be an alcoholic. But if the mere presence of a substance could produce a substance abuse problem, we'd be awash in addicts. We know that a number of issues in people's lives correlate with drug use: a dysfunctional family, problems in school, a tendency toward impulsive behavior, cultural notions of tradition, the approval of peers, even religious sanctions. But even these factors together cannot explain why some people become heavy users while others, after a trial or two, give it up or use it moderately.

From 10 to 15% of substance users have schizophrenia, depression, or an anxiety disorder; some may be trying to treat their own symptoms with substance use. Learning theorists hold that we develop new behaviors by copying what others do. The tobacco companies attract new victims each year solely because their advertisements link cigarette use with beauty, health, and fun. Some shy people find that drugs and alcohol help them make friends, a powerful reinforcer of further substance use. Many studies suggest that, for most drugs, there is an inherited risk for misuse. The neurotransmitters dopamine and serotonin may also play a role in producing both the intoxication and withdrawal states from cocaine and alcohol. In fact, all of these factors are probably important in causing substance abuse; some have even suggested methods of treatment. I especially want to discredit the idea that people drink or use drugs just because they lack willpower or have weak characters.

GETTING THE PATIENT INTO TREATMENT

Persuading abusers to enter treatment can be especially difficult if they don't recognize how destructive a habit has become or if the urge to use is stronger than the desire to stop. (Samuel Taylor Coleridge, a lifelong heavy opium user, wrote of being "chained by a darling passion.") If you use drugs or alcohol and you cannot decide whether you should seek help, discuss the facts and your feelings with a trusted friend—but not someone who drinks or uses with you. You need someone who is involved enough to care but independent enough to be objective. Various forms of coercion and threat—helpful ones—may play a pivotal voice in a user's decision to change.

- **Employee assistance.** Many corporations and government agencies offer professional help through voluntary programs.
- **Work–school coercion.** The threat of job loss or academic expulsion can be a powerful stimulus for change. The military has made especially effective use of this mechanism, as have the professional diversion programs offered physicians as an alternative to loss of license.
- **Spousal leverage.** When Nathan was in college, he had habitually used alcohol, cocaine, marijuana, and tobacco. He met Nan when he was 25 and, after a prolonged courtship, she agreed to marry him—with the understanding that she would leave, taking any children they might have, if he resumed using drugs. Three years later he slipped and began drinking; after 2 weeks Nan packed up her bags and the baby, and stood at the door. That was the last time he used anything; 8 years later he is still clean and sober.

- **Children.** When the user is a minor child, your legal leverage to command evaluation and treatment is strong—assuming you can find and afford them (see Chapter 3 for a list of resources).
- **Court.** Patients who enter treatment in lieu of punishment for crimes or misdemeanors committed while intoxicated do about as well as voluntary patients.
- **Mass persuasion.** A critical mass (at least three or four) of relatives and friends, all expressing the same (even unwelcome) truths, can motivate a user to take action.

For several reasons, however, we hesitate to apply pressure, as Nan did, to save the lives of those we love. Especially if the person is a parent or spouse, it can be wrenching to change roles and become an authority figure. As for friends and co-workers, we are often reluctant to intrude where we are not invited. We also know from experience that, like Del, many people who have used substances casually do not go on to develop serious problems, so we live in hope. Again like Del, who once drove drunk, we may be reluctant to confront an issue when there is so little daylight between ourselves and the person who clearly has a problem.

TREATING SUBSTANCE USE: GENERAL APPROACHES

Some substances, including the inhalants, PCP, and hallucinogens, have no special treatment modalities—drugs haven't been developed, psychotherapies haven't been explored—so we have only general principles to rely on. In the following discussion, I assume that you are the patient, but the principles apply equally to your friends or relatives.

A clinician's first step is to take a complete history and obtain a physical examination. The goals are to be sure that no medical disease has resulted from drug use, to assess how many substances are being abused and to what degree, and to probe the causes of their use. The reasons include peer pressure ("All the kids back then were doing it"), self-soothing ("If I don't have a couple of drinks before bed, I stare at the ceiling and worry"), fun ("For the first time ever, I was the life of the party"). This information may reveal another diagnosis—perhaps depression, social phobia, or another anxiety disorder. When another mental diagnosis (dual diagnosis) is found—which is the case in over half the people who misuse drugs and alcohol—it can impart another dimension to treatment. Another purpose of the initial evaluation is to assess motivation to change, which is essential to recovery. If your commitment to sobriety seems to waver, the clinician might use motivational interviewing to highlight the conflict between life goals and substance use—for example, that you want to be a good provider but, because of drinking, often don't show up for work.

The plan for long-term treatment and prevention outlined below assumes that you have already cleared the hurdles of acute intoxication and withdrawal and any emergencies (suicidal ideas and severe infections are just two of the many possibilities). Of course, you should discuss these general treatment steps with your physician, but they are time-honored practices that nearly every clinician will wholeheartedly endorse.

- Take a week off to organize your thinking. Shield yourself from drug-using friends, but don't be alone—keep your spouse or trusted (non-drug-using) relative or friend with you. Plan how you will change your lifestyle to avoid old habits.
- Abstinence should be the foremost goal of your treatment. For decades people have tried to limit substance use rather than eliminate the substance completely; for the vast majority of users, it simply doesn't work. Your future depends on freedom from, not of, substance use.
- Change your environment. It will be far more difficult to stay off drugs if you live or work someplace that encourages their use. You may need to move away from associates, places, and situations that remind you of drugs.
- Clean house. Get rid of every bit of drug paraphernalia, every hidden bottle, every last gram of drug.
- Deal with family problems. Relatives can facilitate your recovery by becoming involved in therapy and perhaps confronting their own drug or alcohol issues.
- Join a 12-step program. Although there is little research to prove their effectiveness, I strongly recommend the "Anonymous" programs (Alcoholics, Narcotics, Cocaine, Pills). They provide role models, support, and fellowship and cost nothing but time. Some of my most successful patients are those who commit to attend "90 meetings in 90 days," then follow through. For many, especially those who have no other mental disorders, these programs probably work better that conventional psychotherapy. They serve many problems and constituencies around the globe. Some groups disparage *all* forms of drug treatment, so if you need to use medications, shop around for a 12-step group that meets your needs.
- For some of the same reasons that the 12-step programs work so well, your clinician may recommend group therapy, which can increase social support, decrease isolation, and augment education.
- If individual psychotherapy is proposed, a proven technique, such as cognitive-behavioral therapy, is often the best approach.
- Use antidepressant, antianxiety, or antipsychotic medications only for an independent mental disorder, such as a depression that persists many weeks beyond the time you stop using.
- If you do have another diagnosis, it should probably be treated along with the substance use, preferably by the same clinician.
- A big risk for some is furtive use—closet drinking or secretive snorting that eludes detection. If that has been your history, you may need to submit to urine screening to help you comply with the program. Some patients even authorize the

therapist to report them if a urine tests positive for drugs. The threat of negative consequences (being fired or jailed, losing a professional license) provides a powerful incentive to stop using.

- Drug-free programs for cocaine and heroin users combine weekly individual counseling, frequent checks of urine specimens, and group meetings daily or several times a week. Some reward compliance with vouchers that can be exchanged for useful products. They may provide transportation to and from shelters, where the patients actually live, and lunch at the program. After several months, patients can graduate to paid work.

- Therapeutic communities work well for some people. Of these, Phoenix House is perhaps the best known. Patients reside at one of many facilities for 12 to 18 months, receiving education, counseling, individual and group therapy, job training, and work assignments. Though expensive, the cost is usually far less than hospital treatment. Phoenix House allows no substitute drugs, but others, such as the VA domiciliary programs, may be less strict.

Once you are clean and sober, your job has only just begun, for relapse is just a swallow away. One of my most successful patients kept a daily to-do list that was always headed, "Stay sober." Your clinician will help you identify cues that can trigger a relapse: moods, specific situations, and being around certain people. You will need to learn alternative approaches to these situations. Your friends, neighbors, and relatives should be brought into the campaign for your sobriety. Even if you should slip and use again, prevention is important to limit the scope and severity of your abuse. Don't let a slip serve as an excuse to return to full-scale use.

TREATING SPECIFIC ADDICTIONS

Listed in descending order of use, we'll next cover the range of abused drugs. Table 25.2 summarizes recent data on substance use prevalence.

Nicotine

In terms of the sickness and death it wreaks, nicotine is the most deadly addictive substance in the world. The consequences are almost too well-known to list in detail—lung cancer, heart disease, and emphysema, for starters. Nearly half of smokers die of illnesses related to this habit, which cuts 7 years off the average life span. The attractions of tobacco use—glamour, peer acceptance, feeling grown up—are strong enough to make nicotine dependence our most prevalent mental disorder.

Of all smokers, nearly half try to quit each year and about half eventually suc-

TABLE 25.2. Estimated Number of Substance Users in the United States, Based on the 2000 National Household Survey on Drug Abuse

Substance	Lifetime use in millions (%)	Past month in millions (%)
Tobacco	157.5 (70.5%)	65.4 (29.3%)
Alcohol	180.8 (80.0%)	12.5 (5.6%)[*]
Marijuana and hashish	76.4 (34.3%)	10.7 (4.8%)
Cocaine and crack	25.4 (11.2%)	1.2 (0.5%)
Tranquilizers	13.0 (5.8%)	1.0 (0.4%)
Hallucinogens and PCP	26.1 (11.7%)	0.98 (0.4%)
Stimulants	14.6 (6.6%)	0.79 (0.4%)
Inhalants	16.7 (7.5%)	0.62 (0.3%)
Sedatives	7.1 (3.2%)	0.17 (0.1%)
Heroin	2.8 (1.2%)	0.13 (0.1%)
Any illicit drug	86.9 (38.9%)	14.0 (6.3%)

[*]Heavy alcohol users (5+ drinks/day, 5+ days/month).

ceed, sometimes only after many attempts. Some experts call nicotine the most addictive substance in the world; its legal availability can make it harder to quit than heroin for some people. Your clinician will probably suggest several steps to help you; the more previous attempts you've made, the more of these suggestions you may need. First, establish a quit date and stop abruptly, if you can. Get into a group: especially if this isn't your first attempt, the support from others facing the same challenges can give you an extra boost. Seek a therapist who can provide behavior therapy (there is good evidence for the effectiveness of reducing the cues that have meant smoking in the past, such as ash trays in the house and after-dinner coffee). Some therapists recommend rapid smoking to the point of nausea, but the data don't show advantages over other methods, and it does present health risks.

Nicotine withdrawal symptoms occur in about half of those who quit, peaking at 2–3 days and lasting 3–4 weeks. For example, in the days after she went "cold turkey," Miranda felt depressed and irritable and had a ravenous appetite. "I was a hungry, cranky witch," she confessed later at a group support meeting; she also described having insomnia, trouble concentrating, and restlessness. Data show that using medication with behavior therapy will likely give you the best chance of quitting (and of avoiding weight gain that so often accompanies quitting). After a week, Miranda's clinician suggested that she use a nicotine patch, which quieted the withdrawal effects. Other people may prefer nicotine gum, spray, or inhaler. Zyban (the antidepressant Wellbutrin) (p. 140) has been shown to reduce weight gain and the craving for nicotine and to slow the onset of relapse; it can also address depression, which is quite likely to recur in a person who was previously clinically depressed and who stops smoking. If you have repeatedly tried to quit and failed, your doctor may recommend a patch, Zyban, *and* behavior/group therapy as the best chance for success.

Alcohol

The lifetime risk of serious alcohol use problems is about 10% for men, 4% for women. Chronic heavy intake can lead to many problems, including malnutrition and a number of neurological symptoms. Pregnant women who drink risk retarded babies with facial malformations (fetal alcohol syndrome).

A heavy drinker like Stanley could suffer from a number of typical withdrawal symptoms: sweating, tremor, insomnia, nausea or vomiting, rapid heartbeat, agitation, and anxiety. This syndrome will require a benzodiazepine such as Librium, perhaps in heavy doses, to prevent even more serious withdrawal symptoms such as delirium and seizures. Untreated, death occurs in up to 5%. A person with other medical problems or a past history of severe withdrawal symptoms may require hospitalization for several days. However, decades of research have produced no conclusive evidence that inpatient care improves outcome, unless there are serious withdrawal symptoms. A healthy person who isn't heavily dependent, like Eva, may be able to stop with mild symptoms, at most.

Two drugs can help maintain sobriety: Antabuse and ReVia. Antabuse isn't used much anymore, partly because of the risk of side effects. However, because it produces almost immediate nausea and other physical symptoms, it can keep someone sober who is well motivated but tends to slip. ReVia decreases alcohol craving and euphoria and has no severe side effects. As for therapy: although nonspecific psychotherapy hasn't proven very helpful, cognitive-behavioral therapy has. In addition, some patients may benefit from learning social and coping skills. With treatment, the outlook for alcoholism is good, in general, and best for people who don't have personality disorders or use other substances, are socially stable, and who steadfastly pursue their rehabilitation programs.

If you use both tobacco and alcohol heavily, should you try to quit them at the same time? There are two points of view, neither of which is backed by much science. One argues that quitting alcohol alone is hard enough and that the social and physical effects of alcohol are more immediately destructive. The other points out that drinkers often smoke, so that stopping both should improve quit rates of each. Although this question must ultimately be decided by you and your physician, I'd work first on the more immediately destructive alcohol.

Marijuana

The upper leaves, flowering tops, and stems of *cannabis sativa* are made into cigarettes, and the smoke is inhaled deeply and held in the lungs as long as possible. Those who don't smoke sometimes eat it in brownies. Hashish is the dried resinous exudate that collects on the tops and undersides of leaves of female plants. Although worldwide marijuana is the most commonly used of all illegal drugs, over the past two decades, the percentage of teenagers who have tried marijuana in the past year has remained relatively stable at about 35%.

Robin, for example, liked marijuana because it made her feel relaxed and contented. After smoking, she would sit back and enjoy dreamy fantasies. It reduced her sexual inhibitions like alcohol, but without the hangover. In fact, marijuana is most commonly used like alcohol—to facilitate sociability, perhaps a few times in a month. Although any smoking is bad for your lungs, occasional use is relatively harmless—certainly, far less a problem than most other illegal drugs cause. However, heavy use causes what's called the "amotivational syndrome"—apathy, poor concentration, social withdrawal, and loss of interest. In teenagers, heavy use can slow emotional and social development. Marijuana is dangerous if you are driving a car, pregnant, nursing, or have heart or lung disease. Although there is no actual withdrawal syndrome, frequent users may feel irritable or have trouble sleeping; anxiety symptoms during use or in a flashback are by no means rare.

Most marijuana users probably don't need treatment any more than people who drink alcohol occasionally. That can make it hard to persuade your teenager that there is a problem. If marijuana is used frequently, to the exclusion of other activities, group therapy that focuses on drugs probably helps most; benzodiazepines may occasionally be needed short-term to deal with anxiety. Although it has been argued for years that marijuana is a "gateway drug" that leads to the use of other, more dangerous substances, no cause-and-effect relationship has ever been demonstrated satisfactorily. The vast majority of people, like Robin, *don't* go on to abuse other drugs. A better case for gateway status can be made for tobacco.

Cocaine

When Terry was 20, he started using cocaine occasionally with friends. It seemed to enhance his social life (he felt bright and witty and had "dynamite" sex). For a semester, he used it every week or two without problems; then, during summer vacation, he smoked crack again and again, until his supply was gone. Then he would fall into a depressed torpor, with dreams of destruction so realistic he would awaken screaming. After a few days, he would rouse himself and start using again so that he could feel wonderful and self-confident once again.

Cocaine is a stimulant that was first used medically over 100 years ago. Until the dawn of the 20th century it was even an ingredient in Coca-Cola. It was little abused in the United States until the 1970s. Especially when inhaled or injected, cocaine elevates mood and increases alertness and confidence. It is the most powerful reinforcer of drug-taking behavior known. Laboratory rats prefer it to food, water, and the company of other rats; given free access, they'll use it until they die of starvation. Human use is nearly as devastating: though usually intermittent at the start, users escalate to intense runs, during which they consume the drug several times an hour, until it is gone. Then the crash is profound, a depression so intense that the person will do just about anything to escape. It is an irony that Sigmund Freud recommended it for treating alcohol and morphine addiction.

Cocaine can be swallowed, snorted, inhaled, or injected. Heated with sodium bicarbonate, it yields a hard white mass that makes a crackling sound when smoked, hence the term "crack." When injected or inhaled, cocaine produces a sudden rush of pleasure that users sometimes intensify by adding other drugs, such as heroin; this combination, called a speedball, has recently been implicated in numerous deaths. Withdrawal is extremely rapid, generally less severe than with opioids or sedatives, and usually requires no special treatment. Hospitalization may be necessary for someone who is suicidal, severely depressed, or psychotic, or whose previous attempts at rehabilitation have been unsuccessful. It may take weeks for thinking, mood, and sleep to normalize. Cocaine produces intense devotion and high recidivism; chronic use causes long-lasting changes in the brain and memory loss.

Education or pressure from relatives or employers can motivate some people who are less heavily dependent. One study suggests that heavy users may improve with the combination of group and individual drug counseling based on 12-step programs. Relapse prevention therapy (RPT; page 163) has been especially successful. Some addicts (and their therapists) swear by earlobe acupuncture; in 2000, a controlled study found it better than two other treatments, but other studies have failed to find any advantages. Terry joined Cocaine Anonymous, and his parents paid for a course of RPT. He recovered, though it took more than a year, and even now he sometimes thinks how wonderful he would feel if he could smoke a single rock of crack.

Amphetamines

Amphetamines are structurally related to adrenaline, the hormone that prepares our bodies for "fight or flight" when we are aroused. Today they are prescribed for attention-deficit/hyperactivity disorder in children and narcolepsy in adults, and they are even occasionally used in depression. When they were first used clinically in the 1930s, doctors prescribed them for a variety of complaints, including appetite control and impotence; older readers may recall Benzedrine inhalers that were once used to clear stuffy nose. (Interestingly, from 1942 until his death, Hitler took daily amphetamine injections, which may have affected his conduct of the war.)

What appeal does this group of drugs have? Truckers and others who drive for a living may swallow low doses to fend off fatigue. Others use them to produce euphoria, perhaps moving on to very high doses, often by inhaling. Users feel strong, smart, and sexy, leading to speed runs of days or weeks, punctuated by periods of crashing. Experienced users sometimes add sedatives or alcohol to moderate the effects.

The symptoms of intoxication and withdrawal are nearly identical to those of cocaine; patterns of use, treatment, and outcome are also similar. Withdrawal from low doses yields relatively brief fatigue; from higher doses people become restless, talkative, irritable, and preoccupied with getting more drug. Paranoia and overt psychosis, and sometimes death (from stroke or heart failure), can ensue. Obtaining amphetamines can occupy a person's entire attention, obliterating all other considerations and responsibilities, including jobs and children. Many occasional users stop without treatment; hospitalization is indicated only if the person becomes severely depressed, psychotic, violent, or the intake is far beyond control. The general treatment approaches discussed above can liberate many users, though it takes nearly 2 years, on average, to get clean and stay that way.

There is an alphabet soup of amphetamine-like drugs—MDMA (Ecstasy), MDEA (Eve), MDA, and PMA, so-called designer drugs. (Other designer drugs are minor alterations of PCP and opioids; one, MPTP, has caused severe parkinsonism in some users.) Jenny encountered Ecstasy at an all-night rave party, when she accepted a drink from a boy she didn't know. At first, it boosted her self-confidence so high that she grabbed the microphone and started to sing. Then someone grabbed *her* and hustled her into the cool-down room, where she gradually succumbed to anxiety bordering on panic, followed by depression. Her drowsiness, trouble concentrating, and fatigue lasted for several days but subsided without any specific treatment. She was lucky: a 2001 study found that MDMA users can suffer long-term brain damage.

Hallucinogens

LSD wasn't synthesized until 1943, but the ability of natural substances (such as mescaline and the fly agaric mushroom) to produce hallucinations has been recorded throughout history. Nearly 100 such plants have been recognized in the Western Hemisphere alone. With LSD so cheap and easily made in home laboratories, many users came to value it for its mild euphoria and sensory distortions. For example, during her dozen or so experiences with LSD in college, Miriam found that colors seemed brighter, sounds clearer, tastes sharper than normal. She always knew that these sensations weren't "real," and she had never experienced a bad trip—terror or fears of insanity when one seems to melt into the boundaries of the universe.

Because frequent use weakens its effects, most people don't use LSD day after day. There is little tendency toward dependence and there are no withdrawal symptoms, as such. When patients seek treatment, it is usually for depression, anxiety, psychosis, or suicidal ideas. Half or more of frequent users report flashbacks—aspects of a previous trip replay themselves spontaneously, without further drug use. For several months after quitting, Miriam would occasionally see bright colors around the edge of the paper she was writing on, and once she thought that people she encountered at the mall were automatons. "It wasn't scary, but I wanted it to go away."

The LSD experience resolves spontaneously after a few hours, during which the user should avoid stimulants, emotional stressors, marijuana, and over-the-counter drugs; Klonopin or Valium may be needed for a bad trip. If hallucinations persist, antipsychotic agents may be necessary. Then an unresolvable argument often erupts: was the long-term psychosis caused by the drug, or would it have occurred anyway?

Sedatives

Barbiturates and other dangerous sedatives were heavily abused in the 1960s, but strict government controls have led to marked declines in their abuse. Although benzodiazepines have been hugely popular for a variety of indications, especially with those over 55, they are used appropriately for the most part. Those who do abuse them often use other drugs as well. Rarely lethal, even in massive overdose, the symptoms of benzodiazepine abuse are far less severe than those of most other drugs, and the response to treatment is far better. Intoxication and withdrawal are symptomatically very similar to alcohol; withdrawal can precipitate seizures and, in a small percentage, even death.

Tegretol (200 mg twice a day) has been used by some to reduce the withdrawal syndrome. The general steps outlined above can help most long-term benzodiazepine users successfully stop and stay off. Because many patients are prescribed benzodiazepines for anxiety and other disorders, adequate substitute treatment is extremely important.

In recent years, Rohypnol has become notorious as the "date rape" drug. A benzodiazepine legally prescribed for sleep in many other countries, it has been smuggled into the United States and used, often with alcohol, to increase sexual compliance and reduce memory in unsuspecting women. "The last thing I remember was a drink that Ronnie gave me," Cynthia told the policewoman who interviewed her. "A few minutes later I felt dizzy and sick to my stomach, and then I must have passed out. I think I woke up once, and he was raping me, but I couldn't be sure. The next clear memory I have is waking up in his bed."

Education and vigilance are the best means to prevent substance-assisted date rape. Avoid punch bowl concoctions; watch your drink being mixed or drink only from a sealed container; and never leave it unguarded, even to use the bathroom. At a party, enlist a friend in a two-person "neighborhood watch," each to observe the other for symptoms of appearing too drunk and, if needed, to get the victim to some place safe.

Inhalants

Inhalants are something of a contradiction: illicit drugs of abuse that were perfectly legal when originally sold as fuels, paint thinners, solvents in glues, and propellants for paint, shaving cream, and hair spray. They evaporate easily and are usually absorbed by bagging (inhaling from a container into which the substance has been sprayed) or huffing (mouth-breathing through a soaked rag). Either method can keep a user high for hours.

Grade-school and teenage boys, who often use inhalants as a group activity, like them because they are cheap and fast-acting (like everything that is absorbed from the lungs). Dudley, for example, had huffed model airplane glue for 3 years; he liked the high and the way it made the hours flash past so he didn't think about the way his parents were always fighting.

Because they severely reduce the blood's ability to carry oxygen, the inhalants are the most physically destructive of all drugs of abuse. A few people die from inhalant use, while others suffer brain or liver damage, so it is fortunate that few people actually become physically dependent on them. For those who use them only occasionally, education may be all the discouragement needed; the severe dangers of chronic use will make any chronic user want to use all the treatment steps mentioned above as soon as possible. Those who persist should be referred for longer recovery programs that use a variety of treatment modalities. See Appendix A.

Opioids

When someone mentions addiction, heroin often springs first to mind. Heroin is an opioid (that is, a derivative of opium), the class of drug used to control severe pain. It includes methadone, morphine, codeine, and Dilaudid, but heroin is by far the one used most by addicts. Weekly use usually leads to dependence, the fate of perhaps one in four who try heroin.

Although some people begin use when they are given narcotics for pain, most start in their teens or 20s, perhaps encouraged by peers or in progression from other drugs. Tolerance begins with the first few doses, and pursuit and use ("staying well") quickly come to dominate their lives. Withdrawal symptoms—nausea, muscle cramps, tearing, insomnia—are hardly life-threatening to healthy adults, but they are extraordinarily uncomfortable and discourage dependent users from quitting. The typical habit costs $200 a day, which users earn by theft or selling drugs themselves. The overall death rate is enormous, especially from overdose, suicide, and AIDS.

Those who genuinely want to rid themselves of heroin dependence must commit to long-term changes of lifestyle, friends, even location—it may be impossible to stay off drugs if exposed to reminders of former lives. The first step is to get off opioids, and to do that may require withdrawal using methadone or clonidine, which can help suppress the aches, insomnia, lethargy, restlessness, and craving for drugs. The medication will be tapered gradually, a process that can take several weeks. Then the problem is to decide how best to prevent relapse. Some manage with drug-free programs, which feature frequent outpatient groups; some move to therapeutic communities for periods ranging to 18 months; here they are treated by ex-addicts as well as professionals. Counseling, Narcotics Anonymous, and cognitive-behavioral therapy all seem to help many users. Though I know of no absolute proof of their effectiveness, I'd consider any or all in the rehabilitation of an opioid user. Family therapy can help, though its advantage may lie simply in having a supportive family that is committed to rehabilitation.

Ironically, many heroin users require drug maintenance if they are to remain clean. For example, Erik was a 42-year-old veteran who had started using heroin with a lot of friends when he was overseas in the army. Back home, his friends quit, but he kept using. By his own account, all of his paychecks "and a lot else" went into his arm. He had lasted less than a week in several drug-free programs. Finally reduced to selling drugs and burglarizing cars for stereos, he applied to a VA clinic and began methadone maintenance. On 70 mg a day he rapidly stabilized. Although once or twice he relapsed, revealed by his urine samples, he admitted his mistakes and redoubled his commitment to staying drug free. Two years later he was still on methadone but otherwise clean and sober, once more gainfully employed.

The federal government closely regulates maintenance by methadone (or ORLAAM, the longer-acting form). Patients must have been dependent for at least 1 year and failed to quit, using other means. With adequate doses (often 60 mg/day or more), most patients experience decreased illicit drug use, depression, unemployment, and crime. An important negative is that withdrawing from methadone is uncomfortable and can take many months. Without it, however, 75% or more of patients return to illicit use, so most clinicians argue that there should be no arbitrary limit on length of maintenance. You should be a full partner in deciding to stop. If you can't find a methadone program or don't qualify for one, there is ReVia. This opioid antagonist blocks opioid euphoria—without the high, there is less drive to use heroin.

The chances of eventually recovering from opioid dependency actually aren't bad. Many people shake the habit, even without special treatment. Overall, the most important predictive factor is the strength of motivation. For example, a professional person whose license to practice depends on remaining clean and sober has a powerful reason to clean up and stay that way; the strict demands of a spouse or partner may serve the same function. Stable employment and supportive relatives generally improve the likelihood of anyone's success. Life crisis or depression often heralds relapse, which is most likely to occur within the first 3 months. Even someone who has tried unsuccessfully to quit shouldn't give up hope: multiple treatment attempts can add up, eventually leading to success.

PCP

Judging just by the numbers, phencyclidine (PCP, or "angel dust") isn't such a se rious problem, but if you go by the utter destruction it can cause, PCP is a calamity lying in wait. Smoked, snorted, or swallowed, PCP's effects are highly unpredictable. It can produce euphoria or panic, hallucinations and paranoia, drowsiness and disorientation. Nystagmus (back-and-forth flicking of the eyes) is characteristic, and convulsions, coma, and eventual death sometimes result. Most people who use PCP recover—though one man I knew remained strapped to a hospital bed, hostile and rigid, secluded for weeks at a time because any stimulation launched him into a violent rage. Benzodiazepines and antipsychotics may be useful for the acute symptoms, but there is no known, definitive treatment. Angel dust is a devil on a blotter. To ingest this drug voluntarily is the utmost in human folly. If you know someone who uses it, I hope you will use all the suggestions I've given below and on page 305.

RESCUING YOUR SUBSTANCE-USING RELATIVE

In no particular order, here are some of the many actions you can take to help your drug-using relative:

- Learn all you can about the substance. Read books and magazine articles, attend lectures, surf the Internet. If allowed, accompany your relative to medical and counseling sessions.
- Meet denial or lies with facts, not fights. The purpose of denial is to avoid feelings of guilt and shame. Facts calmly presented will help establish you as an ally, not an enemy.
- Boredom is the enemy of sobriety. Encourage participation in new activities as a substitute for drug use. Vigorous exercise, for example, produces a "natural high" without harmful side effects.
- Repeatedly express your support and belief that treatment can help. A lot of each will be needed to get past the demoralization ("What's the use?") so many drug users experience.
- Encourage your relative to attend a 12-step program. You may want to attend an Alanon program yourself. For kids, there's Alateen.
- If the clinician recommends coercion, go with it! Even patients who begin treatment under duress often recover.
- Regard slips as an educational opportunity. ("You've had a lapse, not a relapse; we've learned another situation that is dangerous for you.")
- Don't measure success by duration of total abstinence but as percent time spent substance free.
- Don't treat adult users like children—they need to feel more responsible, not less.
- Read this sentence until you believe it:

Overwhelming evidence proves that substance abusers are sick, not bad.

- If your relative contends that professionals overdiagnose to make more money, recognize the belief as an excuse for continued use. Help the clinician get across just how much of a problem your relative has been having—and causing.
- If recommended, embrace family therapy as a terrific opportunity to

deal with enabling (unconsciously shielding someone from the consequences of drug use). Studies show that recovery is strongly reinforced by support of family members, who need to learn that they are not to blame and that their anger at the user is normal.

- Approach differences calmly and when your relative is sober. When high is not the time for a confrontation—it simply won't register.
- Listening to reasons for using doesn't mean that you agree with them. Be clear that you just want to understand and support your relative in every way possible.
- If you are a nonusing spouse, calmly explain (when your partner is sober) that the relationship won't last if drug use continues. The consequences of continuing drug use must come across as information, not as a threat.
- If there has been violence, ensure your own safety and that of your family. Staying with an abusive user endangers you and may make treatment seem less urgent.
- If you want your partner to quit using alcohol, tobacco, or drugs, you must maintain a drug-free home and avoid these substances yourself, even if your use is moderate. For just one partner to quit while the other continues to use is likely to destroy the sobriety, the relationship, or both.
- Are you worried that your children may take up the use of drugs? The relatives of drinkers tend to drink, but this is a statement, not a life sentence. With education and frank discussion, you can help sow the seeds of sobriety now.
- If your relative is pregnant, redouble your efforts to help her avoid all drugs, many of which can seriously affect the survival and health of the developing baby.
- Once your relative is off drugs, be prepared for depression, irritability, and cravings. You'll also have to deal with your own resentment.
- Finally, if you cannot get the person completely off drugs or alcohol, do what you can to reduce harm (for example, HIV counseling, taking multiple vitamins, using condoms).

RECOMMENDATIONS

For All Drugs

I won't repeat the suggestions I've already covered in the sidebar, the table, and the material beginning on page 305. This information covers symptoms of drug use, basic approaches to treatment, and the steps friends and relatives can take to help. For certain substances, using specific medications make sense.

For Smoking Cessation

- Although you can buy gum and patch without a prescription, see your doctor first to be sure you don't have heart disease, diabetes, high blood pressure, ulcers, or asthma. Use the gum especially if you smoke at certain times of day (for example, after meals, coffee breaks). If you smoke heavily, you may do better with the patch. If you choose gum, you'll probably find that you need the 4-mg sticks; even light smokers may find the 2-mg sticks ineffective.
- Because it is irritating, I'd avoid the nasal spray, except as a second trial or a helper for the patch. The inhaler seems especially inconvenient (though you don't have to stand outside to use it).
- Heavy smokers may need combined methods (for example, patch plus spray). Be sure to consult your physician first.
- On your second or third try, consider using bupropion with the patch to increase your chances of success.

For Alcohol

- For a deeply committed patient or one who is willing to undergo monitoring, I'd try ReVia first, because of its low risk of side effects.
- Antabuse remains an effective agent, though side effects and the Antabuse–alcohol reaction limits its use.

For Opioid Abuse

- Despite its drawbacks, I'd recommend methadone as a first approach. The chances of anyone kicking a serious narcotics habit without help are small.
- Moving later to ORLAAM would be a reasonable choice for well-stabilized patients, though methadone may be somewhat more effective.
- ReVia is worth a try for anyone who cannot get into a methadone program.

APPENDIX A

Resources

With so many disorders to address and so many modalities of treatment, a truly comprehensive resource list could easily stretch to book-length. Therefore, I've selected a few resources that offer good places to start your further research into individual topics. The following resources were up to date at the time of publication.

GENERAL

Books

DSM-IV Made Easy, by James Morrison. New York: Guilford, 1995. Updated in 2001 for DSM-IV-TR criteria changes; presents mental health diagnostic criteria in simplified terms, with over 100 case illustrations.

Diagnostic and Statistical Manual of Mental Disorders. (DSM-IV-TR; 4th edition, text revision). Washington, DC: American Psychiatric Association, 2000. For those who want to learn about diagnosis from the horse's mouth.

Essential Guide to Psychiatric Drugs, by Jack M. Gorman. New York: St. Martin's, 1998. Highly regarded resource presented in everyday language.

Organizations and Websites

The **National Institute of Mental Health** (NIMH) maintains an excellent website for patients and their families, including links to resources for referral, further reading, and in some cases, self-administered tests and clinical trials. The disorders covered include obsessive–compulsive disorder and other anxiety disorders, schizophrenia, bipolar and depressive disorders, posttraumatic stress disorder, social phobia, panic disorder, eating disorders, borderline personality disorder, and several childhood disorders. NIMH Public Inquiries, 6001

Executive Boulevard, Room 8184, MSC 9663, Bethesda, MD 20892-9663; tel: 301-443-
4513; website: *http://www.nimh.nih.gov/publicat/index.cfm#disinfo.*

Medline plus. National library of medicine's website includes a medical encyclopedia, drug
information, access to Medline (summaries of health articles written mainly for professionals): *http://www.medlineplus.gov.*

Established in 1979, **the National Alliance for the Mentally Ill** (NAMI) is a nonprofit, grass-
roots, self-help, support, and advocacy organization of consumers, families, and friends of
people with severe mental illnesses, such as schizophrenia, major depression, bipolar disorder, obsessive–compulsive disorder, and anxiety disorders. NAMI also supports research and
teaching efforts for the mentally ill and their families. National Alliance for the Mentally Ill,
Colonial Place Three, 2107 Wilson Boulevard, Suite 300, Arlington, VA 22201; tel: 703-524-
7600; helpline: 800-950-NAMI (6264); website: *http://www.nami.org/.*

The **National Mental Health Organization** was founded in 1909 by Clifford Beers, who had
experienced episodes of mania and depression. This organization, which is active in all 50
states, advocates for patients with mental illness, including schizophrenia, bipolar disease,
anxiety disorders, and substance use, and supports screening programs. National Mental
Health Association, 1021 Prince Street, Alexandria, VA 22314-2971; tel: 800-969-NMHA
(6642); website: *http://www.nmha.org/about/programs.cfm.*

PHYSICAL TREATMENT

Books

Exercise therapy for various ailments is described in *The Healing Power of Exercise: Your
Guide to Preventing and Treating Diabetes, Depression, Heart Disease, High Blood Pressure, Arthritis, and More,* by Linn Goldberg and Diane L. Elliot. New York: Wiley, 2000.

Physical Activity and Psychological Well-Being, edited by Stuart J. H. Biddle, Kenneth R. Fox,
and Stephen H. Boutcher. New York: Routledge, 2000.

Organizations and Websites

Website devoted to **transcranial magnetic stimulation**; includes links to worldwide contacts
where it is being studied: *http://www.biomag.helsinki.fi/tms/.*

Light boxes. To treat winter depression and other mood disorders, a variety of light-
emitting devices from under $200 are available from Light Therapy Products, 6125 Ives Lane,
North Plymouth, MN 55442; tel: 800-486-6723; website: *http://www.lighttherapyproducts.com/*
or *www.yourneighborhooddoctor.com/light-machines-depression.html.*

Essentially the only location in North America for **psychosurgery** is at Massachusetts General Hospital. For information, address Coordinator, Cingulotomy Assessment Committee,
MGH, 15 Parkman Street, Suite 331, Boston MA 02114; tel: 617-726-3407.

MOOD DISORDERS
Books

Feeling Good: The New Mood Therapy (rev. ed.), by David D. Burns. New York: Avon, 1999. A cogent discussion of cognitive-behavioral therapy for mood disorders.

A Mind That Found Itself: An Autobiography, by Clifford W. Beers. Pittsburgh: University of Pittsburgh Press, 1981. The classic description of bipolar illness from the days before effective treatment.

Mind over Mood: Change How You Feel by Changing the Way You Think, by Dennis Greenberger and Christine Padesky. New York: Guilford Press, 1995. Nuts and bolts of cognitive therapy, spelled out in a step-by-step fashion that shows how you can use these methods in dealing with depression, anxiety, anger, panic, jealousy, guilt and shame.

The Noonday Demon: An Atlas of Depression, by Andrew Solomon. New York: Scribner, 2001. A layman probes the depths in this definitely not depressing survey of the experience of depression and its treatment. Winner of the 2001 National Book Award for nonfiction.

An Unquiet Mind: A Memoir of Moods and Madness, by Kay Redfield Jamison. New York: Knopf, 1995. Written from the unusual viewpoint of someone who is not only a professional in the mental health field but also personally suffers from bipolar disease.

Organizations and Websites

The mission of the **National Depressive and Manic Depressive Association** includes education, support for patients and families, and advocacy for research and to eliminate discrimination. Their website includes listings of clinical trials being conducted at some sites across the nation. National Depressive and Manic Depressive Association, 730 Franklin Street, Suite 501, Chicago, IL 60610; tel: 312-642-0049; website: *http://www.ndmda.org/*

ANXIETY DISORDERS
Books

The Boy Who Couldn't Stop Washing: The Experience and Treatment of Obsessive Compulsive Disorder, by Judith L. Rapoport. New York: Dutton, 1989. Though the treatments are a bit out of date, the descriptions of OCD are timeless.

The Anxiety and Phobia Workbook (2nd ed.), by Edmund J. Bourne. Oakland, CA: New Harbinger, 1995. Concise, practical, comprehensive directory on how to reduce anxiety.

Stop Obsessing! How to Overcome Your Obsessions and Compulsions, by Edna B. Foa and Reid Wilson. New York: Bantam, 1991. Two authorities on the treatment of anxiety disorders present a cognitive-behavioral approach to OCD.

Don't Panic: Taking Control of Anxiety Attacks (rev. ed.), by R. Reid Wilson. New York: HarperPerennial, 1996. Covers the diagnosis and treatment of panic, describing a self-help program for coping with panic attacks.

Social Phobia: From Shyness to Stage Fright, by John R. Marshall. New York: Basic Books, 1994. By a psychiatrist who treats anxiety disorders.

Overcoming Social Anxiety and Shyness, by Gillian Butler. New York: New York University Press, 2001. This self-help guide by a British clinician and researcher uses cognitive-behavioral techniques.

The Broken Mirror: Understanding and Treating Body Dysmorphic Disorder, by Katharine A. Phillips. New York: Oxford University Press, 1998. A definitive description of BDD.

Organizations and Websites

National Center for PTSD; tel: 802-296-5132; website: *http://www.ncptsd.org/*.

Social Phobia/Social Anxiety Association, 2058 E. Topeka Drive, Phoenix, AZ 85024; website: *http://www.socialphobia.org/*. Only 5 years old, the mission of this association is to spread awareness of social phobia.

For information about all the anxiety disorders discussed in this book, contact **Anxiety Disorders Association of America**, 11900 Parklawn Drive, Suite 100, Rockville, MD 20852; tel: 301-231-9350; website: *http://www.adaa.org/Public/index.cfm*. The website includes online tests for several disorders.

Obsessive–Compulsive Foundation, Inc., 337 Notch Hill Road, North Branford, CT 06471; tel: 203-315-2190; website: *http://www.ocfoundation.org/*. Online screening test.

PSYCHOSIS AND SCHIZOPHRENIA

Book

Surviving Schizophrenia: A Manual for Families, Consumers, and Providers, by E. Fuller Torrey. New York: Quill, 2001. Classic descriptions of the disease from a psychiatrist who has studied it for years.

Organizations and Websites

World Fellowship for Schizophrenia and Allied Disorders, 869 Yonge Street, Suite 104, Toronto, Ontario, M4W 2H2, Canada; website: *http://www.world-schizophrenia.org/*.

Links to **support, information, research studies,** chat, and much more is available at *http:// www.schizophrenia.com/.*

ELDERLY SERVICES AND DEMENTIA

Book

The 36-Hour Day: A Family Guide to Caring for Persons with Alzheimer Disease, Related Dementing Illnesses, and Memory Loss in Later Life (3rd ed.), by Nancy L. Mace and Peter V. Rabins. Baltimore: Johns Hopkins University Press, 1999. A new edition of the essential book for caregivers of Alzheimer's patients and others.

Organizations and Websites

AARP Grief and Loss programs offer one-to-one support, group work, public education, a telephone and referral service, and an outlet for rebuilding life as a single person. Tel: 800-424-3410; website: *http://www.aarp.org/griefprograms/types.html.*

The **Alzheimer's Association** is a national organization that serves as a clearing house for dementia-related diseases. With chapters throughout the country, its mission is to promote research on treatment for dementia and to help those who are afflicted. It also provides information about support groups, community resources, assisted living, education, and a helpline. The Alzheimer's Association, 919 North Michigan Avenue, Suite 1100, Chicago, IL 60611-1676; tel: 800-272-3900, 312-335-8700; website: *http://www.alz.org.*

Meals on Wheels provides in-home meals for those who cannot provide for themselves. National Meals on Wheels Foundation, P. O. Box 1727, Iowa City, IA 52244; tel: 319-358-9362; website: *http://www.nationalmealsonwheels.org/.*

Hospice information about end-of-life care, including a referral resource. National Hospice Foundation, 1700 Diagonal Road, Suite 300, Alexandria, VA 22314; tel: 703-516-4928; website: *http://www.hospiceinfo.org/.*

You'll find a tremendous amount of information about Alzheimer's disease on the **National Institute of Aging's** website, or you can write to **Alzheimer's Disease Education and Referral Center,** P.O. Box 8250, Silver Spring, MD 20907-8250; tel: 800-438-4380; website: *http:// www.alzheimers.org/pubs/prog99.htm.*

You can obtain up-to-date state-by-state information about advance directives, along with statutory forms, if they exist in your state, from Legal Counsel for the Elderly (LCE), **American Association of Retired Persons,** P.O. Box 96474, Washington, DC 20090-6474.

The **American Medical Association** has a sample advance directive that you can print from your browser: *http://www.ama-assn.org/public/booklets/livgwill.htm.*

EATING

Books

Dying to Be Thin: Understanding and Defeating Anorexia Nervosa and Bulimia—a Practical, Lifesaving Guide, by Ira M. Sacker and Marc A. Zimmer. New York: Warner, 1987. For people who suffer from an eating disorder or suspect they have one, or who are connected with someone who has an eating disorder, this book provides insight, motivation, and knowledge about the complexity of eating disorders.

Overcoming Binge Eating, by Christopher G. Fairburn. New York: Guilford Press, 1995. A cognitive-behavioral therapy guide to learning to control overeating by a well-known eating disorder expert.

The Golden Cage: The Enigma of Anorexia Nervosa, by Hilde Bruch. Cambridge, MA: Harvard University Press, 2001. The classic work on this disorder.

Organizations and Websites

National Association of Anorexia Nervosa and Associated Disorders (ANAD), P.O. Box 7, Highland Park, IL 60035; tel: 847-831-3438; website: *http://www.anad.org.*

Anorexia Nervosa and Related Eating Disorders (ANRED), P.O. Box 5102, Eugene, OR 97405; tel: 541-344-1144; website: *http://www.anred.com/hlp.html.*

Overeaters Anonymous uses a 12-step program to help members recover from compulsive overeating. Overeaters Anonymous, 6075 Zenith Court NE, Rio Rancho, NM 87124; tel: 505-891-2664; website: *http://www.overeatersanonymous.org/.*

Center for the Study of Anorexia and Bulimia, 1 West 91st Street, New York, NY 10024; tel: 212-595-3449.

National Eating Disorders Association, 603 Stewart Street, Suite 803, Seattle, WA 98101; tel: 206-382-3587; website: *http://www.nationaleatingdisorders.org.* This organization's referral page lists many unvetted providers, with very few physicians represented. Especially for anorexia, medication may be necessary.

SLEEP

Organizations and Websites

American Sleep Apnea Association (ASAA), 1424 K Street, NW, Suite 302, Washington, DC 20005; tel: 202-293-3650; website: *http://www.sleepapnea.org.*

National Sleep Foundation. A great deal of general information on sleep and its disorders. Excellent website. National Sleep Foundation, 1522 K Street, NW, Suite 500, Washington, DC 20005; website: *http://www.sleepfoundation.org/disorder.html*.

SUBSTANCE USE

Books

Alcoholics Anonymous (4th ed.). New York: Alcoholics Anonymous World Services, 2001. Called the Big Book by members, the book describes the recovery program and includes personal testimonies by members from different walks of life.

Sober and Free: Making Your Recovery Work for You, by Guy Kettelhack. New York: Simon & Schuster, 1996. Focuses on maintaining sobriety with discussions of how to manage slips and relapses, and relearning how to create significant relationships.

The Recovery Book, by Al J. Mooney, Arlene Eisenberg, and Howard Eisenberg. New York: Workman, 1992. An older, but still relevant, survey that covers more than just 12-step programs.

Recovery Options: The Complete Guide, by Joseph Volpicelli and Maia Szalavitz. New York: Wiley, 2000. The alternating viewpoints of a therapist and a drug user present the reader with a balanced understanding of how people get into, and out of, drug and alcohol use.

Organizations and Websites

Alcoholics Anonymous, 475 Riverside Drive, 11th Floor, New York, NY 10115; website: *http://www.alcoholics-anonymous.org*.

Narcotics Anonymous World Services, P.O. Box 9999, Van Nuys, CA 91409, tel: 818-773-9999; website: *http://www.na.org/*.

Cocaine Anonymous World Services (CAWSO), 3740 Overland Avenue, Suite C, Los Angeles, CA 90034; tel: 310-559-5833; website: *http://www.ca.org/*.

Al-Anon/Alateen. These organizations help families and friends deal with the effects of problem drinking. Alateen is a recovery group for young people. Al-Anon Family Group Headquarters, 1600 Corporate Landing Parkway, Virginia Beach, VA 23454; tel: 757-563-1600; website: *http://www.al-anon.alateen.org*.

International Institute for Inhalant Abuse, 450 West Jefferson Avenue, Englewood, CO 80110-3536; tel: 303-788-1860.

CHILD MENTAL HEALTH RESOURCES

Book

Straight Talk about Psychiatric Medications for Kids, by Timothy E. Wilens. New York: Guilford Press, 1999.

Organizations and Websites

The **National Institute of Mental Health**; see entry under general resources above.

The **American Academy of Child and Adolescent Psychiatry** (AACAP) is the leading national professional medical association dedicated to treating and improving the quality of life for children, adolescents, and families affected by mental health disorders. The association's members actively research, evaluate, diagnose, and treat psychiatric disorders and pride themselves on giving direction to and responding quickly to new developments in addressing the health care needs of children and their families. Website: *http://www.aacap.org/*.

The **American Academy of Pediatrics** (AAP) and its member pediatricians dedicate their efforts and resources to the health, safety, and well-being of infants, children, adolescents, and young adults. The AAP has approximately 55,000 members in the United States, Canada, and Latin America. Members include pediatricians, pediatric medical subspecialists, and pediatric surgical specialists. More than 34,000 members are board-certified and called Fellows of the American Academy of Pediatrics (FAAP). Website: *http://www.aap.org/*.

University of Iowa virtual hospital maintains some information online on a variety of child mental health topics. Website: *http://www.vh.org/Patients/IHB/Psych/Peds/PedsPsychiatry.html*.

Medication Generic and Trade Names

This table will help you translate from generic to brand names of drugs, and back again. Brand names are capitalized; generics are all lower-case. Drugs commonly prescribed for mental health indications are noted by an asterisk.

Accolate	zafirlukast
acetazolamide	Diamox
Actos	pioglitazone
Adapin	doxepin
Adriamycin	doxorubicin
Akineton	biperiden
Aldomet	methyldopa
Aleve	naproxen
Allegra	fexofenadine
alprazolam*	Xanax
amantadine	Symmetrel
Ambien*	zolpidem
amiodarone	Cordarone, Pacerone
amitriptyline*	Elavil, Endep
amoxapine*	Asendin
Anafranil*	clomipramine
Antabuse*	disulfiram
Anzemet	dolasetron
Aralen	chloroquine
Aricept*	donepezil
Artane	trihexyphenidyl
Asendin*	amoxapine
Ativan*	lorazepam
atorvastatin	Lipitor
Atrelol*	carbamazepine

Avelox	moxifloxacin
Aventyl*	nortriptyline
Benadryl	diphenhydramine
Benemid*	probenecid
benztropine	Cogentin
bepridil	Vascor
Betapace	sotalol
bexarotene	Targretin
Biaxin	clarithromycin
biperiden	Akineton
bupropion*	Wellbutrin, Zyban
BuSpar*	buspirone
buspirone*	BuSpar
Calan	verapamil
Capoten	captopril
captopril	Capoten
carbamazepine	Tegretol, Atrelol, Epitol
Cardene	nicardipine
Cardioquin	quinidine
Cardizem	diltiazem
Catapres	clonidine
cefixime	Suprax
Celexa	citalopram
Celontin	methsuximide
Cerubidine	daunorubicin
cevimeline	Evoxac
Chibroxin	norfloxin
chlordiazepoxide*	Librium
chloroquine	Aralen
chlorpromazine*	Thorazine
chlorzoxazone	Parafon Forte
cholestyramine	Prevalite, Questran, LoCHOLEST
cilostazol	Pletal
cimetidine	Tagamet
Cipro	ciprofloxacin
ciprofloxacin	Cipro
cisapride	Propulsid
citalopram*	Celexa
clarithromycin	Biaxin
Claritin	loratadine
clomipramine*	Anafranil
clonazepam*	Klonopin
clonidine	Catapres
clorazepate*	Tranxene
clozapine*	Clozaril
Clozaril*	clozapine
Cogentin	benztropine
Cognex*	tacrine

Comtan	entacapone
Cordarone	amiodarone
Corgard*	nadolol
Coumadin	warfarin
Crixivan	indinavir
cyclobenzaprine	Flexeril
cyclosporine	Gengraf, Neoral
Cytomel	liothyronine
dalfopristin	Synercid
Dalmane*	flurazepam
danazol	Danocrine
Danocrine	danazol
Darvon	propoxyphene
daunorubicin	Cerubidine
delavirdine	Rescriptor
Depakote, Depakene*	divalproex, valproic acid, valproate
desipramine*	Norpramin, Pertofrane
Desyrel*	trazodone
Diamox	acetazolamide
diazepam*	Valium
didanosine	Videx
Diflucan	fluconazole
Dilantin	phenytoin
diltiazem	Cardizem
diphenhydramine	Benadryl
disopyramide	Norpace
disulfiram*	Antabuse
divalproex*	Depakote
dofetilide	Tikosyn
dolasetron	Anzemet
Dolophine*	methadone
donepezil*	Aricept
dopamine	Dopastat, Intropin
Dopastat	dopamine
Dopram	doxapram
Doral*	quazepam
doxapram	Dopram
doxepin*	Adapin, Sinequan
doxorubicin	Adriamycin, Rubex
doxycycline	Vibramycin
efavirenz	Sustiva
Effexor*	venlafaxine
Elavil, Endep*	amitriptyline
entacapone	Comtan
Epitol	carbamazepine
Eskalith*	lithium
estazolam*	ProSom
ethosuximide	Zarontin

Evoxac	cevimeline
Exelon*	rivastigmine
felbamate	Felbatol
Felbatol	felbamate
Feldene	piroxicam
fexofenadine	Allegra
Flagyl	metronidazole
flecainide	Tambocor
Flexeril	cyclobenzaprine
fluconazole	Diflucan
fluoxetine*	Prozac
fluphenazine*	Prolixin
flurazepam*	Dalmane
fluvoxamine*	Luvox
Gabitril	tiagabine
galantamine*	Reminyl
gatifloxacin	Tequin
Gengraf	cyclosporine
Geodon*	ziprasidone
grepafloxacin	Raxar
guanethidine	Ismelin
Habitrol*	nicotine patch
Halcion*	triazolam
Haldol*	haloperidol
haloperidol*	Haldol
ibuprofen	Advil, Motrin
imipramine*	Tofranil
Imitrex	sumatriptan
indapamide	Lozol
Inderal*	propranolol
indinavir	Crixivan
Indocin	indomethacin
indomethacin	Indocin
Intropin	dopamine
Ismelin	guanethidine
isocarboxazid*	Marplan
isoniazid	Nydrazid
isoproterenol	Isuprel
Isoptin	verapamil
Isuprel	isoproterenol
itraconazole	Sporanox
Kemadrin	procyclidine
ketoconazole	Nizoral
Klonopin*	clonazepam
Lamictal*	lamotrigine
Lamisil	terbinafine

lamotrigine*	Lamictal
Lariam	mefloquine
Larodopa	levodopa
Levaquin	levofloxacin
levodopa	Larodopa
levofloxacin	Quixin, Levaquin
levomethadyl acetate	ORLAAM
Librium*	chlordiazepoxide
linezolid	Zyvox
liothyronine	Cytomel
Lipitor	atorvastatin
lisinopril	Zestril, Prinivil
Lithane*	lithium
lithium*	Eskalith, Lithobid, Lithane, Lithonate
Lithobid, Lithonate*	lithium
LoCHOLEST	cholestyramine
loratadine	Claritin
lorazepam*	Ativan
Lorelco	probucol
lovastatin	Mevacor
loxapine*	Loxitane
Loxitane*	loxapine
Lozol	indapamide
Ludiomil*	maprotiline
Luvox*	fluvoxamine
Manerix*	moclobemide
maprotiline*	Ludiomil
Marplan*	isocarboxazid
mefloquine	Lariam
Mellaril*	thioridazine
Meridia	sibutramine
meropenum	Merrem
Merrem	meropenum
mesoridazine*	Serentil
methadone*	Dolophine, Methadose
Methadose*	methadone
methsuximide	Celontin
methyldopa	Aldomet
metronidazole	Flagyl
Mevacor	lovastatin
mibefradil	Posicor
mifepristone	RU-486
Minipress	prazosin
Mirapex	pramipexole
mirtazapine*	Remeron
Moban*	molindone
moclobemide *	Manerix
modafinil	Provigil

molindone*	Moban
moxifloxacin	Avelox
Mycobutin	rifabutin
Mysoline	primidone
nadolol*	Corgard
naltrexone*	ReVia
Naprosyn	naproxen
naproxen	Naprosyn, Aleve
Nardil*	phenelzine
Navane*	thiothixene
NebuPent	pentamidine
nefazodone*	Serzone
Neoral	cyclosporine
Neo-Synephrine	phenylephrine
nevirapine	Viramune
nicardipine	Cardene
Nicoderm*	nicotine patch
Nicorette*	nicotine gum
nicotine gum*	Nicorette
nicotine nasal spray*	Nicotrol NS
nicotine oral inhaler*	Nicotrol inhaler
nicotine patch*	Nicoderm, Habitrol, Prostep, Nicotrol
Nicotrol*	nicotine patch, inhaler, nasal spray
nifedipine	Procardia
Nizoral	ketoconazole
Norflex	orphenadrine
norfloxin	Noroxin, Chibroxin
Noroxin	norfloxin
Norpace	disopyramide
Norpramin*	desipramine
nortriptyline*	Pamelor, Aventyl
Norvir	ritonavir
Nydrazid	isoniazid
octreotide	Sandostatin
olanzapine*	Zyprexa
omeprazole	Prilosec
Orap*	pimozide
ORLAAM*	levomethadyl acetate
orphenadrine	Norflex, many others
oxazepam*	Serax
oxcarbazepine	Trileptal
Pacerone	amiodarone
Pamelor*	nortriptyline
Parafon Forte	chlorzoxazone
Parnate*	tranylcypromine
paroxetine*	Paxil
Paxil*	paroxetine
Pentacarinat, Pentam	pentamidine

pentamidine	NebuPent, Pentacarinat, Pentam
pentazocine	Talwin
pergolide	Permax
Permax	pergolide
perphenazine*	Trilafon
Pertofrane*	desipramine
phenelzine*	Nardil
phenylephrine	Neo-Synephrine, many others
phenytoin	Dilantin
pimozide*	Orap
pioglitazone	Actos
piroxicam	Feldene
Pletal	cilostazol
Posicor	mibefradil
pramipexole	Mirapex
prazosin	Minipress
Prevalite	cholestyramine
Prilosec	omeprazole
primidone	Mysoline
Prinivil	lisinopril
probenecid	Benemid
probucol	Lorelco
procainamide	Procan, Pronestyl
Procan	procainamide
Procardia	nifedipine
procyclidine	Kemadrin
Prograf	tacrolimus
Prolixin*	fluphenazine
Pronestyl	procainamide
propafenone	Rythmol
propoxyphene	Darvon
propranolol*	Inderal
Propulsid	cisapride
ProSom*	estazolam
Prostep*	nicotine patch
Protopic	tacrolimus
protriptyline*	Vivactyl
Provigil	modafinil
Prozac*	fluoxetine
quazepam*	Doral
Questran	cholestyramine
quetiapine*	Seroquel
Quinadure, Quinidex	quinidine
quinidine	Cardioquin, Quinadure, Quinidex
quinupristin	Synercid
Quixin	levofloxacin
Raxar	grepafloxacin
Remeron*	mirtazapine
Reminyl*	galantamine

Requip	ropinirole
Rescriptor	delavirdine
Restoril*	temazepam
Retrovir	zidovudine
ReVia*	naltrexone
rifabutin	Mycobutin
Rifadin	rifampin
rifampin	Rifadin
Rilutel	riluzole
riluzole	Rilutel
Risperdal*	risperidone
risperidone*	Risperdal
ritonavir	Norvir
rivastigmine*	Exelon
ropinirole	Requip
RU-486	mifepristone
Rubex	doxorubicin
Rythmol	propafenone
Sandostatin	octreotide
Seldane	terfenadine
Serax*	oxazepam
Serentil*	mesoridazine
Seroquel*	quetiapine
sertraline*	Zoloft
Serzone*	nefazodone
sibutramine	Meridia
sildenafil	Viagra
simvastatin	Zocor
Sinequan*	doxepin
Sonata*	zaleplon
sotalol	Betapace
sparfloxacin	Zagam
Sporanox	itraconazole
stavudine	Zerit
Stelazine*	trifluoperazine
sumatriptan	Imitrex
Suprax	cefixime
Surmontil*	trimipramine
Sustiva	efavirenz
Symmetrel	amantadine
Synercid	dalfopristin, quinupristin
tacrine*	Cognex
tacrolimus	Prograf, Protopic
Tagamet	cimetidine
Talwin	pentazocine
Tambocor	flecainide
Tao	troleandomycin
Targretin	bexarotene

Tegretol*	carbamazepine
temazepam*	Restoril
Tequin	gatifloxacin
terbinafine	Lamisil
terfenadine	Seldane
Theo-Dur	theophylline
theophylline	Theo-Dur
thioridazine*	Mellaril
thiothixene*	Navane
Thorazine*	chlorpromazine
tiagabine	Gabitril
Tikosyn	dofetilide
tocainide	Tonocard
Tofranil*	imipramine
tolcapone	Tasmar
Tonocard	tocainide
Topamax*	topiramate
topiramate*	Topamax
tramadol	Ultram
Tranxene*	clorazepate
tranylcypromine*	Parnate
trazodone*	Desyrel
triazolam*	Halcion
trifluoperazine*	Stelazine
trihexyphenidyl	Artane
Trilafon*	perphenazine
Trileptal	oxcarbazepine
trimipramine*	Surmontil
troleandomycin	Tao
Ultram	tramadol
Valium*	diazepam
valproic acid*	Depakote, Depakene
Vascor	bepridil
venlafaxine*	Effexor
verapamil	Calan, Isoptin, Verelan
Verelan	verapamil
Viagra	sildenafil
Vibramycin	doxycycline
Videx	didanosine
Viramune	nevirapine
Vivactyl*	protriptyline
warfarin	Coumadin
Wellbutrin*	bupropion
Xanax*	alprazolam
zafirlukast	Accolate
Zagam	sparfloxacin

zaleplon*	Sonata
Zarontin	ethosuximide
Zerit	stavudine
Zestril	lisinopril
zidovudine	Retrovir
zileuton	Zyflo
ziprasidone*	Geodon
Zocor	simvastatin
zolmitriptan	Zomig
Zoloft*	sertraline
zolpidem*	Ambien
Zomig*	zolmitriptan
Zyban*	bupropion
Zyflo	zileuton
Zyprexa*	olanzapine
Zyvox	linezolid

Index

About the Author

James Morrison, MD, is a psychiatrist who has treated over 15,000 mental health patients. He was educated at Washington University School of Medicine in St. Louis, and is currently Professor of Clinical Psychiatry at Oregon Health and Science University in Portland. He has written numerous other books and scientific papers.